Kennedy, Khrushchev, and the Test Ban

KENNEDY KHRUSHCHEV

and the TEST BAN

GLENN T. SEABORG

WITH THE
ASSISTANCE OF
BENJAMIN S. LOEB

FOREWORD BY
W. AVERELL HARRIMAN

UNIVERSITY OF CALIFORNIA PRESS
Berkeley, Los Angeles, London

University of California Press
Berkeley and Los Angeles, California

University of California Press, Ltd.
London, England

Copyright © 1981 by The Regents of the University of California

Library of Congress Cataloging in Publication Data

Seaborg, Glenn Theodore, 1912–
  Kennedy, Khrushchev, and the test ban.

  Includes index.
  1. Atomic weapons and disarmament. 2. Atomic
weapons—Testing. 3. United States—Foreign relations—Soviet Union. 4. Soviet Union—Foreign
relations—United States. I. Loeb, Benjamin S.,
1914–   . II. Title.
JX1974.7.S414   327.1'74   81-3051
ISBN 0-520-04332-4   AACR2

Designed by Graphics Two, Los Angeles

Printed in the United States of America

1 2 3 4 5 6 7 8 9

To the memory of John Fitzgerald Kennedy
who told us never to negotiate out of fear
but never to fear to negotiate

CONTENTS

Contents

Foreword   xi

Preface   xiii

Sources and Acknowledgments   xv

PART ONE Prologue: Negotiations Pre-Kennedy   1

1 From BRAVO to the Conference of Experts   3
The U.S. on the Defensive/**3** More Modest Approaches/**6**
New Test Ban Proposals: Official and Unofficial/**7** Toward
Technical Discussions/**10** The Conference of Experts/**12**

2 Test Ban Negotiations Begin   14
Early Days of the Geneva Conference/**14** Technical
Challenges/**16** High-Altitude Detection/**19** Impasse over
Technical Data/**20** Agreement Almost Reached/**21**
Reversal/**24**

PART TWO Downward Spiral   27

3 In Search of a Policy   29
First Meetings with the President/**30** Opposing Views/**32**
Were the Soviets Cheating?/**34** War in My Head/**35**
McCloy's Review/**35** The Principals Endorse
Concessions/**37** The President Takes a Hand/**43** A White
House Luncheon/**45** On Decision Making/**49** Off to
Geneva/**51**

4 A Bad Start at Geneva   54
Enter the Troika/**54** Western Concessions Introduced/**55**
The West Tables a Complete Treaty/**57** A New
Atmosphere in Geneva/**59**

5   Internal Debate, External Challenge   61

Differing Views/**61** Weighing the Options/**63**
Confrontation in Vienna/**66** Preparing—While Seeming
Not To/**68** Teetering on the Brink/**73** The Panofsky
Panel/**74** The Gauntlet Thrown/**76**

PART THREE   Reluctant Militancy   79

6   Over the Brink   81

Meetings, Meetings/**81** A New Western Proposal/**85** The
President Decides/**86** A Bad Start/**89** A Drift Toward
Atmospheric Testing Begins/**89**

7   Organization and Disarmament Initiatives   92

An Agency is Born/**92** A Plan for General and Complete
Disarmament/**96** The President at the UN/**98** A Statement
of Agreed Principles/**99**

8   Toward Atmospheric Testing   103

A New Policy Position/**103** I "Meet the Press"/**105**
Negotiations with the British/**108** And with the French/**110**
Decision Delayed/**111** British Interventions/**113** The AEC
Takes a Stand/**114** The Decision to Prepare in the Open/**115**

9   Test Plans and a Summit   116

The Committee on Atmospheric Testing/**116** Quest for
Christmas Island/**117** A Sober Reevaluation/**119** The Geneva
Conference's Last Gasp/**121** An Aside on Public Opinion/**122**
The Test Committee's Program/**123** Preparations for the
Bermuda Summit/**125** Dialogue at the Summit/**126**

10   The Decision To Test in the Atmosphere   132

New Uncertainties/**132** Various Views/**133** Summit
Correspondence/**134** Decision to Test, with an Escape
Clause/**135**

11   Geneva Revisited   140

Preparing the U.S. Position/**140** A New Low at Geneva/**142**
Technical Reevaluation/**144** The Eight-Nation
Memorandum/**147**

12   Operation DOMINIC   150

Overview/**150** Some Public Reactions/**151** Electrons on
High/**152** Final Tests/**157** Evaluation/**158**

PART FOUR   A Turning   159

13   Auguries of Change   161

Weakening of the U.S. Position/**161** Four Significant
Meetings/**164** New Western Proposals/**168**

14   The Missile Crisis and Its Aftermath   **172**

The Course of the Crisis/**172** Reactions to the Settlement/**175**
Enter the Black Boxes/**176** How Many Inspections? A
Misunderstanding/**178** An Anniversary: "Happy
Relationships"/**181** Unproductive Talks/**183**

15   "My Hopes Are Somewhat Dimmed"   **186**

Those Opposed/**186** Further Changes in the U.S. Position/**187**
Continued Deadlock in Geneva/**189** Plans for Further U.S.
Atmospheric Tests/**192** The Proliferation Connection/**193**
My Effort to Save the Plowshare Program/**195** Where is the
Genie?/**198**

16   The Tide Begins To Turn   **201**

My Journey to the Soviet Union/**201** The Hot Line/**206** A New
Western Initiative/**207** Further Moves by the President/**211**
The Speech: Its Genesis/**211** The Speech: Its Content/**213** The
Speech: Its Reception/**216**

17   Preparation for a Mission   **219**

Dissension within the Administration/**219** The President
Abroad/**224** Toward a Limited Treaty/**226** Instructing
Harriman/**228** Uncertainty/**229**

PART FIVE   "A Shaft of Light"   **233**

18   Twelve Days in Moscow   **235**

Arrival/**235** A Good Beginning/**238** Requiem for the
Comprehensive/**240** Gromyko's Aggressive Pursuit of a
Nonaggression Pact/**243** A Trade: Peaceful Uses for
Withdrawal/**244** Accession/**249** Khrushchev: "Up Close and
Personal"/**250** "The Great Man of the Meeting"/**251**

19   Ceremonies and Reactions   **254**

Terms of the Treaty/**254** Initialing/**255** First Reactions/**256**
Giving the Senate a Role/**258** The Delegation/**259** "A Glorious
Day"/**260**

20   The Senate Consents   **263**

Presidential Efforts/**263** The Hearings Overall/**265** Rusk and
McNamara/**266** My Testimony: Could Plowshare
Survive?/**266** The Joint Chiefs and the Four Safeguards/**269**
Edward Teller and Other Scientists/**271** Reservations
Proposed/**273** Political Aspects/**275** The Stennis
Committee/**276** Conflicting Committee Reports/**277** Floor
Debate/**278** Consent/**280**

PART SIX   Epilogue   **283**

21   A Reckoning   **285**

Four Minutes to Midnight/**285** Hopes Fulfilled and
Unfulfilled/**286**

22   Still Needed: A Comprehensive Test Ban   **293**
Partial Steps/**295** Recent Efforts: Near Agreement Once
Again/**296** A Look Back: If Kennedy and Khrushchev Had
Survived/**297**

**Appendix: Treaty Banning Nuclear Weapon
Tests in the Atmosphere, in Outer
Space, and Under Water   302**

Notes   306

Index   311

FOREWORD

As I write early in 1981, the political climate seems unfavorable to major progress in nuclear arms control. This does not alter the conclusion I and others have reached that there must be such progress before very long if there is to be assurance of continued meaningful human life on earth. My experience tells me that the political climate in the world can change rapidly; no alliance or antagonism between nations should be assumed to be permanent. Under these circumstances, it is a great challenge of statesmanship to be able to perceive genuine opportunities for mutually advantageous arms control agreements at the moments, often fleeting, when such opportunities arise. It is a further challenge to be able to act on such perceptions and to bring agreements to fruition notwithstanding the congealed hostilities and rigid postures of opposition that may exist on both sides.

This is what President John F. Kennedy did in 1963 in negotiating the Limited Test Ban Treaty with the Soviet Union. He perceived enhanced opportunities for the long-sought agreement following the world's brush with catastrophe in the 1962 Cuban Missile Crisis and in the Soviet Union's preoccupation with the mounting antagonism between itself and the People's Republic of China.

In negotiating the treaty, President Kennedy insisted on terms that protected the national interest as he perceived it and, just as important, as the U.S. Senate perceived it. At the same time, he was sensitive to the concerns of the negotiators on the other side, led by Nikita Khrushchev, and was skillful in contriving compromises that catered to these concerns without giving way on matters essential to us.

Having reached agreement with the Soviets, President Kennedy then mounted a most effective campaign to explain the treaty to the American people and to persuade them and their congressional representatives of its merits. The result was a treaty that has been universally acclaimed as a great achievement in international relations, and one that still stands as a solid basis for further strides toward a peaceful world when conditions are again ripe.

It is important that the story of the Limited Test Ban Treaty be told, not only for its value as history but also for the guidance this experience can provide for the conduct of future East-West relations. Many Americans seem to regard negotiations with the Soviet Union as a baffling exercise in which we are bound to come out second best. President Kennedy had the good sense to realize that, by negotiating with patience, firmness, and sensitivity, it was possible to reach mutually advantageous agreements. At the base of this policy was the president's perception that not everything that is in the interest of the Soviet Union is necessarily disadvantageous to us. As he so eloquently expressed it: "We all inhabit this small planet. We all breathe the same air. We all cherish our children's future. And we are all mortal."

It is fortunate that one of the participants in the processes that led to the Limited Test Ban Treaty has elected to share his recollections and his further research with us. His account is the more vivid because during the ten years (1961–71) when he was chairman of the U.S. Atomic Energy Commission, Dr. Seaborg kept a detailed daily journal in which he recorded the ebb and flow of discussions and events. I can testify that my part in the final negotiations leading to the treaty has been most faithfully recorded in these pages, as are other aspects of the story with which I am personally familiar.

W. Averell Harriman

Washington, D.C., 1981

PREFACE

The telephone call that changed my life came on the afternoon of January 9, 1961. I was in the Radiation Laboratory of the University of California at Berkeley. It was my habit each Monday to take refuge there from my administrative duties as chancellor of the Berkeley campus in order to follow progress in my own academic field, nuclear chemistry. The call was from President-elect John F. Kennedy. He asked me to acept the job of chairman of the Atomic Energy Commission. Within a few days I accepted, and soon I was plunged into a new kind of chemistry, that of national and international events.

The Atomic Energy Commission has receded rapidly in memory since its demise in 1974.* Many recall the AEC only, and perhaps ingloriously, for its development and testing of nuclear weapons and its sponsorship of nuclear energy as a source of electricity. While these were two of its principal functions, the agency also had major programs for the production of nuclear materials; reactor research and development for the armed services, including the nuclear navy; research in high- and low-energy nuclear physics and in chemistry and biology; production and sale of radioisotopes for use in medicine, agriculture, industry, and research; licensing of the use of nuclear materials for power plants and other peaceful purposes; and international cooperation in developing the peaceful atom.

Although I remained as AEC chairman for ten years, this narrative is concerned only with my early years on the job, corresponding roughly to the "thousand days" of John F. Kennedy's presidency. It focuses, moreover, on only one story, namely, President Kennedy's vigorous, persistent, and ultimately successful pursuit of a nuclear test ban treaty with the Soviet Union.

I believe that the achievement of the treaty can be traced in large part to the deep commitment of President Kennedy, to his persis-

---

*AEC's functions were divided between two new agencies. Its regulatory functions were assigned to the Nuclear Regulatory Commission; its research, production, and development functions to the Energy Research and Development Administration, a forerunner of today's Department of Energy.

tence in pursuing the goal despite numerous discouragements, to his skilled leadership of the forces involved within his administration, and to his sensitive and patient diplomacy in dealing both with the Soviet Union (which meant, basically, with Nikita Khrushchev) and with the United States Senate. It is my view that President Kennedy's performance in this matter had qualities of excellence which are worthy of study and emulation.

At the same time that these pages celebrate an important achievement, the Limited Test Ban Treaty outlawing nuclear tests in the atmosphere, under water, and in space, they chronicle also what must be considered a significant disappointment, the failure to achieve a *comprehensive* treaty ending *all* nuclear testing by the superpowers. Such a treaty was ardently sought by President Kennedy. With but a handful of exceptions, the leaders and the publics of all the nations in the world fervently supported the quest for such an agreement. Nevertheless, despite some near misses, this glittering prize, which carried with it the opportunity to arrest the viciously spiraling arms race, eluded our grasp. It is important, I think, to consider why this happened. Basically, as we know, it was because of massive mistrust between the superpowers, but we will want to observe in some detail how this mutual suspicion has operated until now to thwart the hopes of the largest part of the world community.

I believe that my personal participation and that of others who have generously shared their recollections with me enable this book to contribute some facts and insights not previously published about the Limited Test Ban Treaty. A question that had to be faced very early in the writing was whether to confine the book to new material, or to present the story in more complete detail. I determined on the latter course because I believe that a wider understanding of what is involved in the achievement of an important arms control agreement can be helpful in the current situation of our country and the world.

Sources and Acknowledgments

A large part of this volume is drawn from a personal journal that I maintained every day of my ten years as chairman of the Atomic Energy Commission. The journal, having been written often in haste at the end of a busy day, was not always couched in optimum phraseology. In various places, therefore, I have allowed myself the privilege of altering a word or phrase. As John Kenneth Galbraith noted in justifying similar changes in his fascinating *Ambassador's Journal*, "No historical merit attaches to bad English."

A number of individuals who were engaged in or privy to the events leading to the test ban have been most generous in sharing their recollections and observations with me. Theodore Sorensen, who as special counsel and principal speechwriter was among the closest to John F. Kennedy, contributed some key insights. Norman Cousins, Jerome Wiesner, Franklin Long, Herbert York, and Warren Heckrotte supplied rich detail about important episodes, in some of which they played leading roles. I am most especially indebted to W. Averell Harriman, who not only described the background and details of his climactic negotiations in Moscow in several extended conversations but also permitted access to his personal files.

The staff of the John Fitzgerald Kennedy Memorial Library provided liberal access to the library's rich documentary resources, notably including the remarkable collection of oral history interviews. I am also indebted to the Kennedy Library for a number of the photographs used to illustrate the text.

To make the story as coherent and complete as possible I have made liberal use of government documents—in particular the excellent reports issued on a current basis by the Arms Control and Disarmament Agency—and of books and articles, both scholarly and journalistic. These are cited if they are quoted or if the item involved seems relatively unfamiliar. I did not think it necessary to show sources for better known facts or events.

The completion of this book owes much to a number of people who provided important assistance along the way. Valuable suggestions on substance and style were offered by those who read early drafts: Paul Seabury, Lillian O. Lukaczer, Francis Duncan, Walter G. Leight, Milton Turen, Ellen Loeb, and Jeanne L. Loeb. Lin Lorenz coordinated the preparation of the manuscript, nursing it through its several vintages with critical intelligence and care, unflagging industry, and unfailing good humor. Further administrative support was contributed by Patricia Johnson.

My daughter, Lynne Cobb, provided valuable criticism of an early draft.

Finally, I am indebted, as always, to my wife, Helen, for her encouragement, support, and wise counsel.

G. T. S

Berkeley, California 1981

PART ONE
Prologue: Negotiations Pre-Kennedy

Control of arms is a mission that we undertake particularly for our children and our grandchildren ... they have no lobby in Washington.

—President John F. Kennedy, statement on securing world peace, 1963.

1

From BRAVO to the Conference of Experts

The principal events in this narrative occurred in the years 1961 to 1963, during the administration of President John F. Kennedy. These events are better understood against the background of certain prior occurrences which shaped the situation as Kennedy found it. Some of that background is summarized in this chapter and the one following. The treatment in these two chapters is, perforce, more cursory than in the remainder of the book.

The U.S. on the Defensive

Nuclear weapons tests first became an object of widespread public concern in 1954. On March 1 of that year the AEC detonated a hydrogen bomb, code named BRAVO, as part of a test series at Bikini Atoll in the Pacific. Because of a yield twice that anticipated—equivalent to 15 million tons of TNT, to this day the most powerful explosion ever detonated by the United States—and because of unexpected wind conditions, BRAVO showered a Japanese tuna trawler with radioactive debris. The crew of twenty-three suffered from severe radiation sickness and one crew member subsequently died, allegedly from effects of the radiation. Some inhabitants of the Marshall Islands were also affected, although less severely. The shock of these events was compounded by news that contaminated fish were reaching the Japanese market from the test area and by further fallout on Japan from a Soviet test soon afterward. A wave of protests followed. Highly respected world leaders, including Prime Minister Nehru of India, Albert Schweitzer, Albert Einstein, and Pope Pius XII, joined in the call for an end to nuclear tests.

Notwithstanding this public clamor, test ban proposals did not at once play a large part in national policies or international diplomacy. Instead, discussions continued to focus, as they had since the end of World War II, on a stream of sweeping general disarmament proposals advocated by the leading powers before various organs of the United Nations.

U.S. policy in the early postwar years was based on the "Baruch Plan," as presented to the UN Atomic Energy Commission in 1946. Under this proposal the manufacture of nuclear weapons was to cease, existing weapons were to be destroyed, and their nuclear materials were to be transferred to an international authority for use in peaceful applications. Rigid controls were contemplated, with punishments for violators not subject to a Security Council veto.

While it seemed that the United States was being unprecedentedly generous in offering to surrender a great military advantage, its atomic monopoly, the Baruch Plan was unacceptable to the Soviet Union for a number of reasons: (1) it involved intrusive inspection procedures that conflicted with the Soviet penchant for military and industrial secrecy; (2) any time the plan failed, the United States would have been left with its monopoly of atomic know-how, if not actual weapons; (3) Soviet development of its own atomic capability, which was being pursued vigorously, would have been nipped in the bud; and (4) the United States would have reaped an enormous propaganda harvest.

The Soviet Union responded to the Baruch Plan with a proposal of its own. As presented to the UN by the young Andrei Gromyko, this would have outlawed at once the production and use of atomic weapons. Three months later all existing atomic weapons were to be destroyed. Only after another three months was a control system to be considered, and any penalties for violators were to be meted out by the Security Council, where the great powers had the veto.

Among the many differences between the U.S. and Soviet approaches, clearly one of the most fundamental had to do with the timing of the various steps. We wanted controls to be established first; then disarmament could follow. The Russians said it had to be the other way around: disarmament first and then controls. The United States, finding its exclusive possession of atomic weapons a heavy moral burden, was willing to give up this advantage but needed strong guarantees before doing so. The USSR wanted to exploit what it hoped to be worldwide moral outrage against nuclear weapons in order to blunt the advantage of the United States but was unwilling to accept any physical intrusion on its domain in return.

Disarmament discussions for the next several years focused on efforts to bridge the wide gap between the U.S. and Soviet approaches. There was little chance of agreement, however, especially after the first Soviet nuclear test in 1949 and the onset of the Korean War in 1950. While both East and West offered several new proposals during these years, they seemed designed primarily to influence world opinion, not as bases for serious negotiation.

The international climate improved somewhat beginning in 1953 as the Korean War ended and both superpowers acquired new leadership. The collective leadership that succeeded Josef Stalin and the new administration of Dwight Eisenhower both seemed more flexible in their approaches to disarmament questions.

In June 1954 the British and French introduced a carefully wrought plan for disarmament in three phases, following establishment of a control organ. It proposed sharp reductions in armed forces and conventional arms, to be followed by the destruction and prohibition of nuclear weapons, all under inspection control. The plan made several concessions to the Soviet point of view. On May 10, 1955, the Soviets caused a flurry of excitement by presenting their own detailed set of proposals, which accepted important features of the Anglo-French memorandum. Specifically, the Soviets agreed on the manpower levels to which the major powers would reduce their forces and, in a major concession, on the principle of control by an international agency. Since the Anglo-French proposals with which the Soviets seemed in substantial accord had been endorsed previously by the United States, there was widespread belief that agreement on disarmament was near.

The rejoicing was premature. The Soviet plan contained requirements known to be unacceptable to the United States, such as the dismantling of all bases on foreign soil. More significant, however, was the fact that serious doubts had arisen in the U.S. government about some of the disarmament positions that our representatives had previously espoused or endorsed. The Atomic Energy Commission, for example, questioned whether nuclear disarmament of any kind accorded with U.S. security interests as long as the Soviet Union held a wide lead in conventional arms. Similar views emanated from the Department of Defense. These objections had not been pressed vigorously in earlier years because those holding them did not take the ongoing disarmament negotiations seriously. The near agreement in 1955 changed all that.

Under the pressure of the dissent within his administration, President Eisenhower ordered "a broad reappraisal of disarmament policy," and in September 1955 Harold Stassen, who had been appointed by the president to the new position of special assistant for disarmament, was forced, amid great embarrassment, to "place a reservation on"—in effect, to repudiate—all previous U.S. disarmament positions. World reaction to Stassen's announcement was predictably unfavorable, as witness this query by Phillip Noel-Baker, leading British disarmament advocate: "Have the U.S. Government reached the point reached by the British, French and Germans in 1914? Do they now believe that only armaments can make them safe, and that keeping the lead in weapons and in force is the only way to safeguard the national interest and uphold the peace?"[1]

More Modest Approaches

One of the most important questions asked in the reappraisal of U.S. disarmament policy related to the technical feasibility of controlled nuclear disarmament. In their proposals of May 10, 1955, the Soviets had intimated that atomic weapons could be stockpiled secretly in such a way that no inspection system would discover them. Stassen asked Ernest O. Lawrence, director of the University of California's Radiation Laboratory,* to head a "nuclear task force" that would endeavor to "seek a scientific breakthrough to a means, thus far unknown, of detecting concealed nuclear weapons." Lawrence and his committee agreed in rather short order with the Soviet position: such a breakthrough could not be achieved.

The implications of this finding seemed clear. The sweeping disarmament proposals of prior years, such as the Baruch Plan, were unenforceable. More modest approaches were needed.

These technical findings helped to induce governments to give increased attention to nuclear test ban proposals during the ensuing

---

*Lawrence was a Nobel Prize winner in physics (1939) and inventor of the cyclotron. He pioneered in research on a grand scale, requiring the establishment of large laboratories, such as the one he headed. He was cautiously conservative on arms control issues.

years. This was at the expense of proposals for general disarmament, which, beginning in the late 1950s, received less attention.

The Eisenhower administration's first response to the new technical findings was to concentrate on what the president called "initial confidence-building measures." As a first step, attention was directed to guarding against surprise attack, the possibility of which was felt to be a dangerously destabilizing influence in a nervous world. In July 1955 Eisenhower made his dramatic "open-skies" proposal to the Geneva summit conference of leaders of the U.S., U.K., France, and the USSR. Under this proposal the two sides were to exchange blueprints of military installations and each was to be permitted to make reconnaissance flights over the territory of the other to ensure that no aggressive preparations were in progress. The initial public stance of the Soviets was to reject this proposal as a "crude espionage scheme" intended to pick out bombing targets for the U.S. Strategic Air Command. Despite the Soviet rejection, the United States continued to push the open-skies proposal and, in time, the USSR agreed to consider aerial reconnaissance over a band of central Europe including, however, only a very small part of Soviet territory.

New Test Ban Proposals: Official and Unofficial

While the Big Four could reach no agreements at the Geneva summit meeting in 1955, the atmosphere was affable, giving rise to an expression, "the spirit of Geneva", which symbolized hope for eventual accord.

International interest in a nuclear test ban was heightened by the first British hydrogen bomb test early in 1956.* The Soviets were able to make propaganda capital of this event by proposing a ban directed specifically at hydrogen bomb tests.

Despite continued administration insistence that nuclear weapons testing was essential to national security, there was rising pressure within the United States during 1956 for consideration of a test ban, even if only a partial one. Adlai Stevenson, then in his second campaign as Democratic presidential nominee, advocated a ban on large nuclear tests in a series of speeches, claiming that such an agreement would be self-enforcing. He appeared to be making good headway with the issue until Soviet Premier Nikolai Bulganin proposed an uninspected test ban in a letter to President Eisenhower in October, noting that "certain prominent public figures in the U.S."

---

* The first U.S. and USSR hydrogen bomb tests occurred in 1952 and 1953, respectively.

were advocating a similar procedure. Political observers felt that association with this crude intrusion damaged Stevenson's candidacy severely.

Meanwhile, atmospheric tests by all three nuclear powers continued, eliciting protests from governments and prominent individuals in all parts of the world. President Eisenhower took cognizance of the protests by emphasizing new precautions in U.S. tests to minimize radioactive fallout. In the negotiations at the United Nations Disarmament Commission, however, the United States continued to insist that, in the absence of agreement to eliminate or limit nuclear weapons under proper safeguards, continuation of testing was essential for our national defense and the security of the free world.

During 1957 the scale of protests against nuclear testing reached unprecedented heights. India's Prime Minister Nehru reiterated his views on numerous occasions. The British Labour party introduced a formal antitesting motion in Parliament. Professor Otto Hahn, co-discoverer of nuclear fission, joined seventeen other leading West German nuclear scientists in a declaration that they would have nothing to do with nuclear weapons. The West German Bundestag appealed for a halt to tests. Albert Schweitzer broadcast an appeal that was heard in fifty countries and endorsed by the Pope. Nobel Prize winner Linus Pauling obtained the signatures of more than nine thousand scientists from forty-three countries to an antitesting petition.* Perhaps most significant of all to the administration, the Gallup Poll showed that 63 percent of the American public favored a test ban, as opposed to only 20 percent three years earlier.

On June 14, 1957, the Soviets proposed a two- or three-year moratorium on tests, to be supervised by an international commission utilizing instrumented detection stations on the territories of the nuclear powers. Eisenhower, at first favorably disposed toward the Russian offer, was partly dissuaded when AEC Chairman Lewis Strauss brought prominent nuclear scientists Edward Teller, Ernest Lawrence, and Mark Mills** to the White House. The scientists stated that, with continued testing, U.S. laboratories could develop "clean" (fallout-free) weapons within seven years and that the Soviets could

---

*Pauling won the Nobel Prize in chemistry in 1954 for his work on molecular structure and was to win the Nobel Peace Prize in 1963 for his opposition to nuclear testing.

**Teller was director of the Atomic Energy Commission's weapons laboratory at Livermore, California. A Hungarian immigrant, he has consistently shown much mistrust of the Soviet Union and taken a hard line on preparedness issues. Mills was head of the Livermore laboratory's theoretical division. On Lawrence, see note, p. 6.

negate any test moratorium by undetectable, clandestine tests. It was emphasized that clean nuclear explosives were vital to NATO's strategy for using battlefield nuclear weapons in the event of a Soviet attack in Western Europe and to the U.S. program ("Plowshare") for peaceful uses of nuclear explosives.

Late in August 1957 the United States offered to accept a test suspension of two years, but the proposal was linked to a controlled cutoff in production of nuclear materials for military purposes. We indicated that the test suspension could become permanent when the cutoff was achieved. The Soviet Union perceived such a cutoff as freezing its inferiority in the quantity of fissionable materials, and Soviet spokesmen began to denounce the link between cutoff and test ban as one of the most objectionable aspects of U.S. policy. In contrast, the Soviets advocated prohibition of all nuclear tests as a separate measure, feeling that this could lead in time to a prohibition of the use of nuclear weapons, thus neutralizing American nuclear superiority.

Scientific events toward the end of 1957 had an important effect on future test ban negotiations. The first U.S. underground nuclear test, code named RAINIER, added a new dimension to the problem of each side's ability to detect the other's tests, since underground tests are far more difficult to detect than tests in the atmosphere. More spectacular was the Russian acomplishment of placing into orbit the first earth satellite, Sputnik I, on October 4, followed on November 3 by the half-ton Sputnik II, which carried a dog around the earth. These events sent a shock wave through the Western world. They called into question the presumed scientific superiority of the United States. They had ominous military implications as well, since they seemed to indicate that the Soviets held a lead in the development of long-range missiles.

President Eisenhower responded by moving to strengthen the scientific resources of his administration. On November 7, 1957, he created the White House position of special assistant for science and technology and appointed to it the president of the Massachusetts Institute of Technology, James R. Killian, Jr. Shortly afterward he established a President's Science Advisory Committee (PSAC).

Prior to these appointments the scientific advice received by the president and Secretary of State John Foster Dulles, at least as it affected nuclear arms control matters, had emanated mostly from the scientists in the Defense Department and in the AEC's weapons laboratories at Livermore, California, and Los Alamos, New Mexico. A large part of the advice was filtered to Eisenhower and Dulles through Lewis Strauss, who had dual status as chairman of the AEC and special assistant to the president for atomic energy. Strauss was a deeply convinced advocate of continued nuclear testing, and his guidance to the secretary of state and the president reflected this conviction.

Once Killian and the PSAC scientists were on the scene, a greater diversity of scientific opinion was represented in the policy councils of the administration. Strauss and the viewpoints he represented continued to be heard, but now other voices were heard as well, conveying a different flow of scientific information and expressing judgments that argued for different policies. Thus, to all the arguments about the difficulties of achieving and implementing a test ban agreement the Killian group responded with arguments about the *greater* difficulties that might ensue in the *absence* of an agreement.

One of the most important apparent converts to the new way of thinking was Secretary of State Dulles himself. Up to the middle of 1957 Dulles does not appear to have believed in the efficacy of reaching arms control agreements with the Soviet Union. He had a fervent mistrust of the Russians and tended to rely on supremacy in nuclear weapons as a cornerstone of U.S. foreign policy. After mid-1957, however, Dulles became convinced that the propaganda drubbings the United States was taking on the test ban issue were proving too much of a handicap in the conduct of foreign policy. In his final years (he died in May 1959) Dulles advocated a more forthcoming approach on test ban matters. This brought him more into harmony with the views of President Eisenhower. The latter, while he did not always exercise vigorous leadership in seeking a test ban, was clearly disposed toward one and later remarked that failure to achieve a test ban treaty was his greatest regret about his presidency.[2]

Toward Technical Discussions

As 1957 drew to a close, the Soviet Union again proposed a three-year, uninspected test moratorium. After extended debate in a by now badly split administration, President Eisenhower felt compelled to reject the proposal, incurring in consequence another propaganda defeat for the United States.

The first part of 1958 witnessed a high-level national debate on the test ban question. The forum was the Senate Disarmament Subcommittee chaired by Hubert Humphrey. Each side paraded its best witnesses before the committee and marshaled its most powerful arguments. The widely divergent views presented served to emphasize that some scientists, led by Linus Pauling at one extreme and Edward Teller at the other, were presenting whatever arguments they could find to support their respective political views, sometimes wandering outside the boundaries of their expert knowledge in so doing.

The last part of the Humphrey subcommittee hearings was conducted under the stimulus of two important events in the Soviet Union. The first of these, on March 27, 1958, was the accession of Nikita Khrushchev to the position of premier. The second was the announcement on March 31 that the Supreme Soviet had approved a decree prohibiting further nuclear testing by the Soviet Union, provided other nations did not test. Khrushchev followed up the Supreme Soviet's announcement with letters to President Eisenhower and British Prime Minister Harold Macmillan urging them "to follow suit." While the timing of the Russian move was transparently cynical—they had just completed a major series of tests and the U.S. was just about to start one—it nevertheless earned the USSR much credit in world opinion.

In drafting President Eisenhower's reply to Khrushchev, Secretary Dulles was strongly influenced by a report just submitted by an interagency panel appointed by PSAC Chairman Killian and headed by Cornell University physics professor Hans Bethe.* The panel concluded, after extensive analysis, that the U.S. nuclear arsenal was sufficient to permit a nuclear test ban without endangering national security. They recommended a test ban verified by a system of instrumented and scientifically manned detection stations, supplemented by onsite inspection. They believed such a system would detect all but the smallest tests, whether above or below ground.

Eisenhower's answer to Khrushchev, dispatched on April 8, 1958, proposed that the Soviet Union join the Western nations in an examination of the technical requirements for verification of a nuclear test ban. U.S. experts were prepared to recommend to such a gathering the system advocated by the Bethe Panel. In effect, the United States was signaling its willingness to consider a nuclear test ban as a separate question, not linked as previously with a controlled cutoff in nuclear materials production.

Khrushchev at first rejected the proposal for a technical conference. Eisenhower thereupon repeated the suggestion, adding the following significant sentence: "Studies of this kind are the necessary preliminaries to putting political decisions actually into effect." This seemed to imply a commitment to agree on a test ban if the

---

*Bethe won the 1967 Nobel Prize in Physics for his contribution to the theory of nuclear reactions, especially his discoveries on the energy production of stars. He was one of the most influential advocates of a test ban.

experts could work out a control system and was evidently a powerful lure. On May 9, Khrushchev responded: "Your messages indicate that you attach great importance to having experts study the technical details connected with the control of the execution of an agreement on the cessation of atomic and hydrogen weapons tests. Taking this into account, we are prepared, in spite of the serious doubts on our part, to try even this course."

The Conference of Experts

The agreement to have a technical conference was implemented speedily. The Conference of Experts to Study the Possibility of Detecting Violations of a Possible Agreement on Suspension of Nuclear Tests was convened in Geneva on July 1, 1958. The Western delegation, which included three Americans, two Britons, one Frenchman, and one Canadian, as well as a number of technical advisers, was led by James B. Fisk, then vice-president of Bell Telephone Laboratories.* The experts considered four methods of detecting and identifying nuclear explosions: recording acoustic waves, locating and examining radioactive debris, recording seismic signals, and recording radio signals.

Throughout the conference the Soviets took an optimistic view of the effectiveness of each method, apparently seeking to minimize the number of control stations and inspections that would be needed on Soviet soil in any verification system. The Western delegation presented data giving far less optimistic estimates, thus arguing for more extensive controls.

The conferees terminated their work on August 21, 1958. What the world was waiting to hear was stated in a communiqué issued on that date: "The Conference reached the conclusion that it is technically feasible to set up, with certain capabilities and limitations, a workable and effective control system for the detection of violations of a possible agreement on the worldwide cessation of nuclear weapons tests."

The proposed system, which became known as "the Geneva System," was spelled out in the final report of the conference issued on August 30. Paralleling the system recommended by the Bethe Panel, it would have involved 160 to 170 land-based control posts (later increased to 180), each containing scientific detection appara-

---

*The other two U.S. delegates were Robert F. Bacher, professor of physics at the California Institute of Technology, and Ernest O. Lawrence. Lawrence had to return to the United States during the conference after a flare-up of a previous illness, to which he succumbed in August 1958.

tus and each manned by 30 to 40 persons, several of whom would have to be scientists. Of these posts, 100 to 110 were to be on continents (the number in the Soviet Union was not specified), 20 on large oceanic islands, and 40 on small oceanic islands. In addition, about ten similarly manned and instrumented ships and regular aircraft flights were to be used to patrol the oceans. Special aircraft flights over land were also to be employed to investigate suspicious events; these flights were to be in planes supplied and manned by the country being inspected, with a control system representative aboard as an observer. It was also provided that the international control organization "could" send an onsite inspection group to investigate suspicious events.

The experts' report claimed that the Geneva System would have a "good probability" of detecting atmospheric explosions yielding as little as one kiloton (equivalent to one thousand tons of TNT) if the explosions were detonated at a height below 50 kilometers. (For reference, the Hiroshima bomb yielded 20 kilotons.) Underground, the system was estimated to be able to detect explosions yielding as little as 5 kilotons and distinguish them from earthquakes. The report stated that there would be from twenty to one hundred earthquakes a year in the Soviet Union that would be indistinguishable from underground explosions and that some of these events "could" be made subject to onsite inspection.

Some of the weaknesses of the Geneva System are apparent from the above description. No techniques were provided for detection of explosions detonated at high altitudes. The technical feasibility of concealment was not explored, although U.S. delegates had presented information on this subject. The provisions for onsite inspection were vague, and the possibility that it could be ineffective was not recognized. And, as was to be pointed out later, the system as a whole, with its requirement for the stationing of thousands of scientists in remote locations, was inordinately elaborate and expensive and probably impractical.

Little attention was paid to these weaknesses in the generally euphoric reaction to the results of the conference. In contrast to the communiqué, which was a worldwide journalistic sensation, the details of the report, not released until nine days later, were reported very sparsely and were difficult for the average person to understand. A very strong impression had been created that speedy agreement on a controlled test ban was within easy reach. The future was to tell another story.

2

Test Ban Negotiations Begin

Early Days of the Geneva Conference

President Eisenhower's reaction to the seemingly affirmative findings of the Conference of Experts was swift. On August 23, 1958, only two days after the conference ended and a week before its final report was released, the president proposed that the three nuclear powers meet to negotiate a permanent end to nuclear tests. He announced further that, to create a favorable atmosphere, the United States would abstain from testing for a year from the date when negotiations began.*

On August 30 the Soviet Union agreed to the idea of negotiations beginning October 31 but refused to indicate whether it would suspend tests during the conference. The Soviets insisted on Geneva as

---

*Khrushchev was quick to point out that this offer was of questionable significance since it took about a year to prepare a meaningful test series.

the conference site, not New York as the Western nations had suggested.

As the conference drew near, all three nuclear powers rushed to complete test series. The U.S. series, known as HARDTACK, comprised fifty-four announced tests, eight of which were underground. The United States announced fourteen Soviet tests, two of which occurred after the conference began.* Following these, there were apparently no further tests by the major nuclear powers for nearly three years.

The U. S. delegation to the Geneva Conference on the Discontinuance of Nuclear Weapons Tests was headed by our deputy ambassador to the UN, James J. Wadsworth, an experienced and capable diplomat. The British delegation was led by David Ormsby-Gore, minister of state for foreign affairs, whom President Kennedy once described as the brightest man he ever knew.[1] The chief Soviet delegate was Semyon K. Tsarapkin, whose experience in disarmament matters reached back to the 1946 discussions of the Baruch Plan.

At the outset of the conference the Soviets tabled, that is, placed on the agenda, a draft treaty. It was very brief: the three powers would agree to stop testing, to set up a control system based on the Geneva System, and to dissuade others from testing. (In speaking of "others," the Soviets surely had France in mind.) This draft was objectionable to the West since under its terms a test ban might be placed in effect with only a vague agreement in principle to establish a control system. It was the old Soviet sequence: a treaty first, controls later. The Soviet draft also raised the basic question of whether the Geneva System, with its omissions and lack of precision, was a sufficient basis for a control system.

Senator Albert Gore of Tennessee, a member of the congressional Joint Committee on Atomic Energy, visited the conference during its early days and came away with the feeling that the Soviets would never accept adequate controls. In a widely publicized letter to President Eisenhower he recommended that the U.S. abandon efforts to achieve a comprehensive test ban, one covering tests in all environments, and try instead for a ban limited to atmospheric tests, which would be relatively easy to detect without international controls.

Perhaps in reaction to Gore's letter and other criticisms in the American press, the Soviets agreed on November 29 that basic provi-

---

*The Soviet Union does not make a practice of announcing its own tests. Public knowledge of most Soviet tests comes from announcements by the U. S. government.

sions of a control system could be included in the text of the treaty. This concession opened the way to some genuine negotiation. Both sides began to set forth their views in detail and to narrow their differences.

By its second recess on March 19, 1959, the Geneva Conference had adopted seven articles of a treaty. These dealt mainly with administrative or noncontroversial items, however, or were so phrased as to paper over differences. The two sides remained at odds over several significant issues.

1. The Soviet Union proposed that scientific detection stations, referred to in the negotiations as "control posts," be staffed by nationals of the country in which they were located, except for "one or two" observers from the control organization. The Western powers stated that this amounted to "self-inspection" and was entirely unacceptable. They proposed instead that control posts on the soil of any of the "original parties," the term adopted for the U.S., U.K., and USSR, be staffed 50 percent from the other nuclear side and 50 percent by neutrals.
2. The Soviets demanded that each of the original parties have a veto in voting by the Control Commission that would supervise a test ban. The U.S. and U.K. opposed this, being concerned principally about potential Soviet vetoes of onsite inspections.
3. The Soviet Union insisted that inspection teams be organized on an ad hoc basis and that they be composed entirely of nationals of the country to be inspected. The West wanted to have permanent inspection teams and to have them selected from the international staff of the control organization.

Underlying these disagreements were the basic elements of mistrust that were to persist and eventually to frustrate the quest for a comprehensive test ban: the U.S., and the British to a lesser degree, insisted on extensive controls because of a suspicion that the Soviet Union might attempt to conduct clandestine tests in violation of a treaty; the Soviet Union resisted controls on its own soil because of a suspicion that the United States intended to use them for purposes of espionage. In particular, they may have been concerned that we would learn the location of their missile sites at this time when they had many fewer missiles than we had.

Technical Challenges

As the Geneva Conference was about to resume on January 5, 1959, Ambassador Wadsworth requested an informal meeting with his Soviet counterpart. At this meeting he informed Tsarapkin of certain technical findings reached by U.S. scientists based on the underground tests in the HARDTACK series. These findings indicated that the Conference of Experts had greatly overestimated the ability of seismic instrumentation to detect underground tests and to distinguish them from earthquakes. The Experts had based their conclusions almost entirely on the experience in detecting RAINIER, the only underground test previously undertaken. The HARDTACK tests provided much additional data. The indications now were that the minimum yield of underground tests that could readily be detected and distinguished from earthquakes by the Geneva System was 20 kilotons, not 5 kilotons as the Experts had concluded. One of the implications of the new data was that many more than the 180 manned control stations contemplated by the already elaborate Geneva System would be necessary to achieve the system's anticipated effect. Many of these stations would have to be on Soviet soil, making it virtually certain that the Soviet Union would not agree.

The new information cast a pall over the Geneva Conference. The initial Soviet response was that the data had been fabricated to discredit the Geneva System and that a technical discussion of the data would be a waste of time.

Dismayed about the impasse over a control system for a comprehensive test ban, President Eisenhower wrote to Khrushchev on April 13, 1959, suggesting that an agreement be put into effect in phases, beginning with tests in the atmosphere up to an altitude of 50 kilometers. The president pointed out that such an initial phase would not require the onsite inspections over which the conference was deadlocked.

Ten days later Khrushchev rejected Eisenhower's proposal as a "dishonest deal," since it would have permitted the United States to continue testing in media other than the lower atmosphere. (The Soviets may well have been concerned that underground tests would permit us to make progress with development of the tactical nuclear weapons intended for use by NATO forces in Europe.) As an alternate way to deal with the inspection issue, Khrushchev called attention to a suggestion made by Prime Minister Macmillan on a visit to Moscow in February 1959. Macmillan had suggested that it would be possible to agree to a fixed quota of onsite inspections each year on the territory of each nuclear power and that this number need not be large.

In letters to Khrushchev dated May 5, 1959, both Eisenhower and Macmillan agreed to explore the inspection quota idea. In his letter the president went on to state that, in order for negotiations on a comprehensive test ban to continue, the Soviet Union would have to modify its positions on the veto in votes by the Control Commission and would have to agree also to an early discussion of techniques for detecting high-altitude tests. On May 14, Premier Khrushchev agreed to technical talks on the high-altitude question, while giving evasive answers to the president's other points.

Further technical challenges to the Geneva System lay ahead. On June 12, 1959, Ambassador Wadsworth introduced into the test ban conference the findings of a U.S. Panel on Seismic Improvement. This was a group of prominent American seismologists headed by Lloyd V. Berkner, president of Associated Universities, Inc.* The initial mandate of the Berkner Panel, as it came to be called, was to determine whether, without increasing the number of control posts contemplated by the Geneva System, the effectiveness of the system could be improved. President Eisenhower had called for such a study to recoup some of the ground lost by the HARDTACK findings.

The Berkner Panel's report noted three rather complex and very costly means of improvement utilizing available technology. The first was to increase the number of seismometers at each control post from ten to one hundred. The second was to use analysis of surface seismic waves, as well as those underground, to aid in distinguishing earthquakes from underground nuclear explosions. The third was to place unmanned instrumented stations, so-called black boxes, approximately 170 kilometers apart in earthquake-prone areas of the nuclear powers. It was the panel's opinion that these three techniques would boost the capability of the Geneva System to the point where it could detect and identify 98 percent of underground events having a seismic impact of one kiloton or greater. The panel emphasized, however, that its findings were preliminary and that more research was needed to remedy a paucity of data.

The Berkner Panel's report also had a more somber side. This concerned techniques of evasion. Following the Conference of Experts, Edward Teller had asked Livermore and Rand Corporation scientists to consider ways in which the Geneva System might be evaded by a clever violator. Albert Latter of the Rand Corporation turned his attention to "decoupling," a technique for reducing the seismic impact of an explosion by detonating it in the center of a large underground chamber so that the surrounding earth would not be forcefully impacted by the explosion. Latter's analysis indicated that it was possible to decouple to such an extent that a 300-kiloton explosion would register on seismographs as though it were only one

---

*This organization operated Brookhaven National Laboratory for the AEC and the National Radio Astronomy Observatory at Greenbank, West Virginia.

kiloton. While there was doubt that yields as high as 300 kilotons could be decoupled because of the difficulty and costs involved in building so large a chamber, even scientists friendly to a test ban, such as Hans Bethe, conceded that Latter's analysis was, in general, valid. These findings seemed to have a devastating effect on the Geneva System since they implied that some underground tests could be concealed and that seismograph readings would not necessarily provide a reliable indication of the size of an explosion.

The situation was made worse by a report, also in the spring of 1959, by a panel headed by Robert F. Bacher of the California Institute of Technology. The Bacher Panel concluded that onsite inspection of a suspicious event would have an exceedingly small chance of proving that an underground test had occurred, especially if the perpetrator was bent on concealment. George B. Kistiakowsky, who succeeded James Killian as President Eisenhower's science advisor in July 1959, quoted a member of the panel as saying that they reached this conclusion in response "to the aggressive arguments of Harold Brown"[2] then an associate director of the Livermore laboratory, later to be secretary of defense under President Carter. (It is noteworthy that Brown, one of the persuasive opponents of a test ban at this time, became one of the most effective spokesmen for the Limited Test Ban Treaty after it was presented to the Senate in 1963.)

High-Altitude Detection

In accordance with the agreement reached by Eisenhower and Khrushchev in their correspondence in May, Technical Working Group I of the Geneva Conference was convened on June 22, 1959, to consider the problem of detecting explosions at high altitudes. After some difficult technical arguments, which need not concern us here, the scientists reached agreement and on July 10 published their recommendations for a detection system. It involved placing five or six large satellites in earth orbit at an altitude of over 18,000 miles to detect radiations from nuclear explosions in space.* The satellites would be supplemented by special equipment placed in the 170 manned control posts of the Geneva System.

The fact that the working groups reached agreement did not mean that the problem of high-altitude detection had been solved. Both delegations agreed that the system they recommended would be very costly and technically difficult to put in place. Furthermore, even if a high-altitude explosion were detected, its originator might

---

* The recommended satellites were in fact placed in orbit in the fall of 1963.

not be identifiable. The U.S. delegates pointed out in addition that, if radiation shielding were incorporated in a high-altitude explosive device, that device would probably escape detection by the system. As one commentator noted, the conference had in fact shown that "effective policing of an outer-space ban would be out of reach for many years."[3]

Impasse over Technical Data

Following up on the exchange of letters among the three heads of state regarding an annual quota of onsite inspections, the Soviets began to mention in private conversations that they might find a quota of three inspections per year acceptable. While the West was not yet prepared to offer a number of its own, U.S. delegates began to argue that an annual quota should be determined "scientifically," rather than "politically," that is, it should bear some relationship to the number of seismic events.

During September 1959 Premier Khrushchev visited the United States. Neither his conversations with President Eisenhower at Camp David nor his major address to the United Nations General Assembly provided anything significant with regard to nuclear testing, although the summit talks, after a rocky start, became conciliatory enough to warrant another symbolic "spirit" phrase, this time the "spirit of Camp David."

When the Geneva Conference resumed on October 25, 1959, following one of its periodic recesses, the U.S. continued to press for consideration of the new seismic data revealed in the HARDTACK underground tests and of the implications of decoupling. On November 3, Tsarapkin proposed that a technical working group be convened to work out criteria for the dispatch of onsite inspection teams. He agreed that, as a concession to the spirit of Camp David, the new seismic data and decoupling could be considered at such a meeting.

The group proposed by Tsarapkin was known as Technical Working Group II (TWG II). It began its work on November 25, 1959. Considering the fact that the meeting was a Soviet suggestion, the U.S. delegates were taken aback by some of the obdurate positions adopted by the Soviets. They were willing to acknowledge the theoretical validity of decoupling but not that it would work in practice. They were willing to discuss "objective instrument readings" on the basis of which onsite inspections could be initiated, but they set conditions so strict as virtually to preclude such inspections. While agreeing with two suggested improvements in the Geneva System: adding a new type of seismometer and raising the number of seismometers in each control station from ten to one hundred, they disagreed with every suggestion of inadequacy in the system that implied the need for more onsite inspections. In particular, the Soviet delegates tried to reject or discredit all HARDTACK data implying that the number of earthquakes in the USSR that could be confused with underground explosions was greater than had been estimated by the Conference of Experts. (Warren Heckrotte of the Livermore laboratory, who was then, and is still, a member of the U.S. test ban negotiating team in Geneva, calls my attention to the fact that when the findings of the Defense Department's seismic research program, Project VELA, were released in the spring of 1962, they showed that the Soviet scientists had probably been more correct on this last point than the U.S. scientists.)[4]

The work of TWG II ended on December 18 amid disagreement so profound that it proved impossible to issue an agreed final report, and in an atmosphere of hostility between the delegations that had no precedent in post-World War II East-West scientific negotiations. The outcome of the conference led to an angry statement by President Eisenhower in which he said: "The prospects for a nuclear test ban have been injured by the recent unwillingness of the politically guided Soviet experts to give serious scientific consideration to the effectiveness of seismic techniques for the detection of underground nuclear explosions."

In the same statement the president announced that the United States would no longer be bound by its voluntary test moratorium when it expired on December 31, 1959, but would give advance notice of any intention to resume testing. The president indicated that we would not test so long as the Geneva talks showed promise. The Soviet Union's response was to repeat its pledge not to resume testing unless the Western nations did. The Soviets left unclear whether in this context a test by France would be considered a Western test.

Agreement Almost Reached

Technical Working Group II demonstrated that the Soviet Union would not consent to any major changes in the Geneva System for controlling a fully comprehensive test ban treaty. The Western side adjusted to this reality by adopting a new negotiating position. This was to propose a treaty that would prohibit only those tests that, in the West's judgment, could be verified by the Geneva System, allowing that the prohibitions would be expanded as capabilities for verification were improved through scientific progress. In announcing this proposal for a phased treaty on February 11, 1960, Ambassador Wadsworth indicated that it would prohibit initially all atmospheric and underwater tests, tests in space to the height (unspecified) where detection was feasible, and underground tests producing signals greater than 4.75 on the Richter earthquake-magnitude scale. A joint East-West seismic research program was proposed to make it feasible to lower this threshold on underground tests. On the thorny question of onsite inspections, the West offered the Russians a choice of three formulas, each of which led to a quota averaging about twenty onsite inspections per year on the territories of each nuclear side.

The Soviets appeared to show great interest in the Western proposals, reacting by asking a number of searching questions. Tsarapkin made it clear that their principal objection was to the fact that some tests would still be permitted in space and below the 4.75 seismic threshold underground, particularly the latter.

The formal Soviet response was made on March 19, 1960, in the form of a counterproposal. They agreed with the Western suggestions with three exceptions. They wished to prohibit all tests in space, whether detectable or not. They wanted an agreement that during the joint seismic research program there would be a moratorium on the smaller underground tests not prohibited by the treaty, those below seismic magnitude 4.75; this moratorium would run for four to five years, after which the three nations would confer on whether to extend it. Finally, the Soviets rejected the Western approach under which the number of onsite inspections would be related scientifically to the number of seismic events. While still not suggesting a specific numerical quota, the Soviets insisted, as they were to do consistently from this time forward, that the number of inspections must be a political decision. Their statement on this was emphatic: "We cannot agree about the inspection quota on any other basis."

Public reaction to the Soviet counterproposal within the U.S. was mixed. Hubert Humphrey hailed it as a major step that brought a comprehensive test ban "in sight." He suggested that the only differences between the approaches of the two sides could be compromised if the Soviet Union would accept twenty inspections per year and the West would accept a moratorium on small underground tests for a specified period during a research program. The Federation of American Scientists, an organization generally sympathetic to a test ban, also regarded the Soviet proposal as "an important step." By contrast, John McCone, who had succeeded Lewis Strauss as AEC chairman in July 1958, denied that the Soviet plan constituted a concession. He implied that it would permit the Soviets to conduct clandestine underground tests below the 4.75 seismic threshold, tests that could lead to important progress, especially with decoupling, whereas our open society would prevent such cheating by the United States. Senator Clinton Anderson, chairman of the Joint Committee on Atomic Energy, struck a similar note, contending that the Soviet proposal asked the U.S. to "buy a pig in a poke," foregoing our own tests while relying on trust that the Soviet Union would forego theirs.

Alarmed by such adverse reactions, British Prime Minister Macmillan made a hurried trip to the United States toward the end of March 1960 to confer with President Eisenhower. After a day and a half in conference at Camp David, the two leaders came up with a conditionally favorable response to the Russian plan. They agreed to accept a moratorium on underground tests below seismic magnitude 4.75, but only *after* a treaty barring all verifiable tests had been signed and a coordinated seismic research program arranged. They invited the Soviet Union to join at once in planning such a research program. The moratorium on underground tests would be "of agreed duration" and would be accomplished by "unilateral declaration of the three powers": it would not be part of the treaty. In a press conference held on his return from Camp David, President Eisenhower indicated that the time period for a moratorium suggested by the Soviets, four to five years, was excessive. Other sources indicated that the United States was thinking in terms of a moratorium of no more than one year.

While some differences remained, the two sides seemed at this point to be drawing together, and an agreement appeared in the offing. The momentum seemed so strong that those who were opposed to a test ban came forward in haste to make their positions known. On April 7, President Charles de Gaulle stated that France would abandon its nuclear weapons program only if the three nuclear powers destroyed their nuclear weapons. (The French had detonated their first nuclear device in the Sahara on February 13 and their second on April 1.) On April 10, Premier Zhou Enlai gave evidence of the nuclear intentions of the People's Republic of China and its widening rift with the Soviet Union by stating that his country would not be bound by any accord that it did not sign. The Joint Committee on Atomic Energy called attention to its predominantly negative sentiments through hastily convened hearings on the technical aspects of test ban controls. The hearings began on April 19, 1960, and lasted four days. Some of the testimony dealt with the enormous costs and personnel problems involved in the Geneva System, such as staffing and operating seismic detection stations in remote areas of Siberia and other earthquake-prone locations. Testimony was also introduced about the difficulties involved in conducting an onsite inspection. This led a number of congressmen to conclude that the chance that such an inspection would uncover evidence of a violation was near zero.[5]

President Eisenhower was not persuaded by the domestic opposition to a test ban. With his encouragement, momentum toward an agreement continued at Geneva. The Soviet Union agreed that declarations regarding a moratorium on underground testing need not be part of the treaty. The Soviets also assented to the convening of a Seismic Research Program Advisory Group, to hold its first meeting on May 11. In addition, delegates at the Geneva Conference made considerable progress clearing away minor disagreements and sharpening the definition of the issues that remained. On April 14, Tsarapkin spoke of "the favorable atmosphere which distinguishes the recent stage of our negotiations from their earlier stages." The anticipation was that final agreement might be reached at the forthcoming Big Four summit meeting in Paris, planned to start on May 16.

Reversal

Into this hopeful atmosphere Premier Khrushchev hurled his dramatic announcement on May 7, 1960, that U.S. pilot Francis Gary Powers and his high-altitude U-2 reconnaissance aircraft had been shot down by a Soviet missile over Sverdlovsk six days earlier.

The impact of this incident was not felt at once in Geneva. The Seismic Research Program Advisory Group convened, as scheduled, on May 11, and in a cordial atmosphere. The Soviet delegates at first implied that they would participate in a joint seismic research program by carrying out coordinated explosions, both chemical and nuclear. After the U-2 discord forced cancellation of the Paris summit, however, the atmosphere in Geneva deteriorated sharply. On May 27, Tsarapkin stated that the Soviet Union saw no need to engage in a joint research program since it had "no doubts regarding the validity of the report of the Geneva experts of 1958." With the rug thus pulled out from under its deliberations, the research group disbanded on May 30 without filing a report.

The collapse of the Paris Summit Conference was followed by a general decline in East-West relations. A crisis in the Congo erupted in July 1960, leading to bitter Soviet attacks against the UN Secretary-General, Dag Hammarskjold. The fifteenth UN General Assembly in September was characterized by acrimonious exchanges. President Eisenhower, alarmed by the increased tensions, was reported to have decided to order the resumption of testing if Richard Nixon won the election.[6] After Kennedy's victory, he advised the president-elect to resume testing without delay.[7]

In this deteriorating atmosphere, the delegates at Geneva slogged on. Having held over two hundred sessions between the start of the conference and the collapse of the summit meeting, they held sixty-eight more between May 27, when the conference reconvened, and December 5, its last meeting date in 1960. Little of significance was accomplished. Aside from some minor tidying up of administrative provisions, the conference merely marked time. Both sides seemed reluctant to take new initiatives or to risk major confrontations in the closing days of the Eisenhower administration. On December 5, 1960, the Geneva Conference adjourned to give the incoming Kennedy administration an opportunity to examine its position.

PART TWO

Downward Spiral

3

In Search of a Policy

We now enter the period of my government service in the administration of John F. Kennedy. From here on our review of events is at a slower pace, in greater detail, and from closer vantage points.

Negotiations for a test ban went forward on two levels. There were negotiations within the U.S. government, as senior officials representing the different departments met repeatedly with the president or among themselves to determine what U.S. policy should be toward a test ban under circumstances that were rapidly changing. I was able to record much of this intramural give and take in my daily journal. Test ban negotiations on the international level proceeded in small groups and large, ranging from two-man talks to meetings of the UN General Assembly, and we will examine these through recollections of participants as well as the public record. As the test ban drama quickens, we

*will also be looking more closely at the backdrop of world
events against which it was played out.*

First Meetings with the President

Although I was not sworn in as chairman of the Atomic Energy
Commission until March 1, 1961, I actually began performing the
duties of the office on February 1. Commissioner John S. Graham
served officially as acting chairman from January 20, when John
McCone resigned, until March 1.

My first business meeting with President Kennedy took place on
February 10, 1961. Also present were McGeorge Bundy, who had
been appointed as White House special assistant on national security
affairs, and Jerome Wiesner, designated as special assistant on science
and technology.* Both had been advisers to Kennedy during his years
in the Senate and during the election campaign.

The main purpose of the meeting was to discuss a confidential
weapons matter, but the president also brought up a number of other
subjects. In his State of the Union message he had mentioned the
desirability of building bridges to the Communist East through exchanges of scientists. He asked me not to forget this, mentioning
Poland in particular. We discussed preparations for the resumption of
the Geneva test ban talks at some length, the president indicating
that he wanted a strong team working on disarmament; he had
criticized the prior administration's efforts as insufficient. Then he
said that he would like an early briefing on the work of the AEC and
thought it might be best if he came out to AEC's Germantown,
Maryland, headquarters building for this purpose. I suggested he
come by helicopter, since we had a landing pad at the site. This was
agreed to and the date was set.

The president's visit took place on February 16. It was an event
not soon to be forgotten at the Germantown headquarters, which
pulsated with excitement before, during, and after the visit. I recorded what took place in my journal:

> I accompanied the president on the helicopter flight from the White
> House lawn, along with Bundy, Wiesner, and Kennedy's military aide.
> It was a wintry day. After landing on the pad behind the AEC
> building, we were driven around to the front. The president shook hands
> with the receptionists and greeted everyone he passed on the way to my
> office. Secretaries and other people were doing their best to act like they

*Bundy, a political scientist, had been on the Harvard faculty for twelve years, most
recently as dean of the Faculty of Arts and Sciences. Wiesner, an electrical engineer,
was director of MIT's Research Laboratory of Electronics and an outspoken proponent
of a test ban.

were tending to business, but they were peeking out the various doors in the process. The visitors first sat down around the conference table in my office while I briefed the president on the fundamentals of nuclear energy. The other three commissioners, John S. Graham, Robert E. Wilson, and Loren K. Olson, were present. [There were only three because we still had a vacancy on the five-member commission.] Then we went down the hall to the commission meeting room where we had a program in readiness.

It had been planned and rehearsed that eleven of the principal programs of the AEC would be summarized by their respective directors, with time allotments scheduled so that the whole presentation would last no more than forty-five minutes. The schedule quickly went awry, however, because of the president's numerous questions.

He was interested in the weapons program in some detail. He noted that we had first developed a weapon yielding 20 kilotons (Hiroshima), and now we were talking about one much larger. He asked why. He wanted to know much about the neutron bomb: why we were interested in it, whether it was a radical departure, whether it would kill immediately, what its range would be, whether one could shield against it.

These questions introduced me to a hallmark of the president's style that was to become familiar in the months ahead, namely, that he tried to master the substantive content of important issues by asking probing questions.

A testimonial to this trait of Kennedy's was given by Ambassador George Kennan in his interview for the Kennedy Library Oral History Program:

> President Kennedy was the best listener I have ever seen in high position anywhere. What impressed me I think most of all, as I saw him repeatedly over the course of years, was the fact that he was able to resist the temptation, to which so many other great men have yielded, to sound off himself and be admired. He asked questions modestly and sensibly and listened very patiently to what you had to say. . . . This is a rare thing among men who have risen to very exalted position.

One question the president asked during the AEC briefing reflected a particular preoccupation.

> I passed him a note saying that schedule slippage would necessitate omitting the presentation of Dr. Charles L. Dunham, director of AEC's division of biology and medicine. Kennedy assented, but said he would like to ask Dr. Dunham one question: The president asked Dunham why the American public and press seemed less concerned about radioactive fallout than two years ago. Dunham replied that, while there was still some stratospheric fallout from tests conducted in 1958 and earlier, it was adding radioactivity to the soil at a lesser rate than the radioactive contamination already in the soil was decaying. Consequently, the peak of the fallout hazard from these old tests had now passed. He further stated that the radioactivity levels reached from weapons fallout had

never exceeded one-twentieth of the permissible level established by the National Committee on Radiation Protection [an authoritative scientific body]. Nevertheless, Dunham expressed the personal opinion that had weapons testing been continued at the 1958 rate, "civilized man would have been in trouble."

Kennedy's resolve to achieve a test ban could only have been increased by such a grim appraisal.*

Opposing Views

While in the Senate, Kennedy had made the need for a nuclear test ban agreement a principal personal theme. His views were forcefully expressed on more than one occasion.

In an address at the University of California at Los Angeles in November 1959, then Senator Kennedy expressed his "emphatic disagreement" with Governor Nelson Rockefeller of New York, who had urged that the United States resume testing. Kennedy argued that such a course would be "damaging to the American image" and that it could lead to a "long, feverish testing period" that might threaten "the very existence of human life," bring about Russian breakthroughs to threaten our lead, and, most important, dispose more nations to enter the atomic club. This would "alter drastically the whole balance of power and put us all at the mercy of inadvertent, irresponsible, or deliberate atomic attacks from many corners of the globe." Kennedy proposed a four-point program: (1) continued U.S. test suspension while serious negotiations proceeded; (2) redoubled U.S. efforts to achieve a "comprehensive and effective" test ban; (3) confining resumed U.S. tests, if forced by Soviet resumption, to those that would "prevent a further increase in the fallout menace," that is, underground tests; and (4) intensified "studies of the impact of radioactive fallout and how to control it."

In an address in Washington one month later, Kennedy depicted the frightful arithmetic of the arms race. The U.S. and USSR together, he said, were "in a position to exterminate all human life seven times over." He added, "Both sides in this fateful struggle must come to know, sooner or later, that the price of running this arms race to the end is death—for both." He urged again that we "press forward now

---

*Further background on the president's preoccupation with fallout is contributed by Jerome Wiesner. In the film shown to visitors at the John F. Kennedy Library, Wiesner narrates: "I remember one day when he asked me what happens to the radioactive fallout, and I told him it was washed out of the clouds by the rain and would be brought to earth by the rain. And he said, looking out the window, 'You mean, it's in the rain out there?' and I said, 'Yes.' He looked out the window, very sad, and didn't say a word for a few minutes."

for any practical disarmament agreement within reach. . . . Our job is to bring the peaceful processes of history into play quickly, even though the ultimate resolution may take generations—or even centuries. . . . We should not let our fears hold us back from pursuing our hopes."

I was well aware of these speeches, and knowledge of such views held by Kennedy was one of the factors that made me feel I could be happy and effective as a member of his administration.

Whereas Kennedy and several of his advisers leaned strongly toward achievement of a test ban, this was not true of the constituency I was to represent. The AEC view throughout the Eisenhower period was that a test ban, as an isolated arms control measure, would endanger U.S. security. This view was shared by the Department of Defense.

The AEC was particularly restive about the test moratorium that President Eisenhower had instituted in October 1958 and opposed its extension at every opportunity. One such expression was published in the agency's annual report for 1960, which was released just before I took office. The report alleged that the continued unpoliced moratorium on weapons testing involved "risks to free world supremacy in nuclear weapons" and "a resultant threat to the free world." It stated that "our weapons scientists are convinced that further nuclear testing [by the U.S.] would achieve major advances in weapons design." It contended that great military advantages were available to the Soviet Union from clandestine tests. While acknowledging that a test ban with adequate controls might be a significant step toward better international relations, the statement concluded that it was "quite another matter . . . to continue indefinitely a self-imposed moratorium . . . while the means of detecting violations does not exist."

It was most unusual for an AEC annual report—usually a bland, if sometimes slightly slanted, narrative of the year's activities—to contain so forthright a statement of views on a controversial issue. This in itself testified to how strongly Chairman McCone and the other three commissioners, the same three who were serving with me, felt on the matter, and probably indicated that a majority of the Joint Committee on Atomic Energy felt the same way.

The AEC had also an institutional reason for opposing a test moratorium. This was the fear that it would be impossible to retain top-flight scientists in its weapons laboratories or to attract new ones if there was to be no opportunity for them to seek experimental verification of their ideas and calculations. It was felt that under those conditions scientists would simply drift away into other employments and that the vitality of the laboratories would be drastically impaired. By contrast it was felt that the weapons laboratories in the Soviet Union would be able to retain their scientists by the exercise of governmental largesse or duress, or by conducting clandestine tests, giving the USSR an important advantage in the deadly competition.

Were the Soviets Cheating?

One of the arguments in the AEC annual report against continuation of the moratorium merits additional comment. This was the contention that the Soviets could make important gains through clandestine tests in violation of the moratorium. We have the testimony of Herbert York, director of Defense Research and Engineering during most of McCone's incumbency, that McCone's views were a degree stronger than this. According to York, McCone was apparently convinced that the Soviets were, in fact, already cheating. His view was probably supported by scientists in the AEC weapons laboratories and shared by others in the AEC and in the Joint Committee on Atomic Energy. But York states: "I knew everything that McCone did, and I was convinced that the Soviets were *not* cheating."

Arriving at a judgment on this matter was a complicated process. A "smoking gun" kind of proof was not to be had. Instead, as explained by York, "It gets down to matters of detail. The intelligence on this has to do with keeping track of who goes where, what kinds of messages go from here to there, were there or were there not some strange explosions in such and such a mountain, and all that sort of thing. Nothing is clear-cut, but you take the data and analyze it all these different ways and it is fuzzy enough that there is usually room to get the answer you want."[1]

This disagreement between York on the one hand and McCone and the AEC scientists on the other provides an interesting example of the tendency of scientists to disagree on public questions, a tendency that often proves disturbing to others. One hears from lawmakers or members of the public comments such as: "If the scientists can't agree, how are *we* to decide?" Such comments often misconstrue both the nature of the controversies and the temperament of scientists. As to the controversies: they frequently turn on issues that are not scientific at all but matters of logic and common sense, as in this case of the cheating problem. As to the scientists: the public should know by now that we do not lack the political passions that infect the rest of society. A consequence is that scientists of opposing political convictions may be tempted to take the same body of data and interpret and present it in ways that lead the public toward opposite conclusions.

War in My Head

I tried to bear all this in mind as I assumed my duties as the first scientist-chairman of the AEC. My own predilections were strongly on the side of arms control in general and a test ban in particular. I felt that the future of mankind required such steps to arrest the arms race. Yet I was not inclined to put down those in the AEC community who held opposite views, usually because of strong feelings about the requirements of national safety. They had many good points to make. There seemed little doubt that there were elements of risk in seeking a test ban agreement with the Soviet Union. The question that weighed heavily, however, was whether the risks of *not* reaching an agreement might not be greater, for such reasons as Kennedy had set forth.

The opposing views of the administration leadership and much of the AEC community continued to wage war in my head and conscience for the entire period of the test ban negotiations under Kennedy, more than two and a half years. I tried to play the honest broker between them, calling to the attention of each what seemed to be valid points raised by the other. At all times, for example, I tried to counsel the administration against positions that might alienate the Joint Committee on Atomic Energy. I was in effect playing a double game in a way that I thought served the national interest. It was not easy. Freeman Dyson, who faced similar problems during his own government employment, has described the dilemma of persons placed as I was: "We are scientists second, human beings first. We become politically involved because knowledge implies responsibility. We fight as best we can for what we believe to be right. Often we fail."[2]

That I had my share of failures I freely acknowledge in this volume. Overall, my hope is that I struck approximately the right balance in attempting to nudge the government apparatus toward policies and practices that favored a test ban while still according with the technical and national security realities.

McCloy's Review

When the Geneva Conference recessed on December 5, 1960, it was scheduled to resume on February 7, 1961. One of Kennedy's first acts as president was to ask for a postponement until March 21 to allow time for a thorough review of U.S. policy. The Soviet government acceded to this request.

Kennedy placed great emphasis on thorough preparation. While in the Senate he had on several occasions been critical of this aspect of the Eisenhower administration's conduct of disarmament negotiations. For example, in March 1960 he had pointed out: "We are meeting next week in Geneva with nine other nations in an East-West Disarmament Conference, but we have prepared no plan for our conferees. We are meeting the Russians at the summit this spring to discuss, among other things presumably, disarmament, but we have no idea what our stand will be." [Kennedy was referring to the scheduled Paris summit that aborted disastrously because of the U-2 incident.] As president, Kennedy was determined that, if we were to fail again at Geneva, it would not be because of a similar lack of preparation or leadership.

Review of U.S. policy toward the test ban negotiations began immediately after Inauguration Day. It was spearheaded by John H. McCloy, who had been selected as the president's special adviser on disarmament. McCloy was a Republican attorney who had served successively as assistant secretary of war, president of the World Bank, American high commissioner for Germany, and board chairman of the Chase Manhattan Bank. He was, and is, a man of proven leadership ability and great personal charm. His low-key but persistent approach and his intellectual balance made him an ideal choice for the difficult task assigned to him.

From his own familiarity with the negotiations, Kennedy felt that some concessions could be made to the Soviet Union without trespassing on positions essential to our security. Accordingly, under McCloy's direction a painstaking examination was undertaken of the transcripts of the more than 250 negotiating sessions at Geneva to determine as precisely as possible the exact nature of Soviet complaints against elements in the Western position. A number of concessions seemed appropriate based on this review, and McCloy began to explore these with the U.S. government agencies involved.

McCloy's investigations were guided in a technical sense by an elite group of fourteen experts appointed by him on January 27. The group's principal assignment was indicated by its formal name, the Ad Hoc Panel on the Technical Capabilities and Implications of the Geneva System. Informally, the group was known as the Fisk Panel, after its chairman, James B. Fisk, by that time president of Bell Laboratories. At a time when the American scientific community was

polarized on the test ban issue, Fisk was noted for his cool
objectivity.*

The Geneva System, since it was first proposed in 1958, had
suffered an apparent loss of effectiveness initially as a result of findings in American tests (see chapter two). It had then recouped a part of
this loss through suggested improvements in technique and equipment. It was the task of the Fisk Panel to balance out all the gains and
losses and come up with a current estimate of what the Geneva
System could do.

The panel's report was submitted to McCloy on March 2, 1961. It
was an extensive document, which remains classified to this date. In
general it agreed with prior evaluations that the Geneva System's
capabilities for detecting atmospheric and underwater nuclear explosions were relatively adequate to deter any potential violator if the
system were fully implemented. The real difficulties of the system
were found in the lack of assured detection capabilities in the underground and space environments.

The Principals Endorse Concessions

At McCloy's request, the Fisk Panel's report was submitted just
in time to be available for a March 2 meeting of the Committee of
Principals. This group, little known to the public, was established by
President Eisenhower just before the 1958 Conference of Experts to
coordinate the executive branch's review of arms control policy.
Under Eisenhower it had only five members: the secretaries of state
and defense, the director of central intelligence, the chairman of the
AEC, and the president's science advisor. President Kennedy expanded the membership to include the chairman of the Joint Chiefs of
Staff, the director of the U.S. Information Agency (bespeaking
Kennedy's recognition of the importance of the propaganda aspects of
disarmament and arms control negotiations), the president's special
assistant for national security affairs and, after establishment of
the Arms Control and Disarmament Agency, its director. Under Ken-

---

*Other members of the panel were Hans A. Bethe of Cornell University; General
Austin W. Betts, director of AEC's Division of Military Application; Harold Brown of
AEC's Livermore Laboratory; Spurgeon Keeny, Jr. of Wiesner's White House office;
Richard Latter of the Rand Corp.; General Herbert B. Loper of the Defense Depart-
ment; J. Carson Mark, director of the Theoretical Division at the AEC's Los Alamos
Laboratory; Doyle Northrup of the Department of Defense; Wolfgang K. H. Panofsky
of Stanford University; Frank Press, director, Seismological Laboratory, California
Institute of Technology; General Alfred D. Starbird of AEC; and Herbert F. York,
Director of Defense Research and Engineering.

nedy, the meetings were seldom, if ever, confined to these individuals, as others were invited to participate depending on the problems to be considered.

The meeting of March 2, 1961, had been called for the purpose of drawing up final recommendations to the president on the positions our negotiators would take in the test ban negotiations in Geneva. The meeting was held in the Under-Secretary's Conference Room in the New State Department Building. Seated at the main table were:

> The Secretary of State, Dean Rusk
>
> The Secretary of Defense, Robert S. McNamara
>
> The Chairman of the Joint Chiefs of Staff, Lyman B. Lemnitzer
>
> The Chairman of the Atomic Energy Commission, Glenn T. Seaborg
>
> The Director of the Central Intelligence Agency, Allen Dulles
>
> The Administrator of the National Aeronautics and Space Administration, James E. Webb
>
> The Director of the U.S. Information Agency, Edward R. Murrow
>
> The Special Assistants to the President for:
>> Disarmament, John H. McCloy
>> National Security Affairs, McGeorge Bundy
>> Science and Technology, Jerome B. Wiesner

In addition, there were a number of assistants and observers seated around the room, bringing the total number present to thirty-two.

Rusk, who presided, established the task for the meeting, and for other meetings to follow, in his opening remarks.

> He said that the president had indicated a very serious interest in getting an agreement at Geneva. The Principals had the task of putting Dean* in a position both to get such an agreement and to protect American interests. He noted that, while the history of attempts to achieve disarmament agreements had not been encouraging, many people around the world still hoped that armament levels could be reduced. There were many dangers in disarmament; one was the tendency of democracies to disarm at the drop of a hat. Rusk nevertheless felt that it might be in our interest to accept a test ban if one could be obtained at this time. He then asked McCloy to present his views.
>
> McCloy remarked that the president's request for a postponement

---

*Arthur H. Dean, a New York attorney and an experienced diplomat, whom President Kennedy had selected to be chief U.S. negotiator at Geneva, with the rank of ambassador.

of the opening date for resuming the negotiations meant that the U.S. intended to negotiate in good faith. He noted further that considerable progress had already been made in the Geneva negotiations and that it would be unwise to strike out in a new direction. Interdepartmental discussions had been held on the issues in the negotiations, and the U.S. position had been resolved on several of them. A principal purpose of this meeting was to reach agreement on four still unresolved issues.

The first of these concerned seismic research. McCloy sketched in the background of the issue. Lack of experimental data had, from the 1958 Conference of Experts onward, been a handicap in establishing a control system and defining its capability. The three chiefs of state agreed early in 1960 to cooperate on research to remedy this problem. At the Geneva Conference in May 1960 the Soviets at first undertook to participate in a joint research program utilizing nuclear devices. They reversed themselves following the collapse of the Paris summit. They continued to insist, however, in participating in any U.S. research program involving nuclear devices to ensure that the detonations had no military purpose. The U.S. had offered to allow the Soviets to examine the exterior of the devices and witness the detonations. The Soviets said this was not sufficient and that any U.S. explosions under those conditions would be grounds for them to resume testing. They demanded the right to inspect blueprints and to examine the interior of the devices. McCloy was in favor of acceding to the Soviet demands. He proposed a U.S. position that obsolete nuclear devices be used in seismic research and that the Soviets be invited to open them for inspection before they were detonated.

McNamara and Dulles concurred in the proposal. I pointed out that the proposal was contrary to secrecy provisions in the Atomic Energy Act and that action by the Congress would be necessary before this proposal could be implemented. I said that the AEC would support the proposal on the understanding that the administration would keep in close touch with the Joint Committee on Atomic Energy regarding it. (I, of course, knew that this issue was coming up and had conferred in advance with Joint Committee members.) I suggested further that the devices used be altered so that they could not be called weapons. Rusk agreed with both points. Further, in case the Soviet Union might later claim that the shots were, in fact, weapons tests, I suggested that it might be a good idea to have present a competent neutral or a UN representative who could certify the contrary.

McCloy had difficulty with my last suggestion. He felt it might be considered strange that we could not show a device to the French, a NATO ally, but could show it to a neutral. Rusk asked McCloy to give further thought to the neutral observer suggestion and then noted that otherwise the proposal for opening research devices to the Soviets could be considered approved.

The next item discussed was a proposal that the Soviet Union be granted similar inspection privileges with regard to the inside of Plowshare devices. Plowshare was the expressive name given to

AEC's program for peaceful uses of nuclear explosions,* which were thought to have great potential for such applications as excavating canals and reservoirs and loosening up deep natural gas and oil deposits to make them available for extraction.

When test ban negotiations began in Geneva in 1958, the Soviets declared that the treaty should forbid all nuclear detonations, including peaceful ones. By 1960 they seemed to have developed some interest in conducting peaceful explosions themselves and proposed a treaty article that would have permitted such detonations in proportions of one to one for the two sides. They demanded the same conditions, however, as for the seismic research explosions, namely, the right to inspect blueprints and the interior of U.S. devices.

> McNamara and Dulles concurred in the proposal to allow the Soviet Union to inspect Plowshare devices. I agreed for AEC, objecting only to a further State Department proposal that would have established a limit on the number of Plowshare explosions permitted in specific time periods.** In response to my objection, McCloy suggested that the U.S. need not propose an upper limit initially. McCloy concluded discussion of this item by expressing his feeling that the AEC had made a considerable concession in the interest of achieving an agreement at Geneva.

I was gratified by this appreciation of AEC's position, which was indeed a difficult one. Opening the Plowshare devices to Soviet inspection would have restricted us to using obsolete devices. These were generally satisfactory for a seismic research program but were much less so for Plowshare because of their bulkiness and heavy fallout. (Seismic research could take place at an isolated test site but, ultimately, Plowshare projects might have to be nearer to human habitation.) There were, consequently, strong feelings in the AEC community against allowing the Soviets to inspect Plowshare devices, but I did not feel that this program, important as it was, should be allowed to be a source of discord impeding progress toward a test ban.

The next item on the agenda was the key item of the meeting, probably the key item of the Geneva negotiations at that stage. It concerned the quotas of annual onsite inspections on the territories

---

*"They shall beat their swords into plowshares, and their spears into pruning hooks: nation shall not lift up sword against nation, neither shall they learn war any more" (Isaiah 2:4). Herbert York states that the name Plowshare was coined by Harold Brown when the program was originated at the Livermore Laboratory in 1950 (*Arms Control: Readings from "Scientific American"* [San Francisco: W. H. Freeman & Co., 1973], p. 346).

**Two years later I found myself advancing this same proposal for an annual quota of explosions in a vain effort to save the Plowshare program from the prohibitions of the Limited Test Ban Treaty.

of the U.S., U.K., and USSR. McCloy began by reviewing the history of the proposals and counterproposals on this issue. These included the early Western ideas that *any* unidentified event should be subject to inspection, countered by Soviet insistence that *no* inspection was necessary; Prime Minister Macmillan's suggestion and Premier Khrushchev's acceptance of the idea of an annual quota; the U.S. theme that the number of inspections should be proportional to the number of unidentified seismic events; and Soviet insistence that the issue was political, not scientific. More recently, the Soviets had indicated willingness to accede to an annual quota of three inspections. The West had replaced various "scientific" formulas it had proposed (all seemed to arrive at average annual quotas of about 20) with the single number 20.

This was an issue on which it was particularly difficult to make concessions because the number 20 had become a political fact of life and was almost sacrosanct to some members of Congress. McCloy made a proposal that was ingenious because it retained this number while still offering the Soviets the possibility of a lesser number under certain conditions.

> McCloy proposed a minimum quota of 10 inspections annually on the territories of each of the original parties, with an additional inspection to be added for each 5 unidentified seismic events beyond 50, up to a limit of 20 inspections. He argued that this would mean no significant change in the U.S. position if estimates were correct that there were an average of 100 seismic events in the USSR each year. He noted that scientists had been unable to prove that any specific number of inspections had scientific validity. The Soviets were able to argue that 20 was just as political a figure as their proposal of 3. Furthermore, Prime Minister Macmillan had in a sense pulled the rug out from under us by telling Khrushchev during his visit to Moscow that a lower number of inspections (we thought it was something like 8) would be acceptable to the West. *
>
> McCloy thought it important that we return to Geneva with a fully agreed Western position. He reported that British negotiator Ormsby-Gore felt he could sell the U.K. government on the 10-to-20 proposal.
>
> Dean underscored McCloy's remarks about the importance of Western unity. He felt that if the Soviet Union sensed any disunity on the quota question they would hammer at this point and then the other

---

*Warren Heckrotte of the Livermore laboratory, who was a member of the U.S. delegation, reports: "On one Saturday morning in Geneva after a U.S.-U.K. meeting, while several of us were standing around chatting, I turned and asked a new member of the U.K. delegation just what numbers Macmillan had suggested. He responded, '3 to 15.' Carl Walske, another U.S. delegate, obtained confirmation of this in a London conversation with another U.K. official." [Heckrotte to Seaborg, June 12, 1980.] The appearance of the number 3 in Macmillan's suggestion may help to explain Khrushchev's subsequent offer of 2 to 3 inspections.

moves we were making would lose some of their impact.

Rusk commented that the key point was whether the administration could take the treaty to the country with the sincere conviction that the control system agreed upon was genuine and not a sham. He then asked the other principals for their views.

McNamara stated that he preferred to hear the views of others before commenting.

McCloy added that he felt his proposal constituted a sufficient deterrent to Soviet violation. Wiesner agreed, pointing out that intelligence information would help us to detect clandestine tests and that we also had national capabilities for distinguishing between earthquakes and explosions. He believed that a *single* clandestine Soviet test would not significantly change the power balance and that, with 20 percent sampling, as proposed by McCloy, a *series* of tests could hardly go undetected.

Dulles supported Wiesner's point about intelligence, at least in deciding which events to inspect. This would depend on the amount of work involved in an attempt at clandestine testing. For example, if large amounts of earth movement were necessary to make a "big hole" for a decoupled shot, intelligence might be able to pick up this activity.

I agreed with Rusk about the importance of being able to go to the country with a treaty that would win popular support. I felt that the treaty would be more acceptable if the number of inspections were proportional to the number of unidentified events, without any ceiling. I therefore suggested that the upper limit of 20 inspections per year be deleted.

Wiesner said that he would personally like to hold to the flat number of 20, without the 10-to-20 escalator provision, if the U.K. would go along with us. He had been told by certain Soviet scientists that, if everything else in the treaty were agreed to, there might be no problem with that number of inspections. [In retrospect, it appears unlikely Khrushchev could ever have been persuaded to go that high.]

McNamara said that, because of the fact that in some years there were many more than 100 seismic events in the Soviet Union, he felt it would be desirable to have a cumulative upper limit, a sort of bank account into which we could deposit unused inspections in years when there were few seismic events so that they could be used in years when there were many.

The variety of views expressed by the Principals on this key issue indicated that complete agreement was unlikely. Rusk resolved the matter for this meeting by concluding that the question was so sensitive that, even if agreement could be reached by the Principals, it should be discussed with the president.

McCloy then turned to the fourth and last concession to the Soviet Union being proposed for consideration by the Principals. This was to adopt the Soviet suggestion of a complete ban on weapons tests at high altitudes and in outer space. The ban would be policed by the system—a group of patrolling earth satellites plus special ground equipment— proposed by Technical Working Group I of the Geneva Conference in 1959. The problem was that, as pointed out in the Fisk Panel's report, the proposed space verification system had acknowledged weaknesses, especially in detecting explosions of devices that had radiation shielding. McCloy stated his belief that we did not stand to lose very much by agreeing to this concession. After a brief discussion, the Principals agreed to the proposal.

McNamara then indicated that he would like to raise two questions that were not on the agenda but which he thought the Principals ought to discuss. The first was how we could disengage from a test ban treaty in the event of certain actions by other countries. The second was how we could disengage from the present voluntary moratorium on tests. A member of the Geneva delegation present replied on the first question that there was a clause in the treaty draft providing for withdrawal from the treaty in case it was not being obeyed.* On the second question, McCloy believed that the president did not wish to set a date for ending the moratorium but that he did contemplate a resumption of tests if it became apparent that the Soviets were stalling on reaching a test ban agreement. McNamara wondered whether it would not be possible to plan *how* the moratorium would be broken off in such an event. Wiesner felt that the knowledge such a plan existed would torpedo the Geneva Conference.

Rusk asked how long it would take the AEC to resume testing. Betts** and I replied that tunnels were ready for underground testing and that approximately three to six months would be required for installing instrumentation and making final preparations. Rusk stated that he thought we should stand on statements the president had previously made on the moratorium question.

McNamara then said he would pose the question in a different way: Would we in fact resume tests if agreement in Geneva were not possible? Bundy said this was a poor time to make such a decision. Rusk said he had supposed we would test if there were no agreement.

Bundy remarked that he understood there was a certain urgency about conferring with congressional leaders on test ban policy. He inquired whether the Fisk report on capabilities of the Geneva System should be made available to them. I commented that we could hardly look for favorable legislative action if Congress could not review the report.

After some discussion, the Principals agreed that the president should be consulted on what steps to take next in preparing for the March 21 resumption of talks at Geneva, particularly on the unresolved question about the number of onsite inspections.

The President Takes a Hand

The meeting with the president to consider next steps and the number of onsite inspections took place on Saturday morning, March 4, 1961, in the Cabinet Room of the White House. Those in

---

*This was not completely responsive since McNamara had in mind not only the Soviet Union but also the People's Republic of China, a presumed nonsigner of any test ban treaty.
**General Austin W. Betts, Director of AEC's Division of Military Application.

attendance included Rusk, McCloy, Dean, Lemnitzer, Paul Nitze (assistant secretary of defense for international security affairs), Dulles, Wiesner, Spurgeon Keeny (Wiesner's deputy), and me.

McCloy opened by reporting to the president that there had been general agreement among the Principals on March 2 on instructions to be given to the U.S. negotiators at Geneva. A difference had developed, however, on the number of onsite inspections, and this seemed important enough for the president to resolve. McCloy explained the proposed U.S. position whereby there would be a minimum of 10 inspections per year plus the possibility of 10 more based on the number of events.

This approach was supported by Bundy, Wiesner, and others. Bundy made the point, supported by statistical arguments, that if you inspected some 10 or 20 events, even though each had a probability of only 1 in 3 or 1 in 4 of uncovering a clandestine operation, the chance that you would miss one was very small.

The president asked Lemnitzer for his point of view. Lemnitzer said, but not very forcefully I thought, that the Joint Chiefs would prefer that the number of inspections be strictly proportional to the number of detected events, with no ceiling. [I knew that the Joint Chiefs held this view and had been disappointed that Lemnitzer did not support me when I expressed it at the meeting on March 2.]

Nitze commented that the Department of Defense didn't consider the number of onsite inspections to be of paramount importance. They were more concerned with the composition of the Control Commission and the methods by which certification of an event for inspection would be made. DOD saw loopholes here that might negate the purposes of the treaty. [At Technical Working Group II late in 1959, the Soviets had proposed very rigid criteria that would have to be met before the dispatch of inspection groups.]

I then said that I wanted to be sure that the AEC's point of view was completely understood. I indicated that settling on some arbitrarily negotiated number, like 20, 3, 10, 17, or any of the others that had been discussed, was a political solution that might or might not be adequate in any given year. Adopting strict proportionality between inspections and suspicious events was, we thought, more scientific, more logical, and more likely to win support from the American public and Congress. The average number of detectable seismic events per year in the Soviet Union appeared to be about 100. If the ratio was one inspection for each 5 events, the average number of inspections per year would be 20. But the number of events seemed to vary from year to year by something like a factor of 2; that is, you might have as few as 50 detectable seismic events, or as many as 200. In some years, therefore, on a strict proportionality basis, a formula of one inspection for each 5 events could lead to less than 20 inspections, in some years more than 20.

As the discussion began to move into other subject areas, McCloy brought it back to the differences on numbers of inspections, and the president then said we should stay with the proposed formula, leading to a minimum of 10 and a maximum of 20.

Discussion next turned to how long we should continue to negotiate at Geneva if agreement were not reached speedily. It was agreed that we would not set any hard and fast time limit at Geneva but that the negotiations would have to be terminated after a reasonable time if they ran on without serious negotiation or prospect for agreement.

There was also discussion of John Finney's article in the *New York Times* for March 3, headlined "U.S. Easing Stand on Atom Test Ban", which included the statement that we had decided, if necessary, to fall back from 20 to 17 inspections per year. There was much speculation about the identity of the person "high up in the State Department" who had leaked this story. [It wasn't exactly a leak since no such decision had been made.]

McCloy next raised the question whether the report of the Fisk Panel should be made available to the Joint Committee on Atomic Energy, pointing out that it was necessary to keep them informed if we expected their support. The president said he would like to study the report over the weekend before deciding. [He decided to make it available, as revealed at the luncheon on March 7.]

The discussion turned next to the importance of working closely with members of Congress. I mentioned specifically the need for correct and timely approaches to members of the Joint Committee on Atomic Energy and the particular need to be aware of issues on which they had taken a position. As an example, I called attention to a meeting last summer where some members of the Committee had argued for reciprocity in any disclosure of obsolete weapons to the other side, whereas the present administration position was for unilateral disclosure of devices used in U.S. seismic research and peaceful nuclear explosions.

Bundy pointed out that a luncheon had been set up for next Tuesday, March 7, at which the president could discuss this and other matters with some key Democratic members of the Committee. The president asked whether it wouldn't be better also to include Republican members. In answer to Bundy's observation that this would make the group unmanageably large, the president suggested that there could be two luncheons.

A White House Luncheon

It proved possible to crowd all the desired guests into one congressional luncheon on March 7, despite Bundy's fears to the contrary. Those present from the executive branch included the president, the vice-president, Rusk, Dean, McNamara, Lemnitzer, McCloy, Bundy, Wiesner, Adrian Fisher (McCloy's deputy), and me. The members of Congress present were mostly members of the Joint Committee on Atomic Energy. JCAE Senate members present included the Committee's vice-chairman, Senator John O. Pastore; and Senators Henry M. Jackson, Clinton P. Anderson, Bourke B. Hickenlooper, and Albert Gore. JCAE House members present were Chet Holifield (the committee's chairman), James E. Van Zandt and Melvin Price. Also representing the JCAE was its executive director, James T. Ramey, later an AEC commissioner. Representing the Senate Committee on Foreign Relations were Chairman J. William

Fulbright and Hubert Humphrey. Chairman Thomas E. Morgan represented the House Foreign Affairs Committee. All the members of Congress present were Democrats except Hickenlooper and Van Zandt. This was a most formidable assemblage. It demonstrated once again Kennedy's earnestness and thoroughness in preparing for the resumption of negotiations at Geneva and also his sensitivity in dealing with his former colleagues in both houses of Congress.

The guests assembled in the Red Room of the White House, and after the president arrived and greeted each one individually, we went into the Gold Room for lunch at about 1:00 P.M.

At about 2:00 P.M. Kennedy rose and opened the discussion. He began by praising McCloy and Dean for their patriotic contributions to the government over the last decade. [Both were able to make much larger incomes in the private practice of law than in government service.] He emphasized the importance of the current Geneva negotiations and then asked McCloy to brief those present in greater detail.

McCloy began by saying that, after extensive consultation with those in the government who were particularly involved, he had succeeded in obtaining general agreement on the stance we would take at Geneva. He then went on to point out items in our position that would be of particular interest to Congress.

First of these was the seismic research program. Possibly bearing in mind what I had said about the Joint Committee's preference for reciprocity in the disclosure of nuclear devices, he stated that, should the Soviets decide to participate in seismic research, the understanding was that we would seek reciprocal inspection privileges. He went on to point out that the devices we would use in the research program would be obsolete and that their disclosure to the Russians would not constitute a significant security risk. He then mentioned that the administration was considering asking for a joint resolution of Congress to make this disclosure possible. At this point, and in the ensuing discussion also, the legislators present showed a distinct lack of enthusiasm for the idea of a joint resolution. [The president took due note of this and it became a factor in the following days.]

McCloy noted that a similar problem of disclosure arose in connection with Plowshare (peaceful uses) explosions. Although obsolete devices might be used for this program at the outset, it might be desired in a few years t.) use more sophisticated ones, and the administration proposed that the joint resolution be worded to make this possible.

McCloy went on to describe our proposed new formula, a minimum of 10 per year, a maximum of 20, for onsite inspections. At this point, the president suggested that McCloy make the Fisk Panel's report on the capabilities of the Geneva System available to those congressional leaders who were interested.

Ambassador Dean said that the U.S. delegation would take two or three weeks in Geneva to present its treaty proposals in detail and then would ask for Soviet reaction. He said it was a well-thought-out and fair program, which had been designed to win agreement. He thought it would be inconsistent with the purpose of obtaining agreement to announce any time limit for the negotiations.

Senator Humphrey asked about two issues on which there had been disagreement with the Soviets at Geneva. The first was the composition of the Control Commission. There had been agreement that there should be a seven-member commission, but no agreement on the national origin of the members. The Western formula had been three Westerners, two Easterners, and two neutrals, whereas the Soviets (insisting on parity, as I thought was their due) wanted the proportions to be 3, 3, and 1. McCloy stated that our treaty draft contemplated a Control Commission of 11, 4 from the U.S.-U.K. side, 4 from the Soviet side, and 3 neutrals. This in effect gave the Soviets the parity they sought without placing an intolerable burden on a single neutral, as would have been the case in their proposal of a 3–3–1 ratio.

The second question raised by Senator Humphrey was whether there was to be a veto over the control organization's budget. Early in 1959 the Soviets had put forward a list of "significant" Control Commission actions, including the dispatch of inspection teams, on which unanimity among the three nuclear powers would be required. This requirement was modeled after the veto power held by the five permanent members of the UN Security Council. By the end of 1960 the Soviets had, in response to Western objections, relinquished all but one of the items on their list, the item remaining being the control organization's budget. McCloy indicated that we proposed to concede to the Soviets the right to veto the overall budget, but not individual items.

There was an exchange, involving Senator Anderson and others, concerning what we would do if the Soviets did not agree to our proposed treaty. Dean indicated that our stance was to attempt in good faith to go as far as we could so that, if we failed, we would as a minimum have achieved a good position in the eyes of the world.

Senator Fulbright asked what we intended to do about the French and the Chinese, both of whom had indicated strong opposition to a test ban. Dean's reply was that the first task was to determine whether we could get a meaningful agreement with the Soviets. If we succeeded in that, we could then proceed to consider the difficult question raised by Fulbright, especially with regard to the Chinese. Someone mentioned that Soviet Ambassador Menshikov had asked whether we could deliver the French, in response to which he was asked whether his country could deliver the Chinese. His reply was that the USSR probably couldn't do anything about that until the Chinese were admitted to the United Nations.

Senator Anderson questioned whether the upper limit of 20 onsite inspections was sufficient and asked if it would apply to a year when there might be as many as 300 unidentified seismic events in the Soviet Union as against an average of about 100. Dean's reply was that it would. At this point the president, to my surprise, asked if we couldn't start out by proposing that the inspections be proportional to events, possibly leading to a number greater than 20. I broke in to say that this was precisely my position. Anderson asked what we would do if the Soviets rejected our limit of 20. Humphrey remarked that they had not yet rejected it. A spirited discussion followed among several participants, during which Anderson kept emphasizing the difficulty of getting the Soviets to agree to anything.

At this point, the president made some concluding remarks. With a smile in his voice he thanked those assembled and said he was glad to see that there was agreement on the U.S. side (laughter), and now the task was to get the Russians to agree also. He asked McCloy and Dean to make themselves available to members of the Joint Committee right up to the time of Dean's departure for Geneva—scheduled for March 14—and that they look to members of the committee for advice. The president emphasized how important it was to make a strong effort at Geneva, much more being at stake than just a test ban. The effect on world opinion could be profound. Also, if we could gain agreement on a test ban, it might enable us to move on toward agreement on other East-West issues, such as Berlin and Laos. Conversely, failure to reach a test ban agreement could make agreements on Berlin and Laos more difficult.

As we were leaving the White House, a group consisting of the president, Jackson, Rusk, Bundy, McCloy, Dean, Wiesner, and me gathered in the main White House entrance for some final discussion. Jackson stressed the need for a clear, "intellectually honest" position. The president agreed and emphasized again the fact that more was at stake than a test ban agreement. We had to think, he said, of the path we might have to go down if there were no agreement: accumulation of weapons without limit by the U.S. and USSR, the spread of nuclear weapons to other countries (he mentioned Israel as an example), and the possible consequences of all this. He said again that we had to make a serious effort at Geneva, so that, even if we failed, the watching world would recognize that we had done our best.

In informal conversation during the luncheon I took occasion to reemphasize individually to Rusk, Fisher, McCloy, Wiesner, and Bundy the advantages of having the number of onsite inspections be proportional to the number of observed seismic events, even if we were forced to a reduction in the total number of inspections. I argued that maintaining such a logical position would be more important than people seemed to realize in gaining acceptance of a test ban by Congress, the scientific community, and the general public.

In retrospect I think I made too much of a fuss about this particular point. Along with others, I tended then to exaggerate the effectiveness of onsite inspection as an enforcement tool. Also, I think I was wrong in believing that the general public would react one way or the other to particular inspection formulas. Regrettably, opinion studies seem to reveal that members of the public do not follow the details of arms control debates very closely, preferring to accept the judgments of political leaders with whom they have identified on other issues (see p. 122, for more on this subject).

On Decision Making

The meetings that occurred in early March 1961 seemed to me to represent the Kennedy administration at its best, a coming together of well-prepared, top officials to discuss matters of the highest import and, under presidential leadership, to decide, or help him decide, on significant national policies.

There is at least one prominent dissenting view about this. Henry Kissinger, early in his impressive memoir, *White House Years*, writes:

> If key decisions are made informally at unprepared meetings, the tendency to be obliging to the President and cooperative with one's colleagues may vitiate the articulation of real choices. This seemed to me a problem with decision-making in the Kennedy and Johnson administrations.[3]

I was somewhat surprised, frankly, to read this comment. It does not seem to me to be a just reflection of what actually happened. Not wishing to trust entirely my own recollection and judgment, I sought the opinion of Theodore Sorensen, who had excellent opportunities to observe what went on from his double White House vantage point as special counsel to President Kennedy and as his principal speech writer. Sorensen expressed a view close to my own:

> First of all, I think there is a lot to Kissinger's basic premise, that if serious decisions are made at informal and unprepared meetings, there is a tendency to go along and policy may suffer. However, I doubt the second part of his premise, namely that this was generally true in the Kennedy administration. Undoubtedly, it was true of many lesser decisions, but I believe that the Kennedy administration's serious decisions were made in a serious way. There may not have been the same elaborate machinery that has prevailed in other administrations, but Kennedy was very careful to make certain that all the key people whose input was needed were consulted, heard each other's views, considered all the facts and all the options, and were not rushed unnecessarily into making a recommendation to him or a decision with him.[4]

On the matter of preparation, it should be emphasized that the Committee of Principals was buttressed by a parallel group known as the Committee of Deputies. This group, representing the same agencies as the Principals, consisted of senior officials with special responsibility for arms control. Commissioner Leland Haworth, after his assumption of duties in April 1961, was the AEC member.

The Deputies tended to have longer and more frequent meetings than the Principals, and its members also established an effective network of informal consultation. Consideration by the Deputies, either formally or informally, was often so effective as to obviate further discussion by the Principals, or the Deputies would define issues so sharply that consideration by the Principals could be swift and to the point. Still, there were issues, such as the matter of onsite inspections, on which opinion within the administration was so divided that the Principals were unable to make an agreed recommendation to the president.

Aside from their value in decision making, the committee meetings contributed, I believe, to unity within the administration. Those whose opinions did not prevail tended to feel better about decisions that followed a complete airing of views, including their own. This at least was my own experience.

One must also emphasize the value of Kennedy's scrupulous practice of meeting with congressional leaders to discuss the most important decisions. Such meetings provided additional substantive input from men whose way of thinking the president, a former member of both House and Senate, understood and generally respected. Not least important, the legislators appreciated the fact that there was genuine consultation of their views. Consequently, when it came to significant congressional votes, Kennedy might lose votes because of conviction or politics, but he did not have to incur the additional liability of ruffled feathers.

Unlike Eisenhower and Reagan, Kennedy did not consider his cabinet to be a decision-making body and assembled its members irregularly. He wanted those who gathered for discussion of an issue to be experts on that issue; the background and interests of cabinet members were too diverse for all of them to be expert on most issues.

As will be apparent, Kennedy himself participated in a high proportion of the important meetings on test ban issues. In my 1964 interview for the Kennedy Library Oral History Program, I described the nature of the president's participation:

> He conducted the meetings in an informal manner. He was very pleasant to deal with. You did not have the feeling that, because you were in the presence of the president of the United States, you had to be on your best behavior. You could interrupt. I tried not to interrupt the president, but I'm not so sure that I did not do so on occasion. The president was most skilled in using information as it developed to formulate perceptive questions and thus to derive maximum benefit from the meetings.

The Kennedy Library interview with Adrian Fisher (later the deputy director of the Arms Control and Disarmament Agency) supplies additional description, which accords with my recollection, of the president's behavior at meetings:

> He'd start out by saying, "I've got X questions I want to ask," and after asking them he'd go around the room and ask each person what he thought. Then on the basis of that he'd formulate a JFK consensus. Then he'd say, "All right, what's wrong with that?" He didn't mind being argued with. I think he enjoyed it. He rather felt that the discussion wasn't as thorough as it should be if there were no objections raised.

Fisher adds: "I found the combination of the fact that he was president of the United States and the informality of him absolutely delightful."

Part of the president's informality was his tendency, which became famous, to pick up the phone and call officials, even of subcabinet rank, in order to get firsthand information on issues. To this day there are many stories being told about individuals who received such calls and their incredulous reactions, which apparently delighted the president. On one occasion, when he called me at home, one of my young sons who answered the phone became distracted and delayed informing me that I was wanted on the phone; the president waited patiently for several minutes until I responded.

I felt I could always see the president if I needed to, but I tried not to abuse the privilege. Instead, I frequently dealt with him through his excellent corps of assistants. Of these, Prime Minister Macmillan wrote: "Never has a man been so well or so loyally served."[5]

On test ban matters my contact was usually McGeorge Bundy, formally titled Special Assistant on National Security Affairs but often referred to as National Security Advisor. Bundy provided for me a most trustworthy pipeline to the president's desk and mind. I could always feel confident that the president did indeed learn what I felt needed to be called to his attention and, conversely, that what was transmitted back by Bundy represented the president's thoughts, not—as was sometimes the case under Nixon—those of a poorly informed staff assistant.

Off to Geneva

At the luncheon meeting with the members of the Congress on March 7, it had been suggested that Congress pass a joint resolution authorizing disclosure to the Soviets of the obsolete nuclear devices we might use in a seismic research program. This matter came up again at a meeting I attended at the White House on March 9 with the president, Wiesner, Budget Director David Bell, and Fred Dutton, one of the president's assistants. The meeting had been called primarily to deal with budgetary matters.

> An alternative method of disclosing research devices to the Russians was suggested, namely, simply to declassify the devices, thereby revealing them to other countries as well as the Soviet Union.
>
> I opposed this suggestion. I explained how difficult it would be politically to make an abrupt change of course after having discussed the joint resolution approach with members of the Joint Committee on Atomic Energy but two days before. The president said that, in view of the unenthusiastic reaction of the JCAE members at the luncheon, it would be better if McCloy didn't press now for a decision on a joint resolution. Instead it would be better to come back to Congress after some progress was made in Geneva. Should there be no progress, he and McCloy would not then have put themselves in the position of risking a turndown by Congress before its agreement was needed.
>
> I reminded the president that McCloy was testifying before the JCAE that very afternoon. The president thereupon called McCloy and suggested that he not press for the joint resolution.

On March 15, Joseph Alsop, the very influential and hawkish syndicated columnist, came to see me at my office. He wanted to chat about the test ban negotiations and indicated that the discussion was completely off the record.

> He asked whether I was optimistic, and I reported estimates I had heard that the chances of success at Geneva were about 50-50. He asked whether I thought the Joint Committee on Atomic Energy would agree to let the Soviets examine obsolete weapons used in a seismic research program. I indicated that this was very difficult to assess but that it would be logical for them to agree. He was interested in whether improvements in weapons could be made by clandestine underground testing, and I indicated that they could. He asked whether big weapons could be tested clandestinely, and I pointed out the possibilities in decoupling. He asked how long I thought the U.S. should permit the negotiations to go on. I replied that I thought they should continue as long as the Soviets seemed to be negotiating seriously and that success would depend a great deal on whether Khrushchev seriously wanted an agreement. Alsop closed by saying he was buoyed up by my feeling that there was some hope for the negotiations.

The next day I was interviewed by Earl Voss, a reporter for the *Washington Evening Star*.* This was also for background and off the record.

> We went into detailed issues such as the number of inspections and the disclosure of weapons in a seismic research program. I told Voss that

---

*Voss subsequently (1963) published *Nuclear Ambush: The Test Ban Trap*, which, as the title indicates, was distinctly unfriendly to a test ban. It was published before final agreement was reached on the Limited Test Ban Treaty.

the whole matter seemed to be a balance of risks: on the one hand, the risk of participating in a test ban treaty that the Soviets might violate; on the other hand, the risk of continuing to accumulate unlimited stockpiles of nuclear weapons and of having more countries possess them. There were some who placed more emphasis on the first risk and others who emphasized the second one, and this difference was, and probably would continue to be, a source of great national controversy.

On March 14, Dean and his assistants departed for Geneva. The president issued a statement expressing hope that the new U.S. proposals would "be accepted and that the negotiators [would] be able to proceed with all appropriate speed toward the conclusion of the first international arms control agreement in the nuclear age."

It seemed clear that this U.S. delegation had been thoroughly prepared. As Voss wrote, "It was the first time that a U.S. Administration had agreed within its own house on a complete program for ending nuclear tests."[6] It was frustrating to realize that no amount of preparation by our side could control events that depended so much on the seemingly unpredictable reactions of the other side.

4

A Bad Start at Geneva

Enter the Troika

Any hope that there would be an early agreement at Geneva was soon dashed. The first blow, and a heavy one, fell in the opening speech as the test ban conference resumed on March 21, 1961. It was delivered by Semyon K. Tsarapkin in his capacity as chairman for the day. Despite the Soviet Union's previous agreement on many treaty clauses referring to a single administrator for the control organization, Tsarapkin now proposed a tripartite administrative council composed of one Soviet, one Western, and one neutral member. The council would be able to act only by unanimous agreement. This proposal paralleled a similar Troika* arrangement that the USSR was then advocating to replace the UN Secretary-General, Dag Hammarskjold, whose activities in the Congo they found objectionable. In defending the proposal, Tsarapkin said that in matters "affecting exceedingly sensitive aspects of the national security of States there

*Troika is a Russian term for a vehicle drawn by three horses abreast.

can be no reliance on the will or caprice of one person." He stated that "it is impossible to find a completely neutral person."

While formal response to the Troika proposal was delayed, there was no doubt of the Western powers' position. For example, on April 5 and 6 Vice-President Johnson visited the Geneva Conference and was reported to have said that the United States would never accept a treaty "subject to crippling vetoes."

The formal Western response came on April 20 in a statement by Ambassador Dean. He told the Soviets that the requirement of a unanimous Troika was the complete antithesis of effective control, that no party to a treaty could "let any other party . . . exercise a veto on control operations," and that if the Soviets were unyielding on this issue they would be "ruling out the possibility of a test ban treaty." President Kennedy underscored Dean's statement in a press conference the following day. He said it was obvious that the Senate would not accept a treaty that included the Troika "nor would I send it to the Senate, because the inspection system then would not provide any guarantees at all."

In his opening address on March 21, Tsarapkin also took the occasion to raise the question of the continuing French tests. He accused the U.S. and U.K. of endlessly dragging out the discussions at Geneva to provide France time to conduct tests from which her NATO allies would profit. He mentioned the possibility that the French tests were creating new types of weapons. Russian scientists were probably aware that the French devices were relatively crude. Nevertheless, the Soviets could have been genuinely concerned about the apparent inability of the U.S. and U.K. to restrain the French, thus demonstrating that a test ban confined to the Big Three might fail to prevent the spread of nuclear weapons to additional countries. France's fourth detonation, on April 25, did nothing to allay this concern, although the French government announced immediately afterward that it would conduct no further tests in the atmosphere, a pledge that was subsequently broken.

Western Concessions Introduced

Notwithstanding the discouraging start at Geneva, Ambassador Dean went ahead on opening day, March 21, with the offer of the various concessions to the Soviet Union which had been discussed within the U.S. government and agreed to by the British in the preceding weeks. The concessions included:

1. The proposed length of the moratorium on underground tests below seismic magnitude 4.75, and of the associated seismic

research program, was increased from two to three years. The Soviets had wanted a moratorium of four to five years, apparently feeling that our ability to profit from smaller underground tests exceeded their own.

2. The United States undertook, "if agreement on other treaty provisions was in sight," to seek legislation permitting the Soviets to examine the internal mechanisms of nuclear devices employed in U.S. seismic research and peaceful explosions programs. Dean made it clear that the United States would expect reciprocal rights if there were any Soviet research or peaceful-uses detonations.

3. The West agreed to a total ban on tests in space and to the means of verification proposed by Technical Working Group I, despite the limited effectiveness of the verification system.

4. While preferring a plan providing for twenty-one internationally staffed detection posts on Soviet soil, the West agreed to relocate two proposed posts into neighboring parts of Asia, leaving a total of nineteen in the USSR. The Soviets had said they would accept no more than fifteen on their territory.

5. The West accepted a Soviet proposal that each originating party be assigned an equal quota of onsite inspections. Thus, under the Western proposal, there could be twenty inspections per year in the United States and twenty in the United Kingdom, instead of a total of twenty between the two as previously offered.*

6. The Soviet request that each original party have a veto over the control organization's total budget was granted.

7. Formulas were introduced which met Soviet demands for East-West parity in the staffing of detection stations and of the control organization's Vienna headquarters.

8. Parity was also accepted in the Control Commission by means of the 4−4−3 formula discussed earlier.

These concessions by the West constituted an earnest effort, based on McCloy's painstaking study, to meet such Soviet demands as did not seem to undermine U.S. security or trespass on strong views of U.S. congressional leaders. It was an effort that was to win

*Hubert Humphrey pointed out here a "glaring inconsistency" in the Soviet position. When it came to the number of inspections or to financial contributions, the Soviets wanted the U.S. and U.K. to be reckoned as separate entities, each having a share equal to that of the USSR. When it came, however, to the staffing of the Control Commission headquarters staff and detection stations, the Soviets wanted U.S. and U.K. shares to be pooled so that there would be parity between Soviet representation and that of the U.S. and U.K. combined. (U.S. Congress, Senate, Subcommittee on Disarmament, "Analysis of Progress and Positions of the Participating Parties," 86th Congress, second session, October 1960, intro.)

much praise from commentators around the world. This was indeed one of its purposes; if agreement could not be achieved, President Kennedy was determined at least to reverse previously unfavorable world opinion and swing it to the U.S. side.

The Soviet response was not wholly negative. On April 4, Tsarapkin accepted "in principle" the Western concessions regarding the seismic research and peaceful explosions program. He also accepted the proposals banning high-altitude tests and permitting a veto of the total budget. A week later the Soviets agreed to the 4—4—3 composition of the Control Commission, after initially rejecting it.

Thus, the major U.S. effort had succeeded in reducing somewhat the number of issues dividing the two sides. Wide differences remained, however, on such fundamental issues as:

1. The Soviet Troika proposal versus the Western concept of a single neutral administrator.
2. The annual quota of onsite inspections, the West proposing twenty, the Soviets offering three.
3. The number of detection stations on Soviet soil, the West proposing nineteen, the Soviets offering fifteen.
4. The question of whether detection stations and inspection teams should be manned almost entirely by host country personnel, as the Soviets wanted, or entirely by personnel from other countries, as the West wanted.

The West Tables a Complete Treaty

On April 18, 1961, the United States and United Kingdom introduced at the Geneva Conference a complete draft treaty, embodying "agreements previously reached by the conference" plus the Western position on all the contested issues. Dean and Ormsby-Gore made the further rather theatrical gesture of offering to sign the draft treaty at once. As Tsarapkin later commented, why would they not be ready to sign a treaty drafted by themselves?

The draft treaty, with some still further liberalizing amendments, remained open for signature during the next sixteen months. It thus was part of the diplomatic atmosphere during that period. At the risk of some repetition, it may therefore be useful to summarize it.

The treaty would have banned all nuclear tests in the atmosphere, in outer space, and in the oceans, and all tests underground except those producing signals of less than 4.75 seismic magnitude. (Tests below that threshold were thought to be too small to be detected and identified consistently by the proposed verification system.) It was proposed by the West, though not set forth in the draft treaty, that there would be a three-year moratorium on underground tests below the threshold. The moratorium would be renewable annually while further research was carried out to improve techniques of detection.

The treaty was to be policed by a worldwide detection system operated by a single administrator and an international staff, headquartered in Vienna. Policy direction was to be provided by a Control Commission of eleven members, four from the Soviet side, an equal number from the U.S.–U.K. side, and three neutrals. Commission decisions were to be by a simple majority. The commission was to appoint the administrator.

The detection system was to utilize 180 manned detection stations on land—19 on Soviet soil—and on ships at sea. Each station was to be instrumented to detect illegal tests by their sound, light, and radio waves, nuclear radiations, radioactive fallout, and seismic signals. The detection stations were to be supplemented in doubtful cases by inspection—carried out by an international team of experts—at the site of possible violations. There were to be a maximum of 20 inspections per year on the territory of each of the three original parties. Inspection teams were not to include nationals of the country being inspected, but that country could escort the inspectors and determine the route they traveled.

Detonations for peaceful purposes could be undertaken only with safeguards to ensure that no party would use them to gain a military advantage. The safeguards included disclosure of the devices to, and observation of the detonations by, the other side.

The headquarters staff of the control organization was to be composed one-third of USSR nationals, one-third of U.S. and U.K. nationals, and one-third of nationals of other countries. The same proportions were to be used to staff detection stations. The chief of each detection station on the soil of an original party was to be drawn from the other nuclear side. The technical staff of onsite inspection groups was also to be drawn from the other nuclear side, though the host country might designate observers to accompany the inspection groups.

Annual contributions to the control organization's budget by the U.S. and USSR were to be equal, with the U.K. contributing a lesser amount. Each of the three original powers was to have a veto on the budget as a whole, but not on individual items.

Although he withheld formal response, Tsarapkin declared on April 19 that the proposed treaty was nothing more than a set of old

Western proposals clipped together and that his country refused to sign a comprehensive test ban treaty that would allow the United States to test nuclear weapons underground. One month later the Soviets formally rejected the draft treaty.The USSR negotiating stance seemed so intransigent and unreasonable that some observers (e.g., Earl Voss), bearing in mind what was to follow in late summer, have inclined to the view that the Soviets were trying to goad the West into breaking off the negotiations. Someone less dedicated than Kennedy to achieving a test ban might well have done so. I believe that his insistence on keeping the negotiations open contributed to the final successful result.

On May 29, the Western powers offered to abandon their demand for twenty onsite inspections per year on the soil of each original party. They proposed instead a formula similar, though not identical, to that discussed by the Committee of Principals on March 2. Under this formula the number of inspections might vary from twelve to twenty, depending on the number of unidentified seismic events beyond sixty. In rejecting this proposal on May 31, Tsarapkin asserted that the number of inspections sought by the West was still "artificially high," and he repeated the often-voiced Soviet position that the determination of an acceptable number had to be a political rather than a scientific issue.

A New Atmosphere in Geneva

The first stage of test ban negotiations under the Kennedy administration seemed destined to failure. But something significant had nevertheless happened at Geneva. It had to do with the spirit and pace of the negotiations, with the relative amount of initiative being exercised by the two sides, and with a swing in the tide of world opinion. The change is perhaps best noted in the words of Daniel Lang, a writer for the *New Yorker* magazine, who visited the Geneva Conference repeatedly and recorded his impressions.*

Writing in July 1961, Lang noted:

> In the past year, the atmosphere at the conference has altered considerably. A year ago, as one member of our delegation put it to me quite unofficially the other day, "the United States was dragging its feet." At that point, as nearly everyone connected with the talks realized, it was the Russians who were pushing the conference forward, providing ideas, granting concessions, and displaying a certain restraint in making propaganda capital of an opponent's

---

*They were published seriatim in the *New Yorker* and later collected in a book, *An Inquiry into Enoughness*(New York: McGraw-Hill, 1965).

singularly wavering conduct. . . . At present, though, thanks to a thorough overhauling of our position by President Kennedy and his advisors, it is the Americans who are forcing the action. In contrast to a year ago, British diplomats here are delighted with our burst of initiative, and are no longer chafing at the faltering ways of their formidable partner. It is the Russians who now appear to be dragging their feet, and Western representatives here are quick to offer evidence that this is not their view alone. It was pointed out to me that organizations given to demonstrating publicly against any use of nuclear arms have recently made the Soviet Union the target of critical remarks; sections of the Japanese press that were formerly hostile toward us are writing appreciatively of our new policies; and a similar shift of sentiment has occurred in India, Sweden, and neutral African countries.[1]

Dean, briefly home from Geneva, confirmed this shift in world opinion at a White House meeting on May 2. He said that, for the first time, many newspapers in Europe were commending our stand and our action in tabling the complete text.

The tough policy-making sessions in March at the Committee of Principals, the National Security Council, and the White House had not led to a test ban, but they had contributed to a change in world opinion, and this was not to be despised. As Arthur Schlesinger wrote, Kennedy, "like Wilson and [Franklin] Roosevelt, regarded opinion as a basic constituent of power."[2] Favorable world opinion, however, would not be sufficient to deal with the challenge that lay ahead. Sterner measures would be required.

5

Internal Debate,
External Challenge

Differing Views

While the diplomats held forth in Geneva, voices were being raised at home with comments and suggestions about the course the United States should be taking. My journal entry for March 18 took note of one such expression:

> I had dinner with Leo Szilard at the University Club.* He thinks that attempting to obtain a nuclear test ban treaty is the wrong approach to disarmament; that the U.S. and USSR should first explore the ways and means of getting along in the world in some other way. This might be started by having meetings of high-level, nongovernment groups from both sides. Another, perhaps even better, way would be to have President

---

*Szilard was one of two (Eugene Wigner was the other) scientists who prevailed on Albert Einstein to write the famous letter to President Roosevelt that initiated the World War II atomic energy project. He was a colleague of mine during the war, an eloquent "dove" on issues related to nuclear weapons, including testing, and altogether one of the most brilliant, innovative, and unpredictable people I have known.

> Kennedy and Khrushchev meet to explore the problems on a broad, rather than a narrow negotiating basis.

The latter method was soon to be tried, with dismaying results.

Another segment of opinion that made itself heard throughout this period was that of dedicated idealists who urged that the surest path to world peace was unilateral disarmament by the West. I was visited by an advocate of this view on March 25.

> I met with Don DeVault of the Society for Social Responsibility at 10:00 A.M. in my office. DeVault was an old friend of mine, dating from his graduate school days at Berkeley in the late thirties. His purpose in coming was to tell me in advance of a vigil that was to be conducted at AEC's Germantown headquarters on March 31 by the Witness for Peace Group. He assured me that it would be well-ordered and quiet [as indeed it was] and that these vigils were designed to encourage people to reflect about world problems and the need for disarmament. He asked whether I had any comments or words of advice.
>
> I told him that I doubted, in terms of the facts of life and political reality, that this tactic (vigils) would lead toward achievement of his aims; that, for example, it would probably have little effect on Congress, which would have to implement any movement toward his objective. As far as the objective itself was concerned, I said that there was a fear that uncontrolled unilateral disarmament could cause a loss of freedom and that many people valued freedom more than life itself. He said that freedom to him meant doing what he thought was right, even at the risk of going to jail.
>
> The conversation was very friendly, and he expressed delight that I had become AEC chairman.

The meeting with DeVault haunted me afterward. It seemed to throw into sharp relief an essential dilemma of our time. On the one hand, the humanity in all of us cried out for release from the crushing burden of armaments and the mounting danger of nuclear holocaust. On the other hand, the immediate threat of a hostile nuclear power, the Soviet Union, was there and could not be ignored by a responsible U.S. government. How could the nation's safety and institutions be protected in the short run without losing sight of the larger, more distant goal of a world in which the enormous energies and resources now squandered on armaments could be redirected to bettering the human condition? As I reflected on this, it seemed to me that here was precisely the significance of the president's quest for an end to nuclear testing. A test ban offered, quite simply, a means to arrest the momentum of the nuclear arms race and to begin a momentum heading the other way.

To balance the voices calling for disarmament, there were those urging a prompt resumption of testing by the United States. On April 21:

> John McCone phoned to tell me that he had sat in on a session with McCloy and his staff people yesterday. McCone said he was very disturbed because throughout the discussion there was a kind of feeling that it wasn't important to do any testing. He said that if the Geneva negotiations broke down, as seemed likely, he would oppose our just standing still. He seemed to feel very strongly about this.

On the same day:

> I met with McCloy, Fisher, and others to discuss readiness capability in case it was decided to resume testing. McCloy wanted me to take a position on whether to resume testing, but I said the need of the AEC to develop weapons had to be balanced against so many larger factors that I didn't think AEC's attitude should be given undue weight.

In view of past performances, this must have seemed a most extraordinarily reticent position for an AEC chairman to take.

Weighing the Options

Once he became convinced that there would be no early agreement at Geneva, Kennedy began to consider the options available to him. At a White House meeting on April 22:

> The president asked McNamara how important it was to resume testing. McNamara said that testing was particularly important in three areas: (1) to increase the yield-to-weight ratio of a number of nuclear warheads; (2) to study the effect of the enemy's defensive weapons on nuclear warheads; and (3) to develop the neutron bomb.
>
> The president suggested that McCloy prepare a position paper emphasizing two or three points that could be used by Dean and Ormsby-Gore in a further try at Geneva. This might be followed by a communication from the president to Khrushchev.

Here was clearly indicated the split in the president's thinking: he was at one and the same time considering both the resumption of testing and a harder try for a test ban.

On May 2, I attended another meeting at the White House. At this meeting:

> McCloy gave a brief summary of the situation and ended by suggesting that the Joint Chiefs of Staff might want to prepare a briefing on the possible accomplishments of testing that would be presented to the president, with the secretary of state and myself present. [Such a briefing was presented at a special meeting at the White House on May 19.]

The president was concerned that any suspension of negotiations at Geneva take place in such a way as to reflect the least discredit on the United States. At this same meeting on May 2, he asked Ambassador Dean for his recommendations.

> Dean said that he wouldn't break off negotiations now, but that perhaps the president and the prime minister should send a letter to Khrushchev pinpointing some of the difficulties and suggesting they get down to brass tacks. The letter might be sent about May 22, allowing ten days to two weeks for a reply. Meanwhile the interested agencies could be preparing for the president a comparison of what the U.S. and the Soviet Union stood to gain from resumed testing. Depending on what this showed, the president might announce on or about June 15 that we intended to resume.
>
> Kennedy suggested we might state publicly that we had evidence the Soviets were conducting clandestine underground tests. Dulles said this possibility could not be excluded on technical grounds, but that CIA had no evidence of Soviet tests and that he doubted they were testing because of the political risks involved if they were caught. Dulles acknowledged, however, that Air Force Intelligence did not agree with this point of view.
>
> The president wondered whether he should make a statement before Dean returned to Geneva. Dean thought he should and that the statement should highlight the problems. It was concluded that the president might make some comment, including a hope for progress, at his press conference three days hence.

One should note in passing the reappearance at this meeting of the question about whether the Soviet Union was violating the test moratorium—the matter on which McCone and York had the disagreement mentioned earlier. It is not entirely clear whether the president really believed the Soviets were cheating or merely suggested they were to see what response he would get. Especially interesting is the fact that CIA and Air Force Intelligence appeared to have reached opposite conclusions on this matter. My own view, as I expressed it in my Kennedy Library interview in 1964, was that the Russians were probably not cheating during the moratorium.

As agreed at the meeting on May 2, Kennedy did issue a statement on the negotiations. It came on May 15 and was conciliatory in tone. Still the president conveyed the message that his patience had limits. He observed that the Soviets had put forward their Troika proposal before they had had an opportunity to consider Western test ban proposals. He hoped our proposals would now be considered in a positive manner. He noted that Dean was returning to Geneva that day to resume the negotiations, and concluded, "I have asked Ambassador Dean to report to me within a reasonable time on the prospects for a constructive outcome."

On May 19 the president convened another meeting at the White House. An unusually large number of military people were present. The purpose of the meeting was to hear a classified briefing by Harold Brown, recently appointed director of research and engineering for the Department of Defense, on the kinds of weapons the U.S. could develop through further testing. Following the briefing there was a general discussion.

> The president asked what the Russians needed most from testing. Brown answered that they did not appear to need larger strategic warheads so much as lighter, more maneuverable ones. The president asked Air Force Chief of Staff LeMay whether, if we made a strike, it would be effective enough to prevent retaliation. LeMay said it probably would not be. LeMay suggested that the interests of both the U.S. and USSR lay in the development of smaller missiles. The president asked about the reliability of the Atlas and Polaris missiles, and LeMay gave some estimates.
>
> The president then reported on the answers to a question that had been directed to our embassies around the world. They had been asked to estimate the reaction if we were the first to resume testing. They all said it would be very adverse. *
>
> The president went on to say that all factors bearing on this question must be weighed and that, if the decision appeared to be a close one, perhaps we should wait a while before resuming. On the other hand, if the answer seemed clear, we should begin immediately to think of the steps that should be taken to minimize the adverse reaction.
>
> Bundy made the point that it was very important to obtain better evidence on whether or not the USSR was conducting clandestine tests. Dulles said that technical means of detection simply could not be relied on to obtain evidence of low-yield tests and that whether intelligence could uncover evidence of such tests was a matter of luck. [This of course bore out precisely the position of Herbert York, cited earlier.]
>
> The president then raised the question of where we should do the testing and on what time scale it should be announced if he did decide to resume. He also asked McCloy and Murrow to think about a course of action that would increase public awareness of the problem created by the Russian intransigence in Geneva.

The president seemed at this time to be beset by indecision in resolving the question: to test or not to test. From what we could

---

*Ambassador John Kenneth Galbraith wrote from New Delhi: ". . . a resumption of testing would cause us the gravest difficulties in Asia, Africa and elsewhere. Certainly no other foreseeable problem could cause us so much difficulty in India." (Schlesinger, *A Thousand Days*, p. 455.) The president was doubtless also under heavy pressure from the British. Warren Heckrotte recalls a luncheon in Geneva at about this time where he "was seated between Sir Michael Wright (the head of the British delegation) and Senator Hickenlooper. Sir Michael spent most of the luncheon pleading with the Senator that the U.S. should not resume testing. The British were very concerned that we meant to do so." (Heckrotte to Seaborg, 12 June 1980.)

gather, he seemed to be coming down on the negative side. I commented on this in my Kennedy Library interview:

> I had the impression that the president was not convinced that it was necessary, for purposes of national security, to resume testing. I had a chance to check this impression in a telephone conversation with McCloy the day following the meeting of May 19th, and he and I both agreed that the president seemed to feel . . . that there was no deep military need for nuclear testing at that time. . . .
>
> Then I had a chance to confirm this impression firsthand, more or less by chance, about a week later when I attended the president's birthday dinner. [This was a huge $100-a-plate affair given by the Democratic National Committee at the National Guard Armory.] The president engaged me in conversation about the problem of resuming testing and gave me the impression—in fact I believe he stated it in so many words—that he doubted there was any need for testing nuclear weapons at that time. So if one were trying to assess President Kennedy's posture at that moment—let us say at the end of May 1961—I would say that he was unconvinced, but willing to hear the arguments and to continue to sift the evidence and assess data.

There was soon to occur an event that would change the president's view.

Confrontation in Vienna

Shortly after Kennedy's election, Premier Khrushchev made it known to U.S. Ambassador Llewellyn Thompson that he was interested in an early meeting with the president. At a February 11, 1961, meeting in the White House attended by Thompson and three other former ambassadors to the Soviet Union—Averell Harriman, Charles Bohlen, and George Kennan—along with Rusk and Bundy, it was agreed that an informal get-acquainted meeting would be useful.

The president wrote to Khrushchev on February 22 suggesting such a meeting. The idea was presumed dead after the Bay of Pigs misadventure in April. But on May 12 Kennedy received an unexpected reply from Khrushchev suggesting a meeting in Vienna early in June. The event was scheduled for June 3 and 4, directly after a meeting in Paris with General de Gaulle which the president had been planning for some time.

The Vienna meeting occurred at a time of maximum Soviet self-confidence. They had recently crowned their earlier Sputnik triumphs by sending cosmonaut Yuri Gagarin into orbital flight around the earth, the first such journey by a human being. The United States had suffered its crushing Bay of Pigs reverse in Cuba but five weeks earlier. Communist forces were on the march in Southeast

Asia. The rate of Soviet industrial growth was exceeding our own. Such factors had led Khrushchev to conclude in a truculent speech in Moscow: "There is no longer any force in the world capable of barring the road to socialism."

This mood of bellicose confidence was reflected in Khrushchev's demeanor during the Vienna summit conference. As the president said in a radio-television report to the nation following the meeting, June 3 and 4 proved to be "a very sober two days." The conversation, while civil, was exceedingly tough. Whereas Kennedy appealed for a sort of global standstill that would avoid changes that upset the balance of power, Khrushchev insisted on the Soviet right to support wars of national liberation. The president noted in his report: "We have wholly different views of right and wrong, of what is an internal affair and what is aggression; and, above all, we have totally different concepts of where the world is and where it is going."

Khrushchev's most menacing statements were on the Berlin situation. He announced an intention to sign a peace treaty with East Germany before the end of the year. This would abrogate the West's transit rights to Berlin, and access would then be up to East Germany to grant or deny. If East German borders were violated, force would be met by force.

On test ban matters Khrushchev was adamant. As the president reported:

> Mr. Khrushchev made it clear that there could not be a truly neutral administrator, in his opinion, because no one was truly neutral; that a Soviet veto would have to apply to acts of enforcement; that inspection was only a subterfuge for espionage in the absence of total disarmament; and that the present test ban negotiations appeared futile. [This was an excellent summary of the Soviet position, in very few words.] In short, our hopes for an end to nuclear tests, for an end to the spread of nuclear weapons, and for some slowing down of the arms race have been struck a serious blow. Nevertheless, the stakes are too important for us to abandon the draft treaty we have offered at Geneva.

Averell Harriman told me of the effect of this meeting on Kennedy:

> When I met the president in Paris before his trip to Vienna I told him that he ought to go there to have a good time and that if Khrushchev threatened him he should not take it seriously. Khrushchev could be very crude and tough in the way he talked but there was quite a lot of difference between his threats and his actions. I don't think Kennedy fully understood that. It was the first time he'd seen Khrushchev and he was very much shocked, very much upset, shattered really, by this conversation in Vienna.[1]

Two diplomats experienced in negotiating with the Soviets felt that Kennedy did not acquit himself well in Vienna. George Kennan, who had seen a transcript of the conversation, stated: "I felt that he permitted Khrushchev to say many things which should have been challenged there on the spot. . . . I think this misled Khrushchev, [who] . . . failed to realize on that occasion what a man he was up against. . . ."[2] Kennan went on to speculate that Khrushchev's impression of Kennedy as a "tongue-tied young man who isn't forceful" may have had some influence on the later decision to place missiles in Cuba.

Llewellyn Thompson felt that Kennedy had made a mistake in letting the discussion get off on ideological grounds. Thompson stated:

> The President never quite appreciated the fact that a Communist like Mr. Khrushchev could not yield [on such matters] even if he wanted to. . . . For example, when the president proposed that neither side try to upset the balance of power, Khrushchev pointed out that this was scarcely consistent with . . . their view that victory of Communism was inevitable throughout the world.[3]

Opinion on Kennedy's performance in Vienna is by no means unanimous. Arthur Schlesinger refers to the idea that Khrushchev browbeat and bullied Kennedy at Vienna as a "legend," adding: "A reading of the record dispels that impression. Each made his points lucidly and vigorously. Each held his own. Neither yielded ground."[4]

Those of us who dealt with the president noticed a change after the hard experience in Vienna. I commented on this in my Kennedy Library interview:

> I would say that his meeting with Chairman Khrushchev seemed to be somewhat of a turning point. I do not believe it was ever . . . a right angle change of direction, but I do have the impression that after this meeting he was more inclined to think that the resumption of testing was inevitable. It was something that he did not like to do, but it was one of the matters that had to be faced up to, and perhaps was only a matter of time.

Preparing—While Seeming Not To

Soon after the Vienna meeting, Kennedy began to direct the administration's attention to the detailed practical considerations that would be involved if there were a resumption of testing. The president's concern was that, if circumstances required the United States to resume—and he was still not convinced that this would or should happen—it be done in such a manner as to have the least unfavorable impact on world opinion.

A first consideration was to decide what might be tested. At a Principals meeting on June 16, Defense Secretary McNamara and I received a joint assignment to draw up a plan of weapons to be tested, including their time schedule and priority. As our two agencies worked on this assignment, it became apparent that there were some differences in our points of view. The AEC wanted to conduct only those tests that its laboratories felt to be necessary in order to develop new or improved weapons. Defense wanted to include also some "proof tests" of very large weapons already in the stockpile, not only to determine whether they remained operable but also for the respect such brandishing of U.S. nuclear muscle might inspire among the nations of the world. Because of these differences between the AEC and Defense, it was decided that the two agencies would send separate papers.

There now entered a new element that initiated a difficult juggling act between appearance and reality that was to persist for the next two months. The president wanted to make a further try at Geneva, and while he felt our test preparations should continue, he did not want them to attract undue attention, lest this prejudice the diplomatic outcome. I first learned of this in a phone conversation with McNamara on June 28.

> McNamara reported that the president spoke to him yesterday and indicated he was thinking of starting preparations within three to five weeks on some important tests that might be scheduled for six months from now. McNamara told the president that the Defense Department's paper, already sent forward, had recommended such preparations but had indicated we could test well *before* six months. The president felt it might be politically desirable (with reference to the negotiations and the upcoming UN General Assembly meeting) to defer testing for six months but didn't want to give politics as the reason for the delay. He preferred for us to say we could not get ready for an important test in less time. So that there would be nothing on the record to the contrary, McNamara had withdrawn Defense's paper and I said I would do the same with the AEC paper.

Kennedy's balancing act was difficult to sustain. In view of the hard line taken by the Soviets, both in Geneva and Vienna, pressures on him to order a resumption of testing were mounting in intensity. On June 14 Chairman Holifield of the Joint Committee on Atomic Energy appealed to the president to abandon the test moratorium while at the same time continuing to negotiate in Geneva. Implying that the Soviets might be conducting clandestine tests, Holifield stated: "The time has come when we can no longer gamble with the destiny of the United States and the free world." Holifield said that his views, presented in a House speech and a subsequent news conference, were supported by a majority of the Joint Committee. He further indicated that Kennedy had been informed in advance of his statement, leading to speculation that he was launching an administration "trial balloon."

A further nudge toward test resumption came from the tense situation in Berlin. On July 17 the Western allies rejected Khrushchev's proposals for a German peace treaty and the establishment of Berlin as a demilitarized free city. The Soviet reply on August 3 declared that the West would have to negotiate or accept the consequences of unilateral Soviet action. Ten days later the East German government closed the border between East and West Berlin and began construction of the Berlin Wall.

The news media played a part in complicating the situation. It had been the policy of the AEC since adoption of the test moratorium in 1958 to admit reporters and photographers to the National Testing Site in Nevada. This policy accorded with the U.S. stance as an open society and helped to establish beyond doubt that we were observing the moratorium. When requests for press visitations were received in the early summer of 1961 we granted them as usual, feeling that a reversal of policy at that particular time would arouse suspicion. As a result, considerable publicity was given to the existence at the Nevada site of completed test tunnels. Some of these had in fact been made ready for tests in the VELA seismic research program, but they clearly could be used for underground weapon tests if needed.

Kennedy was quite upset about this publicity since it ran directly counter to his desire to call as little attention as possible to our test preparations. On July 12 Bundy called to voice the president's displeasure:

> Bundy also said that the president had raised the question whether the AEC had commenced unauthorized preparations for testing. I assured him that we had not but then asked, in view of the president's concern, whether we should grant a request that had just been received on behalf of photographers of *Life* magazine. Bundy wanted to refer this question to the president.

Bundy called back the following day to say that President Kennedy had decided that photographers should not be admitted to the test site so long as the test ban negotiations were in a sensitive stage.

Another person who was concerned about the publicity given to the tunnels at the Nevada test site was Hubert Humphrey. Indeed, Senator Humphrey went further, suggesting in a letter he sent to me on July 6 that "the very discussion at the White House level of the renewal of American testing is very apt to encourage the Soviets to prepare to start their own testing forthwith."

On July 14 I went to the Capitol to talk to Senator Humphrey. I noted in my journal:

> He wants very much to take the right stand on testing, and feels he is not at all sure what this should be.

This frank avowal of uncertainty, so characteristic of this utterly honest man, reflected the closeness of the issue. I could not but feel that Senator Humphrey's uncertainty mirrored that felt by the president himself.

While Senator Humphrey may have been ambivalent about the near-term resumption of testing, he was not so about the long-term need for a comprehensive test ban. On that issue he was an ardent advocate. Warren Heckrotte recalls:

> The Senator visited the [U.S. Geneva] delegation during the summer of 1961. We had special staff meetings for him, with the U.K. delegation in attendance. He spoke strongly in favor of a comprehensive test ban and was strongly critical of its principal opponents, whom he identified as the AEC, the Defense Department, certain scientists, generals, etc. He evidently felt that I, as the AEC representative on the delegation, deserved all the criticism—it was heaped on me at length, with an occasional request to explain this or justify that. It was a harrowing experience for me! Afterwards, Charlie Stelle [Ambassador Dean's deputy] suggested that the Senator and I chat privately in Charlie's office. We did, and the Senator was another person—quiet, thoughtful and not at all dogmatic.[5]

I must say that this last is an exact description of the Hubert Humphrey I encountered from time to time: "thoughtful and not at all dogmatic." Perhaps not quiet.

Kennedy must have perceived the problem created by his reluctance to make test preparations in the open, and early in August he moved to resolve it. The occasion was a White House meeting held on August 8, 1961, with Vice-President Johnson, McNamara, McCloy, Bundy, and me in attendance.

> The president began by suggesting two alternative approaches. The first was that he would make a statement saying that, although the decision to test had not been made, we thought we should achieve test readiness and the AEC laboratories were proceeding to attain that position. Alternatively—and the more the president thought of this, the more he seemed to favor it—the AEC would go ahead with test preparations and at the proper time indicate it was doing so to be ready in case the president decided to test. Bundy questioned the need to make such an announcement in the near future, but the president continued to indicate that this might be the best course. I then suggested that I give the

president a memorandum listing the steps that might be needed to achieve a desired state of readiness. The president agreed to this.

I was able to submit the list of preparedness actions in a letter to Bundy on August 10, only two days after the president requested it, because we had been working on such a list in the ordinary course of AEC business. In presenting the list, I had to indicate that the testing schedule I had set forth in the AEC paper written in July was no longer attainable:

> What has happened is this: The sensitivity of even talking about test readiness has caused us to limit the discussions to a relatively few people in AEC's Washington headquarters. Now, as we commence to consult our field headquarters, the many details upon which a test series must finally be based are being uncovered. . . . We must keep in mind that our experience in underground testing is limited and . . . [that it] introduces a new dimension in pre-test preparations.

My letter went on to distinguish between preparedness steps that involved a minimum risk of public disclosure, primarily administrative, technical, and procurement actions, and those that would increase the risk of disclosure. The latter involved excavation and construction activities at the site. To preserve secrecy we had stayed our hand on these.

I concluded my letter with a sober appraisal:

> If the president could be assured of a meaningful test series that could be conducted on relatively short notice, he could be provided a much greater degree of flexibility in dealing with the broader policy questions he must decide. He does not have that flexibility with our present state of readiness.

At the White House meeting on August 8, I had the opportunity to take up another matter with the president. This was to propose a somewhat unorthodox course of action should we decide to resume testing. I had been promoting this idea since late in June, having discussed it in separate conversations with McCloy, McNamara, Bundy, Schlesinger, and Senator Humphrey.

> I pointed out that, historically, weapons work, from design through laboratory experiments, had been carried out secretly and then we had jumped to open tests. A principal reason for this seeming contradiction was that the tests were carried out above ground, so that secrecy was not possible. Now that we were preparing to test underground, we could consider a different procedure. My plan would envisage having the president make an announcement that the United States considered itself free to resume testing, that we were making preparations to do so, that we would test only

such devices as the national security demanded, and that we would not announce individual tests.

The president asked the others what they thought about this. Bundy and McNamara said they agreed with the idea. McCloy seemed generally to agree. The president suggested that it would be impossible to carry out even underground tests without their being reported in the *New York Times*. I agreed that it would not be possible to keep all the tests secret but contended that the plan would decrease the publicity noise level considerably and that it would give us a method of slipping into a testing situation with a minimum of adverse public reaction. The president said he would give the idea serious consideration.

Had we been the first to resume testing, it might well have been done that way. But things were to work out somewhat differently.

Teetering on the Brink

The United States was inching toward a state of readiness for testing. But still there was no apparent resolution in the president's mind of the essential question: Did the national interest require an early resumption of testing? The argument in the country on this issue continued unabated. I myself was exposed to a wide spectrum of views. Thus, on July 24:

> Alvin Graves and William Ogle, in charge of testing at Los Alamos, came in to discuss certain preparations that would be needed if testing were resumed. I asked them if they thought it should be. Graves, while expressing mistrust of the Russians, indicated doubt that there was any test of sufficient importance to justify the resumption of testing. Ogle felt that Russians could not be testing very large weapons if they were testing at all; therefore, there was no urgent need for us to test.

By contrast, on August 10:

> I met with a member of the House Appropriations Committee, Congressman John R. Pillion of New York, regarding AEC's fiscal year 1962 budget. He wanted to put additional money into the budget for testing and urged us to maximize development of the dirtiest possible weapons [i.e., weapons having a maximum of radioactive fallout].

The following day:

> I was interviewed by Joseph Alsop. He felt that delaying the resumption of testing in deference to the upcoming UN General Assembly meeting was nonsense.

Most significantly, a Gallup Poll in July showed more than two-to-one public support for a unilateral resumption of testing by the United States. This contrasted with a Gallup Poll in 1957 showing 63 percent support for a test ban and was a further indication of how mercurial public opinion was on this subject.

In all this debate, Russian intentions constituted a major uncertainty. As to these, ambiguous signals were received by McCloy during a July visit to Khrushchev at his summer house at Sochi, near Yalta on the Black Sea. McCloy had been conferring in Moscow with UN Ambassador Valerian Zorin in an effort to find a basis for resuming disarmament negotiations. Their talks had begun in Washington, and as the Washington phase came to a close on June 30, President Kennedy had invited Zorin to pay him a visit at the White House.

Khrushchev's invitation to McCloy may have been prompted by Kennedy's to Zorin. If so, he greatly exceeded the example in hospitality. McCloy, with his wife, daughter, and niece, were entertained by Khrushchev and various members of his family for two days, July 26 and 27, in a most lavish and cordial manner. Between the bouts of hospitality the two men managed some long and far-ranging talks, the principal topics being disarmament and the Berlin crisis. On nuclear testing McCloy reported two significant, but somewhat conflicting statements by the Russian leader. On the one hand, Khrushchev repeated a pledge made in August 1958 that the Soviet Union would not resume testing unless the West did so. On the other hand, Khrushchev stated that he was under pressure from Soviet scientists and military people to authorize the testing of a weapon yielding 100 megatons.

The Panofsky Panel

It had become customary since World War II to refer troublesome policy questions to technical experts, and the president resorted to this expedient to help resolve the doubt in his own mind about testing. On June 24 he announced appointment of a special panel from the President's Science Advisory Committee under the chairmanship of Stanford University Professor Wolfgang K. H. Panofsky.*
The panel was asked to consider the perennial question of whether or not the Soviet Union could be conducting clandestine tests, and what progress they could make by so doing; also, what progress the United

---

*Other members of this most distinguished group were William O. Baker, vicepresident, Bell Telephone Laboratories; Hans A. Bethe, professor of physics, Cornell University; Norris E. Bradbury, director, Los Alamos Scientific Laboratory; James B. Fisk, president, Bell Telephone Laboratories; John S. Foster, director, University of California Radiation Laboratory (Livermore); George B. Kistiakowsky, professor of chemistry, Harvard University; Frank Press, director, Seismological Laboratory, California Institute of Technology; Louis H. Roddis, president, Pennsylvania Electric Co.; John W. Tukey, professor of mathematics, Princeton University; Walter H. Zinn, vice-president, Combustion Engineering, Inc.

States could make if it resumed testing and whether, if both sides resumed, the Soviets could catch up with the U.S.

The Panofsky panel deliberated for about a month. I recall sitting in on several of its sessions, some of which were held at Camp David. The panel's conclusions did not indicate any immediate need for testing. They reported that it was conceivable that the Soviet Union had conducted secret tests, but that there was no evidence that it had done so or had not done so. They concluded further that, although the absence of testing had introduced certain limitations on U.S. weapons development possibilities, these could in large part be compensated for by other methods. The panel felt, however, that in the long run, if the Soviets were testing secretly, the United States could not continue the test ban moratorium without impairing its military position.

The Panofsky Panel's report was presented and discussed at a meeting at the White House on August 8, 1961. All the key people were present: the president, the vice-president, McNamara, Lemnitzer, Bundy, Wiesner, McCloy, Dean, and others. Significant additions to the usual attendance list were Panofsky and the directors of AEC's weapons laboratories, John Foster, and Norris Bradbury, both members of the Panofsky panel.

> This meeting was convened to consider whether immediate resumption of testing was warranted. Advocates of immediate testing made strong statements. One such was by Lemnitzer who filed a Joint Chiefs of Staff paper challenging the premises and conclusions of the Panofsky report.* Foster argued that immediate resumption of atmospheric tests was needed to develop the neutron bomb. In response, both the president and Wiesner questioned whether development of the neutron bomb had progressed to the testing stage.
>
> The president made it clear that if we were the first to resume testing it would be below ground, after which it could be expected that the Soviet Union would test in the atmosphere. He then directed to Panofsky, Foster, and Bradbury the following question: "If you were satisfied that the Soviet Union was *not* testing, would you favor our resumption underground?" Panofsky and Bradbury answered with somewhat hedged "no's," Foster with an unequivocal "yes."
>
> McCloy argued that we should not resume when the UN General Assembly was about to meet. He had in mind the U.S. and U.K. request that the agenda include an item entitled: "The Urgent Need for a Treaty to Ban Nuclear Weapons Tests under Effective International Control." Also the heads of twenty-five nonaligned nations were scheduled to meet in Belgrade on September 1, and any indication that we intended to resume testing would surely provoke condemnation by this group.

*Arthur Schlesinger's notes of the meeting described the JCS paper as "assertive, ambiguous, semi-literate and generally unimpressive" (*A Thousand Days*, p. 456).

The Gauntlet Thrown

The meeting on August 8 apparently persuaded the president that there was no urgent need for an immediate resumption of testing. The stage was thus set for an additional strong effort at Geneva. The president announced on August 10 that he was asking Ambassador Dean to return to the conference table in two weeks for a decisive test of Russian intentions, adding that if there appeared to be no prospect of agreement, "I will then make the appropriate decisions."

Dean's instructions were determined at a White House meeting on August 17. The principal matter under consideration was whether the West could offer the Soviet Union a further concession relative to the treaty threshold of 4.75 seismic magnitude. It will be recalled that the draft treaty introduced by the West forbade underground tests with an explosive force exceeding this threshold; those below it were to be covered by a voluntary three-year, renewable moratorium. In rejecting this package the Soviets had objected to the fact that it would permit the U.S. to test below the threshold at the end of the moratorium.

At the White House meeting:

> Dean suggested lowering the threshold below the 4.75 limit, or perhaps eliminating it entirely, at the close of the moratorium period. I pointed out that eliminating the threshold could violate the basic U.S. position that the treaty should deal only with enforceable measures. It was finally agreed to take my suggestion to lower the threshold only to the level where verification was feasible. Depending on technology three years hence, this might imply redistribution of manned detection stations in the USSR, and perhaps adding as many as 200 unmanned stations in order to get to a lower threshold.

The concession we decided on was presented by Dean at Geneva on August 28. It provided for convening a panel of scientists six months before the end of the three-year moratorium to propose improvements in the control system and to recommend the degree to which the threshold on underground tests could be lowered, or even eliminated, based on these improvements.

Tsarapkin showed no interest in the Western concession, merely repeating the Soviet litany that a test ban could only be achieved in the context of an agreement on general and complete disarmament. Tsarapkin, like Dean, had shortly before been home conferring with his superiors and arrived back in Geneva at about the same time as Dean did. As Warren Heckrotte recalls: "We on the U.S. delegation assumed (correctly!) that Tsarapkin had returned with a message. Our speculations on what it might be ran the gamut of positive and negative moves. None of us guessed right."[6] Still there had been vague premonitions. Heckrotte again:

> In July the U.K. pressed for an August recess. The Soviets indicated a readiness to recess if we proposed it—their typical approach. I recall Charlie Stelle saying he felt instinctively that a recess could be a mistake. Since he couldn't identify the reasons for his misgivings, however, we sent a message to Washington asking authorization to propose the August recess. And the message came back: stay in session. Charlie's instincts were right, as were also Washington's. If we had recessed, the course the Soviets had chosen would have been a little less awkward for them.[7]

In any case, the reason why Tsarapkin was not interested in the new U.S. concession became evident two days later, on August 30.

> I spent the day at home, supposedly on my vacation. About 6:00 P.M. I received a phone call from Bundy saying that a Tass transmission of items for provincial papers, monitored earlier in the day, had contained a statement, scheduled for release at 7:00 P.M., that *the Soviet Union had decided to resume nuclear testing*!
>
> Bundy's call to me was followed by others from Wiesner and McNamara relating to how soon AEC could perform a weapons test, what tests should be made and under what circumstances, and what should go into a presidential statement.

We were able to learn of the impending Soviet announcement hours before its release because, at about 1:15 P.M., Washington time, an alert monitor at a U.S. listening post in Cyprus fished this item out of reams of copy being teletyped from Moscow to the Caucasus in Cyrillic characters. It was in the hands of the State Department about two hours later, and the president was informed soon after. The round of conferences and consultations, of which the phone calls to my home were a part, then followed, making possible a prompt U.S. response to the actual Soviet announcement.

The announcement came through at 7:00 P.M., right on schedule. It was a long statement addressed "not only to the friends of the Soviet people who correctly understand the peace-loving policy of the Soviet Union, but also to those people in foreign countries who might perhaps judge too severely the carrying out by the Soviet Union of tests of new types of nuclear weapons."

The statement was filled with denunciation of Western policy toward Germany. It was illusory, the statement asserted, to think that a new war would be waged without using thermonuclear weapons. The Soviet government blamed the Western powers for failing to accept its disarmament and Troika proposals. It charged them with failure to adhere to the conclusions of the 1958 Conference of Experts and of encouraging the French tests. It asserted that peaceful explosions were a cover for military developments. The Soviets said that they had designs for a series of superpowerful bombs as well as rockets capable of delivering these weapons to "any point on the globe" and would now proceed to test them.

And so, all at once, we confronted a grim new challenge. To determine the proper response would be far from easy.

PART THREE

Reluctant
Militancy

6

Over the Brink

Meetings, Meetings

President Kennedy was on his way back from a news conference when he was informed of the USSR's decision to resume testing. "His first reaction," reports Theodore Sorensen, who was with him at the time, "is unprintable."[1] His second reaction was to begin to marshall the resources of the government in order to orchestrate the U.S. response.

By virtue of the communications coup through which we had learned of the Soviet decision hours earlier, it was possible for the president to issue a brief statement almost immediately after the USSR's formal announcement on the evening of August 30, 1961. Kennedy's statement was a bitter denunciation of the Soviet decision, which the president said would "be met with deepest concern and resentment throughout the world." He noted that the Soviet resumption of testing was linked "with threats of massive weapons which it must know cannot intimidate the rest of the world." Kennedy concluded by stating that the Soviet decision left the United States "under the necessity of deciding what its own national interests require. Under these circumstances Ambassador Arthur Dean is being recalled immediately from Geneva."

The following day, August 31, I attended a rapid-fire series of meetings convened to help the president determine the exact form and timing of the American response. The first of these meetings took place at 10:00 A.M. in the Cabinet Room of the White House. In addition to the president and vice-president, those present included McNamara, Lemnitzer, Brown, Murrow, Rusk, Bohlen, Bundy, Schlesinger, General Maxwell D. Taylor,* Wiesner, Dulles, and Sorensen.

> The president suggested that one method of proceeding would be for the AEC to announce it was making preparations in case a decision was made to resume testing. This would have the advantage of avoiding a commitment to test so soon after the Russian announcement, thereby allowing our propaganda advantage to run for a while. At the same time it would reassure our own people and our allies that we were not standing still.
>
> Murrow argued strongly for waiting perhaps as much as a few weeks before making any statement that we had decided to test in order to let the Soviet action have its maximum unfavorable effect on public opinion around the world. He felt that this would tend to isolate the Communist bloc.
>
> Rusk favored an immediate commitment to test in order to avoid any impression that the president was being indecisive. The vice-president tended to agree with Murrow that there shouldn't be an immediate test resumption announcement but also pointed out that it would be hard to hold that line very long against congressional pressure; Senators Gore and Symington had made pro-testing speeches already that morning.
>
> McNamara proposed saying to the upcoming meeting of congressional leaders that we saw no military requirement for bombs of 100 megatons. This would be a way of reassuring the legislators that the proposed Russian tests of such large weapons would not place us at a disadvantage.
>
> The primary conclusion of the meeting was that we should defer decision until the president could determine how realistic it was to hope that pro-testing congressional leaders would not stir things up too much over the next few days.

The next meeting, also held in the Cabinet Room, began at 10:45 A.M. It was attended by the president, the vice-president, McNamara, Rusk, Murrow, Lemnitzer, Bundy, McCloy, Dulles, and a large number of congressional leaders, including, among others, Senators

---

*Newly appointed adviser to the president on military and intelligence affairs, later to be chairman of the Joint Chiefs of Staff.

Mike Mansfield, Henry Jackson, J. William Fulbright, Albert Gore, Thomas Kuchel, Stuart Symington, Everett Dirksen, Richard Russell, Leverett Saltonstall, John Pastore, and Hubert Humphrey; and Congressmen Chet Holifield and Charles Halleck.

The president announced that he was directing the AEC to be ready to test before the end of September, but he wanted also to explore the possibility that, by delaying a public announcement of this, we could derive maximum propaganda benefit from the Russian action.

Russell [chairman of the Senate Armed Services Committee] concurred that we should take full advantage of this "God-given" propaganda opportunity and delay any announcements. Gore inquired as to the reaction in Western Europe. Murrow said that it had generally been one of revulsion to the Russian action and favorable to the United States. Gore seemed also to favor delaying any U.S. announcement.

Holifield was concerned about the effect on the British of any long period of silence in which we didn't indicate our intentions. He felt that a public announcement of our intention to resume testing should be made within a few days and that we should be careful to leave open the possibility of atmospheric as well as underground testing.

McCloy thought the U. S. should defer a public announcement but, when the announcement was made, it should leave open the eventual possibility of atmospheric testing.

There then ensued some speculation as to what lay behind the Soviet move. Jackson wondered whether it might not reflect some weakness, such as Khrushchev having internal difficulties or some problem with China. He also mentioned the possibility that they might have a spectacular new device that required testing.

Dulles said that the CIA saw no sign of any rift in the Soviet hierarchy. * Humphrey suggested that Khrushchev might just have yielded to pro-testing pressures in the Soviet Union, pointing out that it had taken tremendous forbearance on the part of President Kennedy to resist such pressures in this country.

Dirksen said he thought the Soviet Union was seeking to gain respect by inspiring the maximum amount of fear. Gore agreed that the Soviet goal was world intimidation; they wanted to break the will of the world to resist, particularly the will of Western Europe. He suggested that the president should state publicly that the United States had a superior stockpile of weapons and that there was no need for alarm.

McCloy said that he was puzzled by the Soviet action since Khrushchev had told him during his Black Sea visit that the Soviet Union would not test until the U. S. did. Something had changed his mind; perhaps the idea that he could frighten the world with the 100-megaton bomb. McCloy thought we should give some time to trying to figure out what was motivating the Russians.

---

*This was another failure of U.S. intelligence to add to the failure to detect Soviet preparations for testing. Recent scholarship has revealed that throughout this period there were sharp differences between a faction led by Khrushchev, which leaned toward serious arms control negotiations, and a hard-line faction supported by the armed forces.

Vice-President Johnson felt the Soviet action might be a reaction to their failure to intimidate the West in the Berlin situation. (He had recently visited Berlin on a morale-building mission.)

The president thanked the congressional leaders and the meeting broke up with a consensus that the AEC would make preparations to resume testing, but that there wouldn't be any announcement until after the Labor Day weekend five days hence.

McGeorge Bundy has written that "of all the Soviet provocations of these two years [1961 and 1962], it was the resumption of testing that disappointed [Kennedy] most."[2] What lay behind this Soviet decision remains something of an open question to this date. Various explanations other than those advanced at the August 31 meeting with congressional leaders have been offered. Thus, a 1966 study for the M.I.T. Arms Control Project indicated that the main military reason for the Soviet resumption of testing probably was the realization that the United States was producing far more nuclear delivery systems than the USSR. A second, more political, reason suggested by the study was the need to demonstrate that the Soviet Union was the military equal of or superior to the United States, thus "enabling Soviet peace propaganda, and, if desirable, Soviet policy, to proceed on the basis of negotiating 'reasonably' from a position of great strength. The resumption of testing also helped to offset criticism of Khrushchev's version of peaceful coexistence as being too soft."[3]

From his vantage point as a member of the U.S. test ban negotiating team in Geneva, Warren Heckrotte offers another possible explanation. Referring to President Eisenhower's announcement, following the end of Technical Working Group II, that the United States would no longer be bound by its voluntary test moratorium when it expired on December 31, 1958, Heckrotte states that this was interpreted by the Soviets as seeming to indicate that the United States intended to resume testing. Heckrotte continues: "I've wondered if this event did not give impetus to the Soviet decision to begin preparations for their extensive test series."[4]

As to whether in resuming testing the Soviets went back on a pledge not to be the first to do so, Heckrotte comments: "The Soviets at Geneva, and perhaps elsewhere, were always careful in their phrasing; they would not test before the 'Western powers.' While some may have tacitly equated 'Western powers' with the United States, the Soviets in Geneva in 1961 said more than once that if France continued to test they might be compelled to resume testing."[5]

Five minutes after the end of the congressional meeting on August 31, I attended another meeting, with many of the same members of the administration present. Kennedy came in toward the end. The purpose of the meeting was to draft a presidential statement, since a high degree of national and world interest was focused on the U.S. government's reaction to the Soviet announcement.

The White House statement, released later that day, read:

> The President met this morning with members of the National Security Council and with Congressional leaders to discuss the resumption of nuclear testing by the Soviet Union. It was recognized that the Soviet announcement was primarily a form of atomic blackmail, designed to substitute terror for reason in the present international scene.
>
> What the Soviet Union is obviously testing is not only nuclear devices but the will and determination of the free world to resist such tactics and to defend freedom.
>
> The President is entirely confident that the size of the U.S. nuclear weapons stockpile and the capabilities of individual weapons and delivery systems are wholly adequate for the defense needs of the United States and of the free world.
>
> The President shares the disappointment registered throughout the world that serious and sustained attempts to ban nuclear testing have come to this abrupt end.

World reaction to the Soviet move was one of shock and dismay, but it did not constitute the enormous propaganda victory for the West that had been hoped for and predicted. Particularly disappointing was the reaction of the heads of twenty-four nonaligned nations whose meeting in Belgrade began on September 1. Although a few of these leaders expressed displeasure that Khrushchev had chosen the eve of their conference as the moment to announce his action, they generally refrained from any direct criticism of the Soviet Union. Instead, they made individual statements of alarm at the world situation and joined in asking Kennedy and Khrushchev to have a summit meeting in order to avert a world war.

On September 1 the Russians conducted their first test, detonating in the atmosphere a weapon yielding approximately 150 kilotons. Following receipt of this news, President Kennedy called me at home (I was still "on vacation") to ask how soon the AEC could conduct a test. I said this could be done in about one or two weeks, but not in such a manner as to derive all the desired information because there was not time to emplace diagnostic equipment.

A New Western Proposal

Kennedy now made a surprise suggestion. I learned about it at a meeting called by Rusk on September 2. Also present were McCloy,

Dean, Bundy, Murrow, Brown, and the following, not previously introduced in these pages:

Herbert Scoville, CIA deputy director for science and technology;

Roswell L. Gilpatric, deputy secretary of defense;

Harlan F. Cleveland, assistant secretary of state for international organization affairs; and

General Earle G. Wheeler, army chief of staff, representing the Joint Chiefs of Staff on this occasion.

> Rusk said that the president had called him from his summer vacation place on Cape Cod to suggest that the United States and Great Britain should propose an immediate atmospheric test ban with no inspection.
>
> The meeting was called to determine if such a pact would have any adverse effects on U.S. preparedness efforts. Gilpatric and Brown noted that the proposed treaty would foreclose U.S. atmospheric tests needed to test antimissile weapons, to test the hardness of our missile-launching sites, and to assess the effect of electromagnetic radiation on these sites. The effect on the peaceful-uses program (Plowshare) was also considered, but it was agreed that the stakes were so high that this could be disregarded.
>
> The consensus was that a treaty forcing both sides to do their testing underground would impede the Russians more than ourselves and that the U.S. and U.K. should go forward with the proposal.

This discussion was most significant since it foreshadowed the debate that would be held two years later on the essentially similar Limited Test Ban Treaty.

The joint U.S.-U.K. release proposing the atmospheric test ban came on September 2. The release said that the aim was to protect mankind from radioactive fallout and to reduce tensions. It stated that the West still wanted a comprehensive test ban treaty and regretted "that the Soviet Government [had] blocked such an agreement." It gave the Soviets until September 9 to reply.

While the U.S.-U.K. proposal was a serious one, there was very little hope that Khrushchev would respond positively. The main expectation was that the proposal would embarrass him and swing world opinion more heavily to our side. The proposal had the added significance that it marked the first time that the West had offered to accept any form of test ban without international control machinery.

The President Decides

Khrushchev soon gave a measure of confirmation to those who believed that his goal in resuming tests was intimidation. In an interview on August 31 at his Black Sea summer home with two left-wing members of the British Parliament, he stated that he had decided to resume testing in order to shock the Western powers into negotiating on Berlin and disarmament.[6]

As the official responsible for conducting U.S. testing activities, it distressed me to find that many on our side wanted to emulate Khrushchev in emphasizing the political effects rather than the military preparedness aspects of testing. The Soviet tests had whipped up a sort of frenzy in which people seemed to reckon each experimental explosion as a blow, strong or weak according to its TNT equivalent, struck for one ideology or its rival. Even the president seemed to be caught up in this contest for a time. From my standpoint, trying to conduct an orderly test program from which the nation could gain the maximum scientific and technical information, this game of kilotons for the sake of kilotons created serious problems. I described some of these in a letter I wrote to Bundy in response to his phone call following the Russian announcement of August 30.

> You inquired how soon we would be able to commence testing, and, from the way you phrased your question, I had the impression you were more or less hoping it would be soon. . . . There are certain things we could test . . . in one or two weeks. On such short notice, however, these would have to be on a "go, no-go basis" [i.e., would the weapons function or would they not?]. . . . Indeed this would be the only information the tests would provide since adequate diagnostic instrumentation could not be emplaced and made operative in time. . . .
>
> I would like to stress again [that] if we proceed on this basis . . . [it would have] the disadvantage of interfering with subsequent tests which are far more important. As you know, there are only a limited number of underground test tunnels now available. It is for this reason that I would suggest that consideration be given to the planned program . . . indicated in my letter . . . of July 19. This program was carefully coordinated with the Department of Defense and could be commenced in about four or five weeks.

All this came up at a September 5 meeting with the president, at which Bundy, General Taylor, Brown, Gilpatric, General Betts, and I were present. The Soviets had by this time conducted a second test in their new series, this one in a range between 10 and 80 kilotons.

> The discussion centered on what was to be the yield of our first test. I indicated we could have one of approximately 20 tons by about September 15.
>
> The president felt that the disparity between a 20-*ton* yield and the first Soviet test of about 150 *kilotons* would invite much adverse comment. He wanted a much larger test, 20 or more kilotons, if possible,

but he did not want to accept any delay. I told him that, while we could ready a device in the desired size range, such a large test conducted so soon would jeopardize the availability of the rest of the tunnel complex where it might be carried out.

General Betts suggested that a proof test of a 2-kiloton guided missile warhead could be conducted by September 15 if approval were given immediately to go ahead with the preparations. The president agreed to this. We told him that the preparations would result in an increase of activity at the test site that could not be hidden from public view. The president said he was prepared to accept whatever press reaction might follow.

Later that same day the president decided he could wait no longer to announce publicly the U.S. intent to resume testing. What changed his mind was news of a third Soviet test. The president's statement, brevity itself, especially as contrasted to the twelve-page statement issued by the Soviet government on August 30, read:

> In view of the continued testing by the Soviet Government, I have today ordered the resumption of nuclear tests, in the laboratory and underground, with no fallout. In our efforts to achieve an end to nuclear testing, we have taken every step that reasonable men could justify. In view of the acts of the Soviet Government, we must now take those steps which prudent men find essential. We have no other choice in fulfillment of the responsibilities of the United States Government to its own citizens and to the security of free nations. Our offer to make an agreement to end all fallout tests remains open until September 9.

It obviously was not easy for the president to take this step, which he had been resisting for so long. Speaking to Adlai Stevenson, then ambassador to the UN, after the decision was announced, the president, as reported by Arthur Schlesinger, said,

> "What choice did we have? They had spit in our eye three times. We couldn't possibly sit back and do nothing at all. We had to do this." Stevenson remarked, "But we were ahead in the propaganda battle." Kennedy said, "What does that mean? I don't hear of any windows broken because of the Soviet decision. The neutrals have been terrible. The Russians made two tests *after* our note calling for a ban on atmospheric testing. Maybe they couldn't have stopped the first, but they could have stopped the second. . . . All this makes Khrushchev look pretty tough. He has had a succession of apparent victories—space, Cuba, the thirteenth of August [the Berlin Wall], though I don't myself regard this as a Soviet victory. He wants to give out the feeling that he has us on the run. The third test was a contemptuous response to our note. . . . Anyway the decision has been made. I'm not saying it was the right decision. Who the hell knows? But it is the decision which has been taken."[7]

A Bad Start

The first U.S. test went off on schedule at 1:00 P.M. Washington time on September 15. I informed President Kennedy approximately five minutes later. Pierre Salinger, the president's news secretary, was informed at about the same time, and he issued an announcement to the press at 1:08 P.M.

At first, all seemed to have gone well, although the shot's yield was 6 kilotons rather than the expected 2 kilotons.

> About an hour later we learned that small amounts of radioactivity had vented from the tunnel into the atmosphere. Still later we learned that some of this radioactivity had reached areas outside the test reservation. The venting semed to have been caused by some followup chemical explosions.
>
> About 4:00 P.M. General Luedecke* and I went to see the president to explain the venting. We met with him in the Lincoln bedroom where he had been taking a nap. Wiesner, Salinger, and Schlesinger were also present. We informed the president that the amounts of radioactivity were very small, but that it could be misunderstood if it became public knowledge. I was particularly concerned because the president's test resumption announcement on September 5 had said there would be "no fallout" from our tests, and the White House announcement of the test had said: "There was no fallout."
>
> The president took it very well. As a separate matter, he decided that the AEC should make a postshot announcement of tomorrow's test.

Kennedy's decision about an announcement was a reversal of his previous position that the United States probably would not announce each test after the first one. This was but one more manifestation of the difficulty that this matter of media relations caused the administration throughout this period. We seemed to be dealing with two conflicting imperatives. On the one hand, there were the needs of a military preparedness program to proceed with a minimum of disruption and also to keep some secrets from the other side. On the other hand, there was the desire to behave in a manner consistent with the institutions of a free society, to be open with our own citizens. It was not easy to reconcile these opposing considerations, and we never seemed to master the problem to our satisfaction.

A Drift Toward Atmospheric Testing Begins

Now that both the U.S. and the USSR were testing, it was inevitable that comparisons would be made between the two test programs. The Soviet program was by far the more impressive. Begin-

---

* Alvin R. Luedecke, AEC general manager.

ning with the start of their series on August 31, the U.S. monitored fifty Soviet atmospheric tests within a period of sixty days. It was the most intense sustained test series the world had yet seen, exceeding in megatonnage the totals reached by all preceding tests of all nuclear nations. The series of tests we began on September 15 seemed relatively puny by comparison. In the remainder of 1961 we conducted only eight tests, in a six-month period only twenty, all underground. The yields of the individual U.S. tests were generally 20 kilotons or below. In contrast to our previous optimism about underground testing, we found it at first to be slow, costly, and replete with unanticipated complications.

One of the complications was the fact that the initial test on September 15, in the process of venting, had contaminated one of the two test tunnels at the Nevada Test Site with radioactivity. It would be many weeks before the tunnel was usable again, in spite of strenuous, three-shift clean-up operations. There were also certain kinds of tests that could not be conducted underground under any circumstances. These included tests at higher yields, those designed to prove the effectiveness of complete weapon systems (including the missiles), and tests of antimissile weapons.

The president became aware of the slowness of underground testing when we sent for his approval a list of proposed tests with their scheduled dates. I heard from Wiesner's office that, while the president had authorized the tests, he was far from happy with the time span required and had said that the program must be speeded up. The president appeared to feel that every day the U.S. was in a test series involved a political price; he wanted to be freed from this burden as rapidly as possible.

On September 19, I departed for a European trip the principal purpose of which was to lead the U.S. delegation to the annual general conference of the International Atomic Energy Agency. Upon my return, I found that Bundy had confirmed in writing the president's request for a speedup of our testing schedule. I accordingly wrote the president on October 7 to give him some bad news, and also to hint at the apparent remedy. I wrote: "This issue has been thoroughly investigated during my absence. . . . It is the conclusion of the Commission that we cannot accomplish any significant speedup in the presently planned program without resorting to atmospheric testing, although it is not the purpose of this letter to make a recommendation for atmospheric testing at this time."

With the UN General Assembly then in session in New York, our testing situation raised diplomatic as well as technical problems.

Resolutions were being discussed that would ask the nuclear powers to declare another test moratorium without controls or, as a variant, to renounce tests in the atmosphere. I wrote to Rusk on October 7 giving the AEC's view that the United States should oppose these resolutions. After relating some of the inadequacies of underground testing, I stated: "In our opinion these factors clearly constitute strong reasons for retaining the President's option to initiate atmospheric testing should he deem it necessary in the interest of national security."

We now initiated with atmospheric testing a cycle remarkably similar to what had prevailed with underground testing but a few months earlier. We were confronting essentially the same questions: Should we begin to make preparations, should the preparations be announced, and finally, should we test in the atmosphere?

Before considering how these issues were resolved, we should pause to catch up with some developments having to do with the government's organization for dealing with arms control and disarmament problems and also with negotiations on "general and complete disarmament," which the Soviets were now insisting must be linked with the test ban question.

7

Organization and Disarmament Initiatives

An Agency Is Born

Long before he became president, John Kennedy had been aware of and had inveighed against this country's lack of preparation to make sustained serious efforts in arms control and disarmament. For example, in a major address to the Senate in June 1960, then-Senator Kennedy said: "Our conferees have consistently gone to the international bargaining table ill-staffed, ill-prepared and ill-advised."

The record appears to substantiate Kennedy's statement. In the years 1945 through 1961 the United States was represented at some seventy international gatherings at which arms control or disarmament were discussed. During this sixteen-year period, U.S. delegations were led by sixteen different officials, frequently individuals who, while they might have distinguished themselves in other fields, knew little about the intricate technical matters at issue.[1] By contrast, there was great continuity in the leadership of Soviet delegations, revolving among a handful of highly trained and experienced individuals. This was true as well of their supporting staffs, which generally consisted of skilled and experienced professionals, whereas U.S. staff teams tended to be recruited hastily on an ad hoc basis.

The relative weakness of the U.S. negotiating teams was particularly great on the political side. This was nowhere more evident than at the 1958 Conference of Experts. The ranking political officer on the U.S. delegation was a thirty-three-year-old foreign service reserve officer, class 4, who had been in the State Department for only three years,[2] while the Russian delegation included Tsarapkin, the senior Russian diplomat who, as we have seen, later became chief Soviet delegate to the Geneva test ban conference. Nor did the U.S. delegates receive any political guidance from senior officials at home. Secretary of State Dulles stated at a press briefing as the delegation was departing for the conference: "I told them to look on their job as a purely scientific technical job. I do not anticipate that there will be any need for political guidance."

The delegates were to learn how naive a view this was when, for example, they were required to take positions on the desired number and location of international seismic detection stations without being told what risks of Soviet evasion the U.S. was prepared to assume.[3] The negotiators were further hampered by the fact that they were unable to obtain decisions from Washington at several critical points during the conference. It is not surprising that the result of the conference's work, the so-called Geneva System, was to prove a source of difficulty and embarrassment as its inadequacies gradually became apparent.

One of the greatest weaknesses in the American approach to arms control and disarmament was a basic shortage of pertinent technical information. While the State Department had a small staff working in this area, the group had no authority to conduct the scientific and technical research necessary for the development of sound proposals. We have already noted how, until the appointment of James R. Killian as scientific advisor in 1957, the bulk of the information about nuclear weapons received by President Eisenhower and Secretary Dulles was filtered through AEC Chairman Lewis Strauss, who reported the results of work at AEC and Defense Department laboratories in accordance with his own strong pro-testing convictions. Later, when the Killian group contributed a more balanced flow of scientific information, it was still often not the type of information needed to support the work of U.S. arms control negotiators.

A further great weakness was the inability to reconcile the divergent opinions inside the government. With the AEC and the Defense Department tugging one way and diplomatic officials another, it was frequently impossible to provide U.S. negotiators with timely instructions. We have noted how great a handicap this proved to be at the 1958 Conference of Experts.

Various attempts were made to rectify the situation. The first serious effort came with the 1955 appointment of Harold Stassen as special assistant to the president for disarmament.* Stassen was able to build a White House staff of some fifty persons and to achieve some independence and prestige for the disarmament function. This latter fact was probably his undoing, however, since Dulles did not take kindly to any dilution of his own preeminence in foreign affairs. Dulles also seemed to feel, as did others, that Stassen's advocacy of agreement with the Russians was excessively enthusiastic, and possibly motivated by his presidential ambitions.

In mid-1957 Stassen was guilty of an indiscretion in showing an American working paper to the Soviet negotiator at the London Disarmament Subcommittee before it had been made official Western policy. The British were greatly upset by this, and Dulles used the resulting diplomatic flap as an opportunity to reassert his personal control over disarmament policy, even appearing briefly in London as chief of the U.S. delegation. While Stassen remained for a while as U.S. negotiator, he was thenceforth under a tight rein, and at the end of 1957 he resigned his post. The White House disarmament staff was then disbanded and the function returned to the Department of State with greatly reduced staff. By mid-1960 the disarmament staff in the State Department numbered no more than twenty. Kennedy complained that when he took office fewer than one hundred individuals in the entire government were concerned even partially with disarmament.

The need for more effective disarmament organization became a subject of increasing study and public attention in 1959 and 1960. A focus for the discussion was the Senate Disarmament Subcommittee chaired by Hubert Humphrey, who was unceasing in his advocacy of an enlarged disarmament effort. In 1960, when both presidential candidates, Nixon and Kennedy, agreed that greater attention to disarmament was needed, the Eisenhower administration responded by establishing the U.S. Disarmament Administration as a small unit wholly within the State Department. This was basically a cosmetic move, however, and changed very little. Essentially the same few people continued to perform the same functions as before.

More far-reaching proposals had begun to surface meanwhile. These focused first on the need for research. In December 1959 the

---

*The term *disarmament* has often been used to encompass not only arms reduction but also arms control measures such as the test ban. That practice is followed at points in this chapter.

Democratic party's Advisory Council proposed establishment of a national peace agency whose functions would have been primarily to undertake research on various aspects of arms control and disarmament, such as inspection and control systems and the effects of radiation on man. In 1960, Senator John F. Kennedy proposed a variant of the peace agency approach by sponsoring legislation to establish an arms control research institute. Kennedy's proposal placed somewhat greater emphasis on economic, social, and political factors but was still limited to research. Congressmen Robert Kastenmeier introduced his own variant of a national peace agency in February 1960. Focused also on research, it added a provision for a center to train personnel for inspection and other disarmament functions.

An important change in concept was originated by John J. McCloy, one of whose assigned responsibilities as President Kennedy's disarmament advisor was to make recommendations on government organization. McCloy agreed with earlier proposals that there should be an independent agency dealing with arms control and disarmament and that it should have extensive powers and resources to conduct research. He added the idea that the new agency should also have the function, closely coordinated with the Department of State, of actually conducting arms control and disarmament negotiations.

Legislation following McCloy's ideas was introduced in June 1961. The Soviets resumed testing before the bill could be debated. Adrian Fisher recalls expressing to Kennedy the hope that the Soviet tests would not cause the administration to withdraw its support for the bill. Fisher remembers the president answering that the administration's support would continue, "but he thought we were dead. He said, 'I don't think it's right; I don't think you should be dead; I think the bill should pass but I doubt it will.' "[4]

In this case the president's usually sharp political sense failed him. The legislation passed both houses by overwhelming margins, and on September 26, 1961, the Arms Control and Disarmament Agency (ACDA) was established as the focal point in government for the planning, negotiation, and execution of international disarmament and arms control agreements. On the same day President Kennedy nominated William C. Foster to be the agency's first director.

Foster was a Republican businessman. He had been vice-president of the Olin Mathieson Chemical Co. Before that, he had been deputy secretary of defense (1951–1953); had served on the Gaither Committee established by President Eisenhower to examine the feasibility of various disarmament measures; and was also chief of the U.S. delegation to the 1958 Conference on Surprise Attack.

With the establishment of the ACDA, McCloy gave up his full-time government employment. While he continued as chairman of the new agency's General Advisory Committee, leadership in day-to-day arms control and disarmament functions thenceforth devolved on Foster and the new agency. So that there would be no ambiguity about Foster's authority, the White House position of special assistant to the president for disarmament, which McCloy had occupied, was left vacant.

A Plan for General and Complete Disarmament

In his June 1960 address to the Senate Kennedy complained that the United States had been "unwilling to plan for disarmament, and unable to offer creative proposals of our own, always leaving the initiative in the hands of the Russians." One consequence, as he said in another speech, was that the Russians were able to "pose as moral leaders." One of the first assignments Kennedy gave to Foster and the new ACDA was to rectify this situation.

In the crisis atmosphere of the summer of 1961, the possibility of negotiating a treaty on general disarmament seemed remote. The administration nevertheless persisted in the formulation of a U.S. "Plan for General and Complete Disarmament in a Peaceful World." It was the assessment of the responsible officials that disarmament negotiations had to be viewed in the long term; if the immediate situation looked unpromising, there was still reason to plan for the future.

A degree of propagandistic motivation for the disarmament plan was explicitly acknowledged within the administration. As stated in an August 1961 memorandum by the State Department: "The primary purpose at this time, in view of the absence of a prospect for serious negotiations on disarmament, is to achieve Allied unity and to win out over the Soviets at the UN and around the world on the public opinion front. This is not the only purpose—for the paper is definitely conceived with an eye to serious negotiations—but at this time, in view of the intransigent Soviet attitude, it is the primary purpose."

Presumably because of this background, the U.S. plan consisted more of a high-sounding statement of principles than of the technical detail of a treaty. It called for a carefully defined and verified transition to complete disarmament through three stages. Stage one would involve the formation of an International Disarmament Organization within the UN to verify progress toward disarmament. Military force levels would be established at 2.1 million men for both the U.S. and the USSR, and at appropriately lower levels for other militarily significant states. (Soviet forces at the time were estimated at about 3.2 million; U.S. forces at about 2.5 million.) Also in stage one: all production of fissionable material for weapons would stop, safeguards would be imposed on the transfer of fissionable materials, and the nuclear powers would be pledged to prevent the spread of nuclear weapons to other nations. There would be an equitable and balanced reduction in the number of vehicles (missiles, planes, and so forth) for delivering strategic nuclear weapons. Procedures would be introduced for advance notification of troop movements or military exercises to reduce the risks of war from accident, miscalculation, or surprise attack.

In stage two, levels of forces and levels of armaments of prescribed types would be further reduced. Excess armaments would either be destroyed or converted to peaceful uses. Specified military bases and facilities would be dismantled. A UN peace force would be established and progressively strengthened.

In stage three "progressive controlled disarmament and continuously developing principles and procedures of international law would proceed to a point where no state would have the military power to challenge the progressively strengthened UN Peace Force, and all international disputes would be settled according to the agreed principles of international conduct." The armed forces of nations "would be reduced to the lowest levels required for maintaining internal order."*

There was only one provision in the paper on which there was prolonged disagreement among the agencies. Both Defense and AEC wanted measures providing for reduction in the number of *nuclear* weapons and delivery systems, where the United States excelled, to be made dependent on concurrent implementation of measures reducing *conventional* forces and weaponry, where the Soviets excelled. The State Department and some other agencies thought the linkage was unnecessary and detracted from the image we sought to create.

This issue was discussed at a Principals meeting on August 17, my notes for which record the following solution:

> It was agreed to resolve this disagreement by recording in the minutes of the meeting that having nuclear and conventional arms scaled down concurrently was the ultimate aim, but this aim would not be recited in the document so as not to impair its near-term propaganda value.

*According to Freeman Dyson, who participated in development of the plan as a summer employee of the ACDA: "Everyone knew that Stages Two and Three were pure moonshine. It would be a major miracle if we ever got to the end of Stage One." (*Disturbing the Universe*, p. 133.)

One should not demean the importance of the propaganda advantages sought through the U.S. disarmament plan. While the word *propaganda* has acquired a negative connotation, the fact remains that world opinion was a major factor in the East-West struggle at this time. Thus, at this same Principals meeting on August 17:

> It was revealed that the main reason for the State Department's viewpoint on a number of these items was the fact that the Indians intended to introduce a UN resolution banning all tests. This motion could be carried unless we improve our position, but State felt that with inclusion of some of the items in the August 11 revision of the disarmament paper the resolution could be defeated.

While the State Department's view prevailed in the Committee of Principals, the Indian resolution nevertheless carried in the General Assembly.

The President at the UN

McCloy and Adlai Stevenson were among those who urged Kennedy personally to unveil the U.S. disarmament plan at the UN General Assembly. Kennedy had his doubts, wondering whether it would seem hypocritical, coming on the heels of our resumption of testing. He already had decided to make the presentation, however, when news came of the death of UN Secretary General Dag Hammarskjold on September 18 in a plane crash in Africa. The president's appearance, which took place one week later, thereupon assumed more dramatic proportions.

Moved by the occasion, Kennedy was at his most eloquent. Referring to the death of Hammarskjold, he said: "The problem is not the death of one man—the problem is the life of this organization. It will either grow to meet the challenge of our age—or it will be gone with the wind, without influence, without force, without respect. Were we to let it die—to enfeeble its vigor—to cripple its powers—we would condemn the future."

On the need for disarmament the president said: "For fifteen years this organization has sought the reduction and destruction of arms. Now that goal is no longer a dream—it is a practical matter of life or death. The risks inherent in disarmament pale in comparison to the risks inherent in an unlimited arms race."

He then outlined the American disarmament proposals. He made signing a test ban treaty the first of his proposals, but was careful to add: "Test ban negotiations need not and should not await general disarmament," thus repudiating the Soviet position linking the two.

The president concluded with a characteristic rhetorical burst:

> We in this hall shall be remembered either as part of the generation that turned this planet into a flaming funeral pyre or the generation that met its vow to save succeeding generations from the scourge of war. . . . The decision is ours. Never have the nations of the world had so much to lose, or so much to gain. Together we shall save our planet or together we shall perish in its flames. Save it we can—and save it we must—and then we shall earn the eternal thanks of mankind and, as peacemakers, the eternal blessings of God.

Kennedy's speech was very well received at the UN, and it greatly enhanced his standing as a world leader. Very possibly because of the president's personal appearance, the General Assembly session was a moderately successful one for the West. The proposal that a Troika replace the UN secretary-general was resoundingly defeated, and U Thant of Burma took his place as successor to Hammarskjold with undiminished powers. As already noted, the Indian resolution urging a renewed moratorium on testing passed. The Soviet bloc joined the West in voting against it, but it carried by seventy-one votes to twenty, with eight abstentions. The assembly also, however, adopted by overwhelming vote a resolution asking the Soviet Union to refrain from its announced test of a superpowerful weapon yielding 50 megatons. Most significantly, the assembly adopted the long-heralded U.S.-U.K. resolution entitled "The Urgent Need for a Treaty to Ban Nuclear Weapons Tests under Effective International Control." The vote was seventy-one to eleven (Soviet bloc and Cuba opposed) and constituted in effect a first endorsement by the world body of the Western position in the test ban negotiations.

A Statement of Agreed Principles

Between March and September of 1961, while the U.S. general disarmament proposals were being worked out within the administration, and while the test ban negotiations were deadlocked in Geneva, another, less-publicized U.S.-Soviet negotiation was taking place successively in Washington, Moscow, and New York. The effort was to find an agreed basis for resuming negotiations on general disarmament, which had been in suspension since the Soviets walked out of the Ten-Nation Disarmament Conference in June 1960.

The negotiations were conducted by John McCloy for the U.S. and Ambassador Valerian Zorin for the USSR. The process was arduous and, at first, seemingly hopeless. The two sides began far apart, with Zorin pushing the Soviet Union's position on a "take-it-or-leave-it" basis. McCloy persisted, however, in his calm and patient way and, over time, the Soviet side became less obdurate. A possible significant factor in their change in attitude was recorded by Arthur Dean, McCloy's alternate during the discussions. Dean wrote: "We had the impression, unsubstantiated but nevertheless strong, that Premier Khrushchev wanted the talks continued to a successful conclusion."[5]

A concession from the U.S. side that, while it seemed relatively trivial to us, may have been important to the Soviets, came on a matter of semantics. The question was what term to apply to the process under discussion. The Soviets had consistently attached the term "general and complete disarmament" to the plans they presented to the UN. We had accepted this term in a 1959 UN resolution but had more recently shifted to "total and universal disarmament" in order to make clear that we were not dealing in the bilateral discussion with the substance of recent Soviet plans. This matter was discussed at a meeting of the Committee of Principals on August 3, 1961.

> McCloy reported that the Soviets were disturbed about our introduction of the new name and wanted to know how it was to be defined. He was convinced that our insistence on the change in terminology would unduly handicap our efforts, especially in the UN, where the old name had become accepted.
> Rusk pointed out that the translations of the two names from English into certain other languages, including Russian, were identical. He said neither "total" nor "complete" disarmament would be achieved for many years under either the U.S. or Soviet plan, so both names were fraudulent. He felt that if there was any difference between the two names it was a metaphysical one and the president should not be placed in the position of having to explain this difference. Rusk stated that the Soviets had made headway by appropriating such terms as *peace* and *freedom*. We could make "general and complete disarmament" our own phrase if it were attached to a realistic and important proposal.
> The committee agreed to substitute "general and complete disarmament" for "total and universal disarmament" throughout the U.S. paper.

This U.S. concession on semantics may have been important in the negotiations by removing a suspicion that we were engaged in some fathomless trickery.

The most difficult issue in the bilateral negotiations, and one that threatened to cause their breakdown, was the issue of how the term *inspection* was to be defined in the Statement of Principles. While much obfuscating language was used, it became apparent that the Soviets were willing to have the term cover only those munitions brought to terminals for destruction, not those that remained. The U.S. position was that both items destroyed and those that remained must be inspected. It was finally agreed that the clause on which the argument centered should be omitted from the Statement of Principles and that McCloy could dispatch a public letter to the missions of all UN members disclosing the differences between the two sides.

With this issue out of the way, the U.S. and USSR were able to submit jointly to the General Assembly on September 20, 1961, their Joint Statement of Agreed Principles for Disarmament Negotiations. The statement had eight operative paragraphs, which I will summarize roughly as follows:

1. The goal of disarmament negotiations was to be general and complete disarmament, accompanied by the establishment of procedures for maintenance of peace.
2. At the end of the process nations were to have only those non-nuclear armed forces needed to maintain internal order.
3. The steps involved in general and complete disarmament were to include, among others, disbanding armed forces, eliminating stockpiles of weapons of mass destruction and their means of delivery, and the end of military expenditures.
4. Disarmament was to take place by stages within specified time limits.
5. Disarmament measures were to be balanced so that no state gained a military advantage.
6. Disarmament was to be implemented under international control, specifically through an International Disarmament Organization (IDO) within the UN. Inspectors of the IDO were to be "assured unrestricted access without veto to all places as necessary for the purpose of effective verification."
7. A UN peace force was to be established with sufficient strength to suppress any aggression.
8. Agreement on disarmament was to be sought at the earliest possible date.

Arthur Dean considers the negotiation of the Statement of Principles to have been significant in two respects:

> "First of all, during the exchange, we began to have a feeling that it might at last be possible to have reasonable negotiations with Soviet representatives on the subject of arms control and disarmament. In this sense it was a kind of turning point, even though the hope was often to be disappointed. In addition, it was during these talks that we were able to achieve an important clarification of the Soviet position on the issue of inspection."[6]

Another result we observed was that, after the Statement of Principles, the Soviets began to harp less on their advocacy of general and complete disarmament. Apparently they felt that there was less of a propaganda harvest to be reaped now that the United States also was identified with this objective.

It is sad that the Statement of Principles did not appear to bring any closer the achievement of general disarmament, which seemed to remain, in Freeman Dyson's phrase, "pure moonshine." In the arena of present reality a more pressing issue continued to be how this country should respond to the massive Soviet series of atmospheric tests, in particular, whether we should reply with atmospheric tests of our own.

8

Toward Atmospheric Testing

A New Policy Position

During the early autumn of 1961, military and diplomatic officials in the administration were at cross purposes to an unusual degree. The military were clearly perturbed by the progress the Russians were making in their atmospheric test series, which preliminary analysis was showing to be surprisingly strong in its scope and variety. There was a feeling of urgency about starting soon to make up the lost ground. The diplomats, by contrast, wanted to avoid any precipitate actions or pronouncements that would prejudice the American position at the ongoing session of the UN General Assembly.

The different approaches of the two groups were evident at a meeting of the Committee of Principals held on October 7.

> McNamara led off by urging that preparations be made for a very early resumption of atmospheric testing, citing as one reason the need for proof testing various weapons in the stockpile. Bundy argued that this

constituted a radical change in the Department of Defense's statement of need—from developmental testing in six months to proof testing in three weeks. Gilpatric acknowledged that Defense had accelerated its recommended program—they had not anticipated the rate of Soviet testing when the previous recommendations were made on September 20.

Nitze pointed out that the extent of Soviet tests had had an effect on the political situation and that conducting proof tests would be a good idea if the Berlin talks failed and the international situation deteriorated. Bundy felt there was an essential difference between tests conducted for political effect and those conducted for significant military reasons.

I supported Defense on the need to prepare for atmospheric tests, comparing the high rate of Soviet atmospheric testing with what was possible for us underground. I did not agree, however, with the need for proof tests. [The AEC and its laboratories realized that President Kennedy would permit only a limited number of tests. We wanted each one to serve some developmental purpose.] McNamara expressed concern about possible Soviet development of an antimissile missile in the next four or five years. Lemnitzer noted that if the Soviets succeeded in doing this it could change the whole picture. I expressed doubt they could succeed.

Dean thought it would help us politically if we could postpone atmospheric tests for the duration of the UN General Assembly but added that the U.S. delegation felt it could handle the political problem if atmospheric tests were considered essential for military purposes. Rusk noted that the political burdens at the UN were heavy and he was not sure, in the light of such issues as Chinese representation and Berlin, that the U.S. could afford to use up much political capital on the testing matter. He said it would greatly help our UN position if we could renew the Kennedy-Macmillan offer of an atmospheric test ban and asked Defense for a realistic assessment of our need for atmospheric testing.

McNamara said that, if the U.S. knew the Soviets would keep an atmospheric test ban agreement, then he could agree to renewing the offer. If the international situation remained tense, however, he thought we would have to assume the Soviets would prepare another test series despite an agreement. If we were caught again in twelve to eighteen months as we had been this last time he thought we would be in serious trouble.

Nitze felt that with another series the Soviets might increase their military capabilities by a factor of three to five over the U.S. and asked if the State Department was prepared to live with this. Both Dulles and Scoville of CIA disagreed on technical grounds that the Soviets could accomplish this.

Rusk asked whether the advantage would still rest with the U.S. if atmospheric tests were to stop at once. McNamara said that it would. Rusk thought that in that case, with preparations for testing publicly announced, we could renew the Kennedy-Macmillan offer. Then the fact of making preparations for testing would not be too difficult for us in the UN.

The upshot of the meeting was a recommendation on October 12 to the president by the Principals, in writing, that the United States reaffirm its offer of a controlled comprehensive test ban but at the same time state we would prepare for atmospheric testing in order to be ready in case such testing were deemed necessary.

Kennedy apparently did not concur that it would be appropriate to renew the offer of an atmospheric test ban. The position on this was made clear in guidelines issued to our UN delegation on October 12. These indicated that we were prepared to sign an atmospheric test ban agreement but would not initiate a new offer "in view of the Soviet refusal to consider the U.S.-U.K. offer of September 3."

The guidelines to the UN delegation also contained this most important paragraph:

> We would state frankly and publicly that, in view of Soviet duplicity in the Geneva talks, we feel compelled to make preparations for atmospheric tests so as to be ready in case it is felt necessary to conduct them. We would say that in our kind of society such preparations cannot be secret, and we are therefore announcing in advance our intention to make them.

This seemed clear and unambiguous enough, and both Adlai Stevenson at the UN and we in the AEC proceeded on the basis that it was established national policy. This was to cause further difficulty in subsequent days because the president, approaching the dread reality of atmospheric testing, drew back again.

I "Meet the Press"

The last paragraph of my biweekly report to the president on October 19 read as follows:

> May I now advert to a new subject. I have accepted a long-standing request (first made shortly after I assumed office) to appear on the TV program "Meet the Press." I had postponed acceptance for many months—twice in recent weeks: first, to avoid appearing just prior to and in connection with our resumption of tests underground; and second, in order not to become involved in the testing issue immediately prior to my arrival in Vienna on a "peaceful uses" mission [as head of the U.S. delegation to the annual general conference of the International Atomic Energy Agency]. I felt reasonably safe as of September 23 in agreeing to appear on Sunday, October 29. Ironically, then, on Tuesday last came Premier Khrushchev's announcement of plans to detonate a 50 megaton device on October 31! Accordingly, I anticipate a number of questions in this area.

On October 28:

> In Bundy's absence I talked to Bromley Smith of the White House staff. I told him that I was appearing on "Meet the Press" tomorrow and needed clarification as to the U.S. position on atmospheric testing. I

pointed out that Adlai Stevenson had stated to the UN, in accordance with the presidential guidelines of October 12, that "we reserved the right to make preparations."

It was agreed that I should discuss this with Rusk, which I did immediately. Rusk said that he expected to see the president in about an hour, would check it out with him, and would let me know. He expressed his own view that I should be authorized to say that preparations were being made.

Rusk called me back later in the afternoon to say that the president did *not* want me to say that we were preparing. Rusk and I then haggled back and forth on possible ways to state the U.S. position, based on some language that the president himself had dictated. He said that he was sure the president would want me to divulge nothing new, but to leave the situation where it was now. He suggested that, as far as my AEC responsibility was concerned, I say that I would carry out the directives of the president, if and when received.

With the press members eager to pry information out of me, and the administration desiring that I divulge nothing, I anticipated a difficult half hour. I was not disappointed.

My four inquisitors were Lawrence Spivak, the permanent member of the "Meet the Press" panel; Marquis Childs, a widely syndicated columnist; John Finney, who covered nuclear matters for the *New York Times*; and Peter Hackes of NBC News. The first colloquy with Spivak elicited approximately the line that Rusk and I had rehearsed, based on the president's instructions.

> SPIVAK: Dr. Seaborg, I know it hasn't been announced, but . . . has a final decision been made yet as to whether or not the U.S. will test in the atmosphere?
>
> SEABORG: The final decision has not been made yet, Mr. Spivak.
>
> SPIVAK: Can you tell us when it will be made?
>
> SEABORG: No, I can't tell you when it will be made—if it will be made.
>
> SPIVAK: Can you tell us what the final decision will be based on?
>
> SEABORG: Well, the final decision will be made by the president, and I suppose that he would want to base it in large part on the result of the analysis of the Soviet tests. I also suppose that he would never take this decision . . . on the basis of political or terroristic considerations, such as has been at least part of the reason for the Russian testing, but would base his decision entirely on the technical need for the information in the interests of national security.

In answer to further questions from Spivak: yes, I thought we were still ahead in nuclear development; yes, if the Russians would sign the treaty we had tabled at Geneva, I would be willing to forego testing entirely.

Childs asked a series of questions about fallout: how great the genetic damage would be from the large Russian tests. I answered that "the scientific basis for a judgment on this is lacking, and there is a rather substantial difference of opinion among scientists as to what the extent of the damage would be."

Finney asked about the 50-megaton bomb: " . . . are you suggesting that it's not really necessary to detonate such a bomb to develop it?"

> SEABORG: That is right, it is not necessary to detonate a full yield of 50 megatons in order to develop it. Tests at smaller yields, yields more in the range of their earlier tests, would be sufficient to develop a bomb of that magnitude or of higher magnitude.
>
> FINNEY: What military uses would there be for a 50- or a 100-megaton bomb, such as Mr. Khrushchev has said the Soviet Union is going to build?
>
> SEABORG: Well, I don't think I'm enough of a military expert to even try to respond to that question.
>
> FINNEY: Well, let's take it in the reverse order then. If the Soviet Union develops a 50- or a 100-megaton bomb, do you feel that it will be incumbent upon the United States to develop similar weapons to have a counterdeterrent?
>
> SEABORG: No, I don't, at least not necessarily.
>
> FINNEY: On this question of atmospheric testing, are we preparing Eniwetok for resumption of atmospheric tests?
>
> SEABORG: I can't respond to that.

Finney wanted more information on who was ahead.

> FINNEY: How much longer do you think that we can maintain our superiority . . . if the Russians continue to test in the atmosphere and we continue under the limitations of underground testing?
>
> SEABORG: I wouldn't want to estimate that time, Mr. Finney.
>
> FINNEY: Well, would you . . . say that eventually they would pull ahead of us if this continued . . .?
>
> SEABORG: I think that . . . if we tested indefinitely underground, and if the Russians tested indefinitely in the atmosphere, they would pull ahead of us.

He wanted me to be more precise, and I said I was "deliberately trying not to be very precise at this time."

There were more queries about fallout in which the questioners' unhappiness with the lack of scientific certainty was evident.

The final colloquy, as the first, belonged to Spivak:

> SPIVAK: Dr. Seaborg, the moratorium with the Russians was on testing but not on production [of nuclear weapons]. Have we been able to improve our weapons during the period of the moratorium?

SEABORG: Yes, we have. We've spent the period digesting data from the HARDTACK [1958] test series, and the computers have been busy, of course, and the physicists and theoreticians have been busy with the computations, so we certainly have been improving our weapons during the moratorium. . . .

BROOKS: [Ned Brooks, the moderator]: I'm afraid at this point we'll have to suspend our questions, and thank you very much, Dr. Seaborg, for being with us.

And so, as the prize-ring expression has it, I was saved by the bell from further punishment.

A week later *Time* magazine carried my picture on its cover, with an accompanying six-page feature story on testing and fallout. The article was reassuring on fallout and generally accurate on the testing situation, although the statement that "the decision [to resume atmospheric testing] has essentially been made by President Kennedy" was premature. The biographical material about me was also reasonably correct, although I didn't particularly appreciate being described as "shambling" and "craggy-faced."

Negotiations with the British

If we decided to resume atmospheric testing, another problem would arise: *where* would we do it?

What had been learned about the dangers of test fallout, and the arousal of U.S. public opinion on this subject, severely restricted the amount and types of atmospheric testing that could be carried out at the Nevada Test Site or anywhere else in the United States.

Some 43 tests had been conducted at the Eniwetok Proving Ground in the Pacific between 1948 and 1958 and, from a technical point of view, Eniwetok was a reasonable choice for further testing since excellent installations were already in place there. However, the Eniwetok Atoll was part of the Marshall Islands Trust Territory, which the United States administered for the United Nations. The State Department predicted that very strenuous objections would be raised in the UN to further testing in the Trust Territory.

Another possibility was Johnston Island, a dot of land owned by the U.S. about five hundred miles southwest of Hawaii. This island had been used for two high-altitude shots during AEC's 1958 series. Johnston had good facilities for tests requiring missile launching. It was AEC's opinion, however, that it could not fully satisfy the needs of a comprehensive and meaningful test program. It was too small.

Where then? Our attention was drawn to Christmas Island, a British possession about 1,000 miles south of Hawaii which the

British had themselves used in previous tests. It was an extensive strip of land and seemed to meet our needs. To gain the use of it, however, seemed a difficult matter since by this time the British public was quite strongly opposed to nuclear testing.

A gingerly feeling out of the situation began during my European trip in September. Preceding the International Atomic Energy Agency's general conference, the main purpose of my trip, I stopped off in London for discussions with Sir Roger Makins, chairman of the United Kingdom Atomic Energy Authority, and other British officials. During these talks Makins inquired as to the possibility of detonating one small U.K. device in the ongoing U.S. underground series at the Nevada Test Site; there were no suitable sites for underground testing in the British Isles.

Upon my return, I wrote both Rusk and McNamara asking their views about the British request. Deputy Secretary Gilpatric, replying for Defense on October 17, made explicit the connection between their request and our need for Christmas Island. He suggested that my reply to Makins indicate, first, that it was technically feasible to include the British device in the Nevada test series and, second, that we might wish to approach the U.K. at an early date regarding the use of Christmas Island.

Rusk's reply also recommended that we tell the British there was no technical objection to their participation in the Nevada series. Before arriving at this conclusion, however, he raised an interesting point indicative of the concern felt about the growing number of nuclear powers. He wrote:

> I am glad that you brought this request to my attention, because it has important foreign policy implications. You will recall that the National Security Council policy toward NATO, approved by the President April 21, states that it would be desirable for the British, in the long run, to phase out of the nuclear deterrent business, since their activity in this field is a standing goad to the French. Over the long run, I believe that we should move to fulfill this policy. I doubt, however, that the present British request is the occasion for this.

Rusk concluded by recommending that British participation in our tests not become publicly known.

I summarized the Defense and State positions and my proposed reply to the British request in a letter to the president on October 19. On October 23 I received from Bundy the president's authorization to proceed along a dual path: (1) indicate to Sir Roger Makins that there was no technical objection to a British underground test in Nevada, and (2) explore with him our possible use of Christmas Island.

I followed through in a communication to Sir Roger on October 30. And so the matter rested until soon it was taken up by the president and the prime minister at the summit.

And with the French

While on my European trip I spent two days conferring with the top officials of the AEC's French counterpart, the Commissariat Energie Atomique. In this case the requests all flowed one way: the French had nothing that we wanted. I reported to the president on these requests both in writing and in a White House meeting with him and Bundy on October 13. I wrote that the French had four requests to make of us:

1. "They desire to participate in the instrumentation aspects of at least one of the weapons tests in the current Nevada series."
2. "They would like U.S. assistance in the construction of a gaseous diffusion plant to separate and produce weapons grade uranium."
3. "They desire to obtain U.S. plutonium for use in their fast breeder reactor program." In the meeting with the president I noted that they had made a similar request of the British. Kennedy's offhand reaction was that it would be better to allow the British to supply the plutonium.
4. "The U.S. has supplied enriched uranium for the French land-based submarine prototype reactor. They now inquire whether the U.S. would supply enriched uranium for a sea-going prototype." I told the president that the French were somewhat amused by the line we tried to draw between land-based and seagoing submarine prototypes.

At the root of U.S. negotiations with the French was the belief that their nuclear weapons program was a net liability to our efforts in arms control. It was an embarrassment to the West in negotiations with the Soviet Union and a hindrance in achieving our objective of preventing further proliferation of nuclear weapons capability.

Some weeks later, on January 4, 1962, having received the views of State and Defense, I wrote to Bundy asking for White House approval of the following disposition of the French requests:

1. We would not grant them access to the current test series.
2. We would allow them to purchase unclassified equipment for use in their gaseous diffusion plant.
3. We would suggest they buy plutonium from the British rather than from us.

4. We would withhold U-235 for their submarine until we learned about the type of submarine they had in mind and to what forces it would be committed, that is, NATO or French. (It was contrary to national policy to support French capability for fabricating missile-bearing nuclear submarines that might be held under French control.)

In due course the White House approved these actions.

It was difficult in the extreme to have to deal so sternly with an ally. That we did so is testimony to the responsibility we felt as a nuclear power to try to prevent the diffusion of nuclear weapons. It must be said that the Soviet Union has acted in a similarly responsible manner, contributing, for example, to the souring of its relations with the People's Republic of China.

Decision Delayed

We now entered a prolonged period of uncertainty regarding preparations for atmospheric testing. A decision would seem to be made one day and withdrawn the next. Kennedy wanted to take a firm stand and be ready; yet he wanted to keep his options open: he was reluctant to take steps that might bar the way to a test ban.

The uncertainty was manifest in a conversation I held with Bundy at the White House on October 13 just before we both met with the president for a report on my recently completed European trip.

> I told Bundy that McNamara had given me the impression that the president had given an OK for all the preparations mentioned in a recent Defense Department memorandum on atmospheric testing. Bundy indicated that this was not the case. I thereupon asked him to give the AEC guidance so that we would know what we should and should not do in preparing for atmospheric testing.

The views held within the AEC were made unusually clear on October 17.

> I spent most of the day in a meeting with the other commissioners, the general manager and members of the AEC staff, the directors of our two weapons laboratories, and officials of the Albuquerque Regional Office to discuss the status of our testing program. It seemed clear to all that underground testing had more severe limitations than we had envisioned and that it would be necessary to go to atmospheric testing to accomplish our objectives.

A dramatic announcement by Khrushchev that same day added to the urgency of the situation. The full Associated Press bulletin read as follows:

> Moscow—Premier Khrushchev announced today that the Soviet Union will explode a nuclear bomb equivalent to 50 million tons of TNT on October 31. It was the first time that the Kremlin had given advance notice of a nuclear explosion. "We have a 100 million ton bomb," Khrushchev told the opening session of the 22nd Soviet Communist Party Congress, "but we do not intend to explode it. If we happen to explode it in the wrong place, we might break our own windows," Khrushchev continued. "May God grant that we never have to explode such a bomb."

Shortly after Khrushchev's announcement was released, I was asked to call the president.

> Kennedy asked me how much fallout we would get from the Soviet 50 megaton explosion and whether it would be enough to warrant his making a denunciatory statement. I told him that I doubted there would be a sufficient basis for a critical statement from the standpoint of fallout.
> I called Bundy and told him that I did not go along with a strong presidential statement about fallout because there was the possibility there would be minimal fallout.

The president was not deterred. A White House statement was issued, and it concluded as follows: "We believe the peoples throughout the world will join us in asking the Soviet Union not to proceed with a test which can serve no legitimate purpose and which adds a mass of radioactive fallout to that which has been unleashed in recent weeks."

In coming days we continued to face the old problem of preparing while seeming not to. On October 19:

> I called Bundy and asked the status of the directive on preparing for atmospheric testing. I said we were being asked questions and the newspapers were carrying articles. Bundy suggested that I say that the president is reviewing the matter and is not ready at the moment to ask AEC to prepare. Bundy feels we have to go ahead with the planning but that we shouldn't move hardware publicly.

I devoted my entire next biweekly report to the president to testing issues. I conveyed to him the views of the AEC's laboratory directors that "in the absence of a test ban treaty with effective controls, and in light of the size and scope of the present Soviet series, and the technical needs for important information, the United States should resume testing in the atmosphere." I noted, however, the general AEC view that underground testing should also be continued because of its advantages in certain situations and also because "there is always the possibility—however remote—that agreement might be reached with the Soviet Union" on an atmospheric test ban.

British Interventions

October 26 brought a new complication.

> Bundy called to tell me that the president had received a proposal from the British prime minister that the two countries announce a six-month moratorium on atmospheric testing.
>
> I said I thought the Commission would feel that six months was a long delay, that there was quite a feeling of urgency. I asked whether the president would go for three months, pointing out that this would give us time to make preparations to do a better testing job. Bundy replied that the president would go for whatever made sense. He emphasized that the main question was the technical one: at what point does it become technically urgent to conduct atmospheric tests?
>
> I asked whether we would be able to make preparations during the proposed moratorium. Bundy replied that one of the reasons for the British proposal was to make it harder for us to resume atmospheric tests, since it was their technical view that such tests didn't amount to much. They could regard preparations as a matter of bad faith.
>
> I said that this proposal would cause unhappiness in the AEC. I predicted that while the Commission members themselves understood that this issue was not a black and white one, they would tend to think that it was technically important to resume atmospheric testing in a shorter period than six months.

This suggestion by Macmillan was finally turned down by Kennedy, but it presaged further interventions by the British prime minister.

Considering their relative unimportance as a military force, particularly in nuclear weapons, it is remarkable to consider how much influence the British had over U.S. arms and arms control policies during this period. Henry Kissinger provides a useful commentary on this:

> When Britain emerged from the Second World War too enfeebled to insist on its own views, it wasted no time in mourning an irretrievable past. British leaders instead tenaciously elaborated the "special relationship" with us. This was, in effect, a pattern of consultation so matter-of-factly intimate that it became psychologically impossible to ignore British views. They evolved a habit of meetings so regular that autonomous American action somehow came to seem to violate club rules. Above all, they used effectively an abundance of wisdom and trustworthiness of conduct so exceptional that successive American leaders saw it in their self-interest to obtain British advice before taking major decisions. It was an extraordinary relationship because it rested on no legal claim; it was formalized by no document; it was carried forward by succeeding British governments as if no alternative were conceivable.

Britain's influence was great precisely because it never insisted on it; the "special relationship" demonstrated the value of intangibles.[1]

In the matters of testing and test ban negotiations, from the Eisenhower period forward the British consistently endeavored, often with success, to exercise a moderating influence on U.S. policy. It would not be correct to say, however, that the British occupied a middle position between the United States and the Soviet Union. They might labor mightily to moderate U.S. positions in intra-West discussions. When it came to a showdown with the Soviet Union, the British loyally and effectively supported their ally.

The AEC Takes a Stand

On October 30, the Russians exploded their 50-megaton weapon. Our analysis subsequently indicated a yield of approximately 57 megatons. It was indicated further that the yield might well have been 100 megatons had the weapon been encased in uranium instead of lead.

On that same day I sent the president a letter summing up the overall situation on atmospheric testing from the AEC point of view. The letter began: "In keeping with your instructions, we have been making plans and limited preparations for atmospheric testing, confining ourselves to such steps as are considered to involve little or no risk of public disclosure of the fact of preparation."

After enumerating some of the steps that had been taken, I pointed out that

perhaps the most important . . . preparations we are *not* making involve the Pacific Islands. . . . While the earliest actions necessary . . . are the obvious operational ones which must be implemented by task forces of the Department of Defense, there are certain AEC actions that also would require attention prior to actual testing. For example, DOD ground crews and AEC technicians must proceed to the island site some weeks prior to a test. . . . While surveys of the applicable islands have been undertaken, no steps toward the transfer of people can be taken until authorized, since it would be almost impossible to keep the fact from becoming public knowledge.

My letter continued with a reiteration of the AEC's views on the desirability of resuming atmospheric testing while continuing underground testing, and concluded: "I respectfully reaffirm our earlier recommendation that the United States forthwith proceed to full-scale preparation for atmospheric tests, and that these preparations be publicly acknowledged, as recommended by the Principals."

It was a rather bold letter, perhaps the most forthright communication I had yet made directly to the president. It expressed the strong feeling pervading the AEC organization, including particularly its weapons development laboratories, that the handicaps of being required to prepare in secret were too great for the political benefits gained, and that the success of an atmospheric test series, should we be asked to carry one out, was being jeopardized by this policy.

The Decision to Prepare in the Open

Kennedy evidently appreciated the AEC's point of view. On October 31, the day after my letter was sent, Sorensen called me to go over a statement the president planned to issue following a meeting at the White House on November 2.

At the meeting:

> It was decided that publicly known preparations would be made for tests that could start in four to six months, that the tests would be of the developmental and effects types and not proof tests [with their psychological overtones] such as the Department of Defense had recommended. We would base them in the Pacific, first at Johnston Island on an interim basis using air drops and then at Christmas Island, if we could get British agreement. Eniwetok would be a second choice, although the serious trusteeship problems at the UN were recognized. We would also look for another site as a third choice. AEC was to have the responsibility of determining the site.
>
> After the meeting Bundy, Vice-President Johnson, Sorensen, McNamara, [Secretary of the Treasury Douglas] Dillon, Adlai Stevenson, and I worked with the president on a statement which he gave to the press immediately following.

In his press statement, Kennedy referred to the Soviet tests with more respect than he had shown previously. While continuing to denounce the "Soviet campaign of fear," the president acknowledged that "these tests are, no doubt, of importance . . . in developing and improving nuclear weapons." Nevertheless, he stated that "in terms of total military strength, the United States would not trade places with any nation on earth. We have taken major steps in the last year to maintain our lead—and we do not propose to lose it." He indicated that we would test as necessary "to maintain our responsibilities for free world security, in the light of our evaluations of Soviet tests."

Then came the key sentence of the statement: "In the meantime, as a matter of prudence, we shall make necessary preparations for such tests so as to be ready in case it becomes necessary to conduct them."

The president's statement concluded with a renewed offer to sign the comprehensive test ban treaty the West had tabled the preceding April in Geneva, an offer that, as we shall soon see, was not so easy to make after the Soviet tests as before them.

9

Test Plans and
a Summit

The Committee on Atmospheric Testing

Following the president's public announcement on November 2, 1961, that the United States was preparing to test in the atmosphere, there was a surge of implementing activity.

A set of joint AEC-Defense Department guidelines was drawn up almost immediately by the White House. Among the principal points were that test readiness was to be achieved in four months and that the test series, if authorized, was to be completed as rapidly as possible thereafter, with a target time of three months. It was emphasized again that the president had authorized preparations only; he had not yet made the decision to test.

A further follow-up to the president's announcement was the establishment on November 13 of a Committee on Atmospheric Testing, with me as chairman. This step resulted from conversations initiated by Bundy with McNamara and with me. Bundy felt, and McNamara and I agreed, that with testing policy basically established—or so we thought—a smaller body than the Committee of Principals or the National Security Council was needed to make the detailed decisions that would now ensue.

The formal White House memorandum establishing the committee named, besides me: Bundy, Wiesner, one senior officer to be selected by State and one by Defense. State named ACDA Director William Foster. Defense named Harold Brown. The president instructed the committee that atmospheric tests were to be considered only on condition that

> (a) The test will provide information of substantial importance to the national defense.
> (b) The information needed can be obtained in no other way, with reasonable time and effort.
> (c) Atmospheric fallout is minimized in all practicable ways.
> (d) The military need for the test outweighs the general desirability of avoiding all atmospheric fallout.

Even if all these criteria were met, the committee was instructed to "submit to the President for decision the carrying out of each atmospheric test."

It was clear from these instructions that Kennedy faced the prospect of atmospheric testing without enthusiasm and that he was determined personally to keep the lid on any U.S. test series.

Quest for Christmas Island

On November 3 Prime Minister Macmillan sent a long letter to the president in which he made formal the British request to conduct an underground test at our Nevada site. The need was to test a weapon designed for use with Skybolt, a missile to be launched from a bomber. (President Eisenhower had agreed in his Camp David conference with Macmillan in 1960 that the United States would develop Skybolt for the British, who would pay only for such operational missiles as they might acquire. The missile failed repeatedly in tests during 1962, after which the agreement was canceled by the U.S., with short-term stormy consequences for the Anglo-American relationship.) Bundy called me the day after Macmillan's letter was received to renew the suggestion that we "pool this request into the Christmas Island issue for whatever bargaining power it might hold." It was decided to send a technical team to London to work with U.S. Ambassador David Bruce in explaining our needs to the British authorities.

The formal request for the use of Christmas Island was conveyed in a letter from the president to the prime minister. Kennedy wrote that he was glad to agree to the use of our facilities for the British underground test. He then went on to state that, should it be necessary for us to have some atmospheric tests, Christmas Island was the only satisfactory alternative to Eniwetok, which, "even though we have no doubt of our legal right to do so . . . we are reluctant to use. It would be of immense assistance in the complex and time-consuming preparations which are necessary, if we could have early assurance that you do not see obstacles to our use of this [Christmas Island] site." The president assured the prime minister that our tests would be kept to the minimum necessary in number, yield, and fallout.

Any hopes we may have had that Christmas Island would fall into our laps on the basis of such a simple request were quickly dispelled by Macmillan's reply. He emphasized the abhorrence of world opinion, including that in the U.K., toward atmospheric testing and shrank from the idea that the West and the Soviets might come to be considered equally reprehensible. He noted that preparations at Christmas Island could not be kept secret. He wanted a clearer picture of what exactly the tests would be and what purpose they would serve. He suggested that it would be advisable to wait at least until the Russian tests had been fully evaluated. He then proposed the following program:

1. A secret reconnaissance of Christmas Island by a "really small Anglo-American party, just two or three a side."
2. A meeting in Washington of experts from both sides in order to obtain "a more precise picture of what your people would propose as a series of tests for 1962, showing the general nature of the tests and the purposes which they would serve."
3. An evaluation of these discussions by himself and Kennedy "when we meet before or after Christmas."

The prime minister's lengthy letter concluded: "I recognize that this programme will involve postponing the start of work at Christmas Island until the New Year. It seems to me, however, that we cannot avoid this if we are to discharge conscientiously our heavy responsibility in this very serious decision."

It was evident that Macmillan meant to use our need for Christmas Island as leverage in an attempt to dissuade us from atmospheric testing. Following receipt of his letter, I spoke to Bundy on the telephone.

> I told Bundy that I felt strongly that we should take a positive approach to the reconnaissance phase and move quickly on the conferences with the British which the prime minister had requested.

On November 18, a group from the AEC and I met with Sir Roger Makins and two members of the British embassy staff.

> After the meeting I called Bundy and told him that obtaining the use of Christmas Island seemed a more complex matter than we had realized. The British were going to want to learn quite a bit about our weapons in order to evaluate the necessity for the tests. This would require some sort of authority for release of the information. [It was classified "Top Secret."]

A memorandum I received from Kennedy on November 21 directed me to "proceed at once for the reconnaissance of Christmas Island. At the same time," the president continued, "I think we should promptly determine just which atmospheric tests we do in fact wish to conduct, if and when I decide that testing should be resumed. For this purpose, I should like to have a report and recommendations from the small NSC Committee which I have asked you to chair not later than November 30th. I shall wish to review these recommendations myself on that day, and when a list is approved, I shall want to send appropriate representatives to England to argue the case for this approved testing program."

In his reply to Macmillan, Kennedy began: "I share your sense of the gravity of a decision to conduct nuclear testing in the atmosphere. The sober picture emerging from analyses to date of more than two score Soviet tests warns us, however, that we may well need to strengthen our nuclear posture."

The president then indicated that we were developing a test program preparatory to having the consultations the prime minister had proposed. "I hope that these consultations will proceed quickly enough to permit us to reach an understanding by the end of the year, and if the idea of a [summit] meeting in Bermuda works out, that would be a good time to deal with the matter." The president repeated for the prime minister the very strict criteria he had laid down to guide my small testing committee. He concluded by accepting the suggestion of a small Christmas Island reconnaissance party, and stated: "Dr. Seaborg will approach your people to make arrangements for immediate dispatch."

A Sober Reevaluation

The evaluation of the Russian tests which the president referred to in his letter to Macmillan was being carried out by a panel of the Air Force Technical Applications Center headed by Hans Bethe. As the results of their evaluation (based on an analysis of radioactive air samples collected from the tests) filtered in, I began to feel some concern that the public statements being made about the tests by the president, myself, and others were not entirely accurate. This seemed particularly so with regard to the relative standing of the Soviet Union and the United States. This point was emphasized at a meeting of the President's Science Advisory Committee which I attended on November 20. A tentative conclusion reached at the meeting was that the Russians might have drawn even with or passed us in some aspects of thermonuclear weapons.

Paradoxically, another new development that caused concern was the fact that the USSR had accepted the U.S.-U.K. invitation to renew test ban negotiations at Geneva. The conference was to resume on November 28, 1961. There were many who felt that the U.S. was not in as favorable a position to sign the test ban treaty we had ourselves tabled as we had been before the Russian tests, when we seemed clearly to be ahead.

These and kindred subjects were discussed at a meeting of the Committee of Principals on November 22.

> Following a briefing on the Soviet tests by Scoville of CIA, Rusk asked me to evaluate the relative positions of the U.S. and USSR in nuclear weapons. I replied that it was almost impossible to give a simple answer, since so many factors entered into the equation. It appeared, however, that in certain aspects of thermonuclear technology the Soviets seemed to have equaled or surpassed us. To Dean's question whether the Kennedy-Macmillan offer of an atmospheric test ban could safely be renewed, I said I would be satisfied to freeze weapons technology at the present state in the U.S. and U.S.S.R., but could see no clear solution to the danger that the Soviets would prepare secretly for another series during the early years of such a treaty.
>
> Rusk concluded that the U.S. should not repeat the Kennedy-Macmillan offer of an atmospheric test ban without controls against secret preparations, and there was no disagreement.
>
> Rusk then raised the question whether it was still in the U.S. interest to sign the comprehensive test ban treaty we had tabled in Geneva. Bundy asked whether there were things that could be added to the treaty to prevent the kind of secret Russian preparations I had mentioned.
>
> Rusk said he believed the situation had now changed and that, whereas until recently the U.S. could have signed the tabled treaty immediately, we now lacked assurance that Congress would ratify the treaty and provide funds for its implementation. He felt, therefore, that Dean could not be instructed to sign the draft treaty until more work had been done with Congress. Foster agreed with this assessment. He stated that we had strongly supported a test ban treaty as the beginning of a process leading to disarmament, but now it appeared that limitations on tests might not be in our best interest; a public change in position, however, would undoubtedly have the most serious consequences.

Bohlen* said that the Soviet note accepting the resumption of negotiations implied that they were not prepared to sign a treaty right away. Nitze said that the Soviet note implied an intent to establish a further moratorium during the negotiations. Rusk replied that there should be no doubt in anyone's mind that we would not accept an unpoliced moratorium and that Dean should describe in no uncertain terms how the Soviet breaking of the previous moratorium had affected the negotiating situation.

Wiesner felt that the key issue was not whether the United States was equivalent to the Soviet Union in every aspect but whether it was missing anything it needed for its security.

Cleveland said that the U.S. position had been based on the understanding that we were so far ahead in nuclear weapon technology that we could sign a treaty to end tests. If this situation had changed perhaps some new balloon should be floated. For example, in the light of new factors, such as the need to inspect preparations, the U.S. might have to move in the direction of combining the test talks with the disarmament.

It was a sobering meeting, one that indicated the extent to which the United States had lost confidence as a result of the Soviet test series. It was also striking that Harlan Cleveland's suggestion that the U.S. might have to seek a test ban in the context of general disarmament exactly mirrored the position until recently adopted by the Soviets. This called to mind the observation I had heard to the effect that the United States and Soviet Union had essentially the same positions on arms control and disarmament; they just didn't have them at the same time.

The Geneva Conference's Last Gasp

Any concern that the Soviets might embarrass us at Geneva by offering to sign the treaty we had tabled was quickly dispelled. When the talks resumed on November 28, the Russians proposed a draft treaty of their own. Its contents were divulged in Moscow a day before the talks opened. The treaty would have prohibited tests in the atmosphere, in outer space and under water, using national means only for verification; there would be no international detection stations or onsite inspection. To this point the Soviet proposal mirrored the Limited Test Ban Treaty that was to be signed in 1963. It went on, however, into ground that was unacceptable to the U.S. It would have bound the parties to abjure underground tests while they negotiated a system of control over such tests. After the bitter experience with the

---

*At this time serving in the State Department as a Soviet expert.

Soviet resumption of testing, another uncontrolled moratorium was something we would not even consider. The Soviets must have known this.* While not at first rejecting the Soviet draft officially, Ambassador Dean felt free to denounce it as "a propaganda proposal," a "piece of sheer effrontery," and "colossal hypocrisy."

The Geneva Conference recessed for the holidays on December 21, 1961, and reconvened on January 16, 1962. On that date the Western delegations officially rejected the Soviet proposal and U.S. delegate Charles Stelle proposed that the test ban negotiations be suspended. The Soviets refused to consider this. At the end of the January 29 meeting, Sir Michael Wright, who was in the chair, declared the meeting adjourned and stated that it would be up to the next chairman to work out a date for the next meeting.

There never was another meeting. After 353 negotiating sessions, the Geneva Conference on the Discontinuance of Nuclear Weapon Tests passed quietly out of existence. When a ban on nuclear testing was next discussed, it was to be in a different forum.

An Aside on Public Opinion

In his November 16 letter to Kennedy, Prime Minister Macmillan drew a contrast between British and American public opinion on the question of testing in the atmosphere. The implication was that Americans generally favored such testing whereas Britons opposed it.

U.S. public opinion on this question did not seem very firm. Analysis of poll results in December 1961 by Samuel Lubell, an outstanding public opinion expert, showed that those who had supported Kennedy in the 1960 election followed the position he took in the campaign and opposed resumption of testing. Conversely, those who had voted for Nixon adopted his campaign line and supported resumption of testing. Lubell interpreted these findings to mean that the public was inclined to follow its leaders on the testing issue, and that it would support President Kennedy if he decided to resume testing.[1]

It appears, therefore, that American public opinion permitted Kennedy considerable freedom of action, more than British public opinion afforded Macmillan. This is an important point to bear in mind in appraising the positions taken by the two leaders in the ensuing months.

---

*The treaty would also have required the signature of France, something we could not deliver.

The Test Committee's Program

The Committee on Atmospheric Testing met on November 28 to put the finishing touches on the test program which the president had requested be submitted by November 30. Besides the five committee members (Seaborg, Wiesner, Bundy, Foster, and Brown), a number of others also attended, including the directors of AEC's Los Alamos and Livermore weapons laboratories.

I submitted a report to the president on behalf of the committee the following day. I reported that, of forty-nine test shots proposed by the AEC laboratories and the Department of Defense, "a minimum of 27" had been selected for inclusion in a three-month series to begin in the spring of 1962.

The report described the stage the nuclear arms race was entering:

> Each potential adversary now has, or soon will have, a stockpile of strategic nuclear weapons such that, if delivered on target, virtual destruction of the enemy would result. Increasingly, therefore, much of the future effort of each side will be directed at measures designed to prevent the delivery of enemy weapons while at the same time preserving the deliverability of one's own weapons in spite of the enemy's preventive measures.

These considerations, the report continued, led to urgent requirements for:

1. increased knowledge of the effects of nuclear explosions on hardened bases, missiles, radar and communications.
2. developments leading to decreased vulnerability of our own offensive missiles.
3. decreased weight-to-yield ratios of strategic missile warheads.
4. developments increasing the effectiveness of our own defensive [antimissile] weapons.

The above applied to strategic weapons only. Separate requirements existed for tactical (battlefield) weapons, including:

1. developments permitting greater diversity of delivery methods.
2. improvements and economies making possible wider deployment.

Our memorandum also recommended that "planning should provide for preparations for a second test series, about a year later, looking for more dramatic advances than are possible in an early time frame."

The committee met with the president on November 30. Vice-President Johnson, John McCone, newly sworn in as director of the Central Intelligence Agency, and the AEC weapons laboratory directors were also present.

> We presented our case for atmospheric testing, using the criteria laid down by the president on November 13 in establishing our committee. Every aspect of confining ourselves to underground testing was explored. We examined the consequences of our not further improving our weapons as much as the Russians were doing to see if this was a tenable position. *The president finally concluded that the United States should resume atmospheric testing but that it would not be announced until shortly before we were to begin the three-month series, about April 1.*

Formal confirmation of some of the president's directives came on December 1 in the form of a memorandum signed by Bundy. It stated, first, that our list of tests was approved for the purpose of proceeding with preparations. We were, however, to review the list "with a view to reduction in the numbers of atmospheric tests, in the length of time of the test series, and in the resulting atmospheric fallout. The Committee . . . should promptly indicate to the President which tests can best be omitted from these points of view." We were instructed to prepare for conducting the series "both with and without Christmas Island," but on the assumption that Eniwetok would *not* be available. Most significantly, our recommendation regarding a second test series, to begin a year later, received a cold reception. Our attention was called to "the possibility that further atmospheric testing after this series may become undesirable for political reasons." And finally: "It must be understood that the President has reserved judgment on the final decision for or against the resumption of atmospheric testing."

This last was curious in the light of the commitment to test I thought I had heard the president make during his meeting with the committee, which I duly recorded (italicized) for my journal as shown above. I am bound to say that while I did not in general find Kennedy to be an indecisive man, he did vacillate on issues related to nuclear testing, contributing to some difficult situations. His vacillation was, quite clearly, not one of objective. It remained evident throughout this period that, even as he contemplated the resumption of atmospheric testing, Kennedy's primary goal, based on intense inner conviction of its necessity for all mankind, was a test ban.

Preparations for the Bermuda Summit

On December 3, I responded to Bundy's memorandum on behalf of the Committee on Atmospheric Testing. We were able to reduce our "minimum" list of twenty-seven by from five to seven by scheduling some as underground tests, consolidating others and, depending on results, eliminating one or two. As to time, the best we could promise the president was a target schedule of April 1 to June 15, 1962, which if achieved meant a series lasting two and one-half months.

Negotiations for the use of Christmas Island now proceeded apace. On December 8, I had lunch with a team of American technical experts preparatory to their meeting with British experts to discuss our need for the island. Rusk was to leave the following night for a Paris meeting of Western foreign ministers where he was expected to discuss the matter with British Foreign Minister Lord Home. If not settled by then, the issue was in all likelihood to be resolved at a summit meeting between the president and prime minister scheduled for December 21 or 22 in Bermuda.

On December 12 I met with Sir William Penney, a member of the British team, to discuss various items of mutual interest. He had the impression that the U.S. representatives "hadn't made a very enthusiastic presentation" on December 8 in behalf of our use of Christmas Island, but he felt the odds were about three to two in our favor.

I reported this to Bundy the following day when he called about the forthcoming Bermuda summit.

> He said he wondered whether the president should take along a technical man and asked about my schedule. I said that I would be available at that time but that probably weight should be given to whom the prime minister brought. He called me later in the day to say that the president was not sure whether he would take a technical person to Bermuda, but if he took anyone, I would be the one.

On December 18, the Principals met to discuss the upcoming Bermuda meeting. It was decided to recommend that we make it clear to the British that the U.S. decision whether or not to test in the atmosphere was independent of whether they granted the use of Christmas Island; we had to retain control of our own test program.

On December 19, Joseph P. Kennedy, father of the president, suffered a stroke while on the golf course, and the president flew to

Palm Beach, Florida, to be with him. This meant that pre-Bermuda strategy sessions were held in Palm Beach rather than Washington. On December 20:

> Bundy, Brown, Rusk, Bruce, I, and others had dinner at the president's Palm Beach home with him and Mrs. Kennedy. I sat next to Jackie Kennedy and so had the opportunity to talk with her during dinner. Our discussion included a good deal of talk about our children, but also included many other topics of the day. I found her to be well informed and a stimulating conversationalist.
>
> After dinner we all briefed the president in connection with the next day's meeting with the prime minister. Brown and I, in particular, briefed him on the Russian tests, the relative U.S.-USSR positions, and the need for atmospheric testing.

The next morning I flew to Bermuda with President Kennedy and his group.

Dialogue at the Summit

The first meeting of the president, the prime minister, and their advisers took place on December 21, 1961, between 5:00 and 6:30 P.M. at Government House. Those present from the American side were the president, Rusk, Bundy, Brown, and I. Representing the British were the prime minister, Foreign Secretary Home, Sir William Penney, and Philip de Zulueta, private secretary to the prime minister. Since I was more spectator than participant at this meeting, I was able to take copious notes.

> Sir William Penney opened with a technical summary. He believed the U.S. was still slightly ahead. He felt both sides might now be forced to attempt setting up an antimissile defense. This would be a fantastically difficult and costly effort. The prime minister was concerned about the piling up of bigger and bigger bombs if the arms race proceeded unchecked. He felt that the U.K. would probably drop out but the two superpowers would go on and on piling up sophisticated weapons. Meanwhile "everyone else" would have simple Hiroshima-type bombs within twenty-five years. This was an intolerable prospect. Mankind could not go on this way. We had to make another effort to reach an agreement.
>
> Macmillan noted that both the United States and Great Britain had made great efforts in the test ban talks. David Ormsby-Gore had spent three years in Geneva, "the dullest city in the world." The talks had almost succeeded and then somebody—he asked me to forgive the allusion—unveiled the "big hole" (he was referring to the decoupling method of evading detection of underground tests under a treaty), and the need for controls on underground tests got out of hand. People were saying that underground tests were not very useful. We might have had an agreement; the failure to get one was a great pity.
>
> Now there was a decision to be made. Should there be a new test series for which the British would allow the use of Christmas Island? Or

should we make a serious new disarmament effort? Could not he and the president and Khrushchev get together and make a great new effort to break the cycle of the arms race? It might fail, but if so we would have lost only a few months. He had been reading Russian novels in order to learn what he could about them and felt that they might come around.

The president commented that Soviet behavior over the last nine months suggested that they did not want an agreement. Was it not true, for example, that they had been preparing since February the tests they initiated in September?

The prime minister asked what a 100-megaton bomb would do to people. Penney replied that it would burn up everyone in even the largest city. The prime minister next asked how many large bombs it would take to destroy England. Penney estimated that eight of the existing multimegaton weapons would be enough to "make a terrible mess" of England. The prime minister continued that he had asked Khrushchev what would happen if all the bombs in the world went off and Khrushchev had said there would be nobody left but the Chinese and the Africans.

The prime minister observed that a large proportion of the U.S. strategic weapons were based in England, and then added: "Every time you lift the phone, Mr. President, I think you may say that you intend to go, and I wonder what answer I would give."

President Kennedy felt that before long the nuclear arms race would come to a standoff where neither side could use these weapons because it would be destroyed if it did. Rusk said this would work only if it were a standoff in which both sides believed. Brown agreed, saying the standoff would have to be psychologically as well as technologically stable.

Macmillan thought the position of the Russians might be changing. Their economic structure was really not very different from that of Western Europe. In both cases railroads and mines were nationalized. They had a ruling class that enjoyed special privileges, including sending their children to schools like the British public schools. In other words the forces of humanity were operating the same in all countries. Couldn't we allow these forces to bring us closer together instead of persisting in the arms race?

Foreign Minister Home observed that the new U.S. plan for general and complete disarmament was basically very similar to the Soviet plan except in the important area of inspection. This being the case, could we not make the impending meeting of the Eighteen-Nation Disarmament Committee a moment of major effort? Perhaps it could be kicked off by the eighteen heads of state.

I remarked that the test ban negotiations might have to be linked with general disarmament because the problem of secret Soviet preparations made it harder and harder for the West to accept a test ban treaty as a separate measure. The President adverted again to the discouraging experiences of recent months. We could not get taken twice. Even though he was a great antitester, he felt we ought to make preparations for a test series and then carry out the tests unless we got something substantial in some other field that helped our security in the world. The president added that there was only one serious issue, the balance of missile/antimissile capabilities.

Lord Home repeated that there must be a major effort to get on with disarmament and stop the arms race. The president replied that the timing was difficult. We could not start atmospheric testing just when we were kindling new hopes for disarmament.

The president summarized the discussion by saying that there appeared to be three questions:

1. Should the U.S. "prepare to test and then test?"
2. Should there be a parallel effort on disarmament?
3. Would the U.K. help the U.S. testing program by making Christmas Island available?

Macmillan then said that he thought the discussion had been most helpful and that he felt better.

Since he had appeared to make no headway at all in deflecting President Kennedy from the course the latter had chosen, it was hard to see why the prime minister felt better. Perhaps it was merely because he had gotten so much off his chest.

Following the afternoon meeting I attended a dinner party for the president, the prime minister, and their delegations, given by the governor-general of Bermuda, Sir Julian Gascoigne, and his wife.

I sat one place removed from President Kennedy at dinner, which gave me the opportunity to talk to him. He invited me to go along on his trip to California to give the Charter Day address at Berkeley on March 23, 1962. He also accepted my invitation to visit the Livermore weapons laboratory at that time. *

Later on, I had the opportunity, over coffee cups, to talk to Kennedy and Macmillan privately about nuclear testing. They both felt that during the test ban negotiations the U.S. had overemphasized what the Soviets could gain from cheating on underground testing and were unhappy that the U.S. had made so much of the "big hole" method of evasion, because it was now apparent that it would have taken the USSR many years to catch up through underground testing. They felt that if less had been made of clandestine underground testing, the treaty would have been consummated and then we would be in a much better position today in the arms race—we would be farther ahead of the USSR—since they would not have had their latest atmospheric series, which had made such a difference.

---

*Charter Day is an annual event on the Berkeley campus commemorating the establishment of the charter of the University of California. I did indeed accompany the president on his visit, which was a huge success. He was greeted by huge crowds at the Alameda airport, along the line of motorcade travel from the airport to the campus, and in the football stadium, where perhaps 80,000 people heard and vigorously applauded his speech after he was awarded an honorary degree. The visit to Livermore never took place, but the president did visit the radiation laboratory on the Berkeley campus, where he talked to scientists from both the Livermore and Berkeley laboratories.

What was extraordinary about this last colloquy was what it seemed to reveal about President Kennedy's personal position. He appeared, in private, to be considerably more in favor of accepting risks and making compromises in order to achieve a test ban than either he or U.S. negotiators ever allowed themselves to be in public. The president's public position was in all likelihood constrained by the realities of American politics, particularly by what the U.S. Senate, through its leadership, had given notice it would be likely to accept.* It was not apparent at the time, but became increasingly so later, that Chairman Khrushchev labored under similar constraints in the need to placate conservative opinion within the Soviet leadership.

The Bermuda conversations resumed the next day with Ambassador Bruce added to the American group and Ambassador Ormsby-Gore to the British.

> The same themes were evident as the day before: the British wanted assurance that there would be one more try for an agreement; the Americans wanted to get down to cases about Christmas Island.
> The prime minister asked how long a time would be needed for preparations on Christmas Island. Brown answered that we would have to start early in January to be ready for testing by April 1. The prime minister remarked that he must have cabinet consent to any decision on these matters. (This came as a bit of a surprise and disappointment; we were hoping to wrap things up in Bermuda.)
> Macmillan repeated his question: Couldn't we make a new effort to reach an agreement? On one side was the Berlin question; it could be settled if people wanted to settle it. On the other side was this testing competition, which seemed to be a "travesty of the purposes of human life."
> Kennedy insisted that the United States had to decide to test but he was willing to couple the decision with another statement of our disarmament proposals. Also, he was willing to hold back any

---

*Theodore Sorensen, when asked about this conversation, made the following comments: "I would be careful about saying flatly that Kennedy was ever willing to settle for 2 or 3 inspections. The fact that he said: 'Yes, wasn't that a shame that we didn't make the most of that at the time?' does not necessarily mean that was his position. I remember once when he was quite upset with Macmillan for having represented to Khrushchev that he, Kennedy, might be thinking along those lines. Kennedy was a multi-faceted individual. By that I don't mean that he was all things to all men. I simply mean that he had a way of engaging the other person, of building bridges to him, of keeping his interest and sympathy without committing himself to the other's view until he had carefully weighed all the options. In this particular situation, Kennedy was determined not to permit himself to buy a test ban agreement which the Senate would reject because he felt that would be a disastrous setback to the whole movement in which he believed so strongly." [Informal communication, July 7, 1980.]

announcement of our decision to test. We would state only that we were making preparations. Kennedy then asked Macmillan if he could agree on Christmas Island now. The prime minister answered that the two countries were partners and the U.K. would back up the U.S. But could we not announce our plans so that "they would seem less a threat than a hope?" Kennedy said we could do this if we were careful not to use words that might trap us in the future.

Home asked if the president intended to make the testing decision dependent on Berlin. Kennedy answered that if a really satisfactory settlement could be worked out on Berlin, he felt that it would be easier for the United States to forego testing at this time. He cautioned that this position should not be published.

It was time then to wrap up the proceedings and reach conclusions.

Ormsby-Gore suggested we could say in a communiqué that the United States had an "absolute justification" for testing, was preparing, but we would make one more try for a treaty before executing the tests. Macmillan said there could meanwhile be a private agreement about Christmas Island subject to cabinet concurrence. [He later gave Kennedy a letter on this.] The president asked Bruce to work with Ormsby-Gore and the technical experts in preparing a communiqué.

At the end of the discussion Sir William Penney and I went into a separate room and quickly agreed on a simple statement of principles governing the use of Christmas Island. It was to be studied further by the lawyers. The prospects looked moderately good that use of the island would be granted.

The final communiqué read as follows:

The President and the Prime Minister . . . took note of the new situation created by the massive series of atmospheric tests conducted in recent months by the Soviet Government after long, secret preparations. They agreed that it is now necessary, as a matter of prudent planning for the future, that, pending the final decision, preparations should be made for atmospheric testing to maintain the effectiveness of the deterrent.

Meanwhile, they continue to believe that no task is more urgent than the search for paths toward effective disarmament, and they pledge themselves to intensive and continued efforts in this direction.

Serious progress toward disarmament is the only way of breaking out of the dangerous contest so sharply renewed by the Soviet Union. The President and the Prime Minister believe that the plans for disarmament put forward by the United States in the current session of the United Nations General Assembly offer a basis for such progress, along with the treaty for ending nuclear tests which the two nations have so carefully prepared and so earnestly urged upon the Soviet Government.

So there it was. The British prime minister had enlisted all his persuasive eloquence for two days in an effort to stay our hand. The president was moved by the prime minister's eloquence, as were virtually all of us. But Kennedy had not come to Bermuda to discuss the future of the world, about which he had concerns as grave as Macmillan's. He had come on a practical mission in behalf of U.S. security interests: to obtain the use of Christmas Island for atmospheric tests should he decide they were necessary. In this he had apparently succeeded.

10

The Decision To Test
in the Atmosphere

New Uncertainties

At the end of 1961, following the Bermuda summit, the decision
to test in the atmosphere seemed to have been made. Yet two more
months were to elapse before the decision was announced. During
this period the president repeatedly sought reassurance, in meeting
after meeting, that it was the right thing to do, that there was no
alternative. He persisted in trying to balance dichotomous goals. In
his State of the Union Message on January 12, 1962, he stressed the
need to improve the nation's defense posture, particularly in conventional forces. At the same time he pledged that his administration
would pursue "a supreme effort to break the logjam of disarmament
and nuclear tests." He continued: "We will persist until we prevail,
until the rule of law has replaced the ever dangerous use of force."

What Kennedy seemed to hope for was some eleventh-hour
agreement with the Russians that would make testing unnecessary.

Shortly after the National Security Council's Committee on Atmospheric Testing was established, the president requested that this committee spawn a subcommittee to plan a program of explanation and justification for the resumption of atmospheric testing. On January 5, 1962, the subcommittee, which was chaired by William Foster, submitted its report to the president.* They recommended a series of forceful presentations that would show atmospheric testing was necessary for U.S. security. They suggested that President Kennedy announce the decision about February 15 and that tests start as early as March 1 with a shot at the Nevada Test Site. They recommended a short time lag between the president's announcement and the first test so there would be no appearance of indecision. They recommended Nevada as the site for the first shot to forestall criticism that the United States was callous about the safety of inhabitants of the Pacific area compared with that of its own citizens.

January 8 brought an intimation that Kennedy still hoped to avoid an early resumption of atmospheric testing. Through Bundy the president requested that the AEC determine the effort required, in money and men, to keep the U.S. in a state of readiness to commence atmospheric testing ("on thirty minutes notice," as Bundy put it) in case the president decided not to resume testing in the coming spring. He might make such a decision in the unlikely event that there was an early test ban agreement like the one the West had proposed in Geneva. The state of readiness was considered necessary because of the defect in that draft treaty to which I had called attention: it contained no provision for monitoring *preparations* for testing. Being ready to resume testing quickly was thought to be a way we could prevent the Soviets from stealing a march on us a second time through secret preparations. The preliminary conclusion within AEC, however—and this was shared by the Defense Department and Wiesner's White House office—was that it would be extremely difficult to maintain a state of readiness such as the president had in mind.

Various Views

During the last half of January 1962 the preparations for testing authorized by the president on November 2 continued, although

*Other members of the group were: AEC Commissioner Haworth, Deputy Secretary of Defense Gilpatric, CIA Director McCone, USIA Director Murrow, White House Adviser Schlesinger, and six officials from the State Department: George McGhee, under-secretary for political affairs; Walt W. Rostow, chairman of the Policy Planning Council; Roger Tubby, assistant secretary for public affairs; Harlan Cleveland, assistant secretary for international organization affairs; Roger Hilsman, intelligence and research director; and Philip Farley, special assistant for atomic energy.

handicapped by uncertainty about whether Christmas Island would be available. Various individuals and groups meanwhile had an opportunity to express their views on different aspects of the situation.

The first anniversary of the Kennedy administration occurred during this period, and there was a certain amount of stocktaking. At a news conference on January 15 the president was asked what were the most rewarding and most disappointing events of his first year in office. He unhesitatingly named "failure to get an agreement on the cessation of nuclear testing" as his greatest disappointment.

On January 18 and 19 the Joint Committee on Atomic Energy held hearings in executive session on the testing program. I testified at these hearings and reported to the president in my regular biweekly report: "There was generally strong sentiment among Committee members in favor of early resumption of atmospheric testing. There was also some surprise expressed at our reticence to test at Eniwetok, with a tendency on the part of members of the Committee to feel that the problem of world opinion and the reaction in the United Nations was secondary to our national security interests."

Kennedy made explicit the dual course he had been following—test preparations while negotiating disarmament measures—in a news conference statement on February 7. He summarized his position as follows:

> So I repeat that these two courses are consistent with each other. We must follow both at once. It would be a great error to suppose that either of them makes the other wrong or unnecessary. I wholly disagree with those who would put all their faith in an arms race and abandon their efforts for disarmament. But I equally disagree with those who would allow us to neglect our defense needs in the absence of effective agreement for controlled disarmament.

Summit Correspondence

February 8, 1962, brought the long-awaited formal agreement granting the use of Christmas Island. It came in the form of a joint U.S.-U.K. statement. Consistent with the position taken by the British at Bermuda—that any agreement on Christmas Island must be coupled with a further major effort to reach an arms control agreement with the USSR—the statement included the following announcement:

> The two Governments are determined to make a new effort to move away from this sterile contest. They believe that a supreme effort should be made at the 18-nation Disarmament Com-

mittee . . . and that the heads of Government [of the three major powers] should assume a direct and personal interest in these negotiations. The President and the Prime Minister have, therefore, addressed a joint communication to Chairman Khrushchev proposing that this meeting be initiated at the foreign minister level and that their foreign ministers should meet before the Conference starts and also be prepared to return as personal participants in the negotiations at appropriate stages as progress is made.

A prime reason for the suggestion that the conference be opened at the foreign minister level was to forestall an expected Soviet suggestion that heads of state should participate. The West did not want to give Khrushchev this platform for denouncing the forthcoming U.S. tests. Khrushchev made the suggestion anyhow. Writing to President Kennedy on February 11, he agreed that the new disarmament negotiations were important—so important that heads of government, not foreign ministers, should attend at the outset.

President Kennedy, answering Khrushchev on February 14, stated: "I do not believe that attendance by the heads of government at the outset of an 18-nation conference is the best way to move forward. . . . Much clarifying work will have to be done in the early stages of negotiation before it is possible for heads of government to review the situation."

Khrushchev responded by charging that the Anglo-American desire to hold the negotiations at the foreign minister level was connected with the intention of the U.S. and U.K. to resume atmospheric testing. He warned that the Soviet Union would respond by further tests if they did so.

In his reply the president argued again for initial participation at the foreign minister level, noting that the Statement of Agreed Principles [on disarmament], "which was worked out so laboriously between representatives of our two countries last year . . . [was] the most that could be expected at this point from a meeting of the Heads of Government." He added a testy comment: "It is strange for the Soviet Union, which first broke the truce on nuclear testing, now to characterize any resumption of testing by the United States as an aggressive act." At length, on March 3, Khrushchev agreed to have the foreign ministers open the conference.

Decision to Test, with an Escape Clause

The president was now in the process of clearing away remaining doubts in his mind about the resumption of atmospheric testing. He asked Secretary Rusk for his recommendation on this issue, and Rusk replied affirmatively on February 20 in a tightly reasoned, five-page memorandum. The secretary noted that Foster and Murrow concurred.

Rusk's method was to evaluate each of the arguments *against* testing. He considered the most important of these to be "the possibility of prejudicing formal or tacit steps toward arms control arrangements by making it more certain that the USSR would again test and thereby further escalate the arms race." While agreeing that there was this danger, he did not believe we could, in the interest of advancing arms control, accept the risk to our national security that would result if the Soviets sought to "capitalize on their recent advances by launching another massive test series." Since ending the arms race would also be in our interest, the secretary advocated that, in addition to testing, we "continue to advocate a comprehensive test ban treaty with adequate international control."

Rusk gave little weight to other arguments against test resumption. He thought losses in our international position would be minimal. The hazards from fallout also seemed minimal "compared with the hazard which might be caused by misunderstandings about our nuclear strength."

The secretary repeated the recommendation made by the subcommittee to the NSC Committee on Atmospheric Testing, that we lead off with shots in Nevada "to alleviate criticism that the U.S. is callous about the safety of inhabitants of the Pacific area."

Rusk concluded by recommending that the resumption of testing be coupled with a vigorous diplomatic offensive at the UN and throughout the world.

On February 27, 1962, there was a climactic meeting at the White House. To clear the way for the announcement he expected soon to issue, Kennedy wished to have one more roundup of views, in the light of the most recent evaluations of the world situation, regarding the two issues uppermost in his mind: the resumption of atmospheric testing, including its timing; and what our position should be on the comprehensive test ban treaty we had ourselves introduced in Geneva the preceding April. At this meeting a strong difference of opinion became apparent between the civilian heads of the Defense Department and the Joint Chiefs of Staff on the issue of a test ban. This was subsequently to become of key importance.

> The president called on various people and others volunteered their comments.
>
> McCone said there were inconclusive indications from the north of Russia and the Sary Shagon missile range that the Soviets might be making new preparations for testing.
>
> Rusk advocated the atmospheric test program because prudence

suggested that we keep alive and alert and stay ahead. The reputation of the United States must not be endangered by suggestions we might be falling behind. He would be willing to sign the draft test ban treaty we introduced last April. The gains from opening the USSR to inspection and the prestige they would lose if they prepared to test under such a treaty made it worthwhile despite the risk. He wouldn't announce tests until we had been at the disarmament conference for from two to four weeks. If testing could stop now the position of the U.S. was satisfactory and thus, if political events of enormous magnitude should occur, such as signing of our test ban treaty or a breakthrough on Berlin, we could decide not to test.

McNamara favored undertaking the test series and signing the test ban treaty. Gilpatric and Brown concurred.

Lemnitzer said that the Joint Chiefs of Staff did not agree that the U.S. should sign the April 1961 treaty because it would not be to our military advantage.

Foster (ACDA) said he would sign the treaty because of the entree this would give us into the Soviet Union. He said we should press for disarmament measures. He disagreed with Rusk on the timing of the announcement and the actual start of tests, feeling that both should occur before the March 14 opening of the disarmament conference.

I said that AEC advocated the recommended series of some twenty-four tests. I pointed out that Rusk's suggestion that an announcement be withheld for two to four weeks after March 14 presented a problem since the test task force required a sailing time of about a month. The starting date would be very late if the announcement were so long delayed. I also supported the value of tests proposed for early March in Nevada.

At this point the president spoke out very vigorously against the tests in Nevada. He thought the political cost of another mushroom cloud visible in the United States would be prohibitive.

Adlai Stevenson felt that a good technical case had not been made for the resumption of testing. If we must test, however, the president should announce as soon as possible, resumption should come after the opening of the disarmament conference, and the U.S. should conduct a "peace offensive" involving the introduction of a modified disarmament treaty.

Dean would still sign the April 1961 treaty, but its three-year delay in putting inspection procedures into effect presented a problem, so he would want to add provisions for inspecting preparations to test. The president said that the three-year delay in beginning inspection might imperil the April 1961 treaty in the Senate and that it perhaps should be updated for that reason.

Vice-President Johnson said he thought the United States should proceed to test without delay. He concluded on the basis of statements made by others that there was military necessity not counterbalanced by political considerations. He inclined toward early announcement and toward having the early tests in Nevada. (This last was noteworthy since it went counter to the president's view, expressed earlier.)

Murrow favored minimum delay between announcement and the start of testing since delay might seem to show indecision. Kennedy asked to see him later in the day to discuss this further.

The president seemed to favor an announcement early in March, leaving open the possibility that the tests would not take place if there were dramatic progress at Geneva or elsewhere.

Following this meeting events moved rapidly. The next day Sorensen, Wiesner, Bundy, Murrow, Brown, Foster, some others and I met in Sorensen's office to discuss the latter's draft of a statement for the president to use on radio and TV. We all worked together on it for hours, right up to the last hour before its delivery on the evening of March 2, 1962. One of our guidelines was that there be nothing in the statement that would be inconsistent with continued negotiation of a test ban treaty.

On the afternoon before his speech, Kennedy called a meeting to brief leaders of Congress.

Present were the president; Senators Anderson, Mansfield, Russell, Pastore, Dirksen, Fulbright, Saltonstall, and Hickenlooper; Congressmen Holifield, Price, McCormack, Van Zandt, and Vinson; McNamara, McCone, Brown, Bundy, and me. The president described the general outline of his announcement. McCone, using charts, described the Russian tests and their significance. Brown outlined the classes of tests in the U.S. program. I emphasized the test at 2,000 kilometers altitude to develop a capability for testing in outer space, and also the respective roles that Johnston and Christmas Islands would play.

The president said that heads of state around the world had been briefed and that the only dissenting comment that needed to be taken seriously was from Japan.

It was the unanimous reaction of the members of Congress, voiced individually by Vinson, McCormack, Mansfield, Dirksen, and Hickenlooper, that the president had made the correct decision in the proper way.

The president's address to the nation that evening was long and thorough in its coverage of the issues. His intent was to present the entire rationale for his fateful decision to announce the resumption of atmospheric testing. It was as though he were addressing the judgment of history.

Kennedy emphasized, as was certainly the case, that no decision of his administration had been "more thoroughly or thoughtfully weighed." He gave a frank assessment of the gains the Soviets appeared to have made in their tests and concluded that "further Soviet tests, in the absence of further Western progress, could well provide the Soviet Union with a nuclear attack capability so powerful as to encourage aggressive designs."

Perhaps with a nod toward the British, the president acknowledged that there were those who had urged the United States not to test. He argued that failure to respond to the Soviet deception would cause many to "lose faith in our will and our wisdom, as well as our weaponry."

The president revealed what may have been one of his prime motivations when he said that the Soviets would be more inclined to negotiate an end to the arms race once they realized that the West would not stand still and let them make progress without response. (Sorensen makes the point that Kennedy had finally become convinced that the resumption of testing was a better route to a test ban than no testing at all.)[1]

The president then referred to the upcoming meeting of the Eighteen-Nation Disarmament Committee and the proposals we would make there, particularly our modified test ban proposal, and stated: "If the Soviet Union should now be willing to accept such a treaty, to sign it before the latter part of April and apply it immediately—if all testing can thus be actually halted—then the nuclear arms race would be slowed down at last—the security of the United States and its ability to meet its commitments would be safeguarded—and there would be no need for our tests to begin."

The president's conclusion undoubtedly mirrored his personal feelings: "It is our hope and prayer that these grim, unwelcome tests will never have to be made—that these deadly weapons will never have to be fired—and that our preparations for war will bring about the preservation of peace. . . . But whatever the future brings, I am sworn to uphold and defend the freedom of the American people—and I intend to do whatever must be done to fulfill that solemn obligation."

For a time now the focus of attention, insofar as nuclear testing was concerned, shifted back to Geneva. There the United States was confronted by a new forum, new participants, and some new approaches.

11

Geneva Revisited

Preparing the U.S. Position

What slim hope Kennedy had of avoiding the tests he had announced on March 2, 1962, rested with the Eighteen-Nation Disarmament Committee, due to resume its sessions in Geneva on March 14.

Meetings of the Committee of Principals were held on March 6 and March 9 to prepare U.S. positions for the conference.

Attending the March 6 meeting were the president and vice-president; from the White House staff: Wiesner and his deputy, Keeney, Carl Kaysen (Bundy's deputy), Schlesinger, and General Taylor; from the Defense Department: McNamara, Nitze, and General Lemnitzer; from the Arms Control Agency: Foster and his deputy, Fisher; from the State Department: Rusk, McGhee, Farley, and Foy Kohler. I attended for the AEC. As noted in my journal:

> The president said we should first discuss the U.S. draft test ban treaty. Foster reported that we had disagreements with the British, who

inclined toward major compromises with the Soviet Union's point of view. He noted, for example, that the British wanted to emphasize national means of verification. Further, while the British still went along with the idea of onsite inspections as a means of identification in doubtful cases, they no longer supported our proposed annual quota of 12 to 20, proposing instead a quota of 3 to 4, close to what the Soviets had previously offered.

Discussion turned to the changes we would now want in the April 1961 treaty draft. The president said there should be a provision for inspections to detect preparations for atmospheric testing, lest we get caught a second time by secret Soviet preparations. Wiesner doubted such a provision was feasible: it would require the Soviets to admit inspectors into their laboratories. Foster mentioned the possibility of extracting from each side a declaration that no preparations for testing were being made.

Foster mentioned, as a second desirable modification, having a shorter time than three years from the signing of the treaty until the first inspection of an underground event would take place.

A third possible modification mentioned by the president was to lower the threshold of 4.75 seismic magnitude which limited the treaty's coverage of underground tests.

On the matter of the number of onsite inspections, I mentioned that, if inspections were insufficient to prevent clandestine testing by the Soviets, the main danger to the U.S. was that the USSR weapons laboratories would thereby maintain greater vitality than their U.S. counterparts. The president asked whether we could safely reduce the quota of inspections. Wiesner suggested that we stay with our 12-to-20 formula but that we redistribute them so that most would take place in the remote, earthquake-prone areas of the USSR, hence reducing the amount of intrusion into the more sensitive industrial areas, which were not earthquake-prone.

The president and vice-president were again in attendance at the March 9 meeting. Most members of the group that had met three days earlier were also present, with CIA Director McCone a significant addition. On this occasion, two of the changes in our position proposed on March 6 were confirmed as U.S. policy while the others remained still in the discussion stage.

Foster said our policy would be to offer to sign the treaty tabled in April 1961, with the amendments offered in May, June, and August. In addition, during the course of negotiations, or in response to situations that might arise, we would propose the following modifications:

1. An inspection system to monitor preparations for testing. It would consist of periodic declarations by the powers that they were not making such preparations, plus the right of each side to inspect the other's declared test sites.
2. Shortening the time between treaty signature and beginning of onsite inspection. By speeding up the construction of control posts,

it might be possible to start inspections within a year of ratification. I said this would be difficult to implement since there were many ways the Russians could delay things.

Foster further indicated that the possible elimination of the threshold of 4.75 seismic magnitude on underground tests would be explored urgently within the next two or three weeks.

The president indicated we might also move in the direction the British wanted by proposing a lesser annual quota of inspections. Two changes since April 1961 made this feasible: first, it didn't seem possible to get as much out of underground tests as had been thought, so there was less to fear from clandestine Soviet tests; second, our seismic research program (VELA) was pointing the way to improvements in the ability to detect and identify underground tests without onsite inspection. [As will be related hereafter, the U.S. ultimately proposed a quota of seven inspections.]

In response to a question from Rusk, I indicated that it probably would not be possible for the Russians to make a major breakthrough in the short term by clandestine underground testing in violation of a treaty.

In anticipating the course the Geneva meeting might take, Rusk said that Gromyko might refuse at the outset to discuss the U.S. draft test ban treaty and that would be the end of it. Bundy urged Rusk to disclose in his very first statement that we had a 1962 treaty version to propose, so this would be on the record regardless of what Gromyko did.

I received the impression that, although the U.S. proposal was being advanced with the hope that it would be accepted, there was also a motive, in the likely case that it was not accepted, of showing the world that we had made every effort toward a test ban before going ahead with atmospheric tests.

A New Low at Geneva

The conference of the Eighteen-Nation Disarmament Committee (ENDC) took place at the Palais des Nations in Geneva, the same building that had housed the Conference on the Discontinuance of Nuclear Weapons Tests.

Three groups of nations had been designated as members of the committee. There were five NATO countries (U.S., U.K., Canada, France, and Italy), five Warsaw Pact countries (USSR, Bulgaria, Czechoslovakia, Poland, and Rumania), and eight nonaligned countries (Brazil, Burma, Ethiopa, India, Mexico, Nigeria, Sweden, and the United Arab Republic). The ENDC differed from a previous UN Ten-Nation Disarmament Committee, which the Soviet Union had terminated by walking out on June 27, 1960, precisely in the addition of the eight neutral nations. The addition was far more than symbolic. "The Eight" were to be an active and innovative force.

In actuality only seventeen nations were represented at the conference. France did not attend. Writing to Premier Khrushchev on

February 19, President de Gaulle stated:* "If negotiations are to have a chance of success, it is in my opinion necessary that they be held by powers that have, or are very soon going to have, nuclear weapons. Indeed, it is difficult to see how participation by States that do not now have any direct responsibility in this matter could lead to positive results." De Gaulle continued to object, moreover, to discussing a test ban separate from disarmament. He proposed talks among the USSR, U.S., U.K., and France, with the immediate aim of agreeing on the destruction and control of means of launching nuclear missiles.

Khrushchev rejected the French bid for talks limited to the Big Four, stating that the problems of disarmament affected the people of other states, "including neutralist ones." The French Foreign Ministry then announced, on March 5, that France would not send any representatives to the conference. The group nevertheless continued to call itself an eighteen-nation committee, as established by the UN, and at each full meeting one chair was conspicuously left vacant for France.

Rusk's prediction of what might happen at the ENDC proved quite accurate. In his opening statement on March 14, Foreign Minister Gromyko reaffirmed the Soviet proposal of a test ban agreement without international controls. The following day representatives of the Big Three discussed the test ban question informally. The Western delegates offered some of the changes that had been discussed by the Committee of Principals. They stated that the U.S. and U.K. were willing to eliminate entirely the threshold of 4.75 seismic magnitude on underground tests, making the treaty fully comprehensive. They proposed to do this without increasing the number of detection stations or onsite inspections. They offered also to allocate inspections so most would occur in earthquake-prone areas remote from the industries of European Russia. To deal with the problem of test preparations, they proposed periodic declarations by heads of state that they were making no preparations. They proposed also that each side be permitted periodically to inspect declared testing sites of the other. These proposals included substantial concessions. Nevertheless, the Soviet delegates rejected the Western proposals in the informal discussions.

At the suggestion of the U.S., the full committee next established a Subcommittee on a Treaty for the Discontinuance of Nuclear Weapon Tests, composed of the U.S., U.K., and USSR. In effect the eighteen were asking the three to resume where they had left off in the previous Geneva conference.

---

*Khrushchev had attempted to enlist de Gaulle's support for his proposal that heads of state open the ENDC.

At the first meeting of the subcommittee the United States formally introduced the new Western proposals. Tsarapkin, for the Soviet Union, formally rejected them and reiterated the Soviet proposal for a test ban relying solely on national means of detection. On March 22, after two negotiating sessions, the subcomittee submitted a report to the full conference expressing regret that it had been unable to make progress toward a test ban treaty.

Technical Reevaluation

The draft test ban treaty introduced by the Soviet Union at the ENDC threw down a technical challenge to the West. In claiming that national means of verification were sufficient to detect and identify tests in all environments, including those underground, the Russians offered certain "proofs." First was the fact that the atmospheric test ban offered by Kennedy and Macmillan on September 3, 1961, would have relied solely on national means. Second was the fact that the Soviet Union's first underground test, on February 2, 1962, had been detected and announced by the United States. (Khrushchev acknowledged in a speech that this test was conducted for the specific purpose of forcing the United States to grant the validity of the Soviet claim that underground tests could be detected by national means.) Third was the fact that the Plowshare program's 5-kiloton GNOME shot of December 10, 1961, which was detonated 1,200 feet beneath the surface in a salt cavern near Carlsbad, New Mexico, had been detected by seismographic stations in Finland, Sweden, and Japan. Aside from demonstrating that relatively small underground tests could be detected by national means, the Soviets alleged that this also disproved the theory of decoupling.

It was easy enough to deal with the Russian "proofs." As Dean pointed out, the Soviet test announced by the U.S. was a large one, relatively easy to detect. Furthermore, it took place far from any seismic area, in fact, near an existing test site, so that there could be little ambiguity as to whether it was a test or an earthquake. The fact that the U.S. GNOME shot had been picked up by seismographic stations in Europe and Japan also proved little. The date and hour of the test had been made known in advance. Furthermore, GNOME was the only one of the U.S. underground shots in 1961 to be recorded in Sweden. Also, the GNOME experience was irrelevant to decoupling since the device was tamped (packed tightly into the surrounding material), not detonated in a large chamber. Finally, the fact that the Kennedy-Macmillan offer of September 3, 1961, involved acceptance of national means of verification for an atmospheric test ban did

During a presidential visit to the Atomic Energy Commission on February 16, 1961, the author briefed the president on some nuclear energy fundamentals before a meeting with staff members for discussion of individual programs. Kennedy listened intently, asked many questions.

W. Averell Harriman with President Kennedy at the White House, March 20, 1961. It would be more than two years before Kennedy would send Harriman to Moscow on the mission that resulted in the Limited Test Ban Treaty.

President Kennedy and Prime Minister Macmillan at the White House, April 8, 1961. They are flanked by Secretary of State Dean Rusk (left) and British Foreign Minister Lord Home.

USSR Premier Khrushchev welcoming President Kennedy on the steps of the Soviet Embassy in Vienna, June 4, 1961, the second day of their get-acquainted summit meeting. Despite the smiles shown here, the talks were grim.

Once inside the Soviet embassy the two leaders posed for this formal portrait.

On March 23, 1962, President Kennedy visited the Berkeley campus of the University of California to take part in the observance of Charter Day. Scientists prominent in the nation's defense effort were assembled to meet the president. He made everyone feel at ease, as is evident from this group photograph. From left, Norris Bradbury, director of the Los Alamos Scientific Laboratory; John S. Foster, director of the Livermore Laboratory; Edwin M. McMillan, director of the Lawrence Radiation Laboratory, Berkeley; the author; the president; Edward Teller, associate director at Livermore; Secretary of Defense Robert McNamara; and Harold Brown, director of defense research and engineering.

The president with the author at his left and Secretary of Defense McNamara at his right arriving at Lawrence Radiation Laboratory, March 23, 1962.

On December 7 and 8, 1962, the author accompanied President Kennedy and others on a wide-ranging tour of AEC and Air Force installations, including Strategic Air Command heaquarters in Omaha, the Los Alamos Scientific Laboratory, the Sandia (New Mexico) Laboratories, and the Nevada Test Site. At the test site we surveyed various points of interest by helicopter and then, as shown, made a tour by car.

Vice-President Lyndon B. Johnson making a point with the president at Los Alamos Scientific Laboratory, December 7, 1962. Laboratory Director Norris Bradbury and Senator Clinton Anderson are in the foreground.

On May 21, 1963, during his trip to the Soviet Union, the author and Chairman Andronik M. Petrosyants of the Soviet Union State Committee on Atomic Energy signed a Memorandum on Cooperation in the Field of the Utilization of Atomic Energy for Peaceful Purposes.

President Kennedy delivering the commencement address at The American University in Washington, D.C., June 10, 1963. This speech greatly impressed the Soviet leadership and had a favorable effect on the test ban negotiations.

famous "Ich bin ein Berliner" speech on June 26, 1963.

President Kennedy looking over the Berlin Wall into the Eastern sector during his visit to West Berlin, June 26, 1963.

During the test ban negotiations in Moscow, W. Averell Harriman and Premier Khrushchev took time off to attend a Soviet-American track meet. They are shown applauding as the two teams circled the field together arm in arm following the competition. Harriman reported that this ceremony, a high point in Soviet-American good feeling, brought tears to Khrushchev's eyes.

The day after the Limited Test Ban Treaty was initialed in Moscow, Averell Harriman called on Premier Khrushchev in the latter's Kremlin office. Khrushchev greeted Harriman warmly, crying "Molodets!" meaning "Bravo!" or "Fine fellow!"

(Credit: United Press International Photo)

Scene as the Limited Test Ban Treaty was signed in the Kremlin on August 5, 1963. Signing at table were, from left, Secretary of State Dean Rusk (not shown), Soviet Foreign Minister Andrei Gromyko, and British Foreign Minister Lord Home. In the front row are, from left, State Department interpreter Alexander Akalovsky, Senator Hubert Humphrey, U.S. Ambassador to the UN Adlai Stevenson, and between them (slightly behind) Senator Leverett Saltonstall, UN Secretary-General U Thant, and Premier Khrushchev. Behind Lord Home and his aide is Edward Heath, British Lord Privy Seal, and beside him, to the left is Soviet Deputy Foreign Minister Valerian Zorin, and beside him and slightly behind to left is Soviet Ambassador to the U.S. Anatoly Dobrynin. To the extreme right, partially shown, is the author

Champagne was in order after the treaty-signing ceremony. Participants included, from left, Senators Fulbright, Aiken, Saltonstall, and Humphrey, and Adlai Stevenson, U Thant, and Premier Khrushchev.

Khrushchev delivering a speech during the reception in the Kremlin's Georgian Hall following the formal signing of the Limited Test Ban Treaty on August 5, 1963. Adlai Stevenson is visible on right.

Having received the advice and consent of the Senate, President Kennedy is shown signing the instrument of ratification of the Limited Test Ban Treaty, October 7, 1963. Standing from left are ACDA Deputy Director Adrian Fisher, Senator John Pastore, Under-Secretary of State W. Averell Harriman, Senator George Smathers, Senator J. W. Fulbright, Secretary of State Dean Rusk, Senator George Aiken, Senator Hubert Humphrey, Senator Everett Dirksen, ACDA Director William Foster, Senator Howard Cannon, Senator Leverett Saltonstall, Senator Thomas Kuchel and Vice-President Lyndon B. Johnson.

THE CONSCIENCE OF THE INTERNATIONAL SCIENTIFIC COMMUNITY	**1947** **7 MINUTES TO MIDNIGHT** The clock makes its first appearance on the Bulletin cover as a symbol of nuclear doomsday.	**1949** **3 MINUTES TO MIDNIGHT** The Soviet Union explodes its first atomic bomb.
1953 **2 MINUTES TO MIDNIGHT** Development of the hydrogen bomb by the United States and the Soviet Union.	**1960** **7 MINUTES TO MIDNIGHT** The Cold War begins to thaw.	**1963** **12 MINUTES TO MIDNIGHT** Signing of the Partial Test Ban Treaty.
1968 **7 MINUTES TO MIDNIGHT** The nuclear weapons club now stands at five, with France, China, Britain, the U.S. and U.S.S.R.	**1969** **10 MINUTES TO MIDNIGHT** Ratification of the Nuclear Non-Proliferation Treaty.	**1972** **12 MINUTES TO MIDNIGHT** Strategic Arms Limitation Talks (SALT) lead to first nuclear arms control agreement between U.S. and U.S.S.R.
1974 **9 MINUTES TO MIDNIGHT** SALT fails to make progress; India joins the nuclear weapons club.	**1980** **7 MINUTES TO MIDNIGHT** Danger of nuclear war increases; irrationality of national and international actions.	**1981** **4 MINUTES TO MIDNIGHT** General deterioration in East-West relations.

The "doomsday clock" on the cover of each issue of the monthly *Bulletin of the Atomic Scientists* is, in the *Bulletin*'s words, "a symbolic warning of the lateness of the hour as mankind confronts (or fails to confront) the urgent problems of our time." As shown here, the minute hand, never far from midnight, has moved ten times since the magazine's first issue. The promise of the Limited Test Ban Treaty set the clock back to twelve minutes to midnight. Failure to achieve the treaty's promise has brought the clock once again to just four minutes to midnight.

not imply that such means were valid to police tests in environments other than the atmosphere.

Disposing of the Soviet arguments based on their lack of technical merit was not a substitute for being able to make a clear presentation of the technical situation to the disarmament conference. Of the eight neutral delegations, Sweden's was the only one with technical advisers. It was consequently necessary to discuss technical points in relatively nontechnical language and in a very patient manner. To deal with this situation, it was decided early in the conference to have a U.S. technical group led by Wiesner come to Geneva and make themselves available to explain the technical situation as the U.S. saw it. This proved a wise decision: the technical delegation did an effective teaching job.

If truth be told, however, the West was somewhat unprepared for a technical challenge at this particular time. The reason was that Project VELA, the seismic research program assigned to the Advanced Research Projects Agency of the Department of Defense, had just produced some preliminary results that needed to be evaluated. In general, the data emerging from VELA seemed to indicate that detection capability was better than had been thought by American experts in the period from 1959 through 1961.

In order to determine whether there had been sufficient improvement in detection capability to warrant a further easing in Western conditions for a test ban treaty, British and American technical delegations met in Washington shortly after the start of the Eighteen-Nation Conference. The American team was headed by Franklin Long, ACDA assistant director for science and technology. The AEC members were Commissioner Haworth and George Kavanagh, my assistant for disarmament.

The upshot of the technical discussions was summarized in a memorandum written by Haworth on March 20, 1962. Based on the latest improvements, he wrote,

> an external system [i.e., one without any detection stations inside the Soviet Union] can probably be made adequate for *detection and localization* purposes after a few years. There is, however, no real evidence that such systems will have any appreciable identification capability [to distinguish earthquakes from explosions] except possibly at the upper end of the yield range. . . .
>
> Of crucial importance is the fact that . . . *there appears to be no prospect of being able to identify an event as an explosion by seismic means alone.* At best, seismic systems can merely reject certain events as being earthquakes, leaving a substantial fraction of the observed events uncertain as to origin.
>
> External systems alone would, so far as can be foreseen, leave this fraction very large. It is, therefore, abundantly clear that *onsite*

inspection is an absolute requirement for any system [Haworth's italics].

The problem of reconciling these technical findings with the political realities at the disarmament conference was discussed at a meeting at the White House on March 28. Those in attendance included the president, the vice-president, Rusk, McNamara, McCone, Foster, Bundy, Wiesner, Robert Kennedy, Fisher, me, and others.

> Rusk reported that the Russians in Geneva had left no room for maneuver on the test ban by declaring that there should be zero inspections. He thought their fear of espionage was a fake since only about 1/2000th of their area would be subject to possible inspection. He was told that, if there were a secret vote by the seventeen nations at the conference, it would be 12 to five against the Soviet position, meaning that the eight neutrals seemed to be convinced of the necessity for some inspection. Nevertheless, Rusk felt that much work remained to be done on persuading the neutrals. He suggested that their embassies be sent an illustrated brochure describing the technical problems. It could show, for example, the similarity in the seismic "signature" of earthquakes and underground explosions.
>
> Rusk proposed that the U.S. stay with the president's March 2 statement and continue to prepare for a test series to start late in April, barring any diplomatic miracle. He said that suggestions for postponing the tests would continue to come from the countries represented at the disarmament conference; however, none had indicated an intent to leave the conference in the event the U.S. resumed testing.
>
> McCone recalled a letter to Eisenhower in April 1959 in which Khrushchev indicated that the Soviets could agree to a low inspection quota if it would lead to a comprehensive test ban. McCone asked if this view had changed. Rusk indicated that it had.

The day following this meeting the president issued a public statement setting forth the U.S. position on the need for inspection. In phraseology obviously aimed at the neutral delegations at Geneva, and echoing the conclusions in Haworth's memorandum of March 20, he pointed out the need to "distinguish carefully between detection and identification. We can detect and locate significant underground events by seismic means, but of course the same seismic means detect many shallow earthquakes. The problem is to identify a particular detected event as an explosion or as an earthquake. . . .the only way we know to perform this identification is to have a scientific team go to the site of the event and examine it."

Kennedy then went on to discuss the Soviet opposition to all inspection and to having any detection posts on its territory, "a sharp and inexplicable regression from the Soviet position of even a year ago." He sought to demonstrate that Soviet fears of espionage were unjustified. The president concluded: "We know of no way to verify underground nuclear explosions without inspections, and we cannot at this time enter into a treaty without the ability and right of international verification. Hence we seem to be at a real impasse. Nevertheless, I want to repeat with emphasis our desire for an effective treaty and our readiness to conclude such a treaty at the earliest possible time."

Rusk's information that a secret vote at Geneva would have found all the neutrals favoring onsite inspection may not have been accurate. It is probably true that the neutrals were persuaded by arguments such as the president had presented that national means alone were not sufficient to distinguish a fair proportion of underground explosions from shallow earthquakes. They were not as convinced, however, that onsite inspection was the answer to the problem. The Swedes in particular were well aware of views expressed by American scientists at the Conference of Experts, in congressional testimony, and in scholarly journals to the effect that onsite inspection would be slow, enormously expensive, and only rarely successful in providing positive identification.[1] Consequently, when the neutrals themselves came up with a plan, it provided for the possibility of onsite inspection *by invitation* but did not by any means make such inspection the cornerstone of their system.

Another aspect of the Western proposals that seemed to leave the neutrals cold was the requirement for an elaborate network of detection stations based on the Geneva System of 1958. As Alva Myrdal, a prominent member of the Swedish delegation at Geneva, commented: "Though the costs [of the proposed control system] were never formally summarized, they must have run into billions of dollars. The staff requirements alone ran into several thousand scientists and technicians, who would be sitting isolated far away, watching day after day and night after night for some suspicious sign—a horrible prospect for any academic."[2] Indeed, the contemplated test ban control organization would have been by far the largest of all UN organizations, and I am inclined , in retrospect, to agree that it was probably impractical. The proposal ultimately advanced by the neutrals rejected this elaborate structure of international control posts.

The Eight-Nation Memorandum

As the declared date ("late in April") for the U.S. resumption of atmospheric testing drew near, danger zones were established and mariners warned to stay clear. The Christmas Island danger zone was to become effective on April 15; the Johnston Island zone, on April 30.

On April 9, the U.S. and U.K. issued a joint statement warning that "if there is no change in the present Soviet position, the Governments of the United States and the United Kingdom must conclude that their efforts to obtain a workable treaty to ban nuclear tests are not now successful, and the test series scheduled for the latter part of this month will have to go forward."

Along with the joint statement of April 9, Prime Minister Macmillan sent a short personal note to Premier Khrushchev asking him to give the statement his "most earnest consideration." Khrushchev's reply of April 12 was one of his more snarling expressions. He charged that the Anglo-American statement had been issued to "divert the wrath of the peoples." He said that the only reason the Western Powers wanted inspection was "for choosing the moment to attack the Soviet Union" and that, if the U.S. and U.K. wished to refute this charge, they could agree to a test ban treaty using national systems of verification.

The eight neutral nations at the ENDC had been increasingly active individually in making suggestions for compromises that might break the impasse between the nuclear powers. Several of these involved an appeal for a moratorium on tests during the conference. The Soviet Union accepted this, but the United States rejected it, stating that it did not intend "to place its security and the security of its allies at the mercy of Soviet on-again-off-again tactics."

On April 16, 1962, the eight presented at Geneva their long-awaited joint memorandum suggesting a compromise solution on the basis of the following ideas:

1. Setting up a control system using existing national observation posts, plus some additional posts to be established by agreement.
2. Establishing an international commission "consisting of a limited number of highly qualified scientists, possibly from non-aligned countries, together with the appropriate staff." This commission would process data received from the control network and would report "on any nuclear explosion or suspicious event." Parties to the treaty "could invite the Commission to visit their territories and/or the site of an event the nature of which was in doubt."
3. If the commission was unable to determine whether a "significant event" was an earthquake or an explosion it would seek clarification from the party on whose territory the event had

occurred. "The party and the Commission should consult as to what further measures of clarification, including verification *in loco*, would facilitate the assessment."
4. After the commission had furnished the parties with its assessment , the parties "would be free to determine their action with regard to [withdrawing from] the treaty."

The eight-nation memorandum was not a model of precision, and the first reaction of the West was to seek clarification on a number of points. The most important of the questions was whether parties would be *required* to accept onsite inspection of unidentified events or whether this would be voluntary. Speaking for the eight, the Ethiopian representative stated that the memorandum would have to stand by itself; the authors would not interpret it. It was intended to be used by the nuclear powers as a starting point of "immediate, new and constructive negotiations," not as a complete blueprint.

The reasons why no clarification was forthcoming were inherent in the circumstances of the memorandum's creation. It represented a series of compromises among the eight and it would probably have been impossible to achieve agreed interpretations. Further, to have been more explicit would have risked being drawn into the arguments of the superpowers involving technical complications which several of the neutral delegates felt were beyond their comprehension.[3]

In the absence of clarification, each side chose to interpret the eight-nation memorandum as favoring its position. The Soviet Union considered the plan a vindication of its position in favor of using only national means of verification and welcomed it as a basis for further negotiations. The U.S. and U.K. held that the memorandum endorsed the principles of international control and onsite inspection. Each side thereupon accused the other of misinterpreting the memorandum.

Thus the impasse continued. Transferring the negotiations to a new forum and introducing the views of the eight neutrals had not succeeded in breaking the deadlock. The U.S. atmospheric test series would go forward.

12

Operation DOMINIC

Overview

The U.S. atmospheric test series, designated Operation DOM-INIC, began April 25, 1962, with an air drop in the intermediate-yield range (20 kilotons to 1 megaton)* off Christmas Island. It was the first U.S. atmospheric test since 1958.

In all, the series comprised forty tests. It included the firing of twenty-nine nuclear devices dropped from aircraft in the vicinity of Christmas and Johnston islands and five detonations of nuclear devices carried to high altitudes by missiles launched from Johnston Island. Two nuclear weapons system tests were also involved—one in the Christmas Island area and one in the eastern Pacific. These

---

*In reporting its own and Soviet tests, the Atomic Energy Commission frequently adopted the practice of reporting yields in size categories rather than as precise numbers. Prior to 1964, the categories and the yield ranges they represented were: low yield, less than 20 kilotons; intermediate, 20 kilotons to 1 megaton; low megaton, 1 to several megatons.

thirty-six Pacific tests were conducted by a joint AEC-Defense Department task force that, at the peak of its activity, numbered over 19,000 men. In addition to the Pacific tests four small tests were conducted near the surface at the Nevada Test Site.

In accordance with the restrictions imposed by the president, the total yield of the series was held to approximately 20 megatons. The Soviet series in the fall of 1961 had yielded almost ten times as much.

By and large, DOMINIC went well. There were, however, certain difficulties.

Some Public Reactions

Despite the administration's careful attention in its actions and pronouncements to the state of world opinion, adverse reactions to the U.S. resumption of testing were inevitable. There remained throughout the world a solid core of sentiment that was bitterly hostile to nuclear tests.

As might be expected, much of this sentiment was found in Japan. Following the first test on April 25, 3,000 demonstrators paraded through the streets of Tokyo, and 2,000 battled police near the U.S. embassy. In London, 350 demonstrators were arrested outside the U.S. embassy.

Our own country was not without its protesters. Opponents of the tests picketed the White House on April 28. One of the pickets was Linus Pauling. He was in Washington to attend a dinner being given the following day by the president and Mrs. Kennedy for forty-nine Nobel laureates and other scientists. (It was at this dinner that we heard Kennedy make his justly famous comment: "I think this is the most extraordinary collection of talent, of human knowledge, that has ever been gathered together at the White House—with the possible exception of when Thomas Jefferson dined alone.")*

The most dramatic protests took the form of attempts by private citizens to disrupt the tests by sailing into the prohibited zones surrounding the Pacific test islands. In the first of these episodes a Committee for Non-Violent Action sent the president a telegram on May 1, informing him that on May 13 a sailing vessel called *Everyman I* would set sail from San Francisco for the Christmas Island test

---

*Robert Kennedy's interview for the Kennedy Library's Oral History Program casts light on the genesis of this line. The interviewer, John Bartlow Martin, reveals that he and Arthur Schlesinger had worked on the president's remarks the afternoon preceding the banquet. "In our remarks," says Martin, "we had the line that this was the greatest, etc.—just a routine, dull, hack line." Martin then asks Robert Kennedy whether it was the president who added the part about Thomas Jefferson. Robert Kennedy answers, "Yes, yes, it was. You can see his notes on a menu card that I've seen."

area. The AEC informed the attorney general and requested that he seek a court order enjoining this contemplated violation of the AEC's regulation prohibiting entry into the test danger zones. On May 25 the assistant U.S. attorney in San Francisco obtained a temporary restraining order. Notwithstanding, the vessel sailed with a crew of three. The Coast Guard apprehended it eighteen miles southwest of the Golden Gate. The crew members were found guilty of criminal contempt for violating the court order and sentenced to thirty days in jail.

On June 11, we learned that a different group from San Francisco, led by a Dr. Steadman of Kaiser Hospital, was threatening to sail from Honolulu in a vessel named *Everyman II*. This time the destination was the Johnston Island danger zone. Once again a temporary re-straining order was obtained, but the vessel nevertheless set sail on June 23. On June 29 *Everyman II* was apprehended by the Coast Guard and brought back to Honolulu. The three crew members were found guilty of contempt of court and fined.

There was to be one more incident. On July 4 *Everyman I* was discovered to be missing from its mooring in Sausalito, California. It had set sail for Christmas Island with a new crew. Once more a court order was obtained, and the vessel was intercepted about twelve miles at sea and brought back to San Francisco. The three crew members, along with two leaders of the Committee for Non-Violent Action, were sentenced to six months in jail. This time *Everyman I* was kept in the custody of the U.S. marshal, lest it sail again.

Electrons on High

One of the grave concerns felt by the administration about the Russian tests of 1961 was that they might have made progress toward an antimissile missile. It was evident from our analyses of the tests that the Soviets had made an effort in that direction.

The implications of this were frightening. If one side could pre-vent penetration by the other side's missiles it would have achieved an enormous and tempting advantage. Concern that the Soviets might be on the way to such an advantage was one of the prime factors motivating the United States to resume atmospheric testing. This concern also led to the inclusion of several high-altitude shots in the U.S. test series. The purpose of these tests was twofold: (1) to determine whether they might black out military radar and com-munications systems, and (2) to determine whether their blast, heat, and radioactivity were capable of destroying incoming missiles, of neutralizing their warheads, or of diverting them by interfering with their guidance systems. Five previous high-altitude tests carried out by the U.S. in 1958 had given some indication that such effects were obtainable.

The plan was to have four high-altitude tests in the 1962 series. Three of these were to be from Johnston Island: BLUEGILL at 50 kilometers; STARFISH at 400 km; and URRACA at 1,300 km; the fourth shot, SMALLBOY, was to take place in Nevada.

Plans for the Pacific high-altitude tests were announced on April 29 by Harold Brown. The announcement brought immediate protests from prominent scientists. The general tenor of the scientists' objection was voiced by Sir Bernard Lovell, director of Great Britain's Jodrell Bank Radio Observatory, who expressed his dismay that nuclear tests were to be conducted in "a region of space which is at present the subject of detailed study."

What Sir Bernard and the other scientists were principally concerned about was the so-called Van Allen radiation belt.* This is an immense cluster of high-intensity charged particles—protons and electrons—which are held in space by the earth's magnetic field at altitudes extending from 500 to 20,000 miles. The phenomenon was named for Professor James A. Van Allen, a physicist at Iowa State University, who first observed it during 1958 rocket experiments. What the protesting scientists feared was that our tests, particularly URRACA, the highest, might add further radiation to the belt, to the detriment of radio communications and space travel; might destroy the inner part of the belt, with unpredictable consequences; or might otherwise cause some permanent modification in the earth's environment.

Professor Van Allen quickly came to the defense of the proposed tests, characterizing them in congressional testimony on May 2 as "magnificent experiments that would add to man's knowledge of the universe." Van Allen's statement touched on another concern of scientists in several countries. If the experiments were to take place, they felt that maximum opportunity should be afforded to scientists around the world to participate. As it was, the tests had been prepared with such speed and secrecy that their potential scientific value was severely limited.

The controversy came to the attention of Kennedy at a White House meeting which I attended on May 8.

> The president brought up the question of the objection by British scientists to our high-altitude explosion (URRACA) from the standpoint of its effect on the Van Allen radiation belt. I told him that,

---

*Scientists have since determined that there are two belts, an inner one and an outer one. While there were some in 1962 who believed there was more than one belt, most public references were to a single Van Allen belt.

although some scientists were worried about this, a larger number felt that the effect would be a temporary one and that the experiment would have great scientific value.

Following this discussion, the president decided to create a committee, including Van Allen, Panofsky, and others, to study the matter. It was further decided to discuss it at a meeting of the President's Science Advisory Committee scheduled for May 15.

The controversy was mentioned at the president's news conference on May 9.

> Q: Mr. President, it has been the stated policy, as you said earlier, for this government to restrict outer space for peaceful objectives only. Will not the proposed H-bomb explosion 500 miles up [URRACA] jeopardize this policy and objective?
>
> A: No, I don't think so. . . . I know there's been disturbance about the Van Allen belt, but Van Allen says it's not going to affect the belt, and it's his! [Laughter]

The president then went on in his answer to indicate that the proposed test was being subjected to "very careful scientific deliberation," which would continue a while longer.

On May 14 I met with a group of scientists to consider the problem. The conclusion was that URRACA would have a negligible effect on the Van Allen Belt.

On May 22, Wiesner called to report a conversation he had had with Kennedy after a meeting of the President's Science Advisory Committee.

> The president had asked Wiesner what the PSAC's judgment had been about URRACA. He told the president he didn't think there was a strong argument for the test but he felt uneasy about suggesting it be dropped because I, Seaborg, thought it was an important test and Defense tended to support my view. He also told the president that the PSAC was willing to go along with the test although they felt the testimony given in support of it was unconvincing. [My recollection is that the PSAC was somewhat divided on this.]

On May 24:

> Haworth and I met with Wiesner, Bundy, and others. It was decided to recommend to the president that URRACA be retained and that a technical release be issued about all the high-altitude tests for the benefit of scientists who might wish to make measurements.

I conveyed the recommendation about URRACA to the president by letter the same day. I noted that preliminary results of the study by the committee he had appointed gave no reason for concern. The two lower-altitude tests, BLUEGILL and STARFISH, were expected to have "no appreciable effects of significant duration on the Van Allen Belt region." URRACA might result in radio noise that would interfere with measurements by radioastronomers within twenty degrees of the magnetic equator, but this noise was expected to disappear after a few days or weeks.

The technical release was issued on May 28, four days before the scheduled date for BLUEGILL, which was to be the first of the high-altitude tests. The release indicated what visual effects observers in Hawaii and Samoa might expect. It stated that the tests might disrupt radio communications on certain bands for short periods and that the Federal Aviation Agency had issued appropriate warnings. It reported the conclusions of scientists about the likely effects on the Van Allen belts—temporary disruption by URRACA only, without hazard to health. "Thus, there is no need for concern regarding any lasting effects on the Van Allen belts and associated phenomena. On the contrary, these tests will give an opportunity to obtain important scientific data regarding the physics of the upper atmosphere, including the nature and cause of the Van Allen belts."

After we had thus alerted the scientific community of the world, it was with acute embarrassment that we learned that BLUEGILL had to be destroyed after launching on June 5 due to a failure of radar tracking. Then on June 20 STARFISH suffered an abort on its Johnston Island launching pad.

These two failures presented us with the problem of what to try next at Johnston Island. General Alfred D. Starbird, the Task Force commander, had already informed me that the fastest he could schedule one missile shot behind another at Johnston Island was fifteen days; that much time was required for pad repair and installation and for checkout of the next missile. The situation was made more uncertain by word, passed to us by Carl Kaysen on June 26, that the president was not inclined to approve URRACA.

Between June 29 and July 1, I visited the Pacific test sites along with Bundy, Arnold Fritsch (my technical assistant at AEC), and Dwight Ink (AEC assistant general manager). On June 30, on Christmas Island:

I arose at 5:15 A.M. and went with others to Observation Point, from which, at 6:20 A.M., we saw an explosion 30 miles south at 5,000 feet, the BLUESTONE event, about 1.3 megatons. It was dropped from an airplane. It was necessary to use dark glasses for the first eight seconds. Upon removing them I found the area brighter than full daylight, an awesome sight.

I spent the morning touring the impressive diagnostic facilities that had been set up in the trailers on short notice.

At 6:40 P.M. we flew by military plane to Johnston Island,
1,100 miles distant, arriving at 10:40 P.M. We were joined there by
Commissioner Haworth.

The next morning General Salet (who was in charge of Johnston
Island), Starbird, and William Ogle (scientific director of the test series)
showed us the facilities on the island, which measures in total approximately one mile by one-quarter mile. We saw the launching pad and the
complicated diagnostic facilities operated by the Air Force and several
laboratories.

After lunch on Johnston, we flew on to Hawaii and then home.

On July 3, bearing in mind the two previous aborts, I sent word to
Starbird not to rush preparations for STARFISH. The shot was post-
poned on July 4, again on July 5, and again on July 7. Finally, on July 9
I could record:

STARFISH went successfully (1.4 megatons, 400 kilometers high)
at 11:09 P.M. last night, local time. It lit the sky all the way to Hawaii and
Australia.

To our great surprise and dismay, it developed that STARFISH
added significantly to the electrons in the Van Allen belts. This result
contravened all predictions. In all the pretest controversy it was
URRACA alone which had been the subject of concern. We had all
been relatively complacent about STARFISH.*

To compound the problems, the second attempt to launch BLUE-
GILL, called BLUEGILL PRIME, proved disastrous. The Thor rocket
burst into flames before lift-off on July 25 and had to be blown up by
the range safety officer. The result, as the AEC announced in a press
release, was such substantial plutonium contamination and other
damage to the launch facility that weeks would be required to make it
operable again. As a consequence, the mariner restrictions around
Johnston Island were lifted temporarily.

The mishaps on Johnston Island raised concern in a strange
quarter. On August 11 we received word that the Soviet Union was
anxious about the safety of its astronaut, Nikolayev, whose orbit
around the earth was expected to last for several more days. They sent
us diplomatic signals that were essentially appeals not to conduct
any tests that might endanger the astronaut's life. Rusk responded
with a public statement: "We wish Major Nikolayev a safe flight and
a happy landing. The United States of course contemplates no activities that would interfere with him in any way."

---

*On more than one occasion when I have met Dean Rusk in subsequent years he has
chided me about the erroneous predictions made by scientists in this case. On such
occasions I have been glad to acknowledge that scientists, like diplomats, make errors.

On August 20, the AEC issued a preliminary assessment of the addition to the radiation belts caused by STARFISH. A more definitive release was issued on September 1.

The first release was an attempt at face-saving of which I am not particularly proud. It indicated that the effects had been "generally anticipated," not acknowledging that the effects anticipated were from another test (URRACA). The second release was more candid. It stated that additional data obtained from the TELSTAR satellite had permitted a more detailed determination of the distribution and intensity of the new radiation belt caused by STARFISH. It lay above the path of current manned space flights, and additional radio noise such as might interfere with radioastronomy would soon disappear. But the intensity of the radiation at higher altitudes was greater than anticipated and might persist for years. The release also stated that electron damage inflicted on their solar cells had destroyed the communications capability of three satellites, TRANSIT IV (a Navy navigation satellite), TRAAC (a Department of Defense satellite), and ARIEL (a British scientific satellite launched by the U.S.). The damage to ARIEL was particularly embarrassing since it had been British scientists who raised the first and loudest objections to our conducting high-altitude tests.

The results of STARFISH should have a sobering effect on any who believe that the earth's outer environment could emerge from a full nuclear exchange without severe damage.

Final Tests

From a national security standpoint we saw little choice but to persist in the high-altitude series that were so important with regard to antimissile capability. Kennedy authorized an extension of DOMINIC beyond its original scheduled closing date, and eleven additional tests were added to the series, three being high-altitude shots. As the president explained in a press conference statement, "as a result of the earlier tests in this DOMINIC series, there are certain things which we would like to prove out." He added, "we have taken some steps to prevent a repetition of the incident which caused an increase in the number of electrons in the atmosphere by lowering the altitude and the yield so that lunar flights will not be further endangered."

At a White House meeting I attended on September 5:

> The president directed that we reduce the number of atmospheric tests to be added to DOMINIC from eleven to eight, and that we sched-

ule the tests so as not to interfere with Astronaut Wally Schirra's September 23 flight. The president suggested dropping URRACA.

At a later meeting dominated by McNamara it was definitely decided to drop URRACA. SMALLBOY, the high-altitude test planned for Nevada, also did not take place, but the others went off as projected. CHECKMATE (less than 20 kilotons, 150 kilometers high) took place on October 20; BLUEGILL (one to several megatons, 50 kilometers high) finally went on October 26; KINGFISH (one to several megatons, tens of kilometers high) took place on November 1; and the series concluded on November 4 with TIGHTROPE (less than 20 kilotons, less than 100 kilometers high).

Evaluation

DOMINIC had so many problems that to relate them may give the impression that the test series was an unproductive fiasco. That was far from the case. We did indeed have more than our share of rather sensational difficulties. They gave us fits at the time, and I would have no motive in failing to recount them now. But DOMINIC also achieved much in improving our weapons capability.

As the series neared its end, I presented a summary evaluation in a letter to the president. A salient portion read:

> The current tests have produced many important successes. They have also yielded some surprises and some failures which confirm that we are indeed experimenting at the frontier of weapons technology. The test successes vindicate, in a large measure, the elaborate computational and certification procedures which were developed during the moratorium [1958−61]. The surprises and failures serve to remind us that our theories and procedures are, at best, only approximate. . . .
> Although not a stated objective of our test program, I believe that one of the most significant results is the fact that our laboratories have become revitalized to a major degree. The importance of this reawakening of our defense posture cannot be overstressed.

DOMINIC in its entirety lasted over six months, far longer than the president had desired. It will be remembered that he had exacted from us an undertaking to try to complete the series in two and a half months. During the period of the tests—April 25 to November 4, 1962—the test ban impasse remained unbroken, but important new initiatives were taken by the United States. Overshadowing all else during this period, however, was a severe crisis that brought the world to the brink of nuclear war and which also, paradoxically, created new diplomatic opportunities.

Part Four

A Turning

13

Auguries of Change

Weakening of the U.S. Position

The wrangles over the interpretation of the eight-nation memorandum of April 16, 1962, left the test ban negotiations in Geneva completely deadlocked. Both sides recognized this and filled the time until June 15, when a month's recess would begin, with aimless bickering. Left to their own devices, the major powers might have terminated the discussions. The eight neutrals, however, insisted on continued efforts to bring the two sides together and tried to find germs of hope in particular statements by Soviet or U.S. representatives. The strategy of the neutrals may have been revealed in the hope expressed by the Brazilian representative that after the U.S. Pacific test series and "other experiments" to follow—another Russian series was considered inescapable—conditions would finally be favorable for fruitful negotiations.

Within the Kennedy administration it was recognized that the

Western position at the disarmament conference had been weakened
by the eight-nation proposal. The Soviet Union gave the appearance
of accepting the proposal more than the West did, and the proposal
was probably in fact closer to the Soviet position than to ours. Foster
(ACDA) was apprehensive that when the conference resumed following the recess the Soviets might table a treaty seemingly based on the
eight-nation memorandum and then seek neutral support for it. He
felt that the United States should also put forward a new treaty draft,
one having some kinship to the ideas of the neutrals.

The U.S. position seemed to be weakened further by the publi-
cation on July 7 of some of the preliminary conclusions of the
Defense Department's seismic research program, Project VELA.
Intimations of these findings had been passed to U.S. negotiators
some time earlier, but now they were made public for the first time.
The findings included the following:

1. It was possible to improve detection capability by placing instruments in deep holes and by reinforcing surface instruments with
   special filtering techniques.
2. Ocean-bottom seismometers also showed promise.
3. The signal strength of underground explosions varied greatly
   depending on the medium surrounding the shotpoint.
4. There were many fewer earthquakes in the Soviet Union that
   might be mistaken for nuclear explosions than had previously
   been thought by U.S. scientists.

The situation was made worse by some confused and uncoordi-
nated responses to the VELA findings on the part of U.S. spokesmen.
At a news conference on July 12, Secretary Rusk acknowledged
"some promising signs that instrumentation can do a better job than
was earlier supposed." He did not think, however, that it provided "a
complete substitution" for control posts inside the nuclear nations or
for onsite inspection. He added that there would have to be a thorough analysis of the data before their effect on U.S. proposals could be
determined. Contrarily, Ambassador Dean was quoted as having
said, upon landing at the Geneva airport on July 14, that if the United
States could get nonnuclear nations to cooperate scientifically, the
VELA findings meant that we could perhaps do without any international detection stations within the Soviet Union.

Dean's remarks caused a sensation, not least in official Washington. Such a change in position as Dean announced had indeed been
discussed in a preliminary way, but there had been no government
decision. In his interview for the Kennedy Library's Oral History
Program, Adrian Fisher describes a telephone call from Rusk after the
secretary read about Dean's remarks in the newspaper. (Foster was

away, so Fisher received the call.) Referring to Dean's reported remarks about not having any control posts in the Soviet Union, Rusk stated: "I haven't been aware of any such change in position." Fisher had to admit that he hadn't either, and he and Rusk worked together on a statement "sort of clarifying the matter." This statement, issued by Rusk, was to the effect that the VELA findings were preliminary and would have to be evaluated before they could be the basis for any modification of prior U.S. proposals.

Fisher continues:

> Now I didn't discuss this with the president directly, but I talked with Mac Bundy about it and, frankly, the president was very upset. He liked to have things done well and the idea that we had made a proposition and now we were saying something else—he had a rather adverse reaction to that, to put it mildly, so he passed the word down: "Now look, let's get things straight. Either we have a position or we don't."

The VELA findings were the prime topic of discussion when the Eighteen-Nation Disarmament Committee resumed its meetings on July 15, 1962. The nature of the discussion forced the U.S. on the defensive as first Indian and then Soviet spokesmen argued that the new data bolstered the position that verification of nuclear tests was possible without international control stations and without onsite inspection. Dean was obliged to repeat Rusk's statement that the findings were preliminary and also to emphasize that they referred primarily to improved possibilities of detecting underground tests but not of distinguishing them from earthquakes. The tenor of this debate was exacerbated by U.S.-USSR recriminations as to which side had done the most to perpetuate the arms race.

On July 21 the Soviet news agency Tass announced the Soviet government's decision to conduct another test series. In this statement the Soviets reiterated their frequent claim that, since the United States had tested first, they had the "right to test last."

It was against this background of events that I faced two correspondents of the American Broadcasting Company—Jules Bergman, science editor, and Robert Lodge, Defense Department correspondent—on the program "Issues and Answers" on July 22, 1962. As in the "Meet the Press" program of October 29, 1961, the preponderance of questions I was asked (more than 75 percent) related to weapons. Among the points I made on weapons testing were the following:

1. The Soviet decision to conduct another test series may have been a result of genuine concern for their security; "they are afraid we may have obtained, in our tests, results that could make the

future dangerous for them. That is one of the difficulties of this testing business. . . . Each side is afraid . . . that the other has been getting ahead. That is what makes it so difficult to call an end to it."

2. Notwithstanding the progress in detection techniques achieved in the VELA program, the United States still required that a comprehensive test ban treaty provide both for internationally manned seismographs within the Soviet Union and for onsite inspections.

3. Whether we would allow the Russians to "test last" before a test ban treaty depended on our evaluation of their tests and whether the treaty had adequate enforcement provisions.

4. The U.S. and USSR could not continue atmospheric testing indefinitely without radiation effects harmful to present and future generations.

Four Significant Meetings

On July 26, 27, and 30 and August 1, 1962, there were four significant meetings—the last three attended by the president—at which the U.S. position in the test ban negotiations was reviewed intensively. The flurry caused by Dean's injudicious airport comments was undoubtedly a factor in stimulating this review.

The first meeting, on July 26, involved the Principals.

Foster contended that the VELA findings of improved detection capability were *not* preliminary, as others were saying. He described the deep interest of various members of Congress in trying to get a test ban treaty based on these detection improvements so as to stop the leap-frogging of test series by East and West. He said that ACDA had prepared a draft of a modified comprehensive treaty employing a combination of national and international means of verification.

Rusk asked which VELA data were still considered preliminary. McNamara said the yield level at which tests could be detected was tentative, but the most important question was what could be accomplished by clandestine underground testing. Rusk asked me to expand on this. I noted that it now seemed possible to detect underground tests of 15 kilotons or greater conducted in alluvium, so the important question was what could be learned in clandestine tests below that level. It appeared that much could be learned since, of our 45 underground tests to date, 37 had yielded less than 10 kilotons.

Rusk asked whether the United States would want a treaty if we knew neither side could test. McNamara and I both answered yes.

There then ensued a colloquy that foreshadowed a turn in U.S. thinking:

Rusk asked why we continued to discuss numbers of onsite inspections since the Russians had said they would tolerate none; perhaps we should just offer an atmospheric test ban. McCone answered that we had already done this. Rusk said again that, so long as the Soviets would tolerate no inspections, it made no sense to keep proposing a comprehensive test ban treaty. Murrow agreed. Wiesner answered that a reason for first trying to get a comprehensive treaty was to stop the spread of nuclear weapons to additional countries; McCone agreed with that.

McNamara said he would like to see the comparative risks put down on paper, that is, the risks to the U.S. of clandestine Soviet tests under a comprehensive treaty versus the risks of proliferation to more countries if both sides continued underground testing under an atmospheric ban. Foster endorsed the idea of such an analysis.

Nitze suggested offering an atmospheric treaty with the understanding that it would be made comprehensive if and when agreement could be reached on inspection.

Keeny suggested that, if we failed to present a proposal with numbers (control posts, inspections, etc.) in it, the eight neutrals at Geneva might come forward with a proposal involving smaller numbers than we could accept.

The remainder of this meeting was taken up with a discussion of steps to be taken in stage one of our plan for "general and complete disarmament."

The next day's meeting took place at the White House, with the president and vice-president both in attendance. At this meeting Kennedy again expressed his irritation at the premature public discussion of the VELA results.

Rusk began by describing the new comprehensive treaty draft that the ACDA was working on. He mentioned the need to educate congressional leaders, especially the Joint Committee on Atomic Energy, regarding this draft.

Rusk said the draft treaty could be introduced at Geneva. He preferred, however, to start with a declaration that the U.S. wanted a comprehensive treaty but that it was impractical to talk about the details of such a treaty so long as the Soviets rejected onsite inspections. Consequently, we should propose an atmospheric test ban while continuing to work toward the comprehensive.

The president, perhaps recalling how Soviet progress in their last series had dimmed our ardor for a test ban, asked whether we might not better wait until the end of the new Russian tests before deciding to offer an atmospheric treaty. Rusk thought we could proceed sooner and then modify our position if the Soviets made a large number of tests before responding.

The president asked why, if VELA results indicated a large reduction in the number of earthquakes that could be mistaken for explosions, we still needed 12 to 20 onsite inspections per year. Foster said one reason was that less of the burden would be carried by control stations in the new treaty than in our 1961 draft; hence, more of the burden would have to be carried by inspections. (We now proposed a total of only 25 control stations, with from zero to 5 in the Soviet Union, whereas the previous Geneva System contemplated 170 stations, with 19 in the Soviet Union.)

I pointed out the importance of the VELA finding that tests yielding less than 15 kilotons might not be detectable by remote national stations. I explained that much could be accomplished by underground tests below 10 kilotons in the areas of (1) tactical weapons, (2) developing detonation mechanisms for large weapons, (3) developing pure fusion weapons (the neutron bomb), (4) tests of effects and vulnerability, and (5) experiments to verify new ideas that came out of the laboratories, with the consequent effect of keeping the laboratories strong.

Bundy said he wasn't sure we should agree to a treaty without internationally staffed posts in the USSR. Rusk pointed out that we might suggest having a neutral scientist present at USSR national stations. The president thought this was a good idea.

The president added that the U.S. had worked itself into a deplorable situation by releasing the VELA data on enhanced detection possibilities before we had had a chance to make policy. He asked whether we could get Dean back for the weekend to go over the situation and this was agreed to.

At the meeting on July 30 there was discussion of the possible effects of a test ban in inhibiting the proliferation of nuclear weapons.

Assistant Secretary of Defense Paul Nitze read from a report the president had requested on the potential spread of nuclear weapons capability in the absence of a comprehensive test ban treaty. Nitze said that many countries could have the bomb in from seven to ten years. He mentioned Sweden, India, West Germany, Italy, China, and possibly South Africa. He said that a test ban would be a necessary, but not a sufficient, condition for inhibiting this proliferation, and that to prevent it would require collaboration by the U.S. and USSR. He added that an atmospheric test ban alone would not be effective in inhibiting the spread of nuclear weapons.

The president asked how much more it would cost and how much longer it would take for a country to develop a nuclear weapons capability when confined to underground testing. Several, including myself, thought that the cost would not be increased. I felt that it might take a couple of years longer, but a number of others doubted it would take any longer.

The president inquired as to the value of the fusion (neutron) bomb, which might be developed in underground testing. Lemnitzer said it would be advantageous to have it. Wiesner said there might be a disadvantage because enemy personnel irradiated by the weapon, knowing they were doomed to early death but were capable of present action, might decide to resort to kamikaze tactics.

Dean, back for the weekend as agreed at the previous meeting, reported that all eight of the neutrals believed that our release of the VELA data on July 7 was a diplomatic signal that we intended to table a revised comprehensive test ban treaty. He predicted that, if we didn't do so within two or three weeks, someone else, such as the Swedes, would do so. He thought we would be in a bad position at the UN General Assembly meeting in September if we hadn't tabled a revised treaty, even one containing some blank spaces. Dean thought he could explore privately with Soviet delegate Valerian Zorin for a couple of days whether they would accept any inspection at all. The president seemed to agree this was a good idea and that we could table a comprehensive treaty without specifying numbers of inspections and control stations.

Bundy conjectured that Congress would be troubled by a comprehensive treaty that relied exclusively on national detection stations. Vice-President Johnson concurred, saying that many senators had talked to him expressing their concern about such a treaty.

Dean mentioned that Zorin had sounded him out about agreeing on a date, such as next January 1 or July 1, after which neither side would test. This was essentially the suggestion that had been pushed at Geneva by the Mexican delegate, Luis Padilla Nervo.

The next meeting occurred two days later at the White House. Significant additions to the group were John McCloy and Robert A. Lovett, both members of ACDA's General Advisory Committee. Lovett, like McCloy, was a distinguished Republican attorney. He had been secretary of defense under President Truman.

The president read a letter from Macmillan in which the prime minister said that he continued to feel that nuclear tests were not needed, that there was urgent need for a test ban, and that a test ban could be fully effective with fewer controls than the U.S. seemed to think necessary. The letter also indicated that possible U.S. reuse of Christmas Island should be negotiated at the time it was needed. [The British thus retained their small amount of leverage over U.S. policy.]

Dean pointed out that Mrs. Myrdal (Sweden) had suggested an atmospheric test ban. The president asked whether we should now agree to a future date for terminating all tests, as Zorin had suggested to Dean. It was agreed that we could accept such a cutoff under proper conditions.

Discussion then turned to the details of a revised comprehensive test ban that the U.S. might explore at Geneva. A memorandum from Foster to the president provided a basis for discussion. It proposed a system based on 25 seismic detection stations, internationally supervised but nationally manned, and a number of onsite inspections lower than the 12 to 20 we had been advocating.

Franklin Long (ACDA) said that, based on the latest knowledge and techniques, the proposed detection system, with about 25 stations, with or without some in the USSR, would do as well as the Geneva System's 170 control stations had been expected to do.

The president asked Dean about his plan for briefing the Geneva delegates on the new U.S. position. Dean said that he planned to keep it on the political level for about a week and then bring U.S. scientists to Geneva about August 9. The president suggested that Dean, Foster, and Rusk start the next day to brief interested congressional committees. [One must observe again how careful the president was to take Congress into his confidence at every significant turn in the road.]

At the end of the meeting, the president asked McCloy and Lovett whether they agreed with the general plan that was evolving, and both said that they did.

It was agreed that what was said to the press regarding this meeting would be limited to what the president would say in his press conference later in the day.

At his press conference the president announced that on the basis of technical advances the United States was prepared to accept a lesser number of control posts, nationally staffed and internationally supervised, but that the requirement for some onsite inspection remained.

New Western Proposals

On August 5, the Soviets conducted a huge atmospheric test, estimated at 30 megatons. It followed several smaller explosions on preceding days. It was against this backdrop of renewed Soviet testing that the United States unveiled in Geneva its new proposals for a test ban treaty.

On August 6, Ambassador Dean presented a private note to Valerian Zorin, describing the revised U.S. proposals. When the three-power Subcommittee on a Treaty for the Discontinuance of Nuclear Weapon Tests met on August 9, he expounded on the proposals in detail. He indicated that Project VELA research findings made it possible to have fewer control stations and fewer inspections than were proposed by the West in its April 1961 draft treaty, but that the keystone to a comprehensive agreement continued to be acceptance of the principle of obligatory onsite inspection. He went on to describe new U.S. proposals for nationally manned, internationally supervised seismographic stations and for an international commission based on the proposals in the eight-nation memorandum. Zorin promptly rejected the U.S. proposals. He contended that they represented only a change in wording from our previous position.

The debate then shifted from the three-power subcommittee to plenary sessions of the Eighteen-Nation Disarmament Committee. At the plenary session on August 27, 1962, the U.S. and U.K. jointly tabled two alternative treaty drafts: one covering testing in all environments, the other limited to tests in the atmosphere, underwater, and in outer space. In a joint statement released that day, the president and prime minister expressed their "strong preference" for the comprehensive treaty. They were willing, however, to accept the limited treaty because it would cause a "downward turn in the arms race . . . make it easier to prevent the spread of nuclear weapons . . . and free mankind from the dangers and fear of radioactive fallout."

The comprehensive treaty draft was a modification of the draft tabled on April 18, 1961, with all its subsequent amendments. The main bases of the changes were the eight-nation memorandum and the new understanding of the technical situation brought about by the VELA seismic research program.

Under this revised treaty, which was to be open to adherence by all nations, the parties were to abstain from *all* nuclear explosions— there was no threshold—and to refrain from helping or encouraging the tests of others. There was one significant exception: peaceful explosions could be carried out by unanimous consent of the "original parties" (U.S., U.K., USSR) or in conformity with provisions that were to be specified in an annex. The annex was not tabled; it had not been possible to resolve administration differences on its terms.

An International Scientific Commission was to collect and report information on all events suspected of being nuclear tests. The commission would consist of fifteen members, four from the West, four from the Soviet bloc, and seven from other countries nominated by the Big Three. The commission was to make decisions by a simple majority. An executive officer, appointed and removable by the commission, and an international staff were to assist the commission. The functions of the executive officer and the size of his staff were considerably reduced from those of the administrator in the April 1961 draft. Also, the provisions in the earlier treaty specifying the nationality distribution of the staff were omitted.

As in the previous Western draft treaty the verification system was to employ seismic verification stations, supplemented by onsite inspections. The seismic stations were to be of three types:

1. Existing national seismographic stations were to be provided and staffed by the Big Three and other parties to the treaty.

2. Additional seismographic stations were to be built by the International Commission at agreed locations: these would be staffed by nationals of the country where they were located but would have observers from the commission. No figures were given as to the number of such stations, although it was made clear that the number on Soviet territory would be many fewer than the nineteen envisaged under the 1961 draft.

3. Additional seismographic stations were to be built and staffed by the commission on territories of parties to the treaty—other than the original parties—which felt unable to build or staff stations themselves.

Onsite inspections could take place upon certification of an unidentified event by the executive officer. There were to be identical annual quotas of inspections on the territory of each of the three original parties. The treaty draft left blank the size of the inspection quotas: a matter for future negotiation. The text did specify that only a limited percentage of the quotas could apply to areas that were not earthquake-prone, such as European Russia. While Western spokesmen implied that they would not seek inspection quotas as high as in the April 1961 draft, the essential terms governing inspection remained the same: from among the events certified by the executive officer the ones to be inspected were to be chosen by the opposing nuclear side, and the inspection team could include no nationals of the country being inspected.

The limited treaty was far less complicated. It would have banned tests in or above the atmosphere and in or beneath the sea. The parties were bound not to abet such tests by others. Peaceful explosions could occur under specified conditions. As in the comprehensive treaty, there was to be an annex specifying these conditions. *

The Soviet Union rejected both treaty proposals immediately and without qualification. The main Soviet objections to the comprehensive treaty, voiced by Deputy Foreign Minister V. V. Kuznetsov, were (1) that it relied on *obligatory* onsite inspection as against the eight-nation memorandum's provision, in the Soviet interpretation, for *invitational* inspection, and (2) that it utilized some "international control posts" instead of relying wholly on national posts.

The Soviets opposed the limited treaty because it allowed continued underground testing. Kuznetsov noted an earlier statement by Dean stressing the military significance of small underground tests. Kuznetsov then said that the Soviet Union was willing to consider a cutoff date after which there would be no more testing, as proposed by the Mexican and other delegations. He proposed January 1, 1963, as this date.

In his press conference two days later, August 29, President Kennedy stated:

> I'm happy to say that the United States government regards [January 1] as a reasonable target date and would like to join with all interested parties in a maximum effort to conclude effective agreements on next New Year's Day. . . . For our part in the United States, such an agreed treaty must be presented to the Senate for ratification. We therefore have no time to lose. [Then, as now, other

---

* The Limited Test Ban Treaty adopted less than a year later was substantially similar to this Western draft treaty. In effect, the Soviet Union was to find acceptable in 1963 what it found unacceptable in 1962.

countries had to be reminded of our constitutional processes.] . . .
But I must point out again that, in order to end testing, we must
have workable international agreements; gentlemen's agreements
and moratoria do not provide the types of guarantees that are necessary. . . . This is the lesson of the Soviet government's tragic
decision to renew testing just a year ago.

Later in the same news conference the president said he would be
willing to sign a test ban treaty on January 1, 1963, regardless of the
progress the Soviets might make in their new test series. He stated:
"We do not believe that they could make sufficient progress in this
series of tests to adversely affect our security." Then, citing the
increased danger to the U.S. "as more and more countries develop an
atomic capacity," he concluded: " . . . the quicker we can get a test
agreement the better off we will be."

Kennedy's concluding comment was evidence that he was beginning now to feel a dread sense of urgency about a test ban, related
primarily to the proliferation problem. This feeling that time was
running out was to become a persistent theme in his public utter-
ances and a prime motivator of his diplomatic initiatives in the
months ahead.

For the first few days of September, debate continued at the
disarmament conference on the new Western test ban proposals. At
the close of the plenary session on September 7, the conference
recessed until November 12 to make way for the UN General
Assembly, which was to convene in New York on September 20.

Before the disarmament conference resumed, the world was to
pass through a period of unprecedented danger which significantly
altered the diplomatic atmosphere.

14

The Missile Crisis
and Its Aftermath

The Course of the Crisis

Periodic intelligence reports since late August of 1962 had revealed the off-loading of military equipment from Soviet ships and an increase in military construction activity at several locations in Cuba. The significance of this activity was variously interpreted, but when it finally became clear through photoreconnaissance that the Soviets were emplacing offensive missiles on the island, it came as a stunning surprise. As had been true when the Soviets resumed testing in 1961, our intelligence establishment had failed to discern Soviet intent. The crisis that followed had a profound effect on test ban negotiations.[1]

The crisis broke on Monday, October 15, when analysis of photographs from reconnaissance overflights by U-2 planes disclosed evidence of a medium-range missile site, though not yet the missiles themselves, in western Cuba.

The president immediately established a top-level group, later formally named the Executive Committee of the National Security Council (EXCOM), to consider policy alternatives and make recommendations to him. The members of this group, which remained in almost continuous session throughout the crisis—some members slept night after night in their offices—included Rusk, McNamara, Robert Kennedy, Gilpatric, Nitze, McCone, Bundy, Sorensen, Dillon, George Ball (undersecretary of state) and his deputy U. Alexis Johnson, General Maxwell Taylor (chairman of the Joint Chiefs of Staff), Edwin Martin (assistant secretary of state for Latin America), Llewellyn Thompson, and, intermittently, Vice-President Johnson, Adlai Stevenson, Ken O'Donnell (special assistant to the president), and Don Wilson (deputy to USIA Director Murrow, who was ill).

By Wednesday, October 17, launchers and missiles could be seen in U-2 photographs, and it was clear that the missiles could be fired within two weeks. EXCOM discussions began to focus on two options: (1) a swift air strike to take out the missiles, or (2) a naval blockade while diplomatic pressure was exercised to get the missiles removed.

By Friday, October 19, the blockade concept appeared to have won out, but with the proviso that an air strike would follow if diplomacy failed. A critical determinant was the statement of General Walter C. Sweeney, who would command the strike. He maintained that we could not be certain of taking out more than 90 percent of the missiles.[2] The next day U.S. warships started moving into their blockade positions. U.S. armed forces around the world were placed on alert.

The president's address to the nation on radio and television, which revealed the extent of the crisis to the world for the first time, took place on Monday evening, October 22. The president described the Soviet deception. He announced the "quarantine": any ship containing offensive weapons would be turned back. He drew a cordon around the hemisphere: "It shall be the policy of this nation to regard any nuclear missile launched from Cuba against any nation in the Western Hemisphere as an attack by the Soviet Union on the United States, requiring a full retaliatory response upon the Soviet Union." He called for meetings of the Organization of American States (OAS) and the UN Security Council.

The OAS met the following day and supported the United States, 19 to 0, with one abstention. This provided the president with the legal basis for his blockade proclamation. He signed it invoking the 1947 Interamerican Treaty of Reciprocal Assistance. On the same day, Senegal and Guinea, the only practical refueling stops for Soviet planes bound for Cuba, agreed to deny landing rights to such planes.

On Wednesday, October 24, UN Secretary-General U Thant asked for suspension of both Soviet arms shipments and the U.S. blockade. By this time half the Soviet ships on the way to Cuba had stopped dead in the water or had changed course. The president replied to U Thant the next day, stating that he would make no bargain: the missiles must be removed. UN Ambassador Adlai Stevenson unveiled photographic evidence of the missiles in a dramatic session of the Security Council.

On Friday, October 26, a Soviet-chartered freighter was boarded, searched, and allowed to proceed. Work on the missile sites meanwhile continued to proceed rapidly. Word was passed to the Soviets that an air strike could be delayed only two days longer. John Scali, an American Broadcasting Company correspondent, was approached by a Russian embassy official and asked if the United States would accept a deal: missiles to be removed in exchange for a U.S. pledge not to attack Cuba. Secretary Rusk authorized Scali to say the deal looked promising but that time was of the essence. Shortly afterward, a long, rambling, secret letter was received from Khrushchev. It generally hinted at the same deal and pleaded for self-control and a peaceful solution.

On Saturday, October 27, a second letter from Khrushchev was received, this one broadcast by Radio Moscow. It demanded removal of U.S. missiles from Turkey as the price for removal of Soviet missiles from Cuba. The second letter appeared to be a group product, whereas the first one seemed clearly to have been written by Khrushchev.

The apparent diplomatic progress was negated when a U-2 plane over Cuba was shot down and its pilot lost. The tension greatly increased. The air strike was scheduled for Monday morning, October 29. Any Soviet missiles that survived might be fired. The Soviets could be expected to retaliate by moving on Berlin, perhaps elsewhere as well. It was hard to conceive that nuclear weapons would not be used on a wide scale. Civilization hung in the balance.

At Robert Kennedy's suggestion, the president answered Khrushchev's first letter on Saturday, October 27, and ignored the second one. He offered a pledge not to attack Cuba if the missiles were removed under UN surveillance. Meanwhile the air strike forces were assembled.

On Sunday, October 28, a message came from the Soviet government agreeing to remove the missiles and agreeing also to UN inspection of the removal. No further mention was made of the missiles in Turkey. (These were quietly removed the following spring.)

Thus ended what Dean Rusk aptly characterized as "the gravest crisis the world has known."

An interesting appraisal of Kennedy's conduct of the missile crisis was jotted down in his diary by Prime Minister Macmillan, who was in almost daily contact with the president throughout the period:

> President Kennedy conducted this affair with great skill, energy, resourcefulness and courage. He answered the Communists with their own weapons—for they always use several and even divergent means to secure their ends. (a) He played a firm military game throughout—acting quickly and being ready to act as soon as mobilized. You cannot keep an "army of invasion" hanging about. It must invade or disperse. President K. did not bluster—but everyone knew that (if no other solution was found) there would be an invasion. (b) He played the diplomatic card excellently. The European and other allies had no real grievance about non-consultation. The flying visit of Dean Acheson to Europe [to inform de Gaulle and Adenauer, chancellor of West Germany] and the information to the NATO Council was more than correctness demanded. (c) He played the United Nations admirably. Kennedy mobilized a lot of UN opinion and used Stevenson to keep UN quiet. If it had come to the point, U.S.A. would not have had majority support in the Assembly. So they wisely never let it get out of the Security Council. In Security Council the Russians made the fatal mistake of barefaced lying. Zorin was still denying the existence of the missiles in Cuba when Khrushchev's message was published offering to swap them for those in Turkey! Altogether, the President did wonderfully well.[3]

Reactions to the Settlement

During the missile crisis, Kennedy and Khrushchev exchanged at least eight messages. They had been engaging since September 1961 in a private correspondence whose contents have to this day never been revealed. But now the pace of the interchange quickened. It was the beginning of a closer relationship between the two men. On Khrushchev's side, it was probably also the beginning of a more respectful attitude. It is doubtful that the missiles would have been shipped to Cuba had not the Soviets judged that Kennedy was too weak to react forcibly. One can only speculate as to the origin of such a misjudgment. Three incidents come to mind: the Bay of Pigs debacle, the failure of the United States to react more forcibly to the building of the Berlin Wall, and the president's performance at the Vienna summit, which, as we have seen, was characterized by some who saw the transcript as relatively ineffectual.

As the Cuban crisis wound down, both leaders alluded to arms control problems in their messages to each other. In his letter of Sunday, October 28, the one in which he agreed to remove the missiles, Khrushchev wrote: "We should like to continue the exchange of views on the prohibition of atomic and thermonuclear weapons, on general disarmament and other problems relating to the relaxation of international tension." Kennedy, replying the same day, agreed that "perhaps now, as we step back from danger, we can make some real progress in this vital field. I think we should give priority to questions relating to the proliferation of nuclear weapons . . . and to the great effort for a nuclear test ban."

This exchange of notes, coming after the display of moderation by both sides that led to the peaceful resolution of the crisis, stimulated considerable optimism that a test ban agreement could be reached. Much significance was attached to the fact that Khrushchev had agreed to UN aerial inspection to verify removal of the missiles.

The UN General Assembly sought to stimulate further momentum toward a test ban by the passage of two resolutions on November 6. The first of these, introduced by thirty-seven nonnuclear powers, including all eight of the disarmament conference neutrals, called for the cessation of all tests not later than January 1, 1963, and the settlement of East-West differences on a comprehensive treaty or, failing that, on a limited treaty accompanied by an interim suspension of underground tests to be verified by an international commission. The vote on this resolution was 75−0, with 21 abstentions (the four nuclear powers and their allies).

The second resolution, introduced by the U.S. and U.K., mirrored the Western proposals at the disarmament conference. It called for a comprehensive treaty with international verification or, failing that, a limited treaty (atmosphere, oceans, space). This resolution passed fifty-one in favor, ten opposed (Soviet bloc only), and forty abstentions. The large number of abstentions was a signal that the jury was still out on the position taken by the West at Geneva.

Enter the Black Boxes

The third session of the Eighteen-Nation Disarmament Committee, which lasted from November 26 to December 20, 1962, began under the stimulus of the UN General Assembly's resolution urging that all tests cease by January 1, 1963. It quickly became apparent that this was an unobtainable objective.

Opening statements attempted to reflect a hopeful atmosphere. Dean, for the U.S., stated that the draft treaties submitted by the West in August were not immutable; reasonable suggestions for change would be considered. Tsarapkin, for the USSR, stated that the positions of the two sides were "considerably closer together." These statements merely glossed over the fact that, on the basic issues of international control and obligatory onsite inspection, the parties remained far apart.

In these circumstances, the neutral eight united behind a Swedish suggestion that a limited treaty be agreed to before January 1, and that underground tests be suspended for a limited period (six months to a year) while negotiations proceeded on a comprehensive treaty. During this period an interim scientific commission from neutral countries would evaluate data received from national observation posts and determine whether any onsite inspection was necessary; if so, the commission itself might undertake it.

The Soviet Union rejected the proposal after a week's consideration. The stumbling block was the provision for inspection—the Soviets would not accept it. Tsarapkin proposed instead that all nuclear powers simply suspend tests de facto dating from January 1, 1963. President Kennedy had already indicated this was unacceptable, and it was rejected promptly by Dean. Never again, he said, would the United States enter into an uncontrolled, uninspected moratorium.

The only really new element to emerge from this session of the conference was a Soviet suggestion that unmanned automatic seismic stations ("black boxes") be employed as a supplement to national means of verification. The Soviet press had commented during November on an agreement alleged to have been reached at the Tenth Pugwash Conference in London in September 1962 about the use of such stations.* On December 10 Tsarapkin proposed to the conference that two or three unmanned stations be established on the territories of each of the nuclear nations, being located in areas most subject to earthquakes. He named three such areas in the Soviet Union. Tsarapkin also announced that the USSR would be willing to have international scientific personnel deliver, replace, and take readings from recording equipment at the stations. The Soviets, however, conditioned their proposal on abandonment by the West of its insistence on international controls and obligatory onsite inspection.

While making clear that the United States could not accept unmanned seismic stations as a substitute for onsite inspection, Ambassador Dean nevertheless sought to arrange scientific talks that

---

*This idea had been proposed for consideration in 1959 by the Berkner Panel on Seismic Improvement. The Soviets rejected it then on the grounds that the foreign personnel who might install and service the black boxes on Soviet territory would have the opportunity for espionage.

would explore their potentialities. The Soviets rejected the idea of such technical talks.

Overall, the black box suggestion did little to resolve the differences separating the two sides. Nevertheless, it was significant as a sign of loosening in the Soviet position.

How Many Inspections? A Misunderstanding

Indication that the president was getting through to Khrushchev to an increasing extent was received late in November 1962. Anastas Mikoyan, first deputy chairman of the Soviet Council of Ministers, reported during a White House visit that Khrushchev "liked the spirit of the President's statements and felt that the United States and the Soviet Union should proceed to a point-by-point negotiation of all outstanding questions."[4]

On December 19, 1962, Khrushchev sent Kennedy a long letter devoted entirely to the test ban situation. The Soviet leader began by saying that the time had come "to put a stop to nuclear tests once and for all, to make an end of them." He stated that "the main obstacle in the way of an agreement" was the insistence of the United States on international control and inspection.

Next came a most significant passage: "I should like to think that you yourself appreciate the truth of our arguments that national means of detection are adequate. . . . But you have been unwilling thus far to recognize this reality openly." One can only speculate on the basis for Khrushchev's belief that the president privately did not feel onsite inspection was necessary. In my own mind I go back to the informal discussion between Kennedy and Macmillan at Bermuda in which both leaders regretted that the United States had made so much of the possibility of clandestine underground testing. It seems to me possible that some of the president's feeling, as expressed in this conversation, may at some time have been communicated to the Soviets by the British.

Next in Khrushchev's letter came a discussion of the best sites within the Soviet Union for installation of three automatic seismological stations. American experts had disputed whether the three locations suggested by Tsarapkin at Geneva would give much seismic information. Khrushchev indicated willingness to let the experts on both sides come to an agreement on these locations, but named the same areas plus two additional sites as being the ones considered the most suitable by Soviet scientists.

He then came to the central issue, the matter of onsite inspections, and here there arose a misunderstanding that was to bedevil the negotiations for several months. Khrushchev wrote:

> You and your representatives, Mr. President, refer to the fact that, without a minimum number of onsite inspections it would be impossible for you to persuade the United States Senate to ratify an agreement on the cessation of testing. This condition, as we understand it, ties your hands and is preventing the signature of a treaty which would enable all of us to turn our backs forever on the nuclear weapons proving grounds. Very well: if this is the only obstacle to agreement, we are prepared to meet you on this point in the interest of the noble and humane cause of ending nuclear weapons tests.
>
> *We have noted that on 30 October 1962, in discussions held in New York with Mr. V.V. Kuznetsov, the First Deputy Minister for Foreign Affairs of the USSR, your representative, Ambassador Dean, said that in the opinion of the United States Government two to four onsite inspections a year in the territory of the Soviet Union would be sufficient.* At the same time, according to Ambassador Dean's statement, the United States would be ready to work out measures to rule out any possibility of espionage being carried out under cover of these inspection visits. Such measures might include the use of Soviet aircraft flown by Soviet crews to transport the inspectors to the site, the screening of aircraft windows, a ban on the carrying of cameras, etc.
>
> We have given consideration to all these points and, with a view to overcoming the deadlock and reaching a mutually acceptable agreement at last, *we would be prepared to agree to two to three inspections a year* being carried out in the territory of each of the nuclear powers, when it was considered necessary, in seismic regions where any suspicious earth tremors occurred. [Emphasis added.]

The misunderstanding, which was evidently sincere on both sides, concerned what Dean may have said to Kuznetsov. Dean insisted that the only number that he mentioned in his discussions with Kuznetsov was a number between eight and ten, and Kennedy was obliged to say this in reply to Khrushchev on December 28, 1962. (Warren Heckrotte comments: "Most of us on the Geneva delegation felt that, irrespective of what Dean thought he said, Kuznetsov's report was a correct appraisal of what he thought he had been told."[5] It should be noted also that when Harold Wilson, head of Britain's Labour party and later prime minister, spoke to Khrushchev on June 10, 1963, he, Wilson, attributed the misunderstanding to the fact that Dean was "often vague.")

The full effect of this misunderstanding on Khrushchev's own attitude came to light some months later. It was revealed in an interview he granted to Norman Cousins, editor of the *Saturday*

Review, at his Black Sea vacation retreat on April 12, 1963. (Cousins's visit to the Soviet Union was in connection with an attempt by various religious organizations to get greater religious freedom within the USSR.) Cousins quotes Khrushchev as follows:

> After Cuba, there was a real chance for both the Soviet Union and the United States to take measures together that would advance the peace by easing tensions. The one area on which I thought we were closest to agreement was nuclear testing, and so I went before the Council of Ministers and said to them:
>
> "We can have an agreement with the United States to stop nuclear tests if we agree to three inspections. I know that three inspections are not necessary, and that the policing can be done adequately from outside our borders. But the American Congress has convinced itself that onsite inspection is necessary and the President cannot get a treaty through the Senate without it. Very well, then let us accommodate the President."
>
> The Council asked me if I was certain that we could have a treaty if we agreed to three inspections and I told them yes. Finally, I persuaded them.
>
> People in the United States seem to think that I am a dictator who can put into practice any policy I wish. Not so. I've got to persuade before I can govern. Anyway, the Council of Ministers agreed to my urgent recommendation. Then I notified the United States I would accept three inspections. Back came the American rejection. They now wanted—not three inspections or even six. They wanted eight. And so once again I was made to look foolish. But I can tell you this: it won't happen again.[6]

Although Khrushchev cited only the Dean-Kuznetsov conversation in his letter to the president, he mentioned to Cousins an additional conversation, between Yevgeni K. Federov, a Soviet scientist, and Wiesner in Washington in October 1962, in which Federov reported Wiesner to have said "that the United States was ready to proceed on the basis of a few annual inspections." Heckrotte testifies that among the delegates in Geneva it was known that Federov felt he had been misled by Wiesner and was "extremely unhappy about it."[7]

When I phoned Wiesner in July 1980, he expressed gratification at the opportunity to tell his side of this story, saying that I was the first person to have asked him. According to Wiesner, he had suggested to Federov that one way to get the negotiations off dead center would be for Khrushchev to state to Kennedy that three or four inspections per year would be acceptable to the Soviet Union. The president might then come back with a counterproposal of some seven or eight inspections per year (which in fact he did!) and this might then be followed by a compromise on some intermediate figure like five or so inspections per year. Wiesner indicated further that he talked to the president with the hope of getting him to lower the U.S. figure. He was unsuccessful in this because Kennedy felt he would not be able to get agreement from Congress. Senator Jackson, in particular, had been extremely negative in his conversations with Kennedy, and Jackson had great influence with his colleagues on military matters. Wiesner conjectures that Federov evidently did not understand the conditional nature of Wiesner's suggestion to him.

President Kennedy was unaware of how the misunderstanding on the number of inspections had affected Khrushchev when, on December 28, 1962, he answered the Soviet leader's letter of December 19. Having stated that the offer of two or three inspections was insufficient, Kennedy indicated that he was encouraged by Khrushchev's statement that the Soviet Union could now "accept the principle of onsite inspections" and that he hoped the Soviet Union would match the movement of the U.S. position, when we went to eight to ten inspections from the previous position of twelve to twenty, by moving upward from the Soviet proposal of two to three.

The president also indicated that the number of automatic seismic stations proposed by the USSR was not sufficient and that the sites suggested were not the most desirable. The president then added: "Notwithstanding these problems, I am encouraged by your letter."* He concluded by suggesting that the Soviets designate someone to meet with ACDA Director Foster in New York or Geneva to try to work out the remaining differences. Khrushchev replied on January 7, 1963, more or less repeating his previously stated positions but agreeing to a New York meeting and designating N. T. Fedorenko and Tsarapkin to meet with Foster.

An Anniversary: "Happy Relationships"

A meeting at the White House on January 22, 1963, corresponded roughly with the second anniversary of the Kennedy administration, and the president used the occasion for a general review during which he did virtually all the talking.

During this summary Kennedy indicated once again that concern with the Chinese nuclear program was a principal driving force behind his quest for a test ban. (It was never quite clear to me how he expected a test ban negotiated between ourselves and the Soviets to affect the Chinese unless it were through the force of world opinion, since the Chinese were quite certain to reject such a treaty.)

---

*Schlesinger says that he was "exhilarated" by it. (*A Thousand Days*, p. 896.)

The president began by giving his impressions of the position of the United States in the major theaters of the world where it had alliances.

He then recapitulated the events of the Cuban crisis. He described the consideration of the key issue from the U.S. side—whether there should be an air strike or a blockade—and indicated the bases for his choice of the latter as an initial position. He emphasized the importance of the time factor in the successful resolution of the crisis. He said that there was a period of forty-eight hours when the Russians were debating their course and were indecisive and that if time had not been available for their consideration something drastic might have happened.

The president then went on to talk about his recent correspondence with Khrushchev and the importance of a test ban in the world situation. An important consideration was the power that the Chinese would have with nuclear weapons and how they would use that power. If a test ban treaty could lessen this prospect, the U.S. should take much forethought before turning it down. He suspected that the Soviets were thinking much the same way about it. He said that a test ban that affected only the Russians and the United States would have only limited value but, if there was a chance that it could affect the Chinese, it could be worth very much indeed. In this sense it was more important to the world situation than it had been a year or two ago. He said that the CIA agreed with this assessment.

The president closed by saying that he was pleased with the happy relationships in his administration and that he hoped they could be maintained.

The president's last comment at the meeting is worth a moment's notice. It certainly seemed true that the Kennedy administration, while it contained a disparity of views on many subjects, had very little of the personal feuding that has characterized other administrations.

In a recent conversation Theodore Sorensen shared some of the insights he had gained on this matter from his vantage point as Kennedy's special counsel. Asked to explain the relative harmony that pervaded the Kennedy administration, Sorensen said:

> In part it resulted from the kind of people that John Kennedy attracted. But it also had to do with the kind of administration he conducted. He was quite careful to keep the White House staff very small and relatively low profile and he made sure the staff members confined their role to being advisers and assistants. This restricted substantially their ability to say on the phone that the president insists that you do this or that. That has been a major source of discord in other administrations. [One thinks of the role of Sherman Adams under Eisenhower or that of H. R. Haldeman and John Ehrlichman under Nixon.]
>
> Second, the president was very good about granting access to any of the top people in the administration who wanted to see him. No one thought he was being shut out or shunted aside.

Next, I think that the press operation was conducted with relative openness and fairness so there was less opportunity for the kind of backbiting that is sometimes leaked into the press.

Finally, I guess it was just because we were all very busy, we all felt useful, and we were all dedicated to the success of the country and the administration and the administration's policies and the administration's leader, the president.

There was of course plenty of criticism within the administration on policy—people who didn't like our policy on civil rights or our foreign policy and so on. There was even relatively little of that because in general the people at the top believed in our policies. But when there was criticism of policy it very seldom took a personal form.

I don't want to pretend the administration was totally free of feuding and backbiting, but there was really very little of it.[8]

To the reasons for harmony which Sorensen offered, and I agree with all, I would add one other. This is that Kennedy did not seem to take himself or his image too seriously. This approach seemed to filter down. The result was that officials in the administration paid relatively more attention to getting the job done and relatively less attention to who got credit or blame. One of the fortunate by-products of this sort of atmosphere was that an official felt he could be a bit daring, that he could stick out his neck without fear that anyone would want to chop it off.

Unproductive Talks

The informal talks between Foster and the Soviet representatives agreed to by Kennedy and Khrushchev began in Washington on January 14, 1963. After several days the talks moved to New York where they were joined by Sir David Ormsby-Gore, representing the U.K.

The president seemed more hopeful now than for some time past that progress could be made. In order to show his interest, and as a gesture of encouragement, he directed the AEC to postpone some underground tests in Nevada. This matter came up following the meeting at the White House on January 22.

The president, Rusk, Foster, Bundy, Kaysen, Wiesner, and I repaired to the Oval Office for further discussion.

The president said he would like the AEC to defer any planned underground tests for two to three weeks while the possibility of a test ban based on his correspondence with Khrushchev was explored in the New York talks.

I indicated that this would have an adverse effect on the AEC laboratories and might also disturb some AEC commissioners because it might seem to be the first step toward another unpoliced moratorium. I thought it might be better if a length of time for the deferral were not established. Foster felt that he might know whether a test ban was in prospect before two or three weeks. It was recognized that the AEC had conducted no tests during the last two weeks because of labor troubles; thus a month had passed since the last test. Nevertheless, there was general agreement that the next underground test should be deferred until test ban prospects could be assessed.

As it worked out, the three-power discussions in New York were generally unproductive. There were some minor agreements. The United States agreed that, under a comprehensive treaty, the manned seismic stations in the international data-collection system could be nationally owned and operated, abandoning its previous position that some of the posts had to be internationally supervised. The United States and Soviet Union also exchanged preliminary lists of the national seismic stations they would nominate to be part of a control system, and they agreed formally that the manned stations would be supplemented by unmanned ones. The Soviets also confirmed their previous offer to allow the unmanned stations to be checked periodically by international personnel.

The Soviet delegates refused to negotiate, however, on either the number or the location of the unmanned stations proposed in Premier Khrushchev's December letter to the president. While the U.S. had repeatedly stated that three stations were not sufficient, its original position in the discussions had been not to fix on any numbers until sufficient data had been received from the Soviets. This position was revised to state U.S. willingness to accept ten locations in the United States and ten in the Soviet Union. Later the U.S. delegates stated that seven unmanned stations would be adequate if they were suitably located and equipped and if the Soviets would agree to build new manned stations where needed.

The Soviets steadfastly defended the three locations in Khrushchev's original offer. In return they requested that unmanned stations be placed at three locations in the United States, these being near Los Alamos, New Mexico; Hanford, Washington; and AEC's Savannah River plant in South Carolina. These selections, all near nuclear establishments, obviously had little to do with seismicity and cast doubt on the sincerity of Soviet intentions.

The discussions about onsite inspections were no more fruitful than those on the black boxes. The Western delegates began by repeating the requirement of a quota of eight to ten inspections annually on Soviet soil. They indicated, however, that they might reduce the quota if they could be satisfied that the procedures used would ensure the effectiveness of the inspections. They wanted to discuss the procedures, including such technical details as the criteria for locating suspicious events, the size and shape of the area to be inspected, and the personnel and techniques to be used. The Soviets, however, refused to discuss technical questions while the numbers were still in dispute, preferring to pass such issues to the Eighteen-Nation Disarmament Committee, which was scheduled to reconvene in Geneva on February 12.

The failure of the New York talks was probably preordained by the fact that the Soviet negotiators seemed to have virtually no freedom of action. An AEC staff analysis reported that they did not appear to have any duty in the negotiations except to determine whether the United States would make concessions as to the number of onsite inspections or the number and location of unmanned seismic stations on U.S. and USSR territory. The staff analysis indicated further that the Soviets hoped to improve their position in world opinion by emphasizing the concessions recently made by Khrushchev and contrasting these with alleged U.S. intransigence. They hoped that the prod of public opinion, including opinion in the United States, would then exercise pressure on us to accept the lower Soviet numbers. When it appeared that the pressures were insufficient to budge the U.S., the Soviets moved to return the negotiations to Geneva, where they felt they could mobilize stronger pressures than in New York.

The momentum generated by the missile crisis had produced some concessions from both sides. But the high hopes that both President Kennedy and Premier Khrushchev seemed to have entertained that the world's brush with catastrophe might hasten a test ban agreement were, for the moment, not realized. The situation was to get worse before it got better.

15

"My Hopes Are
Somewhat Dimmed"

Those Opposed

Following the breakdown of the talks in New York, the United States found itself again in a situation where it needed to reconsider its position preparatory to the next stage in negotiations, this time the reconvening of the Eighteen-Nation Disarmament Committee on February 12, 1963.

As usual, there was a broad spectrum of views in the country to be considered. There was, for example, the view of many on the Joint Committee on Atomic Energy. On January 31:

> Along with Commissioner Haworth, I testified at the JCAE hearing on the weapons situation. Several committee members, especially Senators Jackson and Hickenlooper, attacked the basic idea of having a test ban, claiming that it would hurt the United States. Perhaps Haworth and I didn't defend the test ban as vigorously as we should have. We hung back on the theory that it might be better not to increase the antagonism.

Opposition in the Senate was not by any means confined to the Joint Committee on Atomic Energy. On February 21, 1963, Senator

Thomas J. Dodd, a Connecticut Democrat, made a major speech on the Senate floor criticizing the concessions the U.S. had made in departing from the Geneva System of 1961. Further, Senators Russell, Symington, and Jackson wrote a joint letter to the president saying that they could not approve the latest comprehensive treaty draft presented by the U.S. in Geneva.

Another group that arose in opposition to a test ban during this period was led by Congressman Craig Hosmer of California. Following the exchange of letters between Kennedy and Khrushchev, Hosmer became concerned that the United States would accept the Soviet numbers: three onsite inspections per year and three black boxes on Soviet soil. He felt that such terms seriously imperiled U.S. security. After Hosmer expressed his concerns in a speech on the House floor on January 24, the Republican leadership established a Republican Conference Committee on Nuclear Testing and made him its chairman. This committee sponsored a series of papers, including one by Edward Teller, arguing against acceptance of the Soviet proposals and in favor of continued U.S. testing. The committee continued its activities throughout the spring of 1963.

These expressions of congressional opposition served as a constant reminder to Kennedy that there were limits to how far he could go in compromising with the Russians on the terms of a test ban treaty.

Further Changes in the U.S. Position

On February 1, Carl Kaysen called me from the White House to say that, since the New York talks with the Soviets were ended, the president felt that the AEC should resume its testing schedule. A week later I attended a White House meeting convened to discuss specific positions the U.S. might take at Geneva. Attending were the president and vice-president, Rusk, McNamara, Nitze, Gilpatric, Bundy, Wiesner, McCone, Foster, and Fisher.

> I informed the president that four underground tests had taken place that day without apparent incident. In response to questions by the president, I explained that one of the purposes of conducting them all on the same day was to study the problems of detecting simultaneous tests.
>
> The discussion then turned to the U.S. test ban position at the eighteen-nation conference, for which Foster was going to Geneva tomorrow.
>
> Foster said that the U.S. and Soviet test series in 1962 had not changed the strategic balance. He felt that the only ways in which imbalance might be introduced through testing were by changes in yield-to-weight ratios or by the development of pure fusion (neutron) bombs.
>
> Foster went over the issue of onsite inspections, discussing Soviet

rigidity on the number of inspections and the apparent misunderstanding about the number Dean and Wiesner had said would be acceptable to the United States. Foster said he would like authority to go from 8 to 6 inspections as a fallback position. He traced the reasoning by which the estimated 450 seismic events annually in the USSR could be reduced by national seismographic means to 45 or 50 suspicious events so that, with 6 inspections, we would be inspecting 1 in 7 or 8 suspicious events. He thought that the number of suspicious events per year could be further reduced to 25 or 30 by U.S. intelligence information (attache and agent reports, electronic and photographic surveillance and the like). Nitze contended that the number of suspicious events was larger than stated by Foster.

I pointed out that the procedures specified for inspections were as important as their number. For example, AEC staff felt that the area subject to an inspection should be 500 to 700 square kilometers, not the 300 to 500 previously recommended; also that if the inspection area were elliptical rather than round it might permit some reduction in the area's size.

The president asked McNamara whether he would accept 6 inspections, with a 500 square kilometer area for each, the area to be elliptical in shape. McNamara said he would support the 6 but needed to go into technical aspects of procedures in more detail. Rusk said we should get the technical aspects nailed down before we discussed numbers at Geneva.

The president said 6 should be our rock-bottom number and that it should be left to Foster how and when it would be most advantageous to introduce it.

Nitze indicated that we should try to get back to the arrangement, formerly agreed to by the Soviets, whereby there would be foreign personnel, including Americans, stationed in seismographic control stations on Soviet soil. McCone recalled that two years earlier the question was whether there would be 15 or 21 such stations. He pointed out that members of Congress were concerned about the continued lowering of our numbers. He remembered Killian having once argued that 100 onsite inspections per year in the Soviet Union was the absolute minimum.

The president said that, in his opinion, the principal reason for having a test ban was its possible effect in arresting or preventing the nuclear development of other nations, particularly China. If it weren't for this possible gain, it wouldn't be worth the internal disruption, fighting with Congress, and so forth. He went on to say that we should proceed on the assumption that the USSR would cheat and that we should work out the relative advantages, that is, we should compare what the Soviets might gain by clandestine underground testing under a comprehensive treaty with the advantages the treaty might bring in preventing the spread of nuclear weapons, particularly to China.

I didn't gather from Kennedy's concluding comments that he actually expected the Soviets to cheat; rather he felt it was a prudent basis for national policy to assume that they would. The president's preoccupation with Chinese nuclear development was again apparent.

Continued Deadlock in Geneva

When the Eighteen-Nation Disarmament Committee resumed its sessions on February 12, 1963, both sides made strong appeals for the support of the neutral bloc. Foster contrasted the West's flexibility, as demonstrated by repeated modification in its verification proposals, with the Soviet Union's stubborn refusal to make any change in its numbers of inspections and black boxes. He indicated that he could not understand why the Soviets had agreed to talks in New York if their position was entirely inflexible. Foster also chided the Soviets for their consistent unwillingness to discuss the technical aspects of inspections.

The Soviets responded by claiming that their offers of onsite inspections and unmanned seismic stations on USSR territory were major concessions. They also dwelt again on the private conversations in which they alleged that first Dean and then Wiesner had accepted very low inspection quotas, only to have their positions repudiated by the U.S. government.

In his initial presentations to the full conference Foster insisted that the United States could accept no fewer than eight inspections annually on Soviet soil. On February 19, however, he met privately with Deputy Foreign Minister Kuznetsov. After explaining a new U.S. conception of how an inspection system would operate, Foster indicated that, if this concept were adopted, the U.S. could accept seven inspections per year. He still held in reserve the number six, which the president had authorized him to offer at the proper moment.

The inspection procedures proposed by Foster had been accepted by the Committee of Principals at a White House meeting on February 18. They assigned a greater role to the U.S.-U.K. and the USSR in inspecting each other, and a lesser role to the international authority, than had been the case in prior Western test ban proposals. The procedures actually may have represented some hardening of the U.S. position, a fact that tended to escape notice in all the talk about the reduced number of inspections. The procedures had the following features (this description assumes a seismic event in the Soviet Union):

1. The U.S.-U.K. would submit seismic data to the International Commission regarding an unidentified seismic event no later than sixty days after the event.
2. The USSR would have seven days in which to present supplementary information regarding the event.
3. The U.S.-U.K. would decide within seven more days whether to

designate the event for an onsite inspection within their quota.

4. If it were so designated the USSR would have five days in which to notify the commission of its arrangements for receiving and transporting the inspection team.

5. The maximum size of the area to be inspected would be 500 square kilometers, its shape elliptical.

6. The surface inspection team would consist of fourteen U.S.-U.K. nationals and six others (not from Warsaw Pact countries) selected by the International Commission. The Soviet Union could have observers equal in number to the size of the inspection team.

7. The inspection team would have six weeks to complete its surface inspection, including low-level helicopter flights. If drilling was thought necessary, additional personnel and additional time (three to six months) would be allowed.

8. The report of the inspection team would be due within thirty days after completion of its work.

These procedures were formally submitted to the disarmament conference in a joint Anglo-American memorandum on April 1, 1963. This memorandum also spelled out the Western position regarding automatic seismic stations:

1. The stations would be built by the host countries in accordance with agreed specifications. The other nuclear side would then supply instrumentation, some of which would be sealed in vaults in the stations.

2. Information recorded in unsealed instruments would be forwarded by the host country at frequent intervals to the International Commission and other nuclear states.

3. Personnel from the other nuclear side and the International Commission would have the right to visit each station eight times a year to obtain data from instruments in the sealed vault and for maintenance, calibration, or replacement of instruments.

It was the U.S. position that agreement had to be reached on these procedures before there could be a decision on numbers of inspections and black boxes. The USSR took just the opposite position: numbers had to be decided first. Despite repeated attempts by Foster to persuade the Soviets to discuss the procedures, they persistently refused. Kuznetsov accused the U.S. of bogging the talks down in technical detail to avoid agreement on numbers "it has itself proposed"—another reference to the Dean and Wiesner conversations.

In considering the progress of the negotiations for a comprehensive test ban there has been a tendency to focus on the ebb and flow of offers and counteroffers relating to the number of onsite inspections. From this point of view the two sides seemed near agreement in early 1963 when the Soviet Union appeared willing to offer three inspections and we were willing to accept six. Many felt at that time that this difference was too small to prevent ultimate agreement, considering what was at stake for all humanity. I believe, however, that agreement was not close, because, difficult as it may have been to agree on numbers of inspections, it would have been infinitely more difficult to agree on their modalities.

As indicated earlier, the Soviets consistently refused, both in Geneva and in the New York talks, to discuss the U.S. proposals regarding the technical details of onsite inspections. It may very well have been that the Soviets would not discuss these proposals, with which they were of course familiar, because Khrushchev knew that he lacked sufficient political strength in the Council of Ministers to gain their approval.*

Testimony by Averell Harriman before the Foreign Relations Committee in 1973 tends to confirm this assessment. Mr. Harriman stated:

> At the time some of our experts thought three inspections would be adequate because it would give us a spot check which would make the Soviets unwilling to run the risk of detection. . . . But then when I saw the details of what our experts would demand in the way of the kind of inspection . . . , the large area over which we would have helicopters range, and the number of holes we would have to drill, and that sort of thing . . . I am satisfied they would never have agreed to it. . . . The Russians accepted onsite inspection as a principle, but I am satisfied we would never have come to an agreement on what was really needed in the way of onsite inspection.[1]

Harriman's estimate of the situation is borne out by some of the arithmetic involved in the U.S. inspection proposals. As noted above, the procedures contemplated aerial surveys as large as 500 square kilometers in each inspection. Assuming six inspections, this would have added up to 3,000 square kilometers per year. These would have been concentrated in central Asian areas with frequent earth tremors,

---

*Conversely, President Kennedy may have felt that he lacked political strength in the U.S. Senate to settle for anything less.

which just happened to be one of the USSR's most sensitive strategic zones. It seems to me inconceivable that the Soviet Union would have uncovered its territory to prying eyes to such an extent.

Based on these indications, my own conclusion is that a comprehensive test ban agreement was not close at any time up to the summer of 1963. This is not to say, however, that later developments in science and international relations might not make such an agreement possible in the future.

Plans for Further U.S. Atmospheric Tests

Pessimism about the test ban negotiations was one of the factors that prompted the AEC on February 21, 1963, to request that the president approve June 1, 1964, as a planning date for the beginning of another atmospheric test series. On the same date I wrote to Secretary Rusk asking him to rush negotiations for a freer use of Christmas Island for the projected series, including high-altitude tests. In 1962 these had been launched from Johnston Island.

A letter from Bundy received on March 5 indicated that the president did not wish at that time to approve a starting date for a new test series, but that the AEC should proceed on its own best judgment with preparations.

As to Christmas Island, second thoughts soon supervened. On March 4:

> Bundy phoned asking whether it might not be better to omit Christmas Island in our planning for the next series. He said it was in a sense a political question, that is whether to be hard or soft with the British and, to make such a decision, technical assessment was needed from the AEC. I told him that we could probably use Johnston. Bundy asked if this would be hard on us and I said I thought we could work it out.

Secretary Rusk added his weight to the discussion in a March 16 letter to Bundy. He felt that "our freedom of action would almost certainly be limited" if we had to rely on the use of Christmas Island. Consequently he felt that only U.S. facilities (Johnston Island, ships, and planes) should be used in the next series. He also suggested that it would not be necessary or even advisable to conceal preparations. On the contrary, "if the fact that we are getting ready to test becomes known, this might do more to spur on the test ban negotiations than would any indication of concern about Soviet complaints about these preparations." (As to whether the Soviets really would have reacted this way, see account of my conversation with Dobrynin, in chap. 16.)

The secretary went further. "I firmly believe," he wrote, "that it would be of the highest importance to remain prepared for a resumption of nuclear tests even though a test ban treaty were in effect." He acknowledged, however, that under a treaty the "scale of preparations would have to be completely different."

There was a brief colloquy about testing sites at a Principals meeting on April 17.

> I said that the AEC wanted it known that we regarded Christmas Island as vastly superior to Johnston Island. Bundy said it was his impression that the AEC would not want to accept the kinds of conditions the British were likely to impose for further use of Christmas Island.

On May 6 the president formally authorized the June 1, 1964, readiness date for a new series of atmospheric tests. The authorizing memorandum also stated that:

> Maximum use would be made of Johnston Island.
>
> No further negotiations would be pursued for use of Christmas Island.
>
> Test preparations could be pursued openly but "should not be flaunted." [The president evidently did not share Rusk's view that knowledge of our preparations would spur on the test ban negotiations.]
>
> The level of preparations and the openness thereof would have to be completely reviewed should there be a test ban.

The Proliferation Connection

As was disclosed at the White House meeting on February 8, 1963, and on other occasions as well, the president felt that the main reason to persist in the quest for a test ban was the possibility that it would arrest the spread of nuclear weapons. He referred to this motivation again in a news conference answer on February 21:

> I must say that a good many people are opposed to this effort which is being directed by Mr. Foster in Geneva, and quite obviously it's a matter which we should approach with a good deal of care. But the alternative, if we fail, of increasing the number of nuclear powers around the world . . . that alternative, which I think is so dangerous, keeps me committed to the effort. . . . I think people who attack the effort should keep in mind always that the alternative is the spread of these weapons to governments which may be irresponsible, or which by accident may initiate a general nuclear conflagration.

The connection between a test ban treaty and preventing the proliferation of nuclear weapons was not an obvious one, and this frequent emphasis by the president was probably less persuasive than he wished. The connection, as seen by the administration, was explained in an ACDA memorandum in late February:

> In considering the impact of a test ban on the issue of non-proliferation of nuclear weapons, the question to be considered is not whether a test ban signed by the U.S., USSR and U.K. would solve the non-proliferation problem. It clearly would not. The question is whether the chances of taking other measures which might successfully cope with the problem ... are significantly greater with a test ban than without it.
>
> In estimating the probable effect [of a test ban] on national decisions to embark on a nuclear weapons program, one must take into account primarily the calculations of individual states vis-à-vis their neighbors and other states of similar rank in the power scale. A nation like Sweden quite likely would decide not to acquire nuclear weapons if it had reasonable assurance that other European countries were not going to attempt to acquire them. Similarly, Israel might be expected to refrain from acquiring nuclear weapons if it had reason to think that its Arab neighbors would not acquire such weapons. The continuation of nuclear weapons tests by the French, however, and the initiation of tests by the Communist Chinese would bring pressure on these smaller countries to acquire nuclear weapons. To the extent that a test ban signed by the U.S., USSR and the U.K. would make it more likely that the French and Chinese series would be curtailed, it is one step in the direction of non-dissemination.
>
> It is only one step, however, and the U.S. should immediately begin considering what in addition to a nuclear test ban treaty could be done to provide assurances to the smaller countries that a nuclear arms race will not be initiated in the ranks of the smaller powers. In Europe the multilateral nuclear force is one solution.* In other areas of the world some form of assurance that the U.S. would come to the assistance of states threatened by the rise of a nuclear power in that area might buttress the effect of a test ban treaty. There is also the possibility of pushing ahead strongly with other arms control measures, e.g., a non-dissemination [nonproliferation] agreement, which might have an impact.

This problem of nuclear proliferation was one of the topics I discussed with Senator Pastore of Rhode Island at a breakfast meeting on March 5. Senator Pastore, who was to see the president on March 8, had been chairman of the Joint Committee on Atomic

---

*This was a proposal for a NATO naval force, internationally owned and "mixed-manned," to which the U.S. could commit Polaris nuclear missiles. After much discussion the proposal foundered because of a lack of enthusiasm in most NATO countries and outright rejection by France.

Energy since January 1963. I reported on my conversation with Pastore in a memorandum to the White House in order to prepare Kennedy for the senator's visit.

> Senator Pastore volunteered that he was sympathetic toward attempts to achieve a workable test ban agreement but feels the "Nth" country [proliferation] argument has been overemphasized. He feels that once China develops a nuclear weapons capability the subsequent acquisition of nuclear weapons by smaller countries would be of relatively little importance to U.S. security. I pointed out that . . . the possession of nuclear weapons by impetuous or irresponsible smaller countries could serve as a fuse for a larger conflagration. The senator conceded this was a risk.

Following his meeting with Kennedy, Pastore wrote the president a wide-ranging letter in which he took a somewhat more negative view of a test ban treaty than in his conversation with me. "If the current U.S. proposal [for a comprehensive treaty] were agreed to by the USSR," the senator wrote, "I would do all in my power to secure its ratification by the Senate. However, on the basis of informal discussions with other Senate leaders I am afraid that ratification of such a treaty could only be obtained with the greatest difficulty. I personally have reservations as to whether such a treaty would be in the best interests of the United States at this time. This opinion is based upon expert testimony presented to the Joint Committee in a series of hearings over the past few weeks."

Senator Pastore's letter was perhaps the most definitive indication yet of the difficulties a comprehensive treaty would have in achieving Senate ratification. It helped to tilt the administration further toward the realization that a limited treaty might be the best that could be achieved.

My Effort To Save the Plowshare Program

Another matter in the August 1962 Western treaty drafts which needed attention was the provision for peaceful nuclear explosions. Both the comprehensive and limited treaty drafts provided that such explosions could be carried out in accordance with annexes that were to be provided later. The ACDA drafted such an annex to the comprehensive treaty in February 1963, although it was not formally presented in Geneva. The annex provided that any party to the treaty wishing to conduct a peaceful nuclear explosion must:

1. Give four months notice plus a detailed description of the proposed experiment to the International Control Commission

2. Give full consideration to comments received from members of the commission
3. Invite all parties to the treaty to observe the preparations, instrumentation, and actual firing and to inspect the nuclear device both externally and internally

An exception to item 3 would be possible if all parties to the treaty specifically agreed to the proposed explosion.

On March 8 I wrote to Adrian Fisher about this proposed annex. I pointed out that over the past eighteen months considerable progress had been made in developing the technology of nuclear excavations and that this technology promised to provide large economic benefits in certain types of major construction activities. I mentioned the possibility of a new sea-level canal across Panama, which was "a significant factor in our current relations with the Government of Panama." As I was later to tell the Principals (on April 17, 1963), I had in mind also such projects as extracting oil from oil shales; scientific experiments (such as discovering transuranium elements); building a harbor at Point Barrow, Alaska; digging a canal across the Aleutian Island chain; and deepening the Bering Straits. I added that a number of industrial groups, states, and foreign governments had already approached the AEC concerning Plowshare projects they had in mind.

I then pointed out that the needs of the Plowshare program were incompatible with the requirement in the draft treaty's annex that the other side be permitted to examine the exterior and interior of the nuclear devices. The reason was that, for both safety and economic reasons, Plowshare experiments required devices employing advanced weapon design principles that should not be revealed. One of the things we needed, for example, was a device virtually free of fallout. This was a reversal of our stand in 1961 when we had reluctantly gone along with a proposal for device revelation. Further technological progress and analysis had convinced us that the necessity to reveal devices would virtually bring the Plowshare program to a halt.

As an alternative, I suggested that each side be limited to an annual quota of five or six peaceful nuclear explosions. This was another reversal of position since, two years earlier, under different circumstances, I had opposed the idea of a Plowshare quota when it was suggested by the State Department.

Foster himself undertook on March 28 to reply to my letter to his deputy. He acknowledged the desirability of the Plowshare program but felt that my suggestion of an annual quota raised serious problems. The Soviet Union could use its quota "for improvement of its weapons technology and the basic purpose of the comprehensive treaty would be defeated." He was concerned also that "to make such a proposal would subject us to a barrage of propaganda that we are not sincere in our desire for a test ban." Accordingly, he hoped the AEC would reassess its position.

The AEC remained stubborn about this. We were concerned not only about our Plowshare program but also about the fate in Congress of any test ban treaty that imperiled the program, because we knew that Plowshare had some very ardent support in the Congress, particularly in the Joint Committee on Atomic Energy.

Our stubbornness brought the White House into the controversy. Wiesner called me on March 30 to see if it wasn't possible to reach some compromise. I went over our arguments against revealing the devices and also sent him an in-house analysis paper on the subject.

A Principals' meeting was held on April 17, with the Plowshare issue an important part of the agenda. At this meeting I repeated the arguments I had made in my letter to Fisher. I suggested that, in addition to an annual quota of peaceful explosions, there might be a limit on the yield of each explosion. I mentioned 50 kilotons as a possible limit.

> I acknowledged that there were difficulties in my suggested approach because of the possibility it provided for weapons testing under the guise of peaceful explosions. However, I said that there would also be an adverse congressional reaction to the elimination of Plowshare and that my suggested approach had the advantage that it would eliminate the necessity of going to Congress for authorization to reveal nuclear devices to the Soviet Union. It would be difficult to obtain such authorization, even for obsolete designs.
>
> After a great deal of discussion in which it was emphasized by McNamara, Bundy, Wiesner, Foster, and McCone that adopting my approach would open the door to weapons testing by the Soviets, it was suggested by Rusk that the wording of the annex be reexamined to determine whether it was possible to devise a scheme that would permit Plowshare to go forward.

Discussions with scientists at Livermore, including laboratory director John Foster, enabled the AEC to recommend additional safeguards making it less likely that important weapons progress could be made under the guise of Plowshare explosions. As described in a letter to William Foster on June 11, our proposal was to add to the treaty annex on peaceful explosions the following two provisions:

1. "No diagnostic instrumentation would be permitted in connection with any Plowshare experiment . . .
2. "The nation sponsoring Plowshare experiments would be

required to make debris samples available to the other permanent members of the International Commission."

The additional proposals were discussed at a Principals' meeting on June 14.

> Rusk began by saying he did not see how one could have peaceful explosions and a significant test ban treaty at the same time. He wondered, semifacetiously, whether it would be practical to have the Soviets conduct our Plowshare experiments while we conducted theirs.
>
> McNamara asked whether the AEC proposal was acceptable to the Soviets. Fisher said he thought it was not. Keeny pointed out that the Soviets had in the past been adamant against any proposal other than disclosure of the devices; that we had proposed limits on instrumentation but the Soviets had not agreed. Wiesner thought it would be very disturbing to the negotiations to take a new stand on this issue.
>
> Keeny asked if the AEC proposals (having a small quota and a limit on yield) would allow full Plowshare development. I said that these limits would slow, but not halt, the program's growth.
>
> Rusk asked whether the Plowshare program was based on the proposition that the tasks involved (digging canals, etc.) could be done more cheaply by nuclear than by conventional explosions. I replied that this was so and that in some cases the cost by conventional methods was so high as to be prohibitive. Rusk said that if Plowshare were the only obstacle to a treaty, the cost of foregoing Plowshare would probably be negligible compared with the billions that would otherwise go into a competitive arms race. I said that if Plowshare were the one thing that prevented the treaty I might agree.
>
> It was concluded that the committee was unable to reach agreement about Plowshare and that the whole matter should be left open and reviewed at the proper time as the test ban talks proceeded.

The question of how peaceful nuclear explosions can be reconciled with a comprehensive test ban treaty remains an active issue to this day (see Chap. 22).

Where Is the Genie?

Opposition at home, deadlock in Geneva, imminence of Chinese tests, difficulty in working out the U.S. position—all these factors combined to deepen the president's pessimism. At his March 21 news conference he was asked whether he still really had any hope of arriving at a nuclear test ban agreement.

The president's answer began: "Well, my hopes are somewhat dimmed, but nevertheless I hope." He mentioned the Soviet acceptance of the principle of inspection as a hopeful sign. He referred again to the danger of proliferation as "the reason why we keep . . . working on this question. . . . I see the possibility in the 1970s of the president of the United States having to face a world in which fifteen or twenty or twenty-five nations may have these weapons. I regard that as the greatest possible danger. . . ." Alluding to senatorial critics, the president noted that they would have their chance to vote "aye" or "nay" if a treaty were signed and observed that the necessity to get a two-thirds vote was a "great protection to all of us."

In his May 20 news conference the president added a new element to his pessimistic evaluation, a sense that time was running out. The colloquy went as follows:

> Q: Mr. President, on the test ban issue, do you join those who feel that prospects for a test ban are zero . . . or is there something in your private correspondence which will give you some hope?
> A: No, I'm not hopeful, I'm not hopeful. . . . We have tried to get an agreement on all the rest of it and then come to the question of the number of inspections, but we were unable to get that. So I would say I am not hopeful at all.
> Q: Mr. President, would you assume that we will have another round of testing. . . ?
> A: I would think that if we don't get an agreement that is what would happen. . . . Personally I think that would be a great disaster. . . . If we don't get an agreement this year . . . perhaps the genie is out of the bottle and we'll never get him back in again.

The president had further pessimistic comments to make on May 27, mixed this time with an element of determination.

> Q: Where is the genie, sir? Is it out of the bottle or in the bottle?
> A: Well, it is neither in nor out right now. But I would say that we will know by the end of the summer whether it is finally out. . . . We are going to . . . push very hard in May and June and July in every forum to see if we can get an agreement. . . .

Kennedy's apparent feeling of increased urgency may well have come from a sense that there were enhanced chances for success in the improved political atmosphere that succeeded the Cuban Missile Crisis but that this diplomatic opening would not last long and needed to be exploited quickly. Ingredients in the changed situation included:

1. An improvement in the president's standing in the country and with the Congress, particularly concerning confidence in his willingness and ability to stand up to the Soviet Union.
2. A greater awareness in public opinion of the fearful dangers of nuclear confrontation, giving rise to a general readiness to accept agreements that might push back the danger.
3. A clearer awareness in the Soviet leadership of the president's willingness to use force, even nuclear force, in defense of vital

U.S. interests, possibly leading to a greater willingness on the Kremlin's part to seek compromise solutions.

Whatever his motivation, there was a change in the coming months in the intensity of Kennedy's pursuit of a test ban. He had sought one with persistence and ardor since the first days of his presidency. Now, he decided to *really go for it!*

Happily, I was able to play a part at just this time in moving the process along.

16

The Tide Begins
To Turn

My Journey to the Soviet Union

During the years since 1954, while the United States and USSR were wrangling about nuclear tests, nuclear scientists of the two nations had achieved a measure of cooperation. They came together and exchanged information at UN Conferences on Peaceful Uses of Atomic Energy held in Geneva in 1955 and 1958. They cooperated in the activities of the International Atomic Energy Agency (IAEA), a UN affiliate established in 1957. They exchanged scientific and technical visits.

Late in 1959 AEC Chairman McCone and his Soviet counterpart, Professor Vasily Emelyanov, signed in Washington a "Memorandum on Cooperation between the United States and the Soviet Union in the Field of the Utilization of Atomic Energy for Peaceful Purposes." This memorandum was the culmination of numerous personal discussions between U.S. and USSR scientists and nuclear energy officials. It specified areas in which visits and information were to be exchanged.

Some of the contemplated exchanges were implemented, but difficulties arose with respect to others. I was deeply convinced of the value of scientific and technical exchanges in fostering understanding and friendship between the two countries. After I became AEC chairman I therefore pressed Emelyanov, both in correspondence and when we met at the annual general conferences of the IAEA, to schedule additional visits and information exchanges. In this I had a measure of success.

In February 1962, Andronik M. Petrosyants succeeded Emelyanov as chairman of the State Committee on Atomic Energy of the Soviet Union. (Petrosyants remains in that position to this date, an extraordinarily long tenure.) During the rest of 1962 the Soviets proved more cooperative, and most points of difference were resolved. In this better atmosphere I invited Petrosyants and Emelyanov, who remained active in the work of the state committee, to meet with us in Washington in order to sign a new Memorandum on Cooperation. In reply, recalling that the previous memorandum had been signed in Washington, Petrosyants invited me and my scientific colleagues to come to the Soviet Union for the signing and also for visits to Soviet research facilities. I gladly accepted and, after an exchange of letters, the visit was scheduled for the latter part of May 1963.

On April 13 I received a call from the White House informing me that the president offered the use of his plane for a nonstop flight, Washington to Moscow. The following day I had lunch with Russian Ambassador Anatoly Dobrynin.

> Dobrynin was surprised at our intent to fly nonstop from Washington; this had never been done before.
>
> I told him that in Russia we would want to concentrate on seeing scientists and laboratories and not on dinners and social affairs at night.
>
> He asked why the United States resumed underground testing at such a critical period in February of this year, because this was having an adverse effect on the test ban negotiations. I said there had been a feeling that we couldn't refrain from testing indefinitely during an open-ended negotiation. Also, there had been some thought this might give the Soviet Union greater incentive to conclude an agreement. Dobrynin said the opposite was true. U.S. testing had led Soviet scientists to feel more strongly that they also needed to test to stay abreast. All this was discussed in a most friendly way. *

On May 9:

> I talked again to Dobrynin, this time on the telephone. He had received a cable from Moscow approving all the arrangements for the trip

---

* Henry Kissinger has observed about Dobrynin: "He was especially skilled at evoking the inexhaustible American sense of guilt, by persistently but pleasantly hammering home the impression that every deadlock was our fault." (*White House Years,* p. 140.)

exactly as I had requested. He wished me a pleasant trip.

I sent a letter to the president saying that I intended to invite Petrosyants to pay a return visit to the United States and offering to see the president before my departure.

I met with the president on May 17.

> I told him there would be ten in the party and described the group. I mentioned that we would be flying nonstop and that allowing us to do this was an unusual concession by the USSR. I said that I had given the Soviets a list of places we wanted to visit, including two never before visited by Westerners, and that the entire list had been approved. I mentioned that University of California scientists had named the recently discovered element 101 mendelevium, after the great Russian chemist Dmitri Mendeleev, and thought this might improve our reception in the USSR.
>
> I indicated to the president that the visit might offer an opportunity for improving relations with the USSR and that we were looking forward to this possibility. I had the test ban negotiations in mind although I didn't mention them specifically. The president said he would like to have a report from me when I returned.

My companions in the delegation were Gerald F. Tape, recently appointed an AEC commissioner; Manson Benedict, chairman, AEC General Advisory Committee; Alvin R. Luedecke, AEC general manager; Albert V. Crewe, director, Argonne National Laboratory; Albert Ghiorso, scientist, Lawrence Radiation Laboratory; Alexander Zucker, scientist, Oak Ridge National Laboratory; Algie A. Wells, director, AEC Division of International Affairs; Arnold R. Fritsch, my technical assistant at AEC; and Cecil King, my staff assistant at AEC.

On May 18 we flew from Dulles International Airport (Washington) to Moscow aboard Air Force One in just a little more than eight and one-half hours. It was a wonderful flight. (Somewhere Kennedy is quoted to the effect that anyone who questions why a man would want to be President hasn't experienced travel in Air Force One.)

Petrosyants and I signed a renewal of the Memorandum on Cooperation in Peaceful Uses of Atomic Energy on May 21. Petrosyants confided to me on this occasion that I was the first American he had ever met!

Our stay in the Soviet Union was indeed memorable. Everywhere we went we were treated with the warmest hospitality. Our hosts accepted unhesitatingly the itinerary we had proposed and even included some additional sites they thought would interest us. Throughout the trip we were accompanied by Chairman Petrosyants or by one of his deputy chairmen.

Our journey achieved a number of "firsts." We were the first foreign group to visit the Soviet reactor testing station at Ulyanovsk and the site of the high-energy accelerator at Serpukhov; the first

Western visitors since World War II to visit the Radium Institute in Leningrad; and the first foreign group to see many industrial reactors and certain other scientific equipment.

A high point of the trip took place on May 29.

I had an appointment for an hour and a quarter with Leonid Ilyich Brezhnev, chairman of the Praesidium (president) of the USSR. Two days before, my Soviet hosts proudly told me they had made an appointment for me with an important official of the Soviet government, namely the president. When I indicated a lack of knowledge of this individual—the position of president was considered largely ceremonial—they assured me this was an unusual opportunity because Brezhnev was, in their opinion, destined to play a very important role in the Soviet government.

I found him to be a personable man of pleasant appearance, with more of a Western manner than most Soviet officials. He started the conversation by asking me if this were my first visit to the Soviet Union. When I replied that it was, he said he thought it was a good start, and added: "Good relations require frequent visits." We agreed that the international character of science made it an excellent vehicle for developing and maintaining good relations.

He asked whether I found the atmosphere open during my visit. When I said it was, he said that Petrosyants had wanted it that way and that the government had given him instructions to show me "everything." When I commented that our delegation had been well fed during the trip he observed that Russian cuisine varied from region to region within the country but was generally heavy. We discussed sports in the USSR, and Brezhnev remarked that the Soviet people were passionate soccer fans.

He asked my impressions of the cities I had visited. When I commented on the sameness of Moscow apartment buildings, Brezhnev said that 3.7 million square meters of new housing were being added in Moscow each year and that most Soviet housing construction used prefabricated panels of prestressed concrete. He added that the USSR was now sending its architects abroad to study and that foreign architects would be invited to design new buildings on a competitive basis.

I commented on Brezhnev's apparent technical background, and he discussed his career. He had technical training in metallurgy, which seemed to run in his family. His grandfather, father, brother, sister, and son were all metallurgists, and all worked at the same plant! But he himself had been in party work for more than twenty-five years.

He asked my opinion of what I had seen in our delegation's visits and urged me to criticize boldly. I said that in scientific work a solid base was being built with generous government support and that future results would depend on the people involved. I commented on the similarity in approach of Soviet and U.S. nuclear electric power programs. I said that similar problems were being encountered and that cooperation in solving the problems would help both countries. Brezhnev replied that he would welcome such cooperation. He agreed with my statement that there was a place for nuclear power in the economies of both countries, particularly in areas where other sources of energy were scarce and costly.

I complained mildly that I couldn't learn what the total budget was for peaceful uses of nuclear energy because Petrosyants hadn't responded to my question. Petrosyants, who was present, responded that because of the structure of his state committee they couldn't give me an answer without lying and since they didn't want to lie they didn't give me an answer.

As a memento of our visit, I presented Brezhnev with a paperweight containing a small piece of graphite from the CP-1 (Chicago) reactor in which the first self-sustaining nuclear chain reaction was achieved in 1942. He thanked me with great warmth.

He then said he wanted to depart from the subjects of science and engineering. He said that I would doubtless meet with President Kennedy on my return and wanted me to tell the president that Khrushchev meant what he was saying about peaceful coexistence and cooperation in his speeches and in correspondence with the president. "This is not propaganda," Brezhnev said. "It is the sincere desire of our government, of our people, and of our party, which leads the country. I can't say more than that." Brezhnev then added that, although he didn't know the president, he sent his best wishes to him and his family.

While interesting at the time, my talk with Brezhnev was even more so in retrospect, since his elevation to the post of general secretary of the Communist party occurred less than a year and a half later.

It is symptomatic of the extreme insularity of Russian leaders that, as I was told later, I was the first non-Communist American to meet Brezhnev. The only American to meet him before me had been Gus Hall, head of the Communist party in the U.S.

Our delegation left the Soviet Union on May 30. We stopped over in Paris for technical discussions with French officials and arrived back in the U.S. on May 31.

On June 1, I met with Bundy and Kaysen at the White House. I turned over copies of the signed Memorandum on Cooperation and other documents. We discussed some highlights of the trip, including the conversation with Brezhnev. Bundy promised to inform the president.

On June 3, I held a press conference about my trip, with representatives present from Tass and *Izvestiya* as well as from the U.S. media, including all three television networks. Next I reported to the Joint Committee on Atomic Energy in executive session. Earlier in the day I had breakfasted with Congressman Holifield to bring him up to date.

On June 14, I reported to President Kennedy.

I gave the president the message from Brezhnev and described my talk with him and his possible status as heir apparent. I said it was my opinion that Brezhnev would be easier to deal with than many

Soviets we had had contact with; he had a warm and friendly manner. I
described various Soviet programs as we had observed them.

The president asked if the use of his airplane had been helpful. I
said that it had been and that it made quite an impression when we
arrived in Moscow and were met by Petrosyants and his four deputies. I
observed that comparison of the USSR state committee's organization with AEC's would show that their chairman had much more power
than our chairman.

The president said he was very happy that our trip to the Soviet
Union had been so successful. I said I thought it had contributed to
good relations between the two countries.

In retrospect, I would reaffirm my final observation to the
president. Our visit came at a critical time. The members of our
delegation were keenly aware of their potential role as "ambassadors
of good will" and performed well in this regard. The atmosphere
between us and our hosts, excellent to start with, grew progressively
less reserved and more friendly. It is certain that the progress of our
visit was communicated to the highest levels. I doubt that the interview arranged for me with Brezhnev was routine.

I would not wish to overstate. There were substantial currents
running in the world at this particular time. I like to think that our
visit, coming at a propitious time, helped to reinforce those currents
leading to a relaxation of tensions.

The Hot Line

One of the lessons learned in the Cuban missile confrontation
was the importance of swift, reliable communication between opposing sides during dangerous international crises.

During the crisis the need to code, decode, and translate each
Kennedy-Khrushchev message had made the average transmission
take about four hours.[1] At a time when fateful decisions were being
made several times a day, it was necessary in a number of instances,
including Khrushchev's final offer of withdrawal, to rely on open
broadcasts in order to speed communication.

The Soviet Union showed an awareness of this potential problem
before the U.S. did, and well before the missile crisis. On July 23,
1962, Soviet sources reported that the USSR favored establishment of
a direct phone connection between the Kremlin and the White
House. At his news conference the same day President Kennedy was
cool toward the idea. He said he had no plans for such a phone link,
the basic difficulty between the two sides being "comprehension
rather than communication."

The experience during the missile crisis changed the American
view. On December 12, 1962, Ambassador Dean submitted to the

Eighteen-Nation Disarmament Committee a working paper on pre-
vention of war by accident or miscalculation. Part of this paper was a
proposal of a direct communications connection. Both telephone and
teletype were mentioned as possibilities. In his news conference that
day, the president expressed a preference for teletype.

There was no immediate Soviet response. On April 5, 1963,
however, in a speech at the disarmament conference that was otherwise quite harsh, Tsarapkin announced that the Soviet Union was
ready to consider the U.S. proposal. Technical talks then ensued, and
on June 20, 1963, a memorandum of understanding on establishment
of the so-called hot line was signed. It called for a direct and wholly
private teletype link passing through Helsinki, Stockholm, and
London. Before summer's end the line was operable. The hot line has
been activated in several international crises since its establishment,
as one side or the other has sought to prevent misunderstanding of
some action it had taken or was about to take.

The hot-line agreement was a relatively minor event judged
against the momentous substantive issues being discussed in
Geneva. In retrospect, however, it can be seen as a straw in the wind, a
sign that agreement was possible between the two sides and part of
the mounting trend toward reasonable accommodation of differences.

A New Western Initiative

While the U.S. and USSR did not appear to be drawing any closer
together on test ban issues in the late spring of 1963, their leaders
seemed to be reaching out to each other in an effort to establish
personal trust. As I have described, Khrushchev used my interview
with Brezhnev to pass a message to President Kennedy. For his part,
the president already had adopted a similar technique, utilizing the
opportunity afforded by the interview granted by Khrushchev to
Norman Cousins on April 12, 1963.

We have already touched on the part of the Khrushchev-Cousins
conversation which concerned the misunderstanding about the minimum number of inspections acceptable to the U.S. We must consider
other parts of that conversation now, because it did more than
explain history—it helped to make history.

President Kennedy, knowing Cousins was to see Khrushchev,
had asked him to try to explain the American position on the test ban.
According to his own account, Cousins began this endeavor by
saying: "If the Chairman construed the American position on inspections to mean that we actually did not want a treaty . . . then that
interpretation was in error." Khrushchev indicated disbelief. "If the
United States really wanted a treaty, it could have had one."[2]

Next there ensued the discussion we have already alluded to, leading up to Khrushchev's account of his appeal to the Council of Ministers to authorize three inspections. Khrushchev then said: "We cannot make another offer." At this point he revealed that he was under pressure from his atomic scientists to permit a further series of tests.

At length, Khrushchev relented a bit from the severity of his position, saying to Cousins: "Just so there is no mistake about it in your mind, let me say finally that I cannot and will not go back to the Council of Ministers and ask them to change our position in order to accommodate the United States again. Why am I always the one who must understand the difficulties of the other fellow? Maybe it's time for the other fellow to understand my position. But you can tell the President I accept his explanation of an honest misunderstanding and suggest that we get moving. *But the next move is up to him.*" (emphasis added).[3] The Cousins interview, duly reported to the president, made it clear that the ball was now in the Western court.

In fairness, much of the credit for the next, and ultimately decisive, step must be given to the British. When news came early in March 1963 that negotiations at the Eighteen-Nation Disarmament Committee were deadlocked, Prime Minister Macmillan began casting about for a means to break the impasse. He was determined to make an effort, preferably with the United States but if necessary without us.

On March 16 Macmillan sent one of his voluminous letters to President Kennedy. He reviewed at length the efforts to reach agreement since the Anglo-American summit in Bermuda in December 1961. He acknowledged that there were "strong political arguments" for doing nothing, then added: "But this is not the spirit in which you, who carry the largest responsibility before God and man, have faced your duty." He pointed out the importance a test ban treaty might have: "important in itself and all the more important in what may flow from it." He went over the issues—number of inspections, possibility of Russian cheating—and made light of them.

Then the prime minister came to the point: "How are we to renew the negotiations with a view to bringing them to a satisfactory conclusion?" He mentioned the possibility of a summit meeting but saw the political risk for Kennedy. He brought up the possibility of an offer at Geneva of five inspections but felt a rejection by the Soviets would also hurt the president politically. He thought that a negotiation on the test ban treaty could be made more attractive by offering at the same time a nonproliferation treaty.

Finally, Macmillan suggested that the president might "send

some personal message to Khrushchev . . . or perhaps some emissary such as Averell [Harriman], or even your brother Bobby, who would . . . clear up any misunderstanding . . ." about numbers of inspections. (The president's utilization of the Cousins interview with Khrushchev accorded with this last suggestion from Macmillan.)

The president answered Macmillan on March 28. He ruled out a summit meeting until all technical issues were settled at lower levels. He suggested sending a joint letter to Khrushchev and forwarded a draft. Drafts and redrafts of the joint letter crossed the Atlantic for the next three weeks.

At length, on April 24, U.S. and British ambassadors in Moscow delivered the letter to Khrushchev. It emphasized the importance of a test ban agreement as a step toward other agreements. The current impasse between the two sides was described. The letter then continued:

> We should be interested to hear your suggestions as to how we are to break out of this. For our part we should be quite prepared now to arrange private tripartite discussions in whatever seemed the most practical way. For example, our chief representatives at Geneva could conduct discussions on the questions which remain to be settled. Alternatively, or at a later stage . . . *[we] would be ready to send in due course very senior representatives who would be empowered to speak for us and talk in Moscow directly with you.* [Emphasis added.]

President Kennedy referred to the joint letter in his news conference on April 24. His overriding concern about proliferation and his sense of time urgency were once again evident:

> As we feel time is running out, the Prime Minister and I wrote to Chairman Khrushchev to see if we could develop some means by which we could bring this matter to a climax and see if we could reach an accord which we feel to be in the interest of the . . . present nuclear powers to prevent diffusion [of nuclear weapons to other countries].

Before the Anglo-American letter could be delivered—it was completed on April 18 but not delivered until April 24 because Khrushchev was away from Moscow—the atmosphere was clouded further. Notwithstanding his final conciliatory comments to Cousins, Khrushchev elected to reassume his outraged manner. In an interview on April 20 with the editor of the Italian newspaper *Il Giorno* (broadcast by Radio Moscow to assure the widest dissemination) he repeated the charge that the United States had repudiated its own offer of two to four inspections, and he threatened to withdraw his own offer of two to three inspections.

Khrushchev's initial reply on May 8 to the Anglo-American letter maintained his disagreeable tone. He continued the debate and recriminations about the number of inspections. He accused Kennedy of insincerity on a test ban. He threatened further measures to protect Soviet security. Yet, in a final paragraph, he said the USSR would continue to seek agreement and *would be prepared "to receive your highly placed representatives"* (emphasis added).

President Kennedy appeared discouraged by Khrushchev's reply. It was on May 10 that he said at his press conference: "I'm not hopeful. I'm not hopeful." The British were less disturbed. Taking a cue from the way the United States handled Khrushchev's conflicting communications near the end of the missile crisis, Ambassador Ormsby-Gore urged a response that would ignore the negative and concentrate on the positive: the fact that Khrushchev said he would receive the emissaries. On May 30 such a reply was sent, proposing that emissaries go to Moscow at the end of June or early in July.

History provides as yet no definitive answer as to why Khrushchev reacted as he did during this period, specifically, why he continued his belligerent tone while agreeing to the Western proposal for high-level negotiations in Moscow. It is especially curious that he continued to accuse the United States of reneging on its inspection offer after he told Norman Cousins that he accepted the president's explanation of an honest misunderstanding. One can perhaps find a clue in what he told Cousins about his very limited freedom of action vis-à-vis the central committee. In testimony before the Senate Military Affairs Committee on May 7, ACDA Director Foster ventured a similar explanation. This was before Khrushchev's reply to the first Kennedy-Macmillan letter had been received. Foster said:

> Recently, direct overtures have been made to Chairman Khrushchev by the U.K. and U.S. ambassadors in Moscow. Khrushchev's reaction to these overtures was initially negative, but final word has not yet been received from the Soviet government. . . . Perhaps the uncertainties which have recently [since the missile crisis] been apparent in the position of Khrushchev at the pinnacle of the Communist party and the Soviet government have made it difficult for the Soviets to move in the direction of agreement at this time.

Following along the lines of Foster's testimony, one can conjecture that, for political reasons vis-à-vis his Praesidium and Chinese critics, Khrushchev felt obliged to maintain a tough public stance toward the United States, while privately, through Cousins, in Brezhnev's talk with me, and in his grudging acceptance of the emissaries, signaling that he did not wish his apparent intransigence to be taken literally. Another indication that Khrushchev was serious about a test ban is that, of the two alternatives offered in the Kennedy-Macmillan letter of April 24—further discussion in Geneva or participating himself in direct talks in Moscow—Khrushchev chose the latter. The significance of this may not have been grasped fully at the time.

Further Moves by the President

As we have seen, during the spring of 1963 President Kennedy's mood, as revealed in his press conferences, was a combination of pessimism and determination. The determination resulted in some important initiatives.

On May 6 he addressed a memorandum to the Committee of Principals calling for a reexamination of the U.S. position. This memo said, in part:

> I have in no way changed my views on the desirability of a test ban treaty or the value of our proposals on general and complete disarmament. Further, the events of the last two years have increased my concern for the consequences of an unchecked . . . arms race. . . .
>
> We now expect the Eighteen-Nation Disarmament Committee to recess shortly for six weeks to two months. I should like the interval to be used for an urgent re-examination of the possibilities of new approaches. . . .
>
> I should like to review the results at an appropriate time in the process.

To avoid disturbing the atmosphere for the mission of the Moscow emissaries, the president directed on May 13 that three weapons tests, two of them atmospheric, which together went by the name of FERRIS WHEEL, be postponed indefinitely. They had been scheduled for the end of May in Nevada.

These maneuvers by Kennedy lead one to wonder whether he, like Khrushchev, may not also have been playing a double game during this period. By such an interpretation, the president's game might have been to react pessimistically to Khrushchev's truculence (to calm those in Congress who feared an agreement) while also passing along private assurances (for instance, via Cousins), canceling tests and, as we shall now see, preparing in closely guarded secrecy a masterful speech designed to clear the atmosphere prior to the arrival of emissaries in Moscow.

The Speech: Its Genesis

There is a well-worn homily to the effect that it is not what a politician says that counts, but what he does. Like most such sayings, this one is true only to a degree. Occasionally what a politician says and how he says it are so significant as to have the effect of an important action. This was certainly the case with President Kennedy's commencement address at American University in Washington, D.C., on June 10, 1963, a speech that the *Manchester Guardian* called "one of the great state papers of American history."

The first spark of the idea for the speech might well have come from a telephone conversation that Kennedy had with Norman Cousins. Cousins recalls receiving a phone call from the president on another matter. "I advocated making a breathtaking offer to the Russians and the President said he would think about it, that he would talk about it to Ted Sorensen who might call me. In fact, Sorensen did call me and he and I discussed the idea further."[4]

The possibility of negotiations by emissaries in Moscow provided a further reason for the speech. The June 10 commencement at American University, already on the president's schedule, offered a timely opportunity.

The president and Sorensen worked on the speech in relative secrecy. As Sorensen relates:

> Unlike most foreign policy speeches—none of which was as sweeping in concept and impact as this turned out to be—official department positions and suggestions were not solicited. The president was determined to put forward a fundamentally new emphasis on the peaceful and positive in our relations with the Soviets. He did not want that new policy diluted by the usual threats of destruction, boasts of nuclear stockpiles and lectures on Soviet treachery.[5]

It is doubtful that Kennedy would have taken such an independent course prior to the missile crisis. The enhancement of the president's prestige resulting from his handling of that event was a liberating influence.

Two days before the speech was to be delivered an event occurred that greatly enlarged its significance. This was the receipt of a letter from Khrushchev agreeing to a date for arrival of the Western emissaries in Moscow.

Khrushchev's letter was disagreeable in tone and full of complaint about previous Western behavior in the test ban negotiations. He pointed out that agreement was possible only if neither of the parties attempted to wrest a special advantage from the other, and accused Western representatives of failing to recognize this principle of the equality of the parties. He seemed particularly incensed about the attempt during the recent conversations in New York to draw Soviet representatives into discussing the technical details of inspections when no agreement had been reached on the political principles involved.

Despite all his complaints, Khrushchev did agree to receive the Western emissaries and suggested July 15 as the time for them to arrive in Moscow. He warned, however, that a repetition of such an experience as that in New York "would only damage the matter" and that success depended squarely on what quality of baggage the emissaries brought with them to Moscow.

One can conjecture that some of Khrushchev's churlishness in this letter was motivated by a desire to placate hard-liners in the Soviet leadership. Whatever his reasons and notwithstanding his tone, the significant thing was that he had given the green light to the negotiations. The president now had the opportunity in his speech at American University to affect the atmosphere in which the negotiations would take place.

The Speech: Its Content

The president was in Honolulu on Sunday, June 9, addressing a meeting of the U.S. Conference of Mayors. Sorensen flew out with the draft of the next day's speech, and finishing touches were made on the return flight on Air Force One.* Soviet officials and members of the press at home and abroad were told in advance that the president was about to deliver a speech of major importance. The stage was set; the world was listening.

Kennedy began by defining what he meant by peace. "Not a Pax Americana, enforced on the world by American weapons of war. Not the peace of the grave or the security of the slave. I am talking about genuine peace, the kind of peace that makes life on earth worth living, the kind that enables men and nations to grow and to hope and to build a better life for their children. . . ."

He said: "I speak of peace because of the new face of war. Total war makes no sense in an age when great powers can maintain large and relatively invulnerable nuclear forces and refuse to surrender without resort to those forces." He decried the huge expenditures "on weapons acquired for the purpose of making sure we never need to use them." Peace was therefore "the necessary rational end of rational men."

---

*Sorensen notes in his Kennedy Library Oral History Program interview that "Kennedy made a few changes but basically liked it. Averell Harriman was on the plane, and he liked it very much, which encouraged the President not to change it further."

The president then made a strong plea that Americans reexamine their attitudes toward a number of subjects: "toward the possibilities of peace, toward the Soviet Union, toward the course of the cold war and toward freedom and peace here at home."

As to the first subject, peace, he referred to the widely held view that it was impossible. "We need not accept that view. Our problems are man-made—therefore, they can be solved by man. And man can be as big as he wants. No problem of human destiny is beyond human beings." Kennedy went on to say that he was not thinking of an "absolute, infinite concept of universal peace and goodwill.... Let us focus instead on a more practical and more attainable peace—based not on a sudden revolution in human nature but on a gradual evolution in human institutions—on a series of concrete actions and effective agreements which are in the interest of all concerned."

With such a peace as he sought, the president said, ". . . there still will be quarrels and conflicting interests. . . . World peace . . . does not require that each man love his neighbor—it requires only that they live together in mutual tolerance . . . and history teaches us that enmities between nations, as between individuals, do not last forever."

As to the Soviet Union, he found it "discouraging to think that their leaders may actually believe what their propagandists write." He then quoted some "wholly baseless and incredible claims," such as that "the political aims of the American imperialists are to . . . achieve world domination . . . by means of aggressive wars." He held out such Soviet statements as a warning that Americans should not fall into the same trap of seeing "only a distorted and desperate view of the other side."

"No government or social system," the president continued, "is so evil that its people must be considered as lacking in virtue. As Americans, we find communism profoundly repugnant as a negation of personal freedom and dignity. But we can still hail the Russian people for their many achievements—in science and space, in economic and industrial growth, in culture and in acts of courage.

"Among the many traits the peoples of our two countries have in common, none is stronger than our mutual abhorrence of war. Almost unique among the major world powers, we have never been at war with each other."

Then, in one of the boldest strokes in the speech, Kennedy called attention to Russian sufferings in World War II, revealing what many Americans and most Russians had only dimly realized, that "at least 20 million [Soviet citizens] lost their lives. Countless millions of homes and farms were burned and sacked. A third of the nation's territory, including nearly two-thirds of its industrial base, was turned into a wasteland—a loss equivalent to the devastation of this country east of Chicago."

The president went on to portray with chilling realism the dangers of a hot war and the costs of the cold war. This led to only one conclusion: "In short, both the United States and its allies, and the Soviet Union and its allies, have a mutually deep interest in a just and genuine peace and in halting the arms race. Agreements to this end are in the interests of the Soviet Union as well as ours—and even the most hostile nations can be relied upon to accept and keep those treaty obligations, and only those treaty obligations, which are in their own interest.

"So, let us not be blind to our differences—but let us also direct attention to our common interests and to the means by which those differences can be resolved. . . . For, in the final analysis, our most basic common link is that we all inhabit this small planet. We all breathe the same air. We all cherish our children's future. And we are all mortal."

Kennedy next asked for a reexamination of attitudes toward the cold war. "We are not here distributing blame or pointing the finger of judgment. We must deal with the world as it is. . . . We must conduct our affairs in such a way that it becomes in the Communists' interest to agree on a genuine peace. Above all," he continued, in an obvious reference to the recent Russian adventure in Cuba, "nuclear powers must avoid those confrontations which bring an adversary to a choice of either a humiliating retreat or a nuclear war. To adopt that kind of course in the nuclear age would be evidence only of the bankruptcy of our policy—or of a collective death wish for the world."

Turning specifically to matters of arms control, the president indicated that general and complete disarmament continued to be "our primary long-range interest" in the Geneva talks. A treaty to outlaw nuclear tests was "the one major area of these negotiations where the end is in sight, yet where a fresh start is badly needed. . . . The conclusion of such a treaty, so near and yet so far, would check the spiraling arms race in one of its most dangerous areas. It would place the nuclear powers in a position to deal more effectively with one of the greatest hazards which man faces in 1963, the further spread of nuclear arms."

Kennedy then made two announcements:

> First: Chairman Khrushchev, Prime Minister Macmillan, and I have agreed that high-level discussions will shortly begin in Moscow looking toward early agreement on a *comprehensive* test ban treaty. Our hopes must be tempered with the caution of history—but with our hopes go the hopes of all mankind. [Emphasis added.]

Second, to make clear our good faith and solemn convictions on this matter, I now declare that the United States does not propose to conduct nuclear tests in the atmosphere so long as other states do not do so.

The president next asked that Americans reexamine their attitude toward "peace and freedom here at home," saying that "it is the responsibility of all citizens in all sections of this country to respect the rights of all others and to respect the law of the land." (The long-smoldering issue of civil rights for black Americans had flared into an intense national crisis in 1963 with demonstrations—some huge—in hundreds of communities and the specter of violence haunting the public consciousness.) He related this to his quest for peace: "Is not peace in the last analysis a matter of human rights?"

The president concluded with a pledge to work for the peace he had described. "We do not want a war. We do not expect a war. . . . We shall be prepared if others wish it. . . . But we shall also do our part to build a world where the weak are safe and the strong are just. We are not helpless before the task or hopeless of its success."

The Speech: Its Reception

The American University speech constituted a momentous utterance by the president, a supreme effort on his part to cut through the walls of mistrust that had divided East and West and frustrated earlier efforts to reach arms control agreements to which he felt there was no acceptable alternative.

While Kennedy did not consult the bureaucracy in advance, he tried afterward to ensure that it would support his initiative fully. Thus, I, along with others, received a copy of an unsigned memorandum sent from the White House on the day following the speech. The memorandum, entitled "How We Hope the President's Speech at American University May be Understood," stated:

1. The President's speech is an expression of a concern for peace which he feels deeply in a personal sense and which he has not had an opportunity to express in extended form in many months. The speech is a major Presidential statement of the continuing policy of the Administration.
2. The United States Government thinks it important to keep before the world and the Soviet Union the opportunity of real progress toward disarmament and toward the easing of tensions generally.
3. At the same time, the President has always recognized plainly the difficulty of achieving a sharp turn in Soviet policy, and this speech should not be misunderstood as indicating any weakening in the American resolution to resist the pressures for Soviet expansion.

4. The President is not choosing sides, in any ostentatious way, between Moscow and Peiping, but his speech is designed to emphasize the positive opportunities for a more constructive and less hostile Soviet policy.*

5. The speech emphatically reasserts the commitment of the United States to sustain its mutual obligations and responsibilities with its allies; the President's conviction is that a reliable improvement in relations with the Soviet Union, especially in the field of arms control, is in the interest of *all* states.

6. The discussions in Moscow in July are being undertaken not because there is any clear evidence of the possibility of agreement [pessimism persisted], but rather because it seems important to make every reasonable effort to find a way out of the present disagreement. The President's decision to send an emissary of the experience and distinction of Undersecretary Harriman is intended both to underline the importance of the mission and to increase the chances for its success.

7. The President's decision that the U.S. will not be the first to resume atmospheric testing represents a considered judgment based on confidence in the present strategic posture of the U.S. and a conviction that by selective underground testing, and readiness to resume in the atmosphere if others do, the United States can sustain an effective defensive posture without having to damage the chances for international agreement by testing in the air unless others do so first.

8. The President recognizes that the cooperation of both sides will be needed if progress is to be made along the lines which are set forth in the American University speech. He is well aware that the Soviet Government may not choose to respond affirmatively, and he knows as well as any man in public life that the Soviet Union has in the past shown itself capable of taking a quite opposite course. This makes it all the more essential, in his view, to keep it clear that the U.S. would prefer the path of progress toward durable peace. It goes without saying that the U.S. will be alert to prevent any Soviet effort to engage in new adventures under the cloak of peaceful discussions. The United States thinks that this lesson of the Cuban crisis of October is not lost upon Soviet leaders.

The address drew remarkably little attention at home—it was overshadowed in the media and in public interest by the civil rights crisis at home and a sex scandal in the British cabinet—and not all the

---

*What this seems to say is that the president was taking sides in an *unostentatious* way. It is sometimes forgotten that at this time the Chinese were regarded by many as the less responsible, the more implacably hostile and potentially the more dangerous of the Communist giants. President Kennedy seemed to be one who held this view, perhaps to excess. In recent years, with changes in government attitudes on both sides, relations between the United States and the People's Republic of China have warmed considerably. I am proud to have been able to play a part in this process through participation in the exchange of professional visits and scientific information.

attention it drew was favorable. Some Republicans in Congress criticized the speech for its softness, one terming it "a dreadful mistake."

But on the primary target audience, the leadership of the Soviet Union, the effect appeared to be profound. Khrushchev later confided to Harriman his view that the speech was the best by any American president since Franklin Roosevelt and that it had taken courage on Kennedy's part to make it. Notwithstanding the fact that it contained some criticisms of Soviet policies and Soviet analyses of history, the address was published in its entirety in the Soviet press and rebroadcast in its entirety in the Voice of America translation. It was as though Khrushchev had been looking for a weapon to use against Chinese criticisms of his policies toward the United States and Kennedy had provided it. Others in the Council of Ministers must also have been impressed enough to permit dissemination of the president's words to the Soviet people. Another consequence of the address was that the jamming of Western broadcasts, which had been going on for fifteen years at enormous expense to the Soviet Union, and which had slackened off some in May, now ceased entirely.* While Khrushchev had agreed prior to the speech to receive the Western emissaries, the prevailing diplomatic climate and the tone of his letter of acceptance offered little hope that the talks would succeed. The Soviet response to the American University speech changed the atmosphere.

Another positive development followed later in the month. For some time the Soviet Union had been strongly opposing adoption of a system of safeguards whereby, through record keeping and inspections at nuclear facilities throughout the world, the International Atomic Energy Agency would attempt to prevent diversion of nuclear material from peaceful to military purposes. The purported Soviet objection had been that the safeguards would involve an intrusion on the national sovereignty of the countries owning the reactors. On June 21, 1963, I was able to inform the president and others at a White House meeting that, at a meeting of the IAEA Board of Governors the preceding day, the Soviet Union had reversed itself and voted in favor of IAEA safeguards.

After so many discouraging setbacks there seemed at last to be some hopeful portents. The true significance of the portents remained to be tested, however. This was the task for the coming weeks.

---

*More militant Western broadcasts, such as those of Radio Free Europe and Radio Liberty, continued to be jammed.

17

Preparation for
a Mission

Dissension within the Administration

Having received Khrushchev's invitation to send emissaries to
Moscow on July 15, both President Kennedy and Prime Minister
Macmillan set about designating their principal representatives. The
president turned to perhaps the most experienced of our diplomats in
dealing with the Soviet Union, Undersecretary of State W. Averell
Harriman, who had been U.S. ambassador in Moscow from 1943 to
1946. Harriman was highly respected among the Russians for what he
had contributed in that tour of duty and in general for the consistent,
no-nonsense forthrightness of his approach.

Macmillan's comment on the selection of Harriman underscored the rightness of the choice: "I was very glad to learn that the
President had decided on Harriman. . . . For a task of this kind he had
every quality—infinite patience, tact, courage and complete independence from any political or even administrative pressure."[1]

Macmillan, for his part, selected Lord Hailsham (Quintin Hogg), Minister of Science. Hailsham's official position made his selection logical but in other respects he was not especially well qualified for a tough diplomatic negotiation.

The president and his advisers were now faced once more with the task of formulating an up-to-date position on a test ban, particularly a comprehensive test ban, since that was what the president had announced would be his objective in the Moscow discussions. As this process unfolded, it became apparent that there was a surprising amount of disagreement within the administration itself about the acceptability of the proposals we had ourselves advanced at Geneva. The groups and individuals who now raised questions appeared earlier to have consented to the proposals but, as Theodore Sorensen has pointed out, this consent had been given at a time when "they felt they were discussing an academic question and would never be faced with an actual treaty."[2]

Air Force Chief of Staff Curtis LeMay confirmed this analysis in his Senate testimony on the treaty, saying: "I think we were caught a little bit by surprise at the seriousness of the administration trying to get a treaty signed at the point when Mr. Harriman was going over there. Up until that time we hadn't recognized the seriousness of the approach to this particular treaty."[3]

The extent of the problem became apparent at a meeting of the Committee of Principals on June 14, 1963, the same meeting at which there was the extensive consideration of the Plowshare program discussed in chapter 15.

The discussion at this meeting was unusually spirited, with Rusk in particular voicing great indignation at the newly emergent opposition to the U.S. proposals expressed by General Taylor on behalf of the Joint Chiefs of Staff. The give and take at this meeting is worthy of attention for what it reveals about the difficult intra-government negotiations that are sometimes necessary before inter-government negotiations can begin.

> Rusk began the discussion by pointing out that no great hopes were being entertained, but it was a matter of making the greatest possible effort in Moscow; we did not know that there had been as yet any change in the Soviet position. [Khrushchev had recently reiterated that national systems of verification were adequate and that international onsite inspection was a form of espionage.] The Soviets, however, were preoccupied with their split with China, and there was some chance they might change their position. The U.S. emissaries should therefore have a comprehensive treaty in hand that they could bring forward if warranted.
>
> McNamara said he viewed the matter of trying to achieve a firm government position at this time with mixed feelings. He was concerned

that a fixed position would bring forth arguments from Congress and the public which would restrict the Harriman mission's negotiating flexibility. Also, the Joint Chiefs were due to testify late in June before the Stennis Committee [Preparedness Subcommittee of the Senate Armed Services Committee], and if their testimony related to a specific draft they might have to oppose it. This would then disclose an administration split over the treaty. If the draft treaty were put forward as just one alternative, however, then the Chiefs could say they supported a test ban if it had adequate inspection.

General Taylor said that under the present draft comprehensive treaty the Soviets could make important gains through clandestine testing and that therefore the treaty was not in the security interests of the United States. He said the Chiefs did not look forward to appearing before the Stennis Committee in such a way as to bring out the disagreement within the government. He therefore agreed with the idea of regarding the current draft as only one possibility. McNamara reaffirmed this view, saying that a long series of discussions would be required before the technical issues disturbing the Joint Chiefs could be resolved. He did not want the draft treaty approved prematurely.

Rusk asked whether the Joint Chiefs had ever expressed themselves on a ban limited to atmospheric tests. Taylor said they had not done so formally. However, he thought this would be a better solution than an inadequate comprehensive test ban.

Foster (ACDA) expressed surprise at the way the discussion was going. He said that the test ban position had been discussed for months and that agreed government positions had been reached last summer and again in February. McNamara said that the issues really hadn't been joined; the technical groups had not reached agreement. Foster said he thought the review suggested by McNamara was a tactic of delay. McNamara disagreed, saying that much progress had already been made in technical meetings preparing testimony for the Stennis Committee and that more progress could be made in further discussions. He had been trying to rebut the positions of test ban opponents who were wrong in their facts.

Fisher supported Foster's position, saying that the April 1, 1963, U.S.-U.K. memorandum presented to the disarmament conference reflected a governmental position approved by the president and that he, Fisher, hadn't thought any problems remained other than the Plowshare one. He asked what was in the draft treaty that had not been covered by the April 1 memorandum, which the Department of Defense had approved.

McNamara said that he himself fully supported the draft treaty, but that was not true of the Joint Chiefs. He repeated that we must avoid arguing among ourselves before Congress. McCone supported McNamara to the extent of saying that he hadn't heard the Joint Chiefs agree to the present draft treaty at any meeting.

Abram Chayes* pointed out that the staff of the Stennis Committee had a copy of the April 1 memorandum so there was no way the Chiefs could avoid being asked where they stood on its contents.

---

*Legal adviser to the Department of State.

McNamara said he supported the present draft treaty because he felt that the United States was ahead and that a test ban would freeze our superiority. AEC laboratory directors, however, had made statements concerning the technical facts before the Joint Committee, and the Joint Chiefs relied heavily on the laboratory directors. Wiesner said the laboratory directors were not in a position to judge overall policy considerations.

Rusk said he didn't quite understand the Chiefs' position. He said he would not dare to take a foreign policy position that differed from that of the president. McNamara said this was a complicated problem. There was a clause in the law that enabled the Chiefs to present their personal opinions to Congress. This law was being interpreted by the Congress as *requiring* the Chiefs to give their personal opinions when asked. General Taylor said he would be glad for the president to say that the Chiefs' views were privileged because they were his technical advisers. He did not feel this was practical, however.

Fisher referred again to decisions made at the February 18 White House meeting, as reflected in the document tabled in Geneva on April 1, and wanted to know whether we were withdrawing from those positions. McCone said he saw no purpose in discussing the draft treaty and hadn't understood this was the purpose of the meeting.

Taylor asked whether it was possible to reopen past positions in view of the Harriman mission; he would hate to have the newspapers reporting the Chiefs opposed a test ban while Harriman was in Moscow.

Rusk doubted that any amount of discussion would ever bring the technical people to agree among themselves. McNamara referred to statements by R. W. Henderson, a scientist at Sandia Laboratories, and John Foster, director of the Livermore Laboratory, to the effect that our warheads could not penetrate to Soviet targets unless further tests were undertaken to correct defects. Such statements were inaccurate and had to be refuted on the record. Until this was done it was difficult for the Chiefs to take a different position.

Taylor said one of the AEC laboratories claimed that 80 percent of the testing the Soviets would want to do could be done clandestinely without being detected. Nitze thought this might be true.

Taylor said that the Chiefs were conscientious men sincerely concerned about national security. He invited Foster and his experts to meet with the Chiefs and tell them where they were wrong. Foster accepted the invitation. [I am not aware that such a meeting ever took place.]

Rusk said we were faced with the problem that Harriman was going to Moscow to discuss the test ban within a month and we needed a position. He asked whether there was anything in the draft comprehensive treaty that had not been approved by the president except the Plowshare annex. Fisher said there was not and cited again the February 18 meeting and the April 1 memorandum. McNamara said there was no question about the president's position and the Department of Defense supported it, but the Chiefs had reservations.

Rusk said that the basic position on the test ban had been approved by the president and that Harriman could enter into talks on the basis of this position. It was up to those who wanted a change in the position to take the initiative to seek the change. McNamara said he hoped that

Harriman would not table this particular draft comprehensive treaty in Moscow and that we would not resurface it before the Moscow talks began.

Rusk said that the draft treaty reflected the present U.S. position. Unless the position was changed by the president, it would be the position taken by Harriman. He thought it was consistent with all the interests of the country, including national security. He did not see any question of whether there was an approved position. The question to be discussed was how to handle discussions with Congress on the U.S. position.

McNamara asked whether there was any intention to table a draft treaty before Harriman arrived in Moscow, and Foster said there was not. McNamara hoped the Principals would leave it that way. He wanted to get together with Wiesner next week to draw together the divergent views of the various scientists. Wiesner said this perhaps could be done by updating the reports resulting from the previous meeting of scientists.

Kaysen concluded that discussion with Congress of the basis for the Harriman mission should be avoided if possible.

Nitze stated that, while it was difficult to support the test ban treaty on national security grounds alone, it could be supported on foreign policy grounds. Rusk said it was his impression that the Principals had all agreed that the risks to national security from an unlimited arms race were greater than the risks from a test ban treaty.

On June 21 I attended a further meeting regarding the Harriman mission. This was at the White House, with both the president and Harriman among those present. At this meeting the U.S. position still appeared to be up in the air on a number of detailed points, but the basic issue of whether Harriman could negotiate on the basis of the West's August 1962 draft treaties appeared to have been settled in the affirmative.

The president referred to an article in the *Economist* and inquired whether the British had changed their minds on the need for onsite inspection. Foster said the best British scientists agreed such inspections were needed. The president asked whether we had a mutually acceptable paper with the U.K. on this matter. McNamara replied that we didn't even have such a paper on our own position, including what could be accomplished by clandestine testing. The president said we should have a summary of what the Russians could accomplish in about five to seven years of clandestine underground testing. Bundy said that Sir William Penney had written a paper on the subject and had concluded they would not be able to change the strategic balance.

The president asked whether Harriman would be getting together with Lord Hailsham. Harriman said they planned to meet a day or two before they were due in Moscow.

Foster asked whether Harriman should introduce the idea of granting each side a quota (number and yield) of underground tests under a comprehensive treaty. Bundy pointed out that Congressman Hosmer favored this and that it had some political appeal in the country generally.

The president asked how Harriman might handle the discussion with respect to the Chinese development of nuclear weapons capability. Bundy thought the Russians might insist that the Chinese desist from their nuclear weapons development.

The president asked what the objection was to the nonaggression pact suggested by Khrushchev. Rusk replied that we would need assurance that the Berlin situation would remain unchanged before we could consider such an approach.

The President Abroad

Kennedy left on a trip to Western Europe on June 23, 1963. His first stop was in Bonn where, accompanied by Rusk and others, he called on Chancellor Konrad Adenauer and his ministers. A primary purpose of the call was to brief the Germans on the upcoming Moscow talks. Accounts of this meeting indicated that Kennedy remained deeply pessimistic despite the auguries of hope since his American University speech two weeks before. The president's pessimism was evident at a Bonn news conference, where one of the questions addressed to him was: "Is there any possibility that these Moscow talks will be concerned with the nonspreading of nuclear weapons?" The president responded with his usual characterization of the prospect of more nuclear powers as a "highly dangerous situation." He then added: "When Pandora opened her box and the troubles flew out, all that was left in was hope. Now in this case, if we have a nuclear diffusion throughout the world, we may even lose hope."

Following a stopover and speech in Frankfurt—the speech devoted to issues of Europe and the Atlantic Alliance—the president made a tumultuous visit to West Berlin where he delivered the famous *"Ich bin ein Berliner"* speech. His words here, perhaps born of shock at seeing the infamous Berlin Wall, seemed strangely out of accord with the improving East-West climate and his own hopes for the impending Moscow talks. Most singularly inappropriate seemed to be the following: "There are some who say in Europe and elsewhere that we can work with the Communists. *Lass sie nach Berlin kommen!* (Let them come to Berlin!)" This passage, and others nearly as abrasive, apparently took by surprise and dismayed others in Kennedy's entourage.[4] Later the same day the president himself had second thoughts and made a clarification in remarks at the Free Berlin University: "As I said this morning, I am not impressed by the opportunities open to popular fronts [alliances of parties of the left, including Communists] throughout the world. I do not believe that any democrat can successfully ride that tiger. But I do believe in the necessity of great powers working together to preserve the human race."

After Berlin, Kennedy made a sentimental trip to Ireland, visiting Dublin first and then several small communities where he had familial ties.

On June 29, Kennedy arrived by helicopter at Birch Grove, Macmillan's summer home thirty-six miles southeast of London. Here there was an important U.S.-U.K. discussion of some outstanding problems, principally the test ban negotiations and the proposed mixed-manned NATO nuclear naval force.

On the test ban, there was important ground to cover. The British were concerned that there might be some weakening in the American desire for a treaty, perhaps based on what they had heard about objections by the Joint Chiefs of Staff and the AEC laboratories. Also, as indicated at the White House meeting on June 21, differences in view between the two countries had surfaced during the preceding months on such questions as the number of inspections, and these differences had to be resolved so that there would be a coordinated approach in Moscow.

Very little has been reported about this meeting at Birch Grove. Perhaps this was because, as Macmillan notes in his autobiography: "All the serious discussions took place between him [Kennedy] and me alone, with sometimes Private Secretaries to record decisions."[5]

Not that others were not present at Birch Grove. From the U.S. side there were Rusk, Bundy, Salinger, John McNaughton (general counsel of the Department of Defense), and to handle technical matters Franklin A. Long. For once, the British contingent outnumbered the Americans, including Lord Home, Ormsby-Gore, Lord Hailsham, Lord Privy Seal Ted Heath, Secretary of State for Commonwealth and Colonies Duncan Sandys, and two technical experts, Sir William Penney and Sir Solly Zuckerman.

Long recalls that Kennedy and Macmillan brought out from their meeting a list of technical questions for which they wanted answers by 10:00 A.M. the following morning. He (Long) and McNaughton worked until 3:00 A.M. on the answers, then arose at 6:00 A.M. to confer with the British experts. Thus, an agreed U.S.-U.K. memorandum was presented to the two principals by the 10:00 A.M. deadline.[6]

Macmillan's description of Kennedy's visit, which lasted but twenty-four hours, is poignant indeed:

> From the very first moment when the President's helicopter flew in and landed in the park until his departure there was a feeling

of excitement combined with gaiety.... I can see him now, stepping out from the machine, this splendid, young, gay figure, followed by his team of devoted adherents. . . . Inside the house it seemed more like a play, or rather the mad rehearsal for a play, than a grave international conference. There was none of the solemnity which usually characterizes such meetings. After all, we were all friends and many of us intimate friends. . . .

It was of course sad to realise how illness and pain had already laid their hands on this buoyant and gallant figure. His specially constructed bed had to be brought, on which alone he could get comfort. I obtained, and still cherish, a rocking chair which he used throughout our talks. But none of these disabilities seemed to have the slightest effect upon his temperament. Of our party, as doubtless of many others, he was what is called "the life and soul". . . .

Far too soon, the visit came to an end. It was time to go. He went, as he came, by helicopter. Before he said goodbye we discussed once more our plans for frequent communication, by telegram or telephone; with another meeting before Christmas or, at the latest, in the New Year. Hatless, with his brisk step, and combining that indescribable look of a boy on a holiday with the dignity of a President and Commander-in-Chief, he walked across the garden to the machine. We stood and waved. I can see the helicopter now, sailing down the valley above the heavily laden, lush foliage of oaks and beech at the end of June. He was gone. Alas, I was never to see my friend again.[7]

From Birch Grove, the president went on to the final stop on his European itinerary, Italy, where he met with the Italian leaders of all parties including Communist, and with the pope. When arrangements for the trip were being made, Kennedy had hoped this meeting would be with John XXIII, but that charismatic leader had died but four weeks earlier.

Summing up the trip as a whole, Arthur Schlesinger wrote with pardonable exaggeration: "In the summer of 1963, John F. Kennedy could have carried every country in Europe."[8]

Toward a Limited Treaty

Kennedy's pessimism about prospects for a test ban treaty seemed to stem mainly from the impasse about the modalities and number of onsite inspections, and secondarily from the similar deadlock about the number and location of automatic, unmanned seismological stations. Both of these matters had reference to a *comprehensive* test ban treaty. The president still appeared to give less emphasis to the possibility of a *limited* treaty prohibiting tests only in those environments—the atmosphere, oceans, and outer space—where onsite inspections and the automatic stations would be unnecessary. It is true that the Soviets had rejected the idea of a limited treaty when it was suggested by President Eisenhower in 1959 and again when it was offered in the Kennedy-Macmillan proposal of September 3, 1961. Administration analysis had indicated also that a limited treaty that would permit underground tests would be less effective in restricting the proliferation of nuclear weapons, the president's primary concern. A chain of events was soon to make it clear, however, that a limited treaty might be the only option attainable.

That chain began in the U.S. Senate. During May 1963 Senator Joseph S. Clark of Pennsylvania conducted a private survey of his colleagues. He concluded that the comprehensive treaty then being proposed by the United States would fall ten votes short of the two-thirds needed for ratification. This bore out what Senator Pastore had written to the president in March when he expressed doubt that he would be able, as floor leader, to obtain Senate ratification of the somewhat different comprehensive treaty then being proposed by the West. On May 27 Senators Dodd and Humphrey and thirty-two other senators cosponsored a resolution favoring a limited treaty banning tests in the atmosphere and oceans. This marked quite a turnabout for Dodd, who had previously been an outspoken opponent of any test ban agreement. The senator himself attributed his change in view to a publicized correspondence between himself and ACDA Director William Foster. Dodd found some of Foster's arguments persuasive. Then, on June 10, 1963, Harold Wilson, leader of the British Labour Party, had a three-hour conversation with Khrushchev during which Wilson gained the impression that the Soviet leader was withdrawing his offer of two to three onsite inspections per year and that chances for a comprehensive test ban agreement were therefore faint. Wilson felt that prospects for a limited treaty, however, were quite good. The Joint Chiefs of Staff too were opposed to a comprehensive treaty as then drafted but more amenable to a limited test ban.

The agenda of the Moscow talks was all but sealed by a speech delivered by Khrushchev in East Berlin on July 2. He again accused the West of demanding inspections for espionage purposes and stated that there could be no bargaining on this matter. The Soviet Union would never "open its doors to NATO spies." He then made this important declaration: "Having carefully weighed the situation, the Soviet Union, moved by a sense of great responsibility for the fate of the peoples, . . . [and] since the Western Powers are impeding the conclusion of an agreement on the cessation of all nuclear tests, *expresses its readiness to conclude an agreement on the cessation of nuclear tests in the atmosphere, in outer space and under water"* (emphasis added).Khrushchev proposed that such a limited test ban treaty be coupled with a nonaggression pact between NATO and the Warsaw Pact countries.

Instructing Harriman

On July 9, two days before Harriman's departure, I attended a meeting at the White House intended to reach final understanding on the negotiating positions he was to take. The meeting was attended by the president, vice-president, Harriman, Robert Kennedy, Rusk, McNamara, McCone, Foster, Wiesner, Bundy, Kaysen, Nitze, Taylor, McNaughton, and others. A disturbing disclosure at this meeting was that the Joint Chiefs now appeared to have doubts about whether they could support even a limited test ban.

> Rusk initiated the discussion by referring to a memorandum of instructions to Harriman, then in draft form. He said that one of the problems would be our attitude toward having a limited quota on underground tests for each side under a limited treaty, instead of exempting underground tests from the treaty altogether. Rusk suggested that Harriman should seek further instructions if this question arose. The president asked how many would be a sensible quota. Foster said he thought the idea of a quota was not a good one, although it might be better than no test ban at all. Rusk said he preferred a ban on atmospheric testing together with continued negotiations to broaden it to include underground testing.
>
> Rusk also mentioned the need for a clear understanding of what was meant by an atmospheric test. Foster read the definition from the draft treaty tabled by the West on August 27, 1962. It said that a test that broke the surface of the ground but did not produce radioactivity detectable outside the exploding country's boundaries would not be considered an atmospheric test. I said this was a good definition. [Interpretation of this definition was later to prove of key importance in determining the fate of the Plowshare program.]
>
> There was discussion of Khrushchev's desire to couple a test ban treaty with a NATO-Warsaw Pact nonaggression treaty, and it was agreed that Harriman would make no commitments in this area.
>
> The president suggested that Harriman's reports from Moscow be kept confidential. This would require an agreement with the prime minister on the dissemination of news.
>
> The president raised the question of whether Harriman might actually sign an agreement or whether this should be reserved for a summit meeting, as the British seemed to prefer. Rusk was of the opinion that Harriman should conclude an atmospheric test ban agreement on the spot if this was feasible, but Bundy raised the question of the need to check with the French. The president asked whether anything could be done to bring the Chinese in line, but Harriman said it was doubtful the Soviets would even discuss this problem.
>
> General Taylor said he thought we should study again whether an atmospheric test ban was to the advantage of the U.S. The president said that the standing position of the U.S. was in the affirmative. Taylor said

that perhaps Foster should investigate the pros and cons of an atmospheric test ban both with and without a quota of underground tests. McNamara said he thought a formal government discussion of this problem at this time was not desirable. The president agreed. He said he would be glad to have the individual positions of the Chiefs of Staff, but he didn't want an attempt made to arrive at a collective position. Rusk felt that the time for a review of the desirability of a limited test ban had passed; the decision had already been made.

While Kennedy appeared at this meeting to have repressed the opposition of the Joint Chiefs, a heavy price ultimately would have to be paid for their support of the treaty.

Following the meeting of July 9, the "Instructions for Honorable W. Averell Harriman" were revised and formally issued to him.

The document was broadly couched, as was befitting an emissary of Harriman's experience and judgment. On the specific issue of a test ban, Harriman was told that the achievement of a comprehensive test ban remained the U.S. objective. If that was unobtainable, as seemed likely in view of Khrushchev's July 2, 1963 speech, he was to seek a limited treaty in three environments (atmosphere, water, space) along the lines of the Western draft treaty of August 27, 1962.

Harriman was authorized to explore Soviet intentions about a nonaggression pact but was instructed to keep this matter separate from the test ban treaty.

The instructions concluded by authorizing Harriman to explore any other matters the Soviets wished to raise.

Benjamin Read, undersecretary of state for management in the Carter administration and a long-time associate of Harriman, has testified to the latter's own view of the instructions: " . . . in reminiscing about this in subsequent days, [he] has told me many times that in his opinion these were the absolute ideal instructions. They were to get an agreement and come home. They didn't attempt to tell him all the tactical dos and don'ts in advance as was the case in later days in the Vietnam negotiations."[9]

Uncertainty

Notwithstanding Khrushchev's July 2 remarks in Berlin about his willingness to accept a three-environment test ban, members of the administration, including Harriman himself, were far from certain that such a treaty on terms acceptable to the United States was "in the bag."

It was noted that Khrushchev's July 2 offer of a limited test ban had been coupled with an insistence that a nonaggression pact between NATO and the Warsaw Pact nations be signed at the same time. This proviso had been repeated in a message that Khrushchev sent to Prime Minister Macmillan on July 11. For reasons that were made evident at the conference table, such coupling was unacceptable to the United States, but it was not at all clear whether Khrushchev could be persuaded to abandon it. In the view of some, the nonaggression pact was Khrushchev's primary goal in the talks.

There was also concern that the Soviets would insist on a moratorium on underground tests as a price for the test ban agreement, a requirement that would have ensured defeat of the treaty in the Senate. This concern arose in part from a statement by Khrushchev in his July 2 interview that his offer of a limited test ban repeated a similar proposal made previously. The record showed that the only previous Soviet offer of a limited test ban, in November 1961, had been coupled with a demand for an underground test moratorium. As far as could be determined, there had been no change in Soviet opposition to underground testing.

Ambassador Harriman shared some of the doubts about his mission's prospects. He felt that Khrushchev's choice of July 15 as the date for the talks was so close to the date for impending talks with the Chinese that it might mean he wanted to use the United States in some way as a whipping boy or lever to pry concessions from the Chinese. Harriman believed that China had to be Khrushchev's major preoccupation at this time.

The diplomatic atmosphere may also have deteriorated slightly since its dramatic improvement following President Kennedy's American University speech on June 10. The president's own somewhat belligerent speeches in Germany ("*Ich bin ein Berliner,*" for instance) were in part responsible for this. In his July 11 letter to Prime Minister Macmillan, Khrushchev indicated that he had taken note of these speeches and that they seemed to have been delivered by "quite a different person" from the one who had given the speech at American University.

Another indication that Khrushchev had not made up his mind appeared in a conversation he held with Paul-Henri Spaak, former Belgian prime minister and, from 1957 to 1961, secretary-general of NATO. In a letter to President Kennedy reporting on this conversation, Spaak quoted Khrushchev as saying that he was prepared to negotiate seriously with the West or to be tough depending on the position taken by the United States.

From all this evidence it seems clear that the Harriman mission involved a lot more than merely wrapping up the details on an agreement already achieved in substance, as some media commentators implied. In fact the outcome depended on what transpired at the bargaining table.

Harriman expressed his own uncertainty about the outcome of his mission as he enplaned for Europe on July 11, stating: "President Kennedy has done everything he can to make it clear that he will cooperate in achieving a test ban. If there is a failure, the failure will be on the part of the Soviet Union." Harriman added that it was too early to judge if the three-nation talks would succeed, and he warned Americans not to get their hopes too high.

PART FIVE

"A Shaft of Light"

18

Twelve Days in
Moscow

Arrival

Harriman played a prominent part in selecting the other members
of the U.S. negotiating team. They were Bundy's deputy, Carl Kaysen;
ACDA Deputy Director Adrian Fisher; William Tyler, assistant
secretary of state for European affairs; and John McNaughton, general
counsel of the Department of Defense. It will be noted that there were
no technical specialists in this group. This was deliberate on Harriman's part. He expressed his view on this some years later in Senate
testimony:

> These matters have got to be left to the political leaders of our
> Nation. The expert is out to point out all the difficulties and
> dangers . . .but it is for the political leaders to decide whether the
> political, psychological and other advantages offset such risks as
> there may be.[1]

The negotiators were not without technical support, however.
Accompanying the mission as technical advisers were Franklin A.

Long, ACDA Assistant Director for Science and Technology, and Frank Press, a seismologist at the California Institute of Technology.

The delegation departed for Europe on July 10, 1963. They stopped first in London for discussions with their British counterparts. The full U.S. and U.K. teams met for an hour on July 12. Here Harriman made the acquaintance of Lord Hailsham. *

On July 12, Prime Minister Macmillan gave a luncheon for the U.S. and U.K. negotiating teams, following which he asked Harriman to stay on for a private discussion. During this talk the prime minister agreed to instruct Hailsham to support the U.S. position on any points of disagreement. With the exception of one incident later on, when Hailsham thought Harriman was jeopardizing the treaty by being too tough, the leadership of the United States was thereafter unchallenged.

On the morning of July 15, the date that Khrushchev had set weeks before, the Western delegations arrived in Moscow. Harriman felt that the choice of Moscow as the locus of negotiations was a fortunate one. As he told me:

> I have always thought that Moscow was the place to hold negotiations of this kind. We dealt with Gromyko in the daytime. He obviously couldn't make the important decisions, but he'd consult with Khrushchev that night and then would give us the Soviet decision and be pressuring us for our response the next day. For our part, we were often unable to get an answer before thirty-six hours, partly because of the eight-hour difference in time.[2]

While the U.S. side could not match the Soviets in speed, the way in which Harriman's group in Moscow coordinated its activities with the president and others in Washington contributed to the success of the negotiations.

Kennedy insisted on maintaining very tight security on the progress of the negotiations. Benjamin Read, who was at that time executive secretary of the State Department, described the president's attitude in his Kennedy Library Oral History interview:

> He had worked up a passionate concern that a subject of this importance not be jeopardized by premature leaks. And he knew that the Russians had a similar rabid concern about discussions getting out prematurely. So he was really very, very adamant that this enterprise, which he put great stock in, not be spoiled by indiscreet handling.

* This account of the negotiations relies on cables between the Harriman mission and the State Department released under a Freedom of Information Act request; on Harriman's recollections, refreshed to a degree by the released cables and communicated privately; and on other sources as noted.

Read described the procedures followed on the Washington end:

> Harriman and others in the delegation would dispatch cables to the [State] Department. . . . They would come in frequently, sometimes reporting, but sometimes asking for instructions on how to proceed on a given issue. . . . We fell into the regular practice of going over to the White House at about seven o'clock or eight o'clock in the evening with the Secretary [Rusk], George Ball, and Bill Foster. Bob McNamara would be there. John McCone would be there. . . . The group was added to as the discussions wore on in Moscow; [U. Alexis] Alex Johnson became part of it almost from the beginning. Ed Murrow was called in on a number of occasions. . . . Ted Sorensen sat in on the last two or three days. . . . [Llewellyn E.] Tommy Thompson was brought in as an old Soviet hand whose judgment was respected by the whole group.
>
> We'd meet first in the Cabinet Room, and then usually the president would join us after we'd had a preliminary go-round and would stay with us anywhere from a half-hour to an hour, until we reached agreement on what should be sent out in the way of instructions or guidance to the delegation. . . .
>
> The president showed a devouring interest in the . . . negotiations. He'd delve into the subject with gusto and in considerable detail. And I remember many occasions in which he set the tone of the outgoing instruction very personally and directly in his own words.

While the cables from Moscow were routinely seen only by the handful of officials enumerated by Read, certain others in the administration were kept generally informed and were consulted on matters peculiarly within their sphere of interest or knowledge. I was kept informed, for example, about the discussions on peaceful nuclear explosions.

Harriman, though a veteran of many troubleshooting missions for several presidents, was not prepared at first for the intensity of President Kennedy's interest in the detail of the negotiations. Thus, he recalls being chided on one occasion because his reports were not full enough; on other occasions because they were not prompt.

The procedure of the negotiations in Moscow was described in *Life* magazine:

> The negotiations fell into a daily routine of hard bargaining. Each morning for ten days a drafting committee—made up of disarmament experts from each country: Russia's Semyon Tsarapkin, Adrian Fisher of the U.S. and Charles Darwin (a lineal descendent of the British naturalist)—met at the Spiridonovka Palace and argued out draft versions of the treaty, article by article. Each afternoon this committee presented the results of its effort to a meeting of the full delegations. After the major meeting adjourned, the Western teams went to the U.S. Embassy to plan their next day's tactics in

the privacy of a secure area—an elaborately insulated room designed to foil the Soviet penchant for eavesdropping on important visitors.

This description is incomplete in one important respect. On several days, meetings were held that involved only the three delegation chiefs: Harriman, Hailsham, and Gromyko. Some of the most important deliberations took place at these private sessions.

A Good Beginning

As the negotiations opened on July 15, there were several favorable omens. One was the designation of Foreign Minister Gromyko as the chief Soviet negotiator, indicating a welcome seriousness of purpose. Prior Western speculation had been that the Soviet team might have lesser leadership, possible Kuznetsov or Zorin, each a deputy foreign minister.

Another good omen was the fact that Khrushchev himself remained throughout the first day's discussion, and his good spirits established an unexpectedly relaxed mood for the start of the negotiations. Harriman recalls:

> Khrushchev was very jovial in our first meeting. He said, "Why don't we have a test ban? Why don't we sign it now and let the experts work out the details?" So I took a blank pad which was in front of me and I said, "Here, Mr. Khrushchev, you sign first and I'll sign underneath." That was the jovial way in which we were talking.[3]

At this first meeting, Khrushchev tabled two draft treaties, one for a limited test ban and one for a nonaggression pact. The Soviet test ban draft was simplicity itself. It had only two operative articles. The first said that each party undertook to discontinue test explosions in the prohibited environments: atmosphere, space, and underwater. The second article stated that the agreement would enter into force immediately on signature by the USSR, U.K., U.S., and France.

In response, Harriman gave Khrushchev a copy of the limited test ban treaty the West had introduced in Geneva on August 27, 1962. Harriman and Hailsham then insisted that France be eliminated from the Soviet draft although they agreed that France's ultimate adherence to the treaty would be very important.

While the Soviet draft was somewhat crude in form and indicated that much negotiation over language lay ahead, Harriman was left with the conviction that Khrushchev genuinely wanted an agreement. The discussion about France provided Harriman with an opportunity to raise the question of the potential danger posed by China's budding nuclear weapons program. Khrushchev did not seem disturbed about this. He commented that it would be years before China would have nuclear weapons and that they would not have them in quantities remotely approaching the U.S. and Soviet stockpiles.

Kennedy replied to Harriman's report on the meeting with Khrushchev on the same day, July 15. He stated:

> Your report is encouraging on limited test ban. You are right to keep French out of initial treaty, though I continue to be prepared to work on French if Soviets will work on Chinese, and you should make this clear as occasion offers. I remain convinced that Chinese problem is more serious than Khrushchev suggests and believe you should press question with him in private meeting. . . . I agree that large stockpiles are characteristic of U.S. and USSR only but consider that relatively small forces in hands of people like Chicoms could be very dangerous to us all. You should try to elicit K's view of means of limiting or preventing Chinese nuclear development and his willingness either to take Soviet action or to accept U.S. action aimed in this direction. *

The president began now to demonstrate his political acumen and skill. Feeling that the talks were progressing well, he began to consult senatorial leaders. He also felt that public curiosity required a statement from him and scheduled a news conference on July 18, asking Harriman for guidance as to what he should or should not say. Harriman replied with a warning that both the Soviets and the British would object to any unilateral announcement by the president on the progress of the talks that went beyond what was being given in the daily communiqués. The president accordingly made only a brief statement: "After three days of talks we are hopeful; . . . negotiations . . . going forward in a business-like way; . . . any agreement will be submitted to the Senate; . . . not negotiating on matters affecting [our allies'] rights and interests; . . . negotiations, if successful, should lead on to wider discussions among other nations. . . ." He accepted no questions on this subject from the assembled reporters.

The opening of the negotiations had resolved much of the pre-conference uncertainty and given rise to a general mood of optimism that an agreement would be reached. Nevertheless, difficult issues remained, and the resolution of some of these would require what Harriman described as "bruising struggles." Each side on at least one

---

*The last sentence of this cable possibly indicates that Kennedy might have been thinking in terms of a preemptive strike against Chinese nuclear facilities.

occasion threatened to terminate the talks rather than yield on a point it deemed essential.

Requiem for the Comprehensive

One of the first matters laid to rest in the Moscow negotiations was the small remaining hope for a comprehensive test ban. When Harold Wilson conferred with Khrushchev in Moscow on June 10, he endeavored to persuade the Soviet leader that there had been a genuine misunderstanding of U.S. intentions on the number of inspections. In doing this, Wilson was going over the same ground that Norman Cousins had covered in his visit to Khrushchev. On that occasion Khrushchev had appeared to relent and acknowledge the existence of an "honest misunderstanding." Wilson blamed the misunderstanding in part on Ambassador Dean, who he said was "often vague." Wilson said it would be tragic to lose the possibility of a complete test ban because of such a misunderstanding.

In reply, Khrushchev disclosed his new position. The USSR would continue to accept black boxes but no onsite inspections. If it was a misunderstanding that had led the Soviets to believe that the Americans would accept two or three onsite inspections per year, then it would equally be a misunderstanding of the Americans to think that the Soviets were any longer prepared to offer two or three inspections.

Khrushchev repeated this new position in his July 2 speech in East Berlin. There was some feeling in the administration, however, that he might be taking this position to establish a hard line for bargaining purposes. Thus, Rusk told the French ambassador on July 10: "We do not know the real Soviet attitude on the test ban question. We have no information beyond the Khrushchev speech in East Germany [and] . . . we are prepared to discover that this is not the entire Soviet position. We do not know what the fine print will say on the Soviet side."[4]

It was therefore decided to make one last try for a comprehensive treaty at the Moscow talks. President Kennedy prepared the ground for this effort in a letter to Khrushchev that Harriman delivered personally. The president wrote:

> As Governor Harriman will explain to you, we continue to believe that it will be best if we can get a comprehensive agreement on the end of all nuclear testing and we regret the continuing difference between us on the question of the nature and number of the inspections which would be necessary to give confidence in such a comprehensive agreement. I can only repeat again that there simply is not any interest in using such inspections for espionage of

any sort but I know from your recent statements that you have not accepted this explanation.[5]

Indeed, Khrushchev had not accepted it! He said as much in conversation with Harriman. As the latter remembers it:

Khrushchev said, "The trouble with you is you want to spy. That's your purpose." I said, "That's not true at all." He said, "You're trying to tell me that if there's a piece of cheese in the room and a mouse comes into the room that the mouse won't go and take the cheese. You can't stop the mouse from going for the cheese."[6]

At the Moscow negotiations what little discussion there was of a comprehensive treaty took place during the three-hour meeting with Khrushchev on the first day. In this meeting, Khrushchev ended all doubts about the firmness of his position. An increased number of black boxes would be permitted, but no inspections.

On July 18 there was an exchange between Washington and Harriman that effectively removed the comprehensive test ban from the conference agenda. Harriman's cable reporting the day's developments contained the following:

Question arises how hard to play continuing discussion of comprehensive treaty. Should we make greater efforts to highlight it or leave it at low key? Soviet disposition appears to be along latter lines. Something to be said on both sides. On one hand President has repeatedly stated our goal is comprehensive treaty. Prime Minister has echoed this. Further, it is clear comprehensive ban more effective in preventing diffusion of nuclear weapons. On other side emphasis on comprehensive at this moment appears to diminish value of limited treaty. This undesirable both internationally and at home. . . . Problem arises that undue emphasis on continuing effort toward comprehensive might lead to argument in Senate that ratification should be postponed to await comprehensive. Our own instincts go in direction of low-key treatment.

Washington's reply was to agree with Harriman's recommendation for low-key treatment. Based on this policy, the comprehensive test ban virtually disappeared from the conference agenda.

The finality of this resolution was signaled by the decision to allow seismologist Frank Press to separate himself from the U.S. delegation and return home. Press had been brought to Moscow solely to give advice on the detection and identification of clandestine underground tests, a matter that would not be relevant under a limited test ban.

Before Press departed, an attempt was made to utilize his presence, along with that of the two British scientists, Sir William Penney and Sir Solly Zuckerman, as the basis for a tripartite scientific discussion. This, however, came to nothing, as Harriman reported on July 17.

> Fisher, Penney and Press called on Tsarapkin and asked whether, in view of presence of both U.S. and U.K. scientists there would be any advantage to hold scientific meetings before [Press] left Moscow. Indicated this was not a request to reconsider the decision to work now toward a three-environment test ban but merely preliminary step toward what all sides hope for, namely, ultimate extension . . . to comprehensive ban. For this to be done there would have to be further scientific discussions and the only question was would this be the best time and place.
>
> Tsarapkin replied that Chairman Khrushchev had already indicated they would not accept onsite inspections. Therefore, USSR feels that scientific meetings would serve no useful purpose.

The reader must be aware that I regard the failure to achieve a comprehensive test ban as a world tragedy of the first magnitude. Evidence of the mutual mistrust and suspicion responsible for this unhappy outcome, revolving principally around the issue of onsite inspection, has been repeatedly shown in these pages. To put the matter in its baldest form, the Soviets were persuaded that the United States wanted to inspect in order to spy; many on our side were convinced that without adequate inspection the Soviets would cheat.

While I did not take this position at the time, looking back I tend to agree with those who feel that our concern about Soviet cheating was exaggerated. Certainly the Soviets did not wish to be caught cheating because of the great political embarrassment this would have caused. Since they could not tell with certainty what tests we could detect—and scientific progress in detection techniques had been rapid since the U.S. launched Project VELA in 1959—it is doubtful that the clandestine tests the USSR might have undertaken in violation of a comprehensive treaty would have been militarily significant in the aggregate.

There is still a good possibility that one day there may be a comprehensive test ban treaty, since negotiations to that end have been resumed (see chap. 22). But, as Harriman pointed out to me,

> every time we have failed to come to an agreement and then later resumed negotiations, the new negotiations have been at a much higher and more dangerous level. . . . When you stop to think of what the advantages were to us of stopping all testing in the early 1960s when we were still ahead of the Soviets it's really appalling to realize what a missed opportunity we had.[7]

Gromyko's Aggressive Pursuit of a Nonaggression Pact

When Khrushchev first broached the idea of an East-West non-aggression pact (NAP), Western reaction was mixed. The British responded positively at first. The French and Germans reacted negatively because they felt that a NAP: (1) would imply acceptance of an unsatisfactory status quo, including the division of Germany; (2) would enhance the status of East Germany, even without Western recognition; (3) would make more difficult Western reaction to any Soviet moves against West Berlin; and (4) might create another phony spirit of detente, leading to Western relaxation.

The U.S. position on a NAP was not entirely hostile. A prevailing view was that, framed in a context that assured the present Western position in Berlin, some form of nonaggression arrangement could be advantageous to us by reducing the danger of further Berlin crises.

While the United States thus seemed to have an open mind on the substance of the NAP issue, it was decided before Harriman's departure that we could not negotiate in the Moscow talks on the NAP, since this was a matter that involved our allies as well as ourselves. The most that could be done was to signify willingness to discuss a NAP in an appropriate forum at a later date.

Harriman recalls that when he communicated this position in the negotiations, Gromyko responded in strong negative fashion. He complained that the U.S. and U.K. were not giving sufficient attention to this matter, which was of great importance to his government. Gromyko's reaction was so strong that Harriman felt the Soviets might even withhold agreement on the test ban in order to have their way. Harriman and Hailsham nevertheless insisted that they could see no way of handling the matter in the Moscow negotiations except by mentioning it in the final communiqué as something that the U.S. and U.K. might commend to their allies for sympathetic attention.

Gromyko's first reaction to this suggestion was that mention in the communiqué would not be sufficient. In reply Harriman indicated that the goodwill engendered by a test ban could create an atmosphere favorable to further agreements and pledged that he would report fully and sympathetically on the USSR's interest in a NAP on his return to Washington. (This he in fact did.) Having played out his hand as far as he could, Gromyko then relented. On the basis that the U.S. and U.K. would pursue the NAP idea later on, the Soviet Union would not insist on linking it to the test ban.

After prolonged haggling about language, a communiqué paragraph was agreed to:

> The heads of the three delegations discussed the Soviet proposal relating to a pact of non-aggression between the participants in the North Atlantic Treaty Organization and the participants in the Warsaw Treaty. The three governments have agreed fully to inform their respective allies in the two organizations concerning these talks and to consult with them about continuing discussions on this question with the purpose of achieving agreement satisfactory to all.

In the end there never were serious negotiations about a NATO-Warsaw Pact nonaggression treaty.

A Trade: Peaceful Uses for Withdrawal

Quite early in the Moscow talks the Soviets gave their formal assent to having a three-environment test ban and to much of the language in the U.S.-U.K. draft. They demurred from that draft, however, on two significant points. These concerned its provisions for peaceful nuclear explosions and for withdrawal from the treaty.

It will be recalled that the Western draft of August 27, 1962, provided that peaceful explosions could take place in the prohibited environments if unanimously agreed to and if carried out in accordance with the provisions of an annex which had never been completed. Gromyko argued that having such an exception in addition to permitting underground tests might arouse suspicion in other countries; at least it would reduce the appeal of the treaty. Gromyko also argued that some progress on peaceful uses could be made through underground explosions without having an exception in the treaty. Bearing out Gromyko's point, we made it clear in Moscow that we expected to continue permitted research in this field.

The Soviet position on peaceful uses was something of a surprise since they were thought to have plans at least as extensive as our own for such explosions. Their attitude was made clearer some days later in a conversation between Harriman and Khrushchev while they were watching a Soviet-American track and field competition. In his cable to Washington, Harriman reported:

> He told me of their various long-range plans such as building canals and diverting the Pechora River to flow south to Kazakhstan instead of north to the Arctic. This gave me opportunity to express surprise that he had thrown out our article on peaceful uses. . . . He said he opposed inclusion today since this reservation might be disappointing to world opinion and arouse suspicions. [This was undoubtedly a valid point.] He offered the view that we should have

no difficulty in agreeing on such matters when the subject had been more carefully explored . . . when tensions were relieved by a test ban and reduced by other understandings. Peaceful uses . . . would then meet popular approval.

These comments provide further insight into Khrushchev's vision of the Limited Test Ban Treaty as a beginning step toward a future shorn of much of the existing tension and suspicion. It was basically the same vision President Kennedy held.

A clause in the Western treaty draft provided a procedure for withdrawal if a party determined that some other country had set off a nuclear explosion which the determining party felt might jeopardize its national security. This clause had been included because it was felt that the U.S. Senate, preoccupied with China's nuclear development, would insist on it. Gromyko objected to the clause on grounds that it would raise doubts about the seriousness of the parties' intentions in signing the treaty and, furthermore, because it was unnecessary; the Soviets insistently claimed that it was their inherent right as a sovereign nation to abrogate any treaty if and when their national interest required it. In his view, they did not need a treaty provision to make this possible, nor did we.

In defending the withdrawal clause, Harriman underlined the importance of China to the United States and stated that we could not dispense with an adequate withdrawal provision. Gromyko remained unmoved.

Following these exchanges in Moscow Harriman proposed for the president's consideration that we offer to give up the peaceful uses provision in exchange for Soviet acceptance of a withdrawal clause. In making this suggestion Harriman bore in mind advice given him by Wiesner that the fruition of Plowshare projects was remote in time and that the Plowshare program should not be allowed to stand in the way of a test ban treaty.[8]

Washington agreed with Harriman's approach. The answering cable, as he recalls it, stated that while peaceful explosions had a constituency within the U.S. government, a withdrawal clause was far more important because without it Senate ratification might be jeopardized.

The proferred exchange was agreeable to the Soviets, but once again there had to be some hard bargaining about language. Gromyko objected to the reference in the Western treaty draft to a nuclear test by a signator or nonsignator as the basis for withdrawal from the treaty. He proposed more general language, as follows: "Each party shall in exercising its national sovereignty have the right to withdraw from the treaty if it decides that *extraordinary circumstances* jeopardize the supreme interests of its country." In espousing this language, Gromyko argued that everyone would understand that a nuclear test was the principal "extraordinary circumstance" referred to.

It was unclear in the American delegation why the Soviets objected to a direct reference to a nuclear explosion, but Harriman offered one possible explanation. Bearing in mind that specific mention of explosions by a third party was an obvious reference to China, he cabled: "They want pressure to come on Chicoms from other countries, particularly the underdeveloped, and therefore insist on avoiding language in withdrawal clause which would appear as pressure on China directly by them."

The first reaction of the U.S. delegation, as Harriman recalls it, was to favor accepting the language proposed by Gromyko. The president disagreed. It was the genius of the U.S. organization for this negotiation that the president and his small group of Washington helpers seemed to take on themselves the responsibility of reviewing the matters at issue on the basis of their sense of the U.S. Senate's mind and mood. They would at times see things differently from the hard-pressed diplomats who were faced with the task of wresting concessions from the Soviets.

Kennedy's objection to the Soviet language was that the phrase "extraordinary circumstances" was vague and might lower the value of the treaty in the eyes of senators and the American public by seeming to offer too easy an exit. Harriman was instructed to insist on alternative language provided to him.

Harriman proposed the new language at the next day's meeting: "Each party shall in exercising its national sovereignty have the right to withdraw from the treaty if it decides that any *nuclear explosion* has occurred in the prohibited environments which has jeopardized the supreme interest of its country."

When Gromyko again objected to the direct reference to nuclear explosions, Harriman reacted sharply. He told Gromyko that by rejecting the U.S. language so quickly he was showing a lack of consideration on something about which the United States felt deeply. Harriman recalls further:

> I said, "If we don't have a right of withdrawal, we can't have an agreement," and I picked up my papers and prepared to leave. Hailsham was so concerned that he sent a telegram to Macmillan saying I was so rough with Gromyko that it was threatening to ruin the agreement. Macmillan in turn wired his ambassador, Ormsby-

Gore, who took it up with Kennedy. I heard that when the President got this message all he did was smile. I think his opinion of me rose.

Following this meeting Harriman cabled to Washington that he planned to "sit tight." Washington's answer supported this strategy: "Agree you should sit tight. . . . Suggest temperature might be lowered by informal and discursive discussion of reasons for clause you have proposed."

The suggested discourse revolved about the Western concept of the difference between the *power* to abrogate a treaty and the *right* to withdraw under the terms of a treaty. One can only surmise how Gromyko would have reacted to such a lecture on international law. It did not prove necessary to deliver it. Gromyko, having considered the matter overnight, was ready with a compromise. This was to retain the Soviet phrase "extraordinary circumstances" but to make it more pointed by adding *"related to the contents of this treaty."*

Harriman felt that this was as far as the Soviets could go to meet the U.S. needs without sacrificing the essentials of their own position. He conveyed the recommendation of his delegation that the new Soviet language be accepted. Washington assented subject only to a change in the English translation from *circumstances* to *events*. The word *event* was considered to have special significance in U.S. usage since nuclear explosions were often referred to as nuclear events. It was decided to recommend no change in Gromyko's proposed Russian text since the Russian words closest to *event* did not have the desired connotation.

The Soviets accepted the change in the English translation and another difficult issue had been resolved. It had been done by a considerable exercise of ingenuity on both sides and a clear effort by each to understand the other's problems.

It is ironic to note that when the anticipated trigger event for activating the withdrawal clause—a Chinese nuclear test—occurred in October 1964, withdrawal from the Limited Test Ban Treaty was not even suggested as an appropriate U.S. response. Nevertheless, it is probably fair to say that opponents of the treaty would have made quite a fuss during the ratification debate had the right of withdrawal in response to a Chinese test not been provided in the treaty.

With regard to programs for peaceful nuclear explosions, the years after 1963 have witnessed an odd turn of events. The U.S. program to which the Soviets had objected continued as our negotiators had predicted: experimental explosions were carried out underground to develop economic data and technologies for nuclear excavation and for the extraction of oil and natural gas. The results of these experiments failed to kindle economic enthusiasm in industrial circles, and there were increasing objections from those concerned about the environment and the proliferation of nuclear weapons. Faced with these discouragements, the Plowshare program gradually dwindled and by 1978 had disappeared from the federal budget.

In the renewed negotiations for a comprehensive test ban now going on, it has been the United States, not the Soviet Union, which has argued for a provision outlawing peaceful explosions. Our argument, as stated in the ACDA Annual Report for 1977, was strikingly similar to the argument the Soviets had advanced earlier in objecting to our Plowshare program: "A ban on nuclear weapons tests, to be effective, must be accompanied by a ban on nuclear explosions for peaceful purposes, since no way has been identified to prevent acquisition of significant military benefits in conducting peaceful nuclear explosions."

Continuing the reversal of roles, this time it has been the Soviet Union that has indicated willingness to delay its peaceful nuclear explosions program in order to achieve a test ban agreement.* In November 1977, General Secretary Brezhnev announced that the Soviet Union was prepared to renounce peaceful explosions for a definite period of time at the beginning of a comprehensive ban, with negotiations to continue as to how they might be permitted.

On his return from Moscow Harriman discussed the sacrifice of Plowshare with me. He alluded to the conversation in which Khrushchev offered hope that "if things go as well as we think and tensions are reduced, there is no reason why we couldn't agree on Plowshare projects via an amendment at the appropriate time." As to the ease of amending the treaty, he pointed out that the Soviets had agreed to our treaty provision whereby amendments could be made if approved by unanimous consent of the original three parties plus one-half of the other signers, rather than two-thirds as the Soviets had first proposed.

My conversation with Harriman took place in the context of discussions I was having with Senator Clinton Anderson, who was quite exercised about the exclusion of Plowshare projects from the

---

*With its huge land mass, the Soviet Union is in a favorable position to conduct peaceful explosions without escape of radioactive debris beyond its territorial limits. Between 1965 and 1977 the Soviets are reported to have conducted some forty such explosions. About half were related to oil and gas recovery or storage. Economic data to support claims of the program's success are lacking.

treaty and was threatening to oppose it on this account. Ultimately he supported the treaty, I like to think because of my efforts.

Accession

From the outset both sides had agreed on the importance of having a maximum number of nations adhere to the treaty. In this way it was felt that the treaty might achieve one of its primary objectives, to inhibit the further proliferation of nuclear weapons capability.

To make accession by all nations possible, the conferees readily reached agreement on the following paragraphs as part of Article IX:

1. This Treaty shall be open to all States for signature. Any State which does not sign the Treaty before its entry into force . . . may accede to it at any time.
2. This Treaty shall be subject to ratification by signatory States. Instruments of ratification and instruments of accession shall be deposited with the Governments of the United States of America, the United Kingdom of Great Britain and Northern Ireland and the Union of Soviet Socialist Republics, which are hereby designated the Depositary Governments.

While it was easy to agree on the text of these paragraphs, what was probably the most contentious issue of the negotiations arose on their implementation. The difficult question that arose was how to deal with adherence by nations that one side or the other did not recognize, such as the Republic of China (not recognized by the USSR) and East Germany (not recognized by the U.S.). These countries might not be able to have their instruments of ratification accepted by all three of the depositary governments.

At one point it was suggested that the language of the treaty be modified to permit adherence by all states or government authorities recognized by *any* of the three depositaries. There was, however, a reluctance on both sides thus to call world attention to this awkward problem. Instead, Fisher and McNaughton came up with the idea of leaving the treaty language untouched while reaching an explicit *oral* understanding allowing any one of the three depositary governments to receive the ratification of any country not recognized by all three. The receiving country would then notify the other two and the ratification would be considered valid.

Gromyko indicated that the Soviet Union's interest in having such a provision applied only to one regime, the Republic of China, and that the USSR intended to accept notices of accession by all other parties it did not recognize. As Harriman recalls it, Gromyko said:

"We don't recognize Spain but we acknowledge that it exists. As far as we are concerned, the Republic of China doesn't exist." At another point, Gromyko labeled Chiang Kai-shek's regime "empty space."

Gromyko was concerned that this understanding remain oral, that nothing be written about it. Harriman explained that it might not be possible to prevent all public mention of the agreement since it would have to be explained to the U.S. Senate. Gromyko then said we were free to say whatever we wished about the understanding so long as we stuck to the facts.

Khrushchev: "Up Close and Personal"

During the twelve days of the negotiations in Moscow, Harriman had a number of opportunities to observe Khrushchev in relatively informal circumstances. One of these was at a reception for Janos Kadar, the Hungarian leader. After the formal toasts and speeches Khrushchev called Harriman to join him. A large group of those attending—party officials and diplomats—then gathered round as the two men bantered. It was a situation similar to the famous "kitchen debate" between Khrushchev and Richard Nixon, but this time the conversation was good-humored rather than antagonistic. Harriman recalls that a part of the banter concerned whether he should be considered a capitalist or an imperialist. During the talk Harriman mentioned that he was thinking of going to the track meet between the U.S. and USSR at Moscow Stadium and asked Khrushchev whether he was going. Khrushchev then confided that he had never been to a track meet but that Harriman should certainly go because it was better for the two powers to have foot races than an arms race.

Toward the end of the final day of the track meet, Khrushchev turned up unexpectedly with a large party that included Kadar, Brezhnev, and their wives. Harriman is convinced that Khrushchev came because he knew Harriman was there. Khrushchev asked Harriman to join him in his box high up in the stadium, along with U.S. Ambassador Foy Kohler and Mrs. Kohler. He was in an ebullient mood and grew especially excited when the famous Soviet high jumper, Valery Brumel, broke his own world record. Harriman particularly remembers Khrushchev's reaction to the closing ceremonies when members of the two teams walked around the field together, arm in arm. Harriman recalls: "He and I stood up and there was a tremendous ovation from the crowd which seemed to be watching us as much as the athletes. There were tears in Khrushchev's eyes."

On the afternoon of July 26, Harriman called on Khrushchev at the latter's office for a final conversation. When the talk was finished, Khrushchev suggested that the two of them walk over together to a small dinner party he was giving for the Anglo-American group. On the way from the office to the Great Palace, they ran into quite a large crowd in front of the Palace of Congresses.[9] Harriman cabled what happened next:

> After the afternoon meeting, Khrushchev and I walked across the square in the Kremlin. We passed the new Palace of Congresses on our way to dinner in the Catherine the Great Palace. As we went by there was quite a crowd of people and Khrushchev stopped and talked to them. I remember he pinched a little girl on the cheek, patted another on the head, and shook hands with some of the bystanders who applauded him. He introduced me as Gaspodin Garriman, saying, "We have just signed a test ban and I'm going to take him to dinner. Do you think he deserves it?" They all applauded and cheered. This, together with the way in which he was applauded at the track meet . . . and the crowd which waited to see him . . . and the manner in which in each case he talked to the people, is a fantastic difference from the way Stalin used to live. Stalin never appeared in public and the public was not allowed in the Kremlin. When he went to his Dacha from the Kremlin he travelled at high speed with a car in front and a car behind. . . . The blinds of his car were kept drawn and it had bullet-proof glass.

The picture we get from Harriman's accounts confirms what we learn from other evidence, namely, that Khrushchev was perhaps the most human of all the Soviet chiefs of state, and the most popular.

"The Great Man of the Meeting"

Averell Harriman at the test ban negotiations was a good example of a man who, as the popular expression goes, "hit the ground running." At the moment of his arrival, while still at the airport, he indulged in some gamesmanship, which he later described to me:

> When we arrived at the airport, the press people rushed up and asked all sorts of questions, one of which was, "How long do you think you'll be here?" I felt that if we said that it was a very complicated proposition that would take a long time, the Soviets would have felt a need to string it out a long time or else it would look as if they were giving in to our side. So I said, "Well, now, if Chairman Khrushchev is as interested in having a test ban treaty as President Kennedy and Prime Minister Macmillan are, we ought to be out of here in two weeks." They *got* us out in *less* than two weeks—they were *pressing* us to get out. One cannot be sure but I feel that after reading my remarks Khrushchev may have taken it on himself to prove that he was just as keen for a test ban as the President and Macmillan.

Reflecting on this incident, Harriman added: "A lot of these people who talk so glibly about the Russians don't realize what these men are. They're human beings. They react. If you understand them and know how they react it's much easier to deal with them."[10]

Harriman had, of course, the advantage of being well known to the Russians. During World War II he had served as chief of the U.S. Lend-Lease Mission to both Great Britain and the Soviet Union. After the United States entered the war he was ambassador to the Soviet Union.

Harriman became quite well acquainted with Khrushchev during the latter's visit to the United States in 1959. As Harriman now recalls it: I chanced to be in Moscow a few months earlier and we spent about ten hours together. The talk was forthright. At this time Khrushchev had adopted a very rough manner. He told me that, if we tried to cross the East German frontier to gain access to Berlin after the Soviets concluded the separate peace with East Germany he was threatening to make, then "the rockets would fly and the tanks would burn." I laughed. He asked, "What are you laughing about?" I said, "What you're talking about would lead to war and I know you're too sensible a man to want to have war." He stopped a minute and looked at me and he said, "You're right."

The Soviets had come to expect such plain and direct talk from Harriman and they seemed to appreciate it. Schlesinger quotes someone from the Soviet embassy in Washington as having said to him: "As soon as I heard that Harriman was going, I knew that you were serious."[11]

There is no doubt that Harriman lived up to his favorable advance billing. Khrushchev personally gave voice to this in a letter to President Kennedy which Harriman carried back with him. In addition to comments about the negotiations just concluded and the future of East-West relations, this letter contained the following personal note: "In conclusion I can testify that Mr. Harriman showed himself to be worthy of the recommendation which you gave him in your letter. Furthermore, we never doubted this."[12]

Perhaps most eloquent of all was the testimony of A. Duncan Wilson, a member of the British delegation. His comments, which concerned not only Harriman but the entire U.S. team, were relayed to Robert Barnett of the State Department, who recorded them in a memorandum to Harriman's assistant, William Sullivan.[13] Wilson said that the U.S. delegation was "formidably effective," and that London was "stunned by the power of Governor Harriman's team. Fisher and McNaughton proved to be skillful treaty draftsmen. Carl Kaysen, by virtue of his position in the White House brought to the conversations something which the U.K. delegation could not match. Bill Tyler's knowledge of the whole range of European and Soviet affairs was invaluable."

Of Harriman, Wilson said: "His conduct at the negotiations was impressive. His restraint concealed a capacity for toughness and even anger. With his knowledge of the Russian, the Chinese, the European, the American, and the strictly nuclear elements in the problem at hand, Harriman was the great man of the meeting."

The first night after Harriman returned to his residence in the Georgetown section of Washington, a large group of neighbors gathered outside his house and serenaded him, singing, among other tunes, "For He's a Jolly Good Fellow." It was a touching tribute to a man who had served his country on this as on numerous prior occasions so selflessly and so well.

19

Ceremonies and Reactions

Terms of the Treaty

The official title agreed to in Moscow was "Treaty Banning Nuclear Weapons Tests in the Atmosphere, in Outer Space, and Under Water." Lacking the complications of inspections and other control machinery, the treaty is a relatively brief document, about eight hundred words in total. It consists of a preamble and five articles. (See Appendix for complete text.)

In the preamble the parties state their aim to achieve general and complete disarmament and their intent to continue negotiations for a treaty ending all nuclear tests.

Article I states the principal obligations of the parties. These are (1) not to carry out any nuclear explosions in the prohibited environments and (2) to refrain from abetting any such explosions by others.

Article II states the procedure for amending the treaty. An amendment can be adopted if approved by a mere majority of the parties, provided that all of the three original parties agree. Advice and consent of the U.S. Senate would thus be required before any amendment could become effective.

Article III states that the treaty was to enter into force when ratified by the three original parties. This article also contained the provisions mentioned earlier relating to accession by other nations through the deposit of instruments of accession with the three original parties. The provision by which a nonrecognized regime could make its deposit in friendly capitals only remained an oral understanding.

Article IV contains the clause providing for the right of withdrawal, upon three months' notice, if a party finds that "extraordinary events, related to the subject matter of this Treaty, have jeopardized [its] supreme interests."

Article V deals with authentic texts and the deposit of copies.

When he testified in the Senate Foreign Relations Committee hearings on the treaty, Arthur Dean presented a word by word comparison of the document signed in Moscow with the limited treaty draft tabled by the U.S. and U.K. at Geneva on August 27, 1962. The two texts were basically alike. There were two significant differences. One was the article on withdrawal. Here the difference was primarily semantic. The 1962 draft stated that a party could withdraw if nuclear explosions by another nation threatened its security. The 1963 treaty substituted the euphemism "extraordinary events."

The other difference concerned peaceful nuclear explosions and was more substantial. The 1962 draft provided that explosions for peaceful purposes could take place if unanimously agreed to by the original parties or if carried out in accordance with an annex to the treaty, an annex that had not yet been worked out so that it was not tabled with the draft treaty. The treaty signed in Moscow made no special provision for peaceful explosions. They were dealt with in exactly the same terms as all other nuclear explosions.

Initialing

On July 25 at 4:30 P.M. in Moscow a meeting of the three principal delegates began. The media had been alerted to expect a public initialing ceremony, and newsmen and photographers were waiting outside the meeting room. The discussion, which was devoted to a final consideration of the procedure for accession by unrecognized regimes, took far longer than expected. At length the delegates reached agreement. Harriman felt, however, that he needed authority from Washington to make the agreement final.

If usual procedures had been followed, obtaining Washington's assent might have required as much as thirty-six hours and might have necessitated as much as a two-day delay of the initialing ceremony. This would inevitably have led to press speculation, which both sides wished to avoid, not wanting to focus public attention on the unrecognized regime issue. Kaysen accordingly suggested that authority be sought by telephone and that the call be placed "in the open" from the Spiridonovka Palace in order not to incur delay by calling from the presumably more secure American embassy. Harriman readily assented. As he told me, "I knew they'd be listening whether we called from the one place or the other."

Arrangements were made quickly with the surprised Soviet officials and at 7:00 P.M., Moscow time, Kaysen, with Harriman, Hailsham, and Kohler standing by, placed a person-to-person call to Bundy. At the time Bundy was in the Situation Room with the president, who was speaking to Prime Minister Macmillan on the telephone. Bundy left the line to relay the information to the president. In a short time Bundy returned saying, "Great! Good luck!"

The group then returned to the meeting room, and Harriman immediately asked Gromyko: "Where are the copies of the treaty we are to initial?" Harriman recalls what happened next:

> It was then about 7:15 P.M. Three leatherbound copies of the treaty were distributed, the mineral water bottles were removed from the table, and then the photographers and reporters were admitted. Gromyko, Hailsham and I each made short statements, all to the effect that the treaty was a valuable step that could lead to further good developments. The reporters were intensely curious about why the meeting had taken so long, but Gromyko was able to parry the questions by saying that the important thing was the end result.

Then came the formal initialing. *Life* magazine reported: "As is fitting for an English lord, Hailsham signed the document with a single elaborate letter: *H*. 'Did you see his *H*?' Harriman asked. 'It was very beautiful!' Harriman signed *WAH*, and Gromyko wrote, in Russian letters, *AG*."

First Reactions

On July 26:

> I helped a group work, under the direction of Bundy, on a speech to be delivered by President Kennedy on TV at 7:00 P.M. regarding the atmospheric test ban treaty that was initialed yesterday in Moscow.

President Kennedy's address was a long and thorough review of the case for the treaty, which he described as "a shaft of light cut into the darkness." He made clear the treaty's limitations: the fact that underground tests and nuclear stockpiling could continue; the ease of withdrawal. Nevertheless, while "not the millennium," he considered the treaty "an important first step—a step towards peace—a step towards reason—a step away from war." It could provide the basis for wider agreements. It would arrest the dangers from fallout. It could be a "step toward preventing the spread of nuclear weapons to nations not now possessing them," since the treaty was open for all nations to join. And it could limit the arms race, leaving the United States relatively secure in its nuclear superiority.

Looking forward to the debate over ratification, the president urged his listeners to take part in this legislative process by making their opinions known.

The president concluded:

> . . . now, for the first time in many years, the path of peace may lie open. No one can be certain what the future will bring. No one can say whether the time has come for an easing of the struggle. But history and our own conscience will judge us harsher if we do not now make every effort to test our hopes by action, and this is the place to begin. According to the ancient Chinese proverb, "a journey of a thousand miles must begin with a single step." . . . Let us take that first step.

In the days following the president's address, other world leaders trooped to the microphones to give their assessment of the treaty. Khrushchev's comments, expressed in an interview with *Pravda* and *Isvestiya* correspondents, were notably positive in tone. The excellent impression made by Harriman and the general mood of detente were reflected in Khrushchev's statement: "I should like to pay tribute to the efforts of the Governments of the United States and the United Kingdom and their representatives who were empowered to conduct the negotiations." Like Kennedy, he emphasized that the treaty was only a beginning and urged that the major powers set about "without delay to solve other questions in order to liquidate the cold war."

DeGaulle expressed the view that the treaty had only limited practical importance unless it was the starting point for something else in very different areas. For that reason, while having France's approval, the agreement also awakened its vigilance. He reaffirmed France's intent to proceed with its own nuclear arming.

In an official statement the Peoples' Republic of China characterized the treaty as "a big fraud," since it did not encompass general disarmament or underground tests.

Giving the Senate a Role

Harriman, Hailsham, and Gromyko had merely initialed the treaty. A more formal signing at a higher level had yet to occur.

During the private talk Harriman had with Macmillan on his way to Moscow, the prime minister mentioned that he would like a test ban treaty to be signed at a summit meeting. Khrushchev also was in favor of a signing at a summit meeting, as he indicated in a message to Macmillan on July 11.

Kennedy disagreed with his counterparts on this. He discussed the question with Harriman on the eve of the latter's departure for Europe. The president thought a summit, especially one involving Macmillan as well as himself, would create difficulties in Germany and France. He also bore in mind President Woodrow Wilson's triumphal tour of Europe in 1919, which was followed by the defeat of the League of Nations treaty in the U.S. Senate.

Aside from knowing that he was to oppose a summit, Harriman was ill prepared to make suggestions as to a signing procedure. This was one respect in which the preparation for his mission, otherwise so thorough, fell short. Once a test ban began to seem likely, therefore, attempts began to come to grips with this problem, with the Washington contingent taking the lead.

Emphasis on Senate participation was a prominent feature from the outset. On July 23 Harriman was instructed:

> Advise Soviets that for formalizing of treaty we expect perhaps as many as, but not more than, six Senators to travel to Moscow with Secretary Rusk. It should be left open that the Senators may, repeat may, wish to sign the treaty.

The strategy was obvious. As Harriman recalls telling the Soviets in presenting this proposal, the president's object was to enlist as much senatorial enthusiasm as possible for the treaty, hoping to get a ratification vote far in excess of the required two-thirds. Kennedy felt that the treaty needed to be launched on a strongly positive note to serve its purpose as a first step to a better world order.

Gromyko's initial response to the U.S. suggestion was to make a renewed pitch for a signing by heads of government at a summit conference. He asked if the president would be willing to participate in such an event if it were held somewhere in Europe other than Moscow. When Harriman repeated that the president did not wish to leave the United States for a signing ceremony, Gromyko did not press the summit idea further. The next day he announced that he had discussed the U.S. proposal with Khrushchev and that the Soviet government would be pleased to welcome Rusk and the senators.

The Delegation

Secretary Rusk invited me to be a member of the U.S. delegation attending the signing ceremony in Moscow. We took off aboard Air Force One at 11:00 P.M. on August 2. Besides Rusk and myself, others on the flight were ACDA Director William Foster, Ambassador-at-Large Llewellyn Thompson, UN Ambassador Adlai Stevenson* and, as predicted, six senators. Ambassadors Arthur Dean and Foy Kohler joined the delegation in Moscow.

The six senators had been chosen with a view to having the maximum impact on their colleagues. Those selected came from both parties and were leading figures on the key senatorial committees.

From the Democratic side there were John O. Pastore, chairman of the Joint Committee on Atomic Energy, and the three ranking Democrats on the Foreign Relations Committee which would hold hearings on the treaty: J. William Fulbright, Hubert Humphrey, and John Sparkman. Presaging the hostility of the Armed Services Committee toward the treaty, none of its Democratic members was willing to attend. The Republicans present were Leverett Saltonstall, the ranking Republican on the Armed Services Committee, and George Aiken, the second-ranking Republican on the Foreign Relations Commitee.

Desiring to enlist the maximum in bipartisan support, the administration's first choice among Republicans had been Minority Leader Everett Dirksen and Bourke Hickenlooper, ranking Republican on the Armed Services Committee. Both declined, stating that they desired to preserve their independence.[1]

The near desperation reached by the administration in its efforts to enlist a representative group of senators for the Moscow trip is revealed in Senator Aiken's account of his own recruitment in his interview for the Kennedy Library Oral History Program.

> Around the 26th of July 1963 I received a call from the White House asking if I'd be willing to go to Moscow with a delegation and intimating very strongly that no effort would be made to send a delegation unless I went. The president didn't want a delegation unless it was bipartisan. It was immediately following one of the leadership meetings, and Senator Mansfield [majority leader] had evidently been delegated to call me and I well recall the conversa-

*I have seen in three different books statements to the effect that Stevenson was *not* included in the delegation to avoid stirring up again the partisan feelings engendered by his use of the test ban issue in his 1956 presidential campaign against Eisenhower. But Stevenson was there and showing evident satisfaction at what must have seemed to him a moment of personal vindication. There may at some point have been a tentative decision that Stevenson should not attend but if so it obviously was reconsidered.

tion. Mike started out by saying, "Don't say no; don't say no" until he could tell his story. He finally convinced me that it was important that I should go and, although I would have given anything not to have gone, I agreed.

"A Glorious Day"

Monday morning, August 5, 1963 was but a few hours short (allowing for the difference in time zones) of being exactly eighteen years after the atomic bomb fell on Hiroshima. No notice was taken of this. There was happier business afoot.

Our delegation had an appointment with Gromyko in the Foreign Ministry building from 9:00 to 9:30 A.M. Also present from the Soviet side were Deputy Foreign Minister Kuznetsov, Smirnovsky (head of the American section in the Foreign Ministry), Ambassador Dobrynin, and Tsarapkin.

Reporters and photographers were present in abundance at the beginning. Gromyko and Rusk expressed hope that the Test Ban Treaty would be the first step toward ending the danger of nuclear war. Rusk called on Fulbright, who said he was strongly in favor of the treaty.

From 11:00 A.M. to 12:00 noon the U.S. delegation visited Khrushchev in his Kremlin office. Gromyko, Kuznetsov, Smirnovsky, and Dobrynin were again present. The office was long and narrow. We sat at a table with a green felt top like a pool table. There were windows on the west side, pictures of Lenin and Marx, bookcases.

After an exchange of greetings by Khrushchev and Rusk, Khrushchev said that the Test Ban Treaty was only a first step and that the main problem facing the two sides was Germany. He said that liquidation of the German Democratic Republic would not be a victory for the United States, nor would liquidation of West Germany be a victory for the Soviet Union. A common solution was needed. Rusk agreed that the German problem was fundamental, and he said that he intended to discuss it on this trip with members of the Soviet government. He said we understood the historical reasons why this question was of basic concern to the USSR. We, too, had memories of two world wars. Rusk noted that the German people needed an opportunity for peace so as not to give them reason to start trouble again and observed that there had been a relaxation of tensions in Eastern Europe in the last year.

There was then some bantering back and forth. Khrushchev chided Rusk for referring to certain countries as "the East" instead of as "socialist countries." Rusk said the term *socialist* wasn't definitive since some people in the United States regarded the Kennedy administration as socialist. Khrushchev said: "What kind of a man would say a thing like that!" Rusk observed that the Yugoslav government seemed at times to be less involved in its country's economy than the U.S. government was in the American economy. Khrushchev said that capitalism gave birth to communism, and added: "Let's compete in culture instead of rockets." Rusk echoed this, noting that Seaborg, [Stewart] Udall (Secretary of Interior) and [Orville] Freeman (Secretary of Agriculture) had recently visited the USSR and that advancement of relations continued.

Rusk then called on Fulbright, who recalled Khrushchev's pleasant meeting with the Foreign Relations Committee during his visit to the United States in 1959. He referred to U.S. internal troubles of 100 years ago. These had been overcome and now the South gets along with the "damned yankees." Similarly, the U.S. and USSR could get along—their differences were actually less than many people thought. Khrushchev agreed that the two countries had many common goals. He said, "You go forward on private property, we on common property. We are for everyone, you are for every man for himself." He noted that Udall had praised USSR achievement in power plants. He said that the USSR was spending billions of rubles to solve its agricultural problems. He predicted they would be solved by the 1980s.

Khrushchev invited Rusk to come down to the Black Sea for a dip since his vacation was to begin the following day, whereupon Gromyko said Rusk shouldn't swim toward Turkey, a reference to Turkey's membership in NATO.

On the way out of his office I talked to Khrushchev, and he referred to me as "my old friend." Since we had never met he must have had reference to my recent visit to the Soviet Union, with which he was of course familiar.

Khrushchev impressed me as a very able person. He had an amazingly good sense of timing and was a master of repartee. He seemed to be in the best of physical condition, full of bounce and in unfailing good humor.

Our delegation toured the Kremlin Arms Chamber Museum and other rooms in the large Kremlin palace. We had lunch in the oldest room in the Kremlin, about 500 years old, at a large U-shaped table. There were about 100 guests. Khrushchev, Rusk, Home, and U Thant spoke—all to the effect that the test ban was a symbolic step. After lunch we returned to an anteroom for coffee and brandy. All this ran from 1:30 to 4:15 P.M.

Then at 4:30 P.M., we attended the historic signing of the Limited Test Ban Treaty in Catherine's Hall. Rusk, Gromyko, and Home signed simultaneously. Speeches by each of the signers and U Thant followed. I stood just behind Khrushchev during the entire ceremony, and he and I tipped our champagne glasses together for toasts at least five times. About fifty to sixty press representatives and photographers were present.

At about 5:15 P.M. we attended a huge reception in Georgian Hall (a magnificent chamber!) where Khrushchev pulled a prepared speech out of his pocket and read it. It was a good speech, very much to the point and very well written. It impressed me that on occasions like this the Soviets seemed to be ready with appropriate remarks at the drop of a hat.

Circulating about in the crowd, I had a chance to talk again to Brezhnev and to Petrosyants, Gromyko, Kuznetsov, Dobrynin, Zorin, Tsarapkin, and that grand old military leader, Voroshilov. I noticed that Khrushchev mixed freely among all the people present, maintaining his ebullient good humor.

In the evening I went to the circus and walked through Gorky Park with Senator Pastore.

A glorious day!

And so, in an atmosphere of celebration, the Limited Test Ban Treaty had been brought close to reality. There still lay ahead, however, the hurdle of Senate ratification. With several influential senators declared in opposition, with others (particularly members of the Joint Committee on Atomic Energy) embittered because the treaty made no specific provision for peaceful nuclear explosions, and with the attitude of the Joint Chiefs of Staff in doubt, the outcome in the Senate was far from assured, although most people thought ratification was probable.

20

The Senate Consents

Presidential Efforts

The president transmitted the Limited Test Ban Treaty to the Senate on August 8, 1963, "with a view to receiving . . . advice and consent." In his transmittal message he cogently summarized the arguments for the treaty:

It advanced, though it did not ensure, world peace; it was "a first step toward limiting the nuclear arms race."

By prohibiting assistance to testing by other nations in the prohibited environments and by virtue of being signed by many potential testers, it was "an important opening wedge in our effort to 'get the genie back in the bottle.' "

It would "curb the pollution of our atmosphere."

The treaty could not be amended without consent of the Senate.

American nuclear progress would not be halted. Underground testing, in which the United States had more experience than any other nation, would continue.

The treaty would preserve the relatively favorable nuclear position of the United States, whereas unrestricted testing—"by which other powers could develop all kinds of weapons more cheaply and quickly than they could underground—might well lead to a weakening of our security."

There was little to fear from Soviet cheating: the political risks of detection outweighed the gains a violator might achieve.

The president concluded: "To govern is to choose; and it is my judgment that the United States should move swiftly to make the most of the present opportunity and approve the pending treaty."

Although prospects in the Senate looked favorable, Kennedy persisted in the pessimism that seemed always to pervade his attitude toward this most treasured of goals. As Sorensen noted:

> The president desired an overwhelming vote, but his chief concern was to get the necessary two-thirds, about which he was more pessimistic than many of us thought he should be. He was afraid that the natural opposition of the Republicans, plus the opposition of the Southern Democrats led by Senators Russell and Stennis, whom he knew had great influence, could easily put together one-third of the Senate plus one and prevent consent to ratification altogether. So while he desired an overwhelming vote, his immediate concern was getting the two-thirds vote.[1]

Kennedy had started early and worked hard to put the Senate in a favorable frame of mind. At each turn in the road he and leading members of the administration had been scrupulous about informing and consulting with Senate leaders. While negotiations were in progress in Moscow, Rusk briefed the Senate Foreign Relations and Armed Services Committees as well as the Joint Committee on Atomic Energy. After the treaty was signed, Rusk, Harriman, and Fisher conducted a further series of briefings. Having the bipartisan group of senators attend the signing ceremony was of course an important gesture, although the idea of having senators actually sign the treaty was, for some reason, abandoned.

After the treaty was sent to the Senate, Kennedy personally took a leading part in the drive to influence public opinion. He encouraged the creation of a Citizens' Committee for a Nuclear Test Ban and personally advised its officers, who included Norman Cousins, on the strategy for an effective campaign. As Cousins narrates:

> He reiterated the need for important business support and suggested a dozen names. He said that scientists such as James R.

Killian and George B. Kistiakowsky would be especially effective if they could be recruited. He felt that religious figures, farmers, educators, and labor leaders all had key roles to play and he mentioned a half dozen or more names in each category. Then he went down the list of states in which he felt extra effort was required. He was confident that organizations such as [he named various liberal organizations] were going to continue to give full support to the issue, but he wanted to be sure that they did not make the test ban appear to be solely a liberal cause.[2]

The president also suggested to the committee's leaders which senators might be targeted in a constituent mail campaign. At the appropriate time, as will be noted later, he conveyed assurances to the Senate leadership in order to allay various misgivings. Kennedy also played a leading role in orchestrating the presentations of administration witnesses before the Foreign Relations Committee. For example, the day before I was to testify I went over certain aspects of my statement with the president at the White House.

In sum, Kennedy threw himself into the ratification process with every resource available to him. He did so out of a sense of conviction which he probably felt for no other measure sponsored by his administration. Indeed, he confided to his associates that he "would gladly forfeit his re-election, if necessary, for the sake of the Test Ban Treaty."[3]

The Hearings Overall

The treaty was referred for study to the Committee on Foreign Relations, which began hearings on August 12, four days after the Senate received the president's message. Chairman Fulbright invited members of the Committee on Armed Services and the Joint Committee on Atomic Energy to join his committee during the hearings; certain other interested senators also attended many of the sessions.

The committee hearings and the subsequent discussion on the Senate floor constituted one of the most intellectually demanding debates in the country's history. The matters considered included complex military, scientific, political, philosophical, and psychological questions. To shed light on these questions, thirty-four witnesses, presumed to be specialists in the various fields, were called upon to testify. Written statements from ten other individuals were entered into the record, which occupied more than one thousand printed pages. The Armed Services Committee's Preparedness Subcommittee (the Stennis Committee) also held extensive hearings.

As had become customary, the technical experts disagreed among themselves. Senator Hickenlooper jocularly suggested how senators might resolve any quandary into which this might throw them: "May I call attention to the philosophy stated by one Senator a few years ago? He said, 'Some of my friends are for it, some of my friends are against it, and I always stay with my friends.' "

Rusk and McNamara

The first three witnesses before the Foreign Relations Committee—Secretary Rusk, Secretary McNamara, and I—were each questioned for an entire day.

Rusk, as the leadoff witness, described and interpreted each article of the treaty. He then went over the main arguments for ratification, covering in greater detail substantially the same points the president had made in his transmittal letter.

While acknowledging that the treaty could not ensure against additional countries entering the nuclear club, the secretary noted that "most of the countries with the capability and incentive to develop nuclear weapons over the next decade have already announced that they will accept the self-denying ordinance of the treaty."

The secretary felt that the most important advantage of the treaty was the possibility that it could be a first step toward a better world. "If the promise of this treaty can be realized, if we can now take even this one small step along a new course, then frail and fearful mankind may find another step and another until confidence replaces terror and hope takes over from despair."

In his testimony the next day McNamara made a special point of what might happen in the absence of the treaty, noting that if testing continued indefinitely in all environments the most likely result would be that we would lose our technical lead over the USSR. Also, he felt that, without the treaty and its inhibiting effect on the spread of nuclear weapons, there would be a great threat to world safety through the possible escalation of minor incidents into a nuclear exchange. McNamara saw as the most serious risk in the treaty the danger that it might lead to a kind of "euphoria" that could cause the United States to become lax in its defense efforts.

My Testimony: Could Plowshare Survive?

Without doubt, the most important aspect of my testimony on August 14 had to do with the effect of the treaty on the AEC's Plowshare program for peaceful nuclear explosions. Several senators, perhaps most notably Clinton Anderson, an ex-chairman and a highly influential member of the Joint Committee on Atomic Energy, had let it be known that their support of the treaty had been weakened because its ban on atmospheric testing seemed to exclude the possibility of Plowshare explosions.

When we in the AEC examined the technical facts, however, the situation seemed not so dark. Plowshare was still in an experimental stage. We were not yet ready to embark on the full-scale projects that seemed to have so much promise. (These I described in my testimony as "civil engineering projects such as digging canals, harbors, passes through mountains for transportation purposes and, in general, any application which requires moving vast amounts of material"; also "aids to mining, aids to the recovery of low-grade oil, the development of underground water resources, and above ground water reservoirs . . . within the United States.") The basis for hope that the experimental program could go forward was the confidence that methods could be developed for using nuclear explosives that produced very little radioactivity and for emplacing them in such ways that nearly all the radioactivity would be trapped underground. A small amount of radioactivity might be released but it would "be deposited from the lower atmosphere close to or immediately downwind from the shot site." Consequently, the experiments probably could be conducted if they had a "downwind distance of several hundred miles from the project site to a territorial limit." (Article I of the treaty committed the parties not to carry out any nuclear explosion "if such explosion causes radioactive debris to be present outside the territorial limits of the State under whose jurisdiction or control such explosion is conducted.")

As for the projects themselves, as distinct from experiments, there was always the possibility of a later treaty amendment favorable to peaceful explosions. Even without such an amendment, it appeared that many of the projects could go forward if the experimental program was successful in its development of the requisite technology. Obviously, the excavation of a new Panama canal would be a violation because of the short distance to territorial boundaries, but other projects well inside U.S. territory seemed likely to be permissible.

This optimistic testimony, which had a strong influence in moving Senator Anderson, and perhaps others, from a doubtful to a favorable position on the treaty's ratification, was based on an interpretation of the treaty's language that had been arrived at within the AEC after careful analysis. The key question was what exactly was meant by the treaty's language: "causes radioactive debris to be present outside the territorial limits." If it meant a minute trace of radioactivity that could barely be measured by the most sensitive instruments available, then my testimony could well have been overoptimistic. To us in the AEC it seemed a matter of common sense, however, that the treaty could not, as a practical matter, be enforced if escape of a minute amount of radioactivity—approaching, for example, a single atom, which could cause harm to no one—were considered a transgression. Also, the use in the treaty of the word "debris" seemed to connote a larger amount. Accordingly, we interpreted the intent of the treaty's drafters to be that an underground explosion would be considered a violation only if it "resulted in a quantity of radioactive debris delivered outside of the country's territorial limits *in amounts sufficient to establish that such contamination resulted from a recent test within that country*" (emphasis added).

This interpretation, along with the rest of my prepared testimony, was of course routinely cleared within the executive branch. By April of the following year, however, the Arms Control and Disarmament Agency had come to feel differently about the matter. They became concerned about "possible international political consequences" of adopting criteria of acceptability not agreed to by other parties to the treaty, and called attention to Soviet criticism of the accidental venting of a Nevada underground test. The ACDA began to advocate a very strict and confining interpretation of the treaty. Their point of view prevailed. I was then in a position, looking back, of having seemed to mislead Senator Anderson and others with my optimistic testimony. As will be clear from the foregoing narrative, I did not do so deliberately.

In addition to my comments on Plowshare, I pledged in my testimony that the AEC would continue under the treaty to support vigorous research and development programs in its weapons laboratories and would thus be able to retain able scientists and engineers, attract new ones, and maintain the vitality of the laboratories. This would help the United States to react speedily should the Soviets abrogate the treaty.

The questions asked of me by the senators ranged over a wide ground. The single subject that drew the most questions was the matter of radioactive fallout from weapons tests. I indicated, as I had on other occasions, that the radiation from weapons tests was at a low level, that there was still much scientific uncertainty about the effects of low levels of radiation, that the reduction of fallout was certainly a desirable effect, but that I did not consider the fallout matter to be "as great a problem as some of the other reasons for the test ban."

I understood, of course, the reason for the multiplicity of questions about fallout. A Gallup Poll in early September showed nearly four-to-one support for the treaty among those with opinions; in the Harris Survey the margin was ten to one. Congressional mail and other public expressions made it clear that the fallout question was probably the most important factor leading to this popular support.

The Joint Chiefs and the Four Safeguards

It is fair to say that no testimony was more eagerly awaited than that of General Maxwell Taylor, chairman of the Joint Chiefs of Staff. It was felt that the Joint Chiefs, having the military security of the nation as their prime responsibility, would be certain to point out any military risks the treaty might entail.

General Taylor's prepared testimony was concise and well organized. He began by stating four criteria of acceptability against which the Joint Chiefs had reviewed the treaty:

> First, the U.S. should not accept limitations on testing if the Soviet Union had or could achieve a significant advantage in any militarily important area of nuclear weapons technology which, under the treaty, could not be overcome by the U.S.
> Second . . . clandestine [Soviet] testing should have no seriously adverse effect on the [military] balance.
> Third, the U.S. [should be able] to withdraw without undue delay . . . in the event our national interests were imperiled.
> Fourth, if . . . criteria one and two were not completely met, the treaty must convey adequate compensatory advantages elsewhere.

Taylor then related how the Joint Chiefs had consulted with various officials of the government to help determine whether the treaty met the conditions. I was one of those consulted, having received on July 30, 1963, a letter from the general asking for the judgment of the AEC on a large number of questions.

Regarding the first criterion, the Chiefs found that the United States was clearly ahead in the ability to wage strategic nuclear war and probably also in the ability to wage tactical nuclear war. They concluded that the Soviets might in time catch up in the tactical field and that the treaty might handicap both sides in their development of antimissile missiles and in learning about weapons effects.

As to clandestine testing, the Chiefs felt that the progress the Soviets might make by such means would be "a relatively minor factor in relation to the . . . balance of military strength," especially if adequate safeguards were maintained.

Taylor then recommended four safeguards which the Chiefs thought necessary:

> (a) The conduct of comprehensive, aggressive, and continuing underground nuclear test programs designed to add to our knowl-

edge and improve our weapons in all areas of significance to our military posture for the future.

(b) The maintenance of modern nuclear laboratory facilities and programs in theoretical and exploratory nuclear technology which will attract, retain, and insure the continued application of our human scientific resources to these programs on which continued progress in nuclear technology depends.

(c) The maintenance of the facilities and resources necessary to institute promptly nuclear tests in the atmosphere should they be deemed essential to our national security or should the treaty or any of its terms be abrogated by the Soviet Union.

(d) The improvement of our capability, within feasible and practical limits, to monitor the terms of the treaty, to detect violations, and to maintain our knowledge of Sino-Soviet nuclear activity, capabilities, and achievements.

General Taylor concluded his statement by saying that, if those safeguards were established, the risks inherent in the treaty could be accepted "in order to seek the important gains which [might] be achieved through a stabilization of international relations and a move toward a peaceful environment in which to seek resolution of our differences."

In their questioning of Taylor, several senators sought assurance that the Joint Chiefs had been given full opportunity to comment on the treaty in its formative stages and during the negotiations and that no pressure had been brought on them at any time to reach a favorable conclusion. Taylor was unequivocal in giving these assurances, reciting the extent of the Chiefs' participation in considerable detail.

General Taylor indicated that his presentation represented the "agreed views of the Joint Chiefs of Staff." The committee nevertheless insisted on hearing testimony from the individual Chiefs. Each of them indicated that he had participated in preparation of General Taylor's statement and, with the safeguards Taylor had enumerated, each stated that he supported the treaty. Each also volunteered that no pressure had been put on him to adopt this position.

One surprising aspect of the Joint Chiefs' testimony was the importance they attached to the political effects of the treaty. In doing this they departed from the mold into which senators sought to cast them: of being concerned exclusively with military matters. A revealing colloquy along these lines occurred between Senator Hickenlooper and General Curtis LeMay:

> SENATOR HICKENLOOPER: It has been my impression . . . that the primary responsibility of the Joint Chiefs of Staff . . . is to take care of the military security of the country, that is, the physical security from the military standpoint.
>
> GENERAL LEMAY: That is correct, sir, and we so regard it.

SENATOR HICKENLOOPER: Which . . . was the controlling consideration in the arrival at your conclusion to support the treaty? Was it the military security and advantage to this country that moved the Joint Chiefs or was it the political implications or arguments of a broad nature that had their effect?

GENERAL LEMAY: I would say probably the key factor was political in this case. We examined the military and the technical aspects and came up with a net disadvantage in that field.

SENATOR HICKENLOOPER: In the military?

GENERAL LEMAY: In the military; yes, sir. Then we examined the political gains that were possible, and we came up with a net advantage there which we thought offset the [military] disadvantages if we were able to reduce those disadvantages by the proper safeguards.

SENATOR HICKENLOOPER: General, let me ask you this. I don't mean this question to have disrespectful connotation, but weren't you getting a little out of your field when you let the so-called political advantages, which are basically out of your professional and technical field . . . cause you to come up with an answer which, if left solely to the area of your major competence, would have been a . . . disadvantageous decision?

GENERAL LEMAY: No, sir; I think I must disagree with you there. We have a broader duty, I think, to the country than just considering military questions. . . . We must consider political factors in the solution of our military problems, because they are important, and they do have a bearing on our solutions.

In adopting their broad approach, the Joint Chiefs were probably influenced by President Kennedy. He had talked with them as a group on July 23, 1963, after having discussed the treaty with each Chief individually the week before. In these conversations Kennedy is reported to have asked the Chiefs to weigh both military and political considerations in their evaluation.[4] The president's support of the four safeguards probably also had its genesis at this time. While this support may have obtained the favorable testimony of the Joint Chiefs, it was at a very heavy price for the cause of disarmament.

Edward Teller and Other Scientists

In the estimation of Chairman Fulbright, the most effective testimony against ratification was that presented on August 20 by Edward Teller, at that time associate director of the Livermore laboratory. Teller stated the factors on which he based his opposition:

The treaty was based on prediction in a field that had repeatedly proved itself unpredictable.

It would prevent the U.S. from acquiring knowledge of weapons effects needed for developing a ballistic missile defense, knowledge which Teller believed the Soviets had acquired in their 1962 tests.

Lacking knowledge, we would tend to "substitute brawn for brains," that is, we would rely for safety not on advancing the quality of our weapons but on multiplying their numbers. This would not arrest the arms race—it would stimulate it.

Since underground testing was permitted and was not very costly, the treaty would not deter proliferation.

The prohibitions of the treaty could sow dissension between the U.S. and its NATO allies since it would prevent our allowing them to have control over nuclear weapons in time of need.

Since most peaceful explosions would result in measurable radioactivity, the treaty, unless amended, would severely wound the Plowshare program.

Teller's testimony was presented without any prepared text or notes and was delivered with his usual great force and conviction. Largely for this reason he received far more attention from press and television, particularly the latter, than any other witness. To blunt the effect of Teller's appearance, proponents of ratification, particularly Fulbright and Humphrey, were at pains to lead succeeding scientific witnesses through the points raised by Teller, with a view to refuting them one by one.

The first of these witnesses was Harold Brown. Brown took issue with Teller on the need for atmospheric testing to develop an antiballistic missile (ABM). He felt that our ABM efforts were on a par with those of the Soviets and doubted that an effective ABM system was feasible for either side. He argued that the answer to the ABM problem was to "continue to develop relatively small warheads which would . . . assure penetration by saturation, even of sophisticated and very elaborate ballistic missile defenses." Brown also denied that the Soviets had more knowledge of weapons effects than the United States. Under questioning by members of the committee, Brown stated that he had access to all the information available to Teller, but that the reverse was not true.

Brown obviously was somewhat uncomfortable about being repeatedly pitted against Teller by the questions of the committee members, stating at one point: "I have known Edward Teller for a dozen years. I have been not only a close professional associate, but he has been a dear personal friend of mine. I have had, and do have, the greatest respect for him, and I have had, and do have, a deep personal affection for him. On this matter we disagree. He thinks I am wrong. I obviously think he is wrong."

Technical testimony along the same lines as Brown's was offered by Herbert York, Brown's predecessor as director of defense research and engineering, and George B. Kistiakowsky, who had been President Eisenhower's last science adviser. Kistiakowsky urged the committee to give special weight to the testimony of Brown, whom he characterized as the only witness who could speak with real authority on the ABM problem. York observed that steadily increasing military power had brought steadily decreasing national security: our increases were matched by the Soviets and each advance in the quantity and quality of Soviet weapons raised the potential number of U.S. casualties in a nuclear exchange. He felt that this dilemma had "no technical solution." He agreed with Brown that the answer to the ABM problem was to build an offense that could saturate any defense. He added that "even if we do wish to put great emphasis on our own ABM, the problems lie in the areas of detection, identification and interception, and not in nuclear weapons technology."

Norris Bradbury, director of the Los Alamos Scientific Laboratory, made an eloquent witness. He acknowledged that the treaty had risks, but, "speaking for the majority of the Los Alamos staff," he felt that the risks could be minimized by testing underground and preparing for testing above ground. He characterized the treaty as "the first sign of hope that international nuclear understanding is possible. . . . If now is not the time to take this chance, to count on this hope, what combination of circumstances will ever produce a better time?" Bradbury urged senators, before they became "too bemused with megatons and multimegatons . . . [to] look again at the pictures of Hiroshima and Nagasaki in 1945 after 15 and 20 kilotons, not megatons."

John Foster, Bradbury's counterpart at Livermore, expressed serious misgivings about the treaty, making substantially the same points as had Teller, his close associate. (This disagreement between the directors of Los Alamos and Livermore carried forward a long-standing difference in emphasis between the two laboratories.)

Reservations Proposed

Several witnesses suggested that the treaty be approved only with reservations. Former AEC Chairman Lewis Strauss, who saw no advantage in the treaty but felt that its ratification was likely, urged the Senate to require reservations: (1) making it unnecessary for the United States to give three months advance notice to abrogate the treaty and (2) making special provision for Plowshare projects, both within our own territory and that of friendly nations. Willard Libby, who had been an AEC commissioner when Strauss was chairman, also wanted a Plowshare reservation.

Ex-President Eisenhower submitted a written statement urging a reservation "that in the event of any armed aggression endangering a vital interest of the United States, this Nation would be the sole judge of the kind and type of weaponry and equipment it would employ as well as the timing of their use." The concern of Eisenhower and others who had urged a similar reservation was aroused by certain words in paragraph 1 of Article I:

> Each of the Parties to this Treaty undertakes to prohibit, to prevent, and not to carry out any nuclear weapons test explosion, *or any other nuclear explosion*, at any place under its jurisdiction or control. [Emphasis added.]

The ex-president and the others feared that the words "or any other nuclear explosion" had the effect of prohibiting the use of nuclear weapons in war. In fact, the words in question had been inserted to prevent peaceful nuclear explosions in the prohibited environments. The president, the secretary of state, the State Department's legal adviser, and others had given repeated assurances that there was nothing in the treaty relating to the use of nuclear weapons in war. Nevertheless, the disquiet on this issue was difficult to still.

Harriman recalls being apprised of senatorial worries on this matter during the Moscow negotiations. He then raised the question of including some language in the treaty to cover the point. Gromyko, however, would have none of it, stating that by its terms the treaty related only to nuclear tests and that specifically authorizing the use of nuclear weapons in war was both unnecessary and likely to create an unfavorable impression. Harriman tended to agree with Gromyko and dropped the matter.

The fact that this concern persisted, despite apparent logic and repeated assurances, was testimony to the nervousness felt by many in American public life that any treaty agreed to by the Soviets must involve some hidden trap.

The testimony of Arthur Dean put a damper on the various reservation proposals. He pointed out that any reservation voted by the Senate "would have to be negotiated not only with the Soviet Union but with all of the nations who have already deposited their assent to this treaty." He estimated the number of nations that had signed or signified an intention to sign as approximately 100. Dean urged the senators to "think twice" about making changes in view of the possible consequences, which might include "throwing away any possibility of further negotiations with the Soviet Union." He thought it would be wise "not to be too cynical" about the possibility of further agreements.

This led to a colloquy with Senator Hickenlooper, who pointed out that the Senate had coequal authority with the president in the making of treaties and asked: "What is so sacred about the executive language in this treaty? Why don't we have the right to put language in the treaty or interpret it if we see fit?" Dean agreed that the Senate had that right. He alluded, however, to a line-by-line comparison between the signed treaty and the draft introduced by the West in Geneva on August 27, 1962. Dean pointed out that the wording of the latter had been gone over with the Foreign Relations and other Senate committees and that, except for the absence of a Plowshare annex and for a changed withdrawal clause, the two documents were virtually identical. In effect Dean was arguing that the Senate already had had repeated opportunities to have an impact on the language of the treaty.

Several senators nevertheless remained extremely resentful that the treaty had been opened for adherence by all nations before the Senate hearings on it even began. Senator Jack Miller of Iowa said he considered it "most unfortunate that those who gave Ambassador Harriman his instructions . . . failed to see to it that the treaty provide that until the [three] parties to the negotiations . . . had all ratified the treaty, no other country would be permitted to join. . . ."

Senatorial pique on this matter was widely and deeply felt and led ultimately to an unnecessary but relatively harmless amendment to the instrument of ratification reasserting senatorial prerogatives.

Political Aspects

Marshall Shulman (then a professor at the Fletcher School of Law and Diplomacy, more recently a State Department special adviser on Soviet affairs, and currently a professor at Columbia University) analyzed the treaty from the point of view of Soviet policy and the international political aspects of the relationship between the Soviet Union and the United States.

Shulman felt that the Soviet leadership was seeking a reduction of international tensions in order to consolidate its leadership, both domestically and within the Communist bloc. Turning to U.S. policy, he contended that "if we simply are preoccupied with trying to build security through maximizing our strategic military superiority over the Soviet Union, we can . . . raise doubts about our own intentions which will stimulate response on the part of our adversaries as well as qualms on the part of some of our allies. This may have the effect of diminishing our actual security."

Shulman felt that the major affirmative function of the treaty was to demonstrate that there was an area of mutual interest, that not everything the Soviets thought to be in their interest was necessarily detrimental to ours.

Harold Stassen urged ratification of the treaty to help stop the spreading of nuclear arms and as a first step toward world peace. He noted that the Soviets did not always violate the treaties they signed, having abided, for example, by the Austrian Peace Treaty and the Antarctic Treaty.

Norman Cousins, recounting for the committee members some of the details of his 1963 visit with Khrushchev, expressed the view that Khrushchev had tied his political future to the success of the treaty. It made it possible for him to show some fruits of his policy regarding the Cuban missiles and, by reducing the dangers of war, freed him to deal with the Chinese Communists. He urged the Senate to accept the treaty as one of those things that "might yet make this planet suitable for human habitation."

As its hearings neared an end, the Foreign Relations Committee received testimony from persons representing various groups. Those favoring the treaty included, among others, the AFL-CIO (George Meany); the Federation of American Scientists; the Friends Committee on National Legislation; the Physicians for Social Responsibility; the National Council of the Churches of Christ; the International Union of Electrical, Radio and Machine Workers; and the Cooperative League of the U.S.A.

One of the individual witnesses who testified in opposition to the treaty was Phyllis Schlafly, who was later to achieve prominence as a leader of the opposition to the Equal Rights Amendment. With characteristic restraint Schlafly stated: "If the Senate approves this Moscow Treaty,* then America, the last, best hope of mankind, may be at the mercy of the dictators who already control a third of the world."

The Stennis Committee

The situation in the Senate was complicated by the fact that, while the Foreign Relations Committee was conducting its hearings, the Stennis Committee was continuing its own test ban hearings underway since May 7. These hearings initially addressed the Western comprehensive treaty draft, the focus of the Geneva negotiations

---

*It was the custom of the more extreme treaty opponents to refer to it always as "The Moscow Treaty."

and the preferred objective of the administration. Following the successful Harriman mission, the committee shifted its attention to the limited treaty signed in Moscow.

Eight of the thirteen witnesses who appeared before the Stennis Committee also appeared before the Foreign Relations Committee. These included the chairman and three members of the Joint Chiefs of Staff, as well as Bradbury, Brown, John Foster, and Teller. The remaining five witnesses were active or retired military officers hostile to the treaty.

General Thomas Power, commander of the Strategic Air Command, expressed strong opposition. He argued that the security of the United States depended on having overwhelming superiority over the Soviets and that atmospheric testing was needed to achieve such superiority. Retired Admiral Arleigh Burke, former chief of Naval Operations, was opposed because the treaty did not provide for inspection within the Soviet Union, among other reasons. Retired Air Force General Nathan F. Twining, formerly chairman of the Joint Chiefs of Staff, felt that under the treaty the Soviets would catch up to and surpass the United States in all fields where they did not already lead. Both he and Admiral Burke urged that, if the treaty were ratified, the Senate insist on strict implementation of the four safeguards recommended by the Joint Chiefs.

Conflicting Committee Reports

Both the Foreign Relations Committee and the Stennis Committee published reports on their hearings early in September. The reports conflicted sharply.

The Foreign Relations Committee recommended ratification of the treaty by a vote of sixteen to one, the lone dissenter being Senator Russell Long of Louisiana. The committee's report emphasized political aspects. It acknowledged that a "good part of the Committee's time and attention during the hearings was devoted to military considerations" but then dismissed much that they had heard. The report noted that much of the highly technical testimony was "sharply conflicting." This made it necessary for the committee to bear in mind that "some witnesses had the advantage of possessing all the relevant information." The report identified those witnesses as the secretaries of State and Defense, the AEC chairman, the CIA director, the Joint Chiefs of Staff and the director of defense research and engineering. By inference the committee thus rejected the testimony of Edward Teller.

The Foreign Relations Committee report endorsed the safeguards recommended by the Joint Chiefs and stated the committee's "clear understanding" that the safeguards would be implemented for as long as they were needed. The report emphasized that, on balance, the military testimony the committee had heard should give reassurance to the American people. For example, the testimony had revealed that the nuclear strike forces of the United States were "superior in number and variety" to those of the Soviet Union. Based on such testimony, the committee considered the military risks of the treaty to be acceptably low.

The report concluded:

> The maintenance of a strong military position is clearly essential to the national security of the United States. But exclusive, or excessive, reliance on military considerations could undermine national security by encouraging comparable military efforts by others, thereby strengthening the destabilizing forces adrift in the world, possibly creating new ones. The treaty offers the prospect of a gradual lessening of tensions, of a start toward the progressive elimination of the danger of a nuclear war. Thus, the committee recommends that the Senate give its advice and consent to the ratification of the pending treaty.

The Stennis Committee reached quite different conclusions. This was to be expected; they approached the problem from a different point of view.

An underlying premise in the Stennis Committee's approach was stated early in its report when it stressed "very strongly" that "Soviet secrecy and duplicity require that this Nation possess a *substantial margin* [emphasis added] of superiority in both the quality and the quantity of its implements of defense." Starting from this premise, the committee found that the treaty involved "serious—perhaps even formidable—military and technical disadvantages to the U.S." by obstructing the attainment of "the highest quality of weapons of which our science and technology are capable." It felt that the Soviet Union would not be similarly inhibited.

The Stennis Committee's report was signed by six of its seven members. Senator Saltonstall dissented, stating that the report was "overly pessimistic." Senator Symington signed the report but announced his intention to vote for ratification, saying that, while he was worried about the treaty, he was more worried about the possibility of a nuclear exchange.

Floor Debate

Having received a favorable report from the cognizant committee—Foreign Relations—the Senate began its formal floor debate on September 9.

By the time the treaty reached the floor, its ratification seemed a foregone conclusion. The main uncertainties appeared to be the margin of victory and whether the treaty would be approved without damaging amendments or reservations. As I have noted previously, these were matters of great concern to President Kennedy and, shortly after the floor debate began, he made a strong move to bolster the treaty's prospects. On September 10, he wrote a letter to the majority and minority leaders, Senators Mansfield and Dirksen, respectively, giving certain "unqualified and unequivocal assurances to the members of the Senate, to the entire Congress, and to the country." In this letter Kennedy pledged the administration anew to implementation of the four safeguards requested by the Joint Chiefs of Staff and in addition addressed himself to certain other misgivings that had been raised during the committee hearings.

The following excerpts from the president's letter summarize the assurances given: *

1. Underground testing ... will be vigorously and diligently carried forward, and the equipment, facilities, personnel and funds necessary for that purpose will be provided. *
2. The United States will maintain a posture of readiness to resume testing in the environments prohibited by the present treaty * ... [and] retains the right to resume atmospheric testing forthwith if the Soviet Union should conduct tests in violation of the treaty. [That is, we would not feel bound to wait three months, as per the treaty's withdrawal clause.]
3. Our facilities for the detection of possible violations of the treaty will be expanded and improved. *
4. I am glad to emphasize again that the treaty in no way limits the authority of the Commander-in-Chief to use nuclear weapons for the defense of the United States and its allies, if a situation should develop requiring such a grave decision.
5. ... if [Cuba] should be used either directly or indirectly to circumvent or nullify this treaty, the United States will take all necessary action in response.
6. The treaty in no way changes the status of ... [U.S. nonrecognition of] East Germany.
7. This Government will maintain strong weapons laboratories in a vigorous program of weapons developments * ...[and] strategic forces fully ensuring that this nation will continue to be in a position to destroy any aggressor, even after absorbing a first strike by a surprise attack.
8. The United States will vigorously pursue its ... [Plowshare] programs within the terms of the treaty and, when such developments make possible constructive uses of [peaceful] explosions ... will seek international agreement under the treaty to permit such explosions.

* Asterisk denotes a safeguard requested by the Joint Chiefs of Staff.

In a consummate political stroke, it was decided that the president's letter should be read to the Senate by the minority leader, whose credentials as a conservative were unchallenged. After reading the letter, Senator Dirksen announced his support for the treaty. He pointed out that the 1960 platform of the Republican party had advocated such a pact. Referring to his age (sixty-seven), Dirksen said: "I should not like to have written on my tombstone: 'He knew what happened at Hiroshima but he did not take a first step.' . . . If there be risks I am willing to assume them for my country."*

A key senator because of his influence with his colleagues on matters of military policy was Henry Jackson of Washington. He had been an opponent of a comprehensive treaty, and it was greatly feared that he would oppose the limited test ban as well. Jackson finally announced that he found the treaty acceptable despite its risks, provided it was firm policy to preserve the U.S. deterrent and to use the right of withdrawal to guard the nation's interests.

The favorable statements of Dirksen and Jackson, both of whom had been thought likely to oppose ratification, were undoubtedly the most influential ones made in the floor debate. Staunch supporters of the treaty, such as Senators Humphrey and Wayne Morse, of course took a most vigorous part in the debate, emphasizing that the assurances in the president's letter obviated any military risks. Notwithstanding that the debate lasted two weeks, very little of substance was brought forward on the Senate floor that had not been thoroughly aired in the committee hearings.

Consent

At length, on September 23, it came time to vote. First to be considered were a number of amendments and reservations. Most of

---

*An intriguing but unverifiable tale related to Dirksen's support of the treaty is told by Bobby Baker in his book, *Wheeling and Dealing: Confessions of a Capitol Hill Operator* ([New York: W. W. Norton & Co., 1978], pp. 97–99). Baker writes that a federal grand jury in Philadelphia was on the verge of indicting President Eisenhower's former aide, "Joe Jones," for income tax evasion. (Writing of this incident in his book *Robert Kennedy and His Times*, p. 403n, Arthur Schlesinger makes it clear that "Jones" was Sherman Adams.) Mrs. Eisenhower feared that "Jones" might commit suicide. Eisenhower asked Dirksen to intervene with his friend, President Kennedy, authorizing him to say that if the indictment were put in the deep freeze, Kennedy would have a "blank check in my bank." After what Baker describes as a hot exchange, the president prevailed on his brother, the attorney general, to drop the indictment. A few weeks later, Baker continues, Kennedy called Dirksen to the White House to say that what he wanted for his blank check was a public endorsement of the test ban treaty by both Dirksen and Eisenhower. In Dirksen's case, this amounted to a reversal of position, since he had previously spoken out against the treaty. Baker implies that but for Dirksen's endorsement the treaty would have been lost in the Senate. One can doubt this, but the margin of victory was almost certainly affected.

these were what, in congressional parlance, are known as "killer amendments." Certain to be unacceptable to the Soviet Union, their passage would have resulted either in the demise of the treaty or required its renegotiation.

All the "killer amendments" were defeated. One, introduced by Senator Barry Goldwater, would have made the treaty's implementation contingent on the removal of the USSR's military presence from Cuba. Another, introduced by Senators Jack Miller and John Tower, would have delayed the treaty's implementation until the USSR paid the arrears on its UN dues. Tower also proposed an amendment adding an onsite inspection provision to the treaty.

One amendment was approved. Introduced by Senator Russell, it did not change the language of the treaty—thereby avoiding diplomatic repercussions. Instead, it added language to the resolution of ratification asserting the Senate's constitutional prerogative to pass on all future amendments. Since this prerogative seemed securely embedded in U.S. constitutional law, and had, in fact, been specifically mentioned in the president's letter transmitting the treaty to the Senate, Russell's amendment seemed unnecessary. Majority Leader Mansfield read into the record a letter from Secretary Rusk to this effect. Senator Fulbright argued that such an amendment would be a precedent calling for similar amendments to all treaties. He produced a second letter from Rusk stating the view that the amendment "would not be in the interests of the United States." The Senate brushed aside all this argumentation and passed the Russell amendment by a vote of 79 to 9.

The reason for this rebellious outburst was undoubtedly to be found in the resentment of the Senate, including those who favored the treaty, that so many nations had adhered to it before the Senate had its opportunity to act. In introducing his resolution Senator Russell related it to that situation. It can be considered an act of statesmanship on Russell's part that he provided this relatively harmless vehicle for the expression of senatorial outrage.

On September 24, 1963, the momentous vote on the treaty itself was taken. Every able-bodied senator was present. The treaty was approved by a vote of 80 to 19. This was 14 votes more than the required two-thirds majority, a margin that satisfied the president's desire for a strong endorsement. Senator Engle, too ill to be present, announced that he also would have voted aye.

The eighty senators who voted for the ratification included fifty-five Democrats and twenty-five Republicans. Of the nineteen opposed, eleven were Democrats, eight were Republicans. All the Democrats who opposed the treaty were Southerners except Senator

Lausche of Ohio. All the opposed Republicans were from west of the Mississippi except Margaret Chase Smith of Maine.

Immediately following the Senate's action, President Kennedy issued a statement expressing his gratification at "this highly satisfactory vote." The following day, September 25, the Praesidium of the Council of Ministers formally ratified the treaty for the USSR.

On October 7 the president signed the documents of ratification for the United States. In his remarks delivered in the Treaty Room of the White House he looked to the future, saying in part:

> This small step toward safety can be followed by others longer and less limited, if also harder in the taking. With our courage and understanding enlarged by this achievement, let us press onward in quest of man's essential desire for peace.

Three days later on October 10, 1963, the U.S., U.K., and USSR certified to one another, by depositing instruments of ratification in Washington, London, and Moscow, that they had in fact ratified the Limited Test Ban Treaty, and it entered into force. Thus was taken the first successful step in disarmament in nearly eighteen years of negotiations with the Soviet Union.

"No other accomplishment in the White House," wrote Sorensen, "ever gave Kennedy greater satisfaction."[5] In this feeling Kennedy was at one with Harold Macmillan who, I am told, considers the Limited Test Ban Treaty to have been his greatest achievement as prime minister.[6]

PART SIX

Epilogue

"We are running a race between catastrophe and understanding."

JEROME WIESNER

21

A Reckoning

Four Minutes to Midnight

It is now more than eighteen years since the Limited Test Ban Treaty went into effect. By the end of 1980, 125 nations had signified their assent to the treaty, either by signing it, by depositing instruments of ratification or accession, or both. (Significant holdouts include China, Cuba, France, Libya, North Korea, Vietnam, and various Persian Gulf states, including Saudi Arabia.) The advent of the treaty was greeted by rejoicing throughout the world. The belief was widespread, even among thoughtful and sophisticated people, that a true turning in the road had occurred, a first step toward a better world, as Secretary Rusk had termed it. Symptomatic of this belief was the fact that the "doomsday clock" on the cover of the *Bulletin of the Atomic Scientists*, which had stood at seven minutes to midnight, was set back to twelve minutes to midnight. The expectation at the time clearly was that , if the treaty lived up to its promise, the clock would be set farther back at repeated intervals as the world, in

Kennedy's phrase, stepped away from danger. Alas for the world, the clock stands today at four minutes to midnight, a reversal that characterizes reasonably well the trend of events in the intervening years.

Hopes Fulfilled and Unfulfilled

What went wrong?

One way to seek an answer to this question is to review the hopes held out for the treaty at its inception and the extent to which each of these hopes has been fulfilled.

The principal hopes for the treaty appeared to have been as follows:

1. It would significantly reduce the hazard to human health from radioactive fallout.
2. It would act as a brake on the arms race between the superpowers.
3. It would be followed by further arms control agreements leading ultimately toward the beginning of genuine nuclear disarmament.
4. It would slow the proliferation of nuclear weapons.

These were the hopes. What has been the performance?

FALLOUT

On the matter of test fallout, the treaty has had its anticipated beneficial effect. Neither the United States nor the Soviet Union appears to have conducted an atmospheric test since the treaty entered into force. While a few U.S. and Soviet underground tests have vented into the atmosphere, the resultant releases of radioactivity have been very small.* The United States has reported atmospheric tests by other powers—France, China, and India. While there has been measurable fallout from these tests, the total amount has remained at such low levels as to constitute a negligible biological risk.

SLOWING THE ARMS RACE

Ironically, the end of the fallout menace may have had a negative effect on the achievement of the treaty's other objectives. The fear of radioactive fallout (as noted in earlier chapters) was the primary basis of popular concern about nuclear testing after the U.S. BRAVO test in

---

*While these apparently inadvertent infractions of the treaty have led to exchanges of notes and requests for explanation, neither side has chosen to make major incidents of them.

1954. As a result persistent pressure was brought to bear on the nuclear powers by influential leaders and popular movements throughout the world. With the fallout worry put aside by the treaty, nuclear tests ceased to be a burning public issue. As George Kistiakowsky and Herbert York commented,[1] the elimination of concern about fallout "made the continuation of uninhibited weapons development politically respectable."

To the extent that there were political pressures in the United States on the subject of nuclear testing after the treaty, their primary emphasis was on implementing the four safeguards that had been required by Joint Chiefs of Staff as the price for their support. To recall, the four safeguards were: (1) continued underground tests; (2) high-level maintenance of U.S. weapons laboratories; (3) continued readiness to resume atmospheric testing; and (4) improvement of our national means of detecting any Soviet treaty violations.

Even before the effective date of the treaty, but after its ratification seemed assured, some members of Congress began to press hard for specific measures to implement the safeguards. Congressman Craig Hosmer of California, for example, wrote to President Kennedy on September 24, 1963, urging a list of safeguards measures whose total cost he estimated at $1 billion in capital outlays and $250 million annually in operating costs. These amounts were far in excess of any being contemplated by the administration. Hosmer's letter was referred to me for reply. When my answer indicated that President Kennedy was requesting only a $17.5 million addition to the AEC's plant and equipment budget for the ensuing year, Hosmer wrote again to the president questioning whether safeguards were "being taken seriously by those who may be advising you." Symptomatic of the mood of Congress was the fact that on the same day that it ratified the treaty the Senate gave unanimous approval to the largest peacetime military appropriation in the nation's history.

Pressure for vigorous implementation of the safeguards continued during the administration of Lyndon Johnson. On March 25, 1964, the joint Senate-House Republican leadership issued a statement requesting that Johnson reaffirm the essential safeguards commitments made by Kennedy. The statement also requested that the president provide semiannual reports on the steps being taken, noting that "some Members of Congress have questioned whether or not a sufficient portion of the overall defense budget is being expended in this field."

Noteworthy signs of the changed emphasis appeared in Johnson's statement issued July 30, 1964, to commemorate the first anniversary of the signing of the treaty. Having made passing mention of the fact that "a year without atmospheric testing has left our air cleaner," the president's statement placed greatest emphasis on the fact that, because of the safeguards programs, the treaty had not impaired the military strength of the nation. He was careful to point out that the Joint Chiefs of Staff were satisfied with the military progress being made.

In the changed political atmosphere, it is not surprising that the pace of U.S. testing has remained at a high level in the years following the advent of the Limited Test Ban Treaty. The number of announced U.S. nuclear detonations for the period 1945–1980 was 638. Of these, 345, or 54 percent, took place after the effective date of the Treaty.* The Soviets, although relatively new to underground testing in 1963, seemed to master its problems quickly and have also continued a high rate of testing. Of the 298 Soviet tests announced by the U.S. through 1980, 168, or 56 percent, took place underground after 1963. As to the motivation behind the strong Soviet effort, one can look instructively to a remark made by Deputy Foreign Minister Kuznetsov to John McCloy when they were negotiating the removal of Soviet missiles from Cuba following the 1962 missile crisis. Kuznetsov said: "You Americans will never be able to do this to us again!"[2]

Based on the pace of testing, it is not surprising that in the years since 1963 both sides have added significantly to the variety and sophistication of their nuclear weapons. The Soviet Union has also made substantial increases in the number of its missiles and warheads, which the United States seems determined to match. Thus, while the absence of atmospheric testing may have impeded the acquisition of some weapons knowledge, it cannot be claimed that, overall, the Limited Test Ban Treaty has had the effect of slowing the arms race between the superpowers.

FURTHER ARMS CONTROL AGREEMENTS

There have indeed been, since 1963, a series of further East-West agreements that can be related to arms control, and it seems worthwhile to summarize these.

The Outer Space Treaty became effective on October 10, 1967. It bars the placement of weapons of mass destruction in earth orbit and the use of the moon and other celestial bodies for military purposes.

The Treaty for the Prohibition of Nuclear Weapons in Latin

---

*These figures, which are from the U.S. Department of Energy, do not include a small number of tests undertaken jointly with the U.K.

America entered into force in April 1968. It was the first treaty to establish a nuclear-free zone in a populated area. Under this treaty, the Latin American signators agree to use nuclear materials for peaceful purposes only and to submit to international inspection to verify their compliance. Nuclear-weapons states, for their part, agree not to contribute to any act that would violate the treaty and not to use, or threaten to use, nuclear weapons in the zone. Unfortunately, this treaty is not fully effective. Cuba has not signed it, Argentina has not ratified it, and Brazil and Chile have stipulated in their ratifications that the treaty will not be effective for them until all eligible countries have ratified.

The Non-Proliferation Treaty, which entered into force March 5, 1970, is addressed in a separate subsection of this chapter since it relates directly to a principal purpose of the Limited Test Ban Treaty.

A Biological Weapons Convention signed by the U.S., U.K., and USSR entered into force in January 1975. It calls for the actual destruction of biological agents or toxins accumulated in quantities not needed for peaceful purposes and of any armaments designed to use such materials in war. It needs to be emphasized that there has been no parallel action with regard to chemical weapons, which continue to be developed and accumulated.

The Seabed Treaty, a parallel to the Outer Space Treaty, entered into force in May 1972. Its terms are quite well described by its full title: "Treaty on the Prohibition of the Emplacement of Nuclear Weapons and Other Weapons of Mass Destruction on the Seabed and the Ocean Floor and in the Subsoil Thereof." It is effective outside a twelve-mile coastal zone.

Also in May 1972, President Nixon and General Secretary Brezhnev signed the SALT I accords; they entered into force on October 3, 1972. There were two distinct parts to the SALT I package. One was the Antiballistic Missile (ABM) Treaty, which, as amended by protocol signed in 1974, prohibits either side from installing ABM's on more than one site and limits the number and range of the missiles at that site. Although ABM's are defensive weapons, the fear was that if widely deployed they might encourage an aggressor by making him feel relatively invulnerable to retaliation.

The second SALT I accord, the Interim Agreement on Strategic Offensive Weapons, provided that for five years neither side would deploy a larger number of strategic missile launchers than were already deployed or under construction when the agreement entered into force. An intent of this agreement was to give each party the confidence that its force of strategic missiles could not be wiped out in a first strike.

The SALT II Treaty, negotiated by both the Ford and Carter administrations, was signed by President Carter and General Secretary Brezhnev on June 18, 1979. It sets equal limits on each side's aggregate number of strategic delivery systems; requires further reductions in the overall ceiling before the treaty expires; limits the number of warheads allowed on each missile; and restricts each side to one new type of strategic missile. The two nations also entered into agreements to ensure that each side's ability to verify the other's compliance would not be impaired. President Carter ceased to press for Senate ratification of SALT II following the Soviet invasion of Afghanistan in December 1979 and the Reagan administration shows no inclination to revive it.

By and large, the array of agreements reached in the wake of the Limited Test Ban Treaty is an impressive one. There is no doubt that the treaty itself contributed in an important way to the atmosphere that made these other agreements possible. The difficulty is that the agreements in their totality have accomplished so little toward damping down the arms race. As Herbert York points out, "Many of the treaties are peripheral to the main problem and in effect prohibit actions that no nation particularly wanted to take anyway."[3]

Certain of the treaties, such as SALT, do apply brakes—one has to stop the train before it can be put into reverse—but significant disarmament remains a distant goal.

INHIBITING PROLIFERATION

It was always the view of Kennedy and his advisers that a comprehensive test ban would be far more effective than a limited test ban in preventing the proliferation of nuclear weapons. There was hope that the Limited Test Ban Treaty might have some effect in the sense that any nation adhering to the treaty might find the permitted underground tests technically difficult and prohibitive in cost. This was a rather slim hope, however, and the nuclear powers, as well as a large number of other UN members, decided to approach their desire to deter proliferation more directly. This was done in the Treaty on the Non-Proliferation of Nuclear Weapons (NPT), which entered into force March 5, 1970. The NPT was the culmination of nearly ten years of effort within the United Nations. The chief stumbling blocks during these negotiations were:

> Soviet objections to proposed nuclear-sharing defense arrangements in NATO, such as the mixed-manned, multilateral, nuclear naval force.

Concern among nonnuclear nations that they would be at a disadvantage in developing nuclear energy for peaceful use.

A feeling among nonnuclear states that their renunciation of nuclear weapons should be balanced by more serious efforts toward disarmament by the major powers.

A fear by nonnuclear states that they could in the future be subject to nuclear intimidation.

Against this background, intensive negotiations led to a treaty in which:

Nuclear weapon states undertook not to transfer nuclear weapons to any nation or to assist any nation to make or acquire such weapons.

Nonnuclear states agreed not to make or receive nuclear weapons.

Nonnuclear states undertook to allow the International Atomic Energy Agency to monitor their compliance.

The parties agreed to share the benefits of the peaceful uses of nuclear energy equitably among all nations.

The parties agreed to pursue nuclear disarmament negotiations in good faith.

In addition, the UN Security Council adopted a resolution, companion to the treaty, asserting the council's intention to provide assistance to any nonnuclear-weapons state subject to threats of nuclear aggression.

As of February 1981, 113 nations were parties to the NPT. An ominous portent, however, is the number and identity of those who have not signed. This list includes Argentina, Brazil, China, Cuba, France, Israel, India, Pakistan, various Persian Gulf states (such as Saudi Arabia), and South Africa.

India's nuclear explosion and rumored nuclear development activities by others among the nonadherents have produced great alarm that the "genie" may be "out of the bottle," greatly increasing the number of places and circumstances from which a world-engulfing conflagration could emanate.

The nuclear powers, particularly the United States, have tried from time to time to persuade various of the nonsigners to change their minds. The nonsigning nations have been quick to point out an apparent element of hypocrisy in this endeavor. On the one hand, the nuclear powers continue to strengthen their own nuclear arsenals; on the other hand, they urge nonnuclear nations to accept permanent and increasing inferiority compensated only by protection under a superpower's nuclear umbrella. This is a very difficult package to accept, particularly for nations concerned about the intentions of neighbors with whom they have uneasy relations. It has been made clear repeatedly to the nuclear powers that their bargaining position would be significantly strengthened if they themselves would make some commitment to reduce their nuclear arsenals. The single action most often urged as an earnest of such a commitment has been the signing of a treaty banning all nuclear tests.

And so we must end as we began, considering once more, in the final chapter, the unfulfilled quest for that keystone in the structure of peace, the comprehensive test ban.

22

Still Needed:
A Comprehensive Test
Ban

The key place of the comprehensive test ban in the structure of international relations has been recognized by political leaders throughout the world for more than twenty years. While it may be evident from the text thus far, or from the reader's own appreciation of the issues, I should like to summarize here why a treaty banning all nuclear tests seems of such vital importance to so many concerned people throughout the world. The main considerations seem to me to be three in number:

First, an agreement to end all nuclear testing would impede further qualitative improvements in the nuclear arsenals of the major powers, improvements that can lead to dangerously de-stabilizing new weapon systems. (In the parlance of the nuclear arms race, *destabilization* refers to any presumed margin of superiority or inferiority that offers an inducement to one side or the other to launch its missiles in a first strike.)

Second, the end of all testing would lift from the shoulders of mankind a part of the crushing economic burden of nuclear weapons development, an activity Prime Minister Macmillan so rightly decried at the 1961 Bermuda summit conference as a "travesty of the purposes of human life."

Third, the termination of all nuclear testing by the major powers would provide evidence, thus far missing, that they are committed to the control of nuclear arms and would thus provide a better climate in which to strengthen international efforts to prevent further proliferation of nuclear weapons.

Fourth, a comprehensive nuclear test ban is an essential preliminary to any realistic effort to achieve genuine disarmament in the modern world.

Prompted by these considerations, responsible voices in the international community have been unrelenting in calling on the major nuclear powers to make progress toward a comprehensive agreement. Nor did the achievement of the Limited Test Ban Treaty lead to any relaxation of this pressure. The treaty was of course warmly welcomed. The Eighteenth UN General Assembly approved a resolution to that effect in November 1963. The resolution noted further, however, that the "original parties" had committed themselves in the treaty to continue negotiations for a comprehensive agreement, and the assembly went on record as desiring that such negotiations proceed "with a sense of urgency." The vote on the resolution was 104 to 1 (Albania).

The U.S. and USSR made it clear in statements to the Assembly that, for the moment, a comprehensive agreement was remote; they remained far apart on the issue of verification. For the United States, Ambassador Adlai Stevenson asserted that onsite inspection was still needed to "make it possible to dispel doubts as to the nature of certain seismic events." The Soviet delegate countered by stating that his government would "not be prepared to accept any inspections inasmuch as they are not necessary." He reiterated that Khrushchev's earlier offer of two to three inspections per year had been a political gesture to placate President Kennedy and the U.S. Senate and that it was now withdrawn.

The pressure continued also at the Eighteen-Nation Disarmament Committee. The Brazilian delegate proposed a gradual approach beginning with the prohibition of underground tests to a limit already verifiable by national means, with the threshold to be lowered progressively as scientific progress was made. Other delegates urged that this approach be discussed by the nuclear powers, either by reconvening the former subcommittee of three or in an East-West scientific conference. The Big Three responded generally by restating their positions. A year later the neutral eight in the disarmament committee submitted a joint memorandum in which they expressed regret that no progress was being made toward a comprehensive agreement. In 1965 the full UN Disarmament Commission passed a resolution urging the nuclear powers to "take all immediate steps toward an agreement."

The major nuclear powers continued to compare their positions on a comprehensive test ban in various forums. In the late 1960s significant progress in verification capabilities was made in the U.S. VELA Program, leading the Western powers to abandon the requirement for a network of internationally manned detection stations on Soviet soil. They continued to insist, however, that some obligatory onsite inspection was needed, while the Soviet Union stayed with its contention that national means of verification were sufficient.

Repeated efforts were made to bridge this gap, with nonaligned nations playing a prominent part, but the fundamental disagreement remained. Still, the international community would not let the issue die. It was in large part due to international pressure that the preamble to the Non-Proliferation Treaty contained a further reference to the "determination" of the parties to achieve a comprehensive test ban.

Partial Steps

Unable to reach full agreement on a comprehensive test ban, the U.S. and USSR decided in the spring of 1974 to pursue bilateral negotiations toward some restrictions on underground testing. In July of that year at a summit meeting in Moscow, President Nixon and General Secretary Brezhnev signed the Threshold Test Ban Treaty under which both sides undertook: (1) not to conduct underground tests yielding more than 150 kilotons; (2) not to interfere with each other's national means of verification; and (3) to exchange detailed data on all tests and test sites in order to facilitate verification.

The Threshold Test Ban Treaty was expected to go into effect on March 31, 1976, and both nations claim to have observed it from that time forward. Formal ratification was delayed, however, because of the need to deal with the problem of peaceful nuclear explosions (PNEs). By this time it was the Soviet Union, not the United States, which was chiefly interested in having a PNE program. Beginning in the fall of 1974, negotiators labored more than a year to arrive at terms whereby PNEs of more than 150 kilotons might be allowed, but they concluded that the verification problem—to assure that the explosions were indeed peaceful ones from which no military benefits might flow—was too difficult. Accordingly, a further agreement, the Peaceful Nuclear Explosion Treaty, was signed in May 1976. Under its terms, individual PNEs were required to be within the 150-kiloton limit imposed by the Threshold Treaty. In addition, each side was to have the right to observe grouped PNEs by the other side which had an aggregate yield greater than 150 kilotons, and no grouped PNEs could yield more in total than 1.5 megatons.

The Threshold and PNE treaties were submitted together to the U.S. Senate in July 1976. During hearings in the Foreign Relations Committee the Threshold Treaty was repeatedly decried as a sham by those favoring a comprehensive treaty. Chairman Frank Church and Senator Claiborne Pell, for example, contended that the limit of 150 kilotons was far in excess of military need. Wolfgang Panofsky stated that the limit had been established at a level that would have no adverse effect on the work of weapons designers and that the treaty was worse than nothing. The Federation of American Scientists felt the treaty would only serve further to postpone a comprehensive test ban. In consideration of such views and of the upcoming presidential election, the Foreign Relations Committee delayed action on the treaties.

Recent Efforts: Near Agreement Once Again

The Carter administration at its inception decided not to press for ratification of the Threshold and PNE Treaties but to push on instead for the full prize, the comprehensive test ban. President Carter announced this intention in an address to the United Nations in March of 1977. In July 1977 formal tripartite (U.S., U.K., USSR) negotiations on a comprehensive treaty resumed in Geneva. Reports emanating from the negotiations indicated that both sides had made concessions and that prospects for an agreement were improved. This impression was confirmed in July 1980 when the three powers presented a progress report to the UN Committee on Disarmament.

This report plus other information communicated to the writer by Herbert F. York, [1] the head of the U.S. negotiating team during the last two years, indicate that the main outlines of a treaty had been worked out. It would rely on automatic national seismic detection stations on the territories of the three powers: ten each in the United States and the USSR and a lesser number in the United Kingdom. There would be a system of voluntary onsite inspections that would include an arrangement for a sequence of challenges and responses designed to ensure that any claim of a possible violation would be based on serious information and that any rejection would be similarly based. If, notwithstanding this arrangement, the two sides failed to agree, there could be ultimate recourse to argument before the UN Security Council.

The treaty would be for a fixed number of years, during which there would be a moratorium on peaceful nuclear explosions (a Soviet concession). During the moratorium there would be joint studies (a U.S. concession) on ways to allow such explosions, at the same time ensuring they would not lead to military advantages.

Although the report to the UN was issued in July 1980, indications are that virtually all the progress reported occurred in the first year and a half of the resumed negotiations, that is, between July 1977 and the end of 1978. Little progress has been made since because of a weakening in the political will to proceed on both sides.

The Carter administration was said to have been hesitant at first to press for the test ban agreement until SALT II had been achieved. In addition, test ban opponents succeeded later in reaching President Carter with arguments against the treaty which persuaded him it would be more difficult to obtain Senate approval than he had anticipated. It is hoped that the Reagan administration may see fit to revive the negotiations. As of June 1981, however, no formal statement had been made as to the administration's intentions.

The rationale behind Soviet hesitancy on the test ban is of course unknown to us, but it is reasonable to presume that it is in large part related to the failure of the United States to accept the SALT II agreement.

A further comment on the matter of onsite inspection: The reader will recall it was primarily this issue that prevented achievement of a comprehensive test ban in earlier years. It is sadly ironic that, when mutual compromise and skillful negotiation recently brought about agreement on this question in Geneva, other issues had arisen to bar the road to a treaty.

And so, we find ourselves where we have been before, close—but not close enough—to the much sought-after, desperately needed agreement on a treaty banning all nuclear tests.

A Look Back: If Kennedy and Khrushchev Had Survived

I am one of those who believe that, if John F. Kennedy had lived and served out a second term, and if Nikita Khrushchev had survived in office, significant further steps in arms control, including a comprehensive test ban, would have ensued.

There can be little doubt that Kennedy would have exerted himself in this direction. Averell Harriman has told me of a conversation in which Kennedy said that if he won a second term its principal thrust would have been to seek improved relations with the USSR. It is logical to believe that a comprehensive test ban would have been the centerpiece of his efforts.

Whether Kennedy could have enlisted support in the country and the Congress is, of course, open to question. Opposition doubtless would have persisted in some military and other circles. Much would have depended on whether verification provisions sufficient to overcome widespread mistrust of the Soviets could have been negotiated. Given the rapid progress made in detection techniques in Project VELA, I believe that verification would have proven less of a stumbling block in Kennedy's second term than it was in his first. The president's own enhanced prestige after the Cuban Missile Crisis and the popular enthusiasm engendered by the Limited Test Ban Treaty might well have enabled him to carry the country along with him on this issue.

The greater uncertainty is what Khrushchev might have been disposed to seek and been able to deliver had he survived in office. Decision making in the Kremlin, past and present, remains a mysterious process that Western intelligence and scholarship decipher with the greatest difficulty. One recalls Winston Churchill's apt characterization of Soviet policy as "a riddle wrapped in a mystery inside an enigma."

While current Soviet decision making still retains much of the aspect of mystery Churchill ascribed to it more than thirty years ago, scholars in recent years have succeeded in making some sense of the historical record by ingenious use of the available clues. Soviet policy toward arms control during the Khrushchev years has lent itself particularly well to this type of scholarly problem solving.[2] The story that has emerged is one of rather fierce infighting, with Khrushchev and a few allies in the power structure pressing fairly consistently for serious arms control negotiations against opposition from military and other conservative elements.

Khrushchev's fortunes in this continuing debate tended to ebb and flow depending on events on the world scene and the resulting changes in the perception of the United States held by Soviet leaders. Following his visit to the United States in September 1959, Khrushchev, who was favorably impressed by President Eisenhower, launched an offensive in favor of a comprehensive test ban agreement. The evidence suggests that Khrushchev, along with other world leaders, expected that an agreement might be reached shortly after the upcoming Paris summit conference.

The U-2 incident of May 1960 was a great embarrassment to Khrushchev, who had gone out on a limb in praising Eisenhower's peaceful intentions. Shortly afterward there was a leadership turn-over in which Khrushchev supporters were demoted and conservatives promoted. Khrushchev himself became relatively silent on the test ban issue for over a year. Preparations for the Soviet Union's September 1961 test resumption must have begun early in this period.

Following the Soviet test series, there was some movement toward a softer line. Early in 1962 Khrushchev pressed within the Soviet hierarchy for consideration of a nationally controlled test ban treaty separate from general disarmament. Military spokesmen, however, persisted in linking the two questions, a faintly concealed way of expressing opposition to a test ban.

Following the Soviet backdown in the Cuban Missile Crisis, Khrushchev again experienced a period of weakness. Conservative elements led by Frol Kozlov began to exercise dominance in policy decisions. It was during this period that Khrushchev complained to Norman Cousins about the difficulty he had in persuading his colleagues to accept two to three inspections per year and the pressure he was under to authorize further tests.

When Kozlov suffered a heart attack late in April 1962, Khrushchev recovered some initiative and began to press harder for a test ban. Even during this period, however, military spokesmen, particularly Chief of Staff Marshal Malinovsky, continued their coolness toward even a partial test ban.

Even after the agreement on the Limited Test Ban Treaty there was a lack of enthusiasm for it in the Soviet leadership. This was made strikingly evident when only three Praesidium members other than Khrushchev were present at the signing ceremonies in the Kremlin which I attended. These three, Brezhnev, Kirilenko, and Podgorny, were known to be Khrushchev's strongest supporters in the Praesidium. Just two days after the treaty was initialed, Marshal Malinovsky failed to refer to it in a Soviet Navy Day Order of the Day in which he discussed Soviet peace initiatives. Instead, he included a ban on nuclear tests in a list of "unsolved problems."[3]

From this review it is evident that the conflict of opinion on the test ban issue in the Soviet Union had similarities to that in the United States. President Kennedy seemed to recognize fully the similarity of his position to that of Khrushchev. As he told Norman Cousins:

> One of the ironic things about this entire situation is that Mr. Khrushchev and I occupy approximately the same political positions inside our governments. He would like to prevent a nuclear

war but is under severe pressure from his hard-line crowd, which interprets every move in that direction as appeasement. I've got similar problems. Meanwhile, the lack of progress in reaching agreements between our two countries gives strength to the hard-line boys in both, with the result that the hard-liners . . . feed on one another, each using the actions of the other to justify his own position.[4]

The resolve of both Kennedy and Khrushchev to make progress on arms control was strengthened greatly by the searing experience of the Missile Crisis. Khrushchev in particular seems to have been persuaded by that experience to recognize that the enormous power at his disposal gave him responsibilities not only to the Soviet Union but to all mankind. He became increasingly a responsible world leader.

The Missile Crisis also had a dramatic effect on the relationship of the two men. Their attitudes toward each other show evidence of having been somewhat ambivalent before the crisis. That brush with calamity seems to have forged a bond between them. They appeared now to understand each other better, to buttress each other's efforts, to avoid making the other look bad. They began to consult each other more frequently, to work together on problems of common interest. This was done in large part through their private, and as yet unpublished, correspondence, the pace of which quickened after the Missile Crisis.

We can of course only speculate on how the increasingly close relationship of Kennedy and Khrushchev might have affected the chances for further agreements had they both remained in office. One thing quite clear was that they both understood only too well what a fragile underpinning the Limited Test Ban Treaty provided in building toward further disarmament goals, and that a more substantial structure could only be built slowly, as confidence grew. Khrushchev expressed this somewhat wistfully in an interview he granted to the editors of *Pravda* and *Izvestiya* on the Limited Test Ban Treaty's first anniversary. He noted that the treaty had not solved the basic problems of disarmament. It had merely helped "to get close to those positions from which it is easier to set about the solution of that most important problem." Asked what should be done to build on the progress toward easing of tensions that the treaty had initiated, Khrushchev answered:

> In my view the year which has passed . . . has enriched international life with new experience; with the creation of a certain fund of confidence it is possible to move further toward reducing international tension . . . it is particularly important to protect this fund of confidence and not allow it to be exhausted but, on the contrary, to strengthen and extend it in every way.

To build on the "fund of confidence," the two leaders needed what neither was granted: time. When Khrushchev made this statement Kennedy was, of course, already gone. Within two months, Khrushchev was gone as well—not dead, but removed from office. The opportunity to reach a comprehensive agreement in the 1960s was thus denied us by removal of the two key figures who, working together, might have brought it about.

Now five American presidents and one Soviet Party Chairman later, there is again an opportunity in the sense that the negotiating positions of the two sides on a comprehensive test ban treaty seem quite close together. What stands in the way as a huge obstacle is a mountain of mistrust and political ill will. The fund of confidence has been sorely depleted. If this should change—and the world has seen many startling political reversals in recent years—an agreement banning all nuclear tests can follow.

Such an agreement today might well not have the saving power—in ensuring stability in the arms race, in moderating its costs, and in preventing proliferation of nuclear weapons—which a similar agreement would have had in the 1960s. As Averell Harriman pointed out, we are negotiating at a higher and more dangerous level. If we allow the present opportunity to slip away, however, the next one, if there is a next one, will be at a level still higher and still more dangerous.

The hour is late. Let us hope not too late.

APPENDIX

Treaty Banning Nuclear Weapon Tests in the Atmosphere, in Outer Space and Under Water

*Text of treaty done at Moscow
on August 5, 1963.
U.S. ratification deposited October 10, 1963.
Entered into force October 10, 1963.*

The Governments of the United States of America, the United Kingdom of Great Britain and Northern Ireland, and the Union of Soviet Socialist Republics, hereinafter referred to as the "Original Parties,"

Proclaiming as their principal aim the speediest possible achievement of an agreement on general and complete disarmament under strict international control in accordance with the objectives of the United Nations which would put an end to the armaments race and eliminate the incentive to the production and testing of all kinds of weapons, including nuclear weapons,

Seeking to achieve the discontinuance of all test explosions of nuclear weapons for all time, determined to continue negotiations to this end, and desiring to put an end to the contamination of man's environment by radioactive substances,

Have agreed as follows:

Article I

1. Each of the Parties to this Treaty undertakes to prohibit, to prevent, and not to carry out any nuclear weapon test explosion, or any other nuclear explosion, at any place under its jurisdiction or control:

(a) in the atmosphere; beyond its limits, including outer space; or underwater, including territorial waters or high seas; or

(b) in any other environment if such explosion causes radioactive debris to be present outside the territorial limits of the State under whose jurisdiction or control such explosion is conducted. It is understood in this connection that the provisions of this subparagraph are without prejudice to the conclusion of a treaty resulting in the permanent banning of all nuclear test explosions, including all such explosions underground, the conclusion of which, as the Parties have stated in the Preamble to this Treaty, they seek to achieve.

2. Each of the Parties to this Treaty undertakes furthermore to refrain from causing, encouraging, or in any way participating in, the carrying out of any nuclear weapon test explosion, or any other nuclear explosion, anywhere which would take place in any of the environments described, or have the effect referred to, in paragraph 1 of this Article.

Article II

1. Any Party may propose amendments to this Treaty. The text of any proposed amendment shall be submitted to the Depositary Governments which shall circulate it to all Parties to this Treaty. Thereafter, if requested to do so by one-third or more of the Parties, the Depositary Governments shall convene a conference, to which they shall invite all the Parties, to consider such amendment.

2. Any amendment to this Treaty must be approved by a majority of the votes of all the Parties to this Treaty, including the votes of all of the Original Parties. The amendment shall enter into force for all Parties upon the deposit of instruments of ratification by a majority of all the Parties, including the instruments of ratification of all of the Original Parties.

Article III

1. This Treaty shall be open to all States for signature. Any State which does not sign this Treaty before its entry into force in accordance with paragraph 3 of this Article may accede to it at any time.
2. This Treaty shall be subject to ratification by signatory States. Instruments of ratification and instruments of accession shall be deposited with the Governments of the Original Parties—the United States of America, the United Kingdom of Great Britain and Northern Ireland, and the Union of Soviet Socialist Republics—which are hereby designated the Depositary Governments.
3. This Treaty shall enter into force after its ratification by all the Original Parties and the deposit of their instruments of ratification.
4. For States whose instruments of ratification or accession are deposited subsequent to the entry into force of this Treaty, it shall enter into force on the date of the deposit of their instruments of ratification or accession.
5. The Depositary Governments shall promptly inform all signatory and acceding States of the date of each signature, the date of deposit of each instrument of ratification of an accession to this Treaty, the date of its entry into force, and the date of receipt of any requests for conferences or other notices.
6. This Treaty shall be registered by the Depositary Governments pursuant to Article 102 of the Charter of the United Nations.

Article IV

This Treaty shall be of unlimited duration.

Each Party shall in exercising its national sovereignty have the right to withdraw from the Treaty if it decides that extraordinary events, related to the subject matter of this Treaty, have jeopardized the supreme interests of its country. It shall give notice of such withdrawal to all other Parties to the Treaty three months in advance.

Article V

This Treaty, of which the English and Russian texts are equally authentic, shall be deposited in the archives of the Depositary Governments. Duly certified copies of this Treaty shall be transmitted by the Depositary Governments to the Governments of the signatory and acceding States.

IN WITNESS WHEREOF the undersigned, duly authorized, have signed this Treaty.

DONE in triplicate at the city of Moscow the fifth day of August, one thousand nine hundred and sixty-three.

For the Government of the United States of America	*For the Government of the United Kingdom of Great Britain and Northern Ireland*	*For the Government of the Union of Soviet Socialist Republics*
Dean Rusk	Home	A. Gromyko

NOTES

One: From BRAVO to the Conference of Experts

1. Phillip Noel-Baker, *The Arms Race*, quoted in Bernford G. Bechoefer, *Postwar Negotiations for Arms Control* (Washington, D.C.: The Brookings Institution, 1961).
2. Herbert York and G. Allen Greb, "The Comprehensive Nuclear Test Ban," California Seminar on Arms Control and Foreign Policy, 1979.

Two: Test Ban Negotiations Begin

1. Arthur M. Schlesinger, Jr., *A Thousand Days: John F. Kennedy in the White House* (Boston: Houghton Mifflin Co., 1965), p. 208.
2. George B. Kistiakowsky, *A Scientist at the White House* (Cambridge, Mass.: Harvard University Press, 1976), p. 6.
3. Earl H. Voss, *Nuclear Ambush: The Test Ban Trap* (Chicago: H. Regnery Co., 1963), p. 324.
4. Heckrotte to Seaborg, 12 June 1980.
5. Harold Karan Jacobson and Eric Stein, *Diplomats, Scientists and Politicians: The United States and the Nuclear Test Ban Negotiations* (Ann Arbor: University of Michigan Press, 1966), p. 253.
6. Ibid., p. 263.
7. Dwight D. Eisenhower, *Waging Peace 1956–1961* (New York: Doubleday & Company, Inc., 1965), p. 481.

Three: In Search of a Policy

1. Herbert L. York, interview for the Kennedy Library Oral History Program.
2. Freeman Dyson, *Disturbing the Universe* (New York: Harper and Row, 1979), p. 8.
3. Henry Kissinger, *White House Years* (Boston: Little, Brown & Co., 1979), p. 40.
4. Private communication, 7 July 1980.
5. Harold Macmillan, *At the End of the Day, 1961–1963* (New York: Harper and Row, 1973), p. 472.

6. Voss, *Nuclear Ambush*, p. 459.

Four: A Bad Start at Geneva

1. Daniel Lang, *An Inquiry into Enoughness* (New York: McGraw-Hill, 1965), p. 51 f.

2. Schlesinger, *A Thousand Days*, p. 482.

Five: Internal Debate, External Challenge

1. Informal communication, 22 February 1980.

2. Inverview, Kennedy Library Oral History Program.

3. Interview, Kennedy Library Oral History Program.

4. Arthur M. Schlesinger, Jr., *Robert Kennedy and His Times* (Boston: Houghton Mifflin Co., 1978), p. 459 n.

5. Heckrotte to Seaborg, 12 June 1980.

6. Ibid.

7. Ibid.

Six: Over the Brink

1. Theodore C. Sorensen, *Kennedy* (New York: Harper & Row, 1965), p. 619.

2. McGeorge Bundy, "The Presidency and Peace," *Foreign Affairs* (April 1964), p. 359.

3. Lincoln P. Bloomfield, Walter C. Clemens, Jr., and Franklyn Griffiths, *Khrushchev and the Arms Race: Soviet Interests in Arms Control and Disarmament, 1954–1964* (Cambridge, Mass: MIT Press, 1966), pp. 156, 160.

4. Heckrotte to Seaborg, 12 June 1980.

5. Ibid.

6. *New York Times*, 2 September 1961, p. 1.

7. Schlesinger, *A Thousand Days*, p. 482.

Seven: Organization and Disarmament Initiatives

1. Congressman Robert Kastenmeier, remarks to Research Conference on Disarmament, Columbia University, 1961.

2. Jacobson and Stein, *Diplomats, Scientists and Politicians*, p. 55.

3. Ibid., p. 66.

4. Interview, Kennedy Library Oral History Program.

5. Arthur Dean, *Disarmament and Test Ban: The Path of Negotiation* (New York: Harper and Row, 1966), p.31.

6. Ibid., pp. 31–32.

Eight: Toward Atmospheric Testing

1. Kissinger, *White House Years*, p. 90.

Nine: Test Plans and a Summit

1. Remarks to Research Conference on Disarmament, Columbia University, 1961.

Ten: The Decision to Test in the Atmosphere

1. Informal communication, 7 July 1980.

Eleven: Geneva Revisited

1. Alva Myrdal, *The Game of Disarmament: How the United States and Russia Run the Arms Race* (New York: Pantheon Books, 1976), pp. 91–92.
2. Ibid., p. 90.
3. Jacobson and Stein, *Diplomats, Scientists, and Politicians*, p. 375.

Fourteen: The Missile Crisis and its Aftermath

1. The story of the crisis has been narrated in detail in several books. I recommend particularly Robert F. Kennedy's *Thirteen Days* (New York: W. W. Norton Co., 1969) and Elie Abel's *The Missile Crisis* (Philadelphia: J. B. Lippincott, 1966).
2. Abel, *The Missile Crisis*, p. 84.
3. Macmillan, *At the End of the Day*, p. 219.
4. Sorensen, *Kennedy*, pp. 725–726.
5. Heckrotte to Seaborg, 12 June 1980.
6. Norman Cousins, "Notes on a 1963 Visit with Khrushchev," *Saturday Review* (7 November 1964), p. 21.
7. Heckrotte to Seaborg, 12 June 1980.
8. Informal communication, 7 July 1980.

Fifteen: "My Hopes are Somewhat Dimmed"

1. U.S. Congress, Senate, Committee on Foreign Relations, *To Promote Negotiations on a Comprehensive Test Ban Treaty, Hearings before the Subcommittee on Arms Control, International Law and Organization*, 93d Cong., 1st session, 1 May 1973, p. 107.

Sixteen: The Tide Begins to Turn

1. Sorensen, *Kennedy*, p. 727.
2. Norman Cousins, "Notes on a 1963 Visit with Khrushchev," p. 20.
3. Ibid., p. 58 [Emphasis added]
4. Informal communication, 11 July 1980.
5. Sorensen, *Kennedy*, pp. 730–731.

Seventeen: Preparation for a Mission

1. Macmillan, *At the End of the Day*, p. 470.
2. Interview, Kennedy Library Oral History Program.
3. U.S., Congress, Senate, Committee on Foreign Relations, *Nuclear Test Ban Treaty: Hearings*, 88th Congress, 1st sess., August 1963, p. 382.
4. *New York Times*, 28 June 1963, p. 1.
5. Macmillan, *At the End of the Day*, p. 474.
6. Informal communication, August 11, 1980.
7. Macmillan, *At the End of the Day*, p. 472 ff.
8. Schlesinger, *A Thousand Days*, p. 888.
9. Interview, Kennedy Library Oral History Program.

Eighteen: Twelve Days in Moscow

1. U.S. Congress, Senate, Committee on Foreign Relations, *To Promote*

Negotiations on a Comprehensive Test Ban Treaty, Hearings before the Subcommittee on Arms Control, International Law and Organization, 93d Cong., 1st sesson, 1 May 1973, p. 106.

2. Informal communication, 22 February 1980.

3. Ibid.

4. Memorandum of conversation in Kennedy Library.

5. Copy in Harriman files.

6. Informal communication, 22 February 1980.

7. Ibid.

8. Averell Harriman, *America and Russia in a Changing World* (New York: Doubleday & Company, Inc., 1971), pp. 96–97.

9. Ibid., p. 99.

10. Informal communication, 22 February 1980.

11. Schlesinger, *A Thousand Days,* p. 905.

12. Copy in Harriman files.

13. Copy in Harriman files.

Nineteen: Ceremonies and Reactions

1. Ronald J. Terchek, *The Making of the Test Ban Treaty* (The Hague: Martinus Nijhoff, 1970) p. 145.

Twenty: The Senate Consents

1. Interview, Kennedy Library Oral History Program.

2. Norman Cousins, *The Improbable Triumvirate* (New York: W. W. Norton & Co., 1972), p. 135.

3. Sorensen, *Kennedy,* p. 745.

4. Terchek, *The Making of the Test Ban Treaty,* p. 30n.

5. Sorensen, *Kennedy,* p. 740.

6. Informal communication from Alistair Horne (British biographer of Macmillan), November 1980.

Twenty-One: A Reckoning

1. George Kistiakowsky and Herbert York, "Strategic Arms Race Showdown Through Test Limitations," *Science* (2 August 1974), p. 404.

2. Quoted in Charles E. Bohlen, *Witness to History 1929–1969* (New York: W. W. Norton and Co., 1973), pp. 495–496.

3. Herbert F. York, "The Great Test-Ban Debate," *Scientific American* (November 1972) reprinted in *Arms Control* (Readings from *Scientific American*), p. 301.

Twenty-Two: Still Needed—A Comprehensive Test Ban

1. Informal communication, 5 May 1981.

2. See, for example, Christer Jönsson, *Soviet Bargaining Behavior, The Nuclear Test Ban Case* (New York: Columbia University Press, 1979).

3. Jönsson, *Soviet Bargaining Behavior,* p. 198.

4. Cousins, *The Improbable Triumvirate,* p. 114.

INDEX

Acheson, Dean, 175

Adams, Sherman, 182, 280n

Adenauer, Konrad, 175, 224

Aiken, George, 259–260

Air Force Technical Applications Center, 119

Alsop, Joseph, 52, 73

American University speech (Kennedy): content of, 213–216; genesis of, 212; interpretation of, 216–217; reception of, 217, 218

Anderson, Clinton P., 23, 45, 47–48, 138, 248–249, 266–267, 268

Antiballistic missiles, 104, 152, 271–272, 273

Antiballistic Missile Treaty (1972–74), 289

Argentina, 289, 291

Arms Control and Disarmament Agency (ACDA), 94–95, 96, 268. *See also* Fisher, Adrian; Foster, William C.

Arms race. *See* Nuclear arms race

Associated Universities, Inc., 18

Atmospheric test, definition of, 228, 267–268

Atmospheric Testing, Committee on, 116–117, 123–124, 133

Atomic Energy Commission (AEC): differences with Defense on test programs, 69, 104; headquarters visited by Kennedy, 30–32; positions taken by, pre-Kennedy, 5–6, 33–34; recommends resumption of atmospheric testing (1961), 112–113, 114; weapons laboratories, 9, 33–34, 123, 183, 268, 273. *See also* Seaborg, Glenn T.

Bacher, Robert F., and Bacher Panel, 12n, 19

Baker, Bobby, 280n

Baker, William O., 74n

Ball, David E., 51

Ball, George W., 173, 237

Barnett, Robert, 252

Baruch Plan, 4, 6

Bay of Pigs (Cuba), 66

Benedict, Manson, 203

Bergman, Jules, 163

Berkner, Lloyd V., and Berkner Panel (Panel on Seismic Improvement), 18–19, 177n

Berlin crisis, 67, 70, 84, 129, 130, 252

Berlin Wall, 70, 88, 224

Bermuda summit (Kennedy-Macmillan, 12/61), 125, 126–131

Bethe, Hans A., and Bethe Panel, 11, 12, 19, 37n, 74n, 119

Betts, Austin W., 37n, 43, 87

"Big hole." *See* Decoupling

Biological Weapons Convention (1975), 289

"Black boxes" (unmanned seismic stations), 18, 177–178, 184, 190

Bohlen, Charles E., 12, 66, 82, 121

Bradbury, Norris E., 74n, 75, 273, 277

Brazil, 289, 291

Brezhnev, Leonid I., 204–205, 206, 248, 261, 290, 295, 299

Brooks, Ned, 108

Brown, Harold, 19, 37n, 65, 82, 86, 117, 126, 127, 129, 138; Senate testimony on treaty, 272–273, 277

Bruce, David, 117, 129, 130

Bulganin, Nikolai, 7–8

Bulletin of the Atomic Scientists, 285, 286

Bundy, McGeorge, 74, 84, 87, 110, 116, 117, 126, 225, 256; communications with, 51, 113, 117, 118, 125, 192; at meetings on U.S. policy, 30, 38, 43, 45,

48, 71, 72, 73, 75, 82, 86, 87, 138, 146, 173, 183, 187, 192, 197, 223
Burke, Arleigh, 277

California, University of, 128
Carter, Jimmy, 290, 296
Chayes, Abram, 221
Childs, Marquis, 106, 107
Chile, 289
China, People's Republic of: attitude on test ban, 23, 257; as factor in test ban negotiations, 43, 47, 194, 228, 238–239, 245, 246; nuclear weapons program of, 181, 182,194, 195, 217, 224, 245, 247, 286; relations with USSR, 111, 217, 230, 246, 276; tests by, 247
China, Republic of, 249–250
Christmas Island: agreement granting U.S. use of, 134–135; quest for use of, 108–109, 117–119, 125, 126–131 passim; reuse of after DOMINIC considered, 167, 192, 193
Church, Frank, 296
Churchill, Winston, 298
Citizens Committee for a Nuclear Test Ban, 264
Civil rights crisis (1963), 216
Clandestine tests, gains possible from, 33, 42, 142, 164, 166, 188, 222, 223, 242
Clark, Joseph S., 227
Cleveland, Harlan F., 86, 121, 133n
Committee of Principals. *See* Principals, Committee of
Committee on Atmospheric Testing, 116–117, 123–124, 125, 133, 136
Comprehensive test ban: chances for Senate ratification of, 195, 227; failure to achieve, tragedy of, 242; near agreement in 1963, 191, 192; negotiations after Kennedy, 292, 295, 296, 301; pressure for, from international community, 294–295; relation to proliferation, 165,166, 188, 193, 195; try for in Moscow negotiations, 240–242; why needed, 293–294. *See also* Test ban issues; Test ban proposals
Conference of Experts (Geneva, 1958), 11, 12, 13, 93. *See also* Geneva System
Conference on Discontinuance of Nuclear Weapon Tests. *See* Geneva Conference
Congressional Joint Committee on Atomic Energy, 23–24, 34, 35, 39, 45, 48, 52, 133, 134, 186, 197, 205
Cousins, Norman, 212, 264–265, 299; interview with Khrushchev (1963),

179–180, 240, 308–309; Senate testimony of, 276
Crewe, Albert V., 203
Cuba, 66, 289, 291
Cuban Missile Crisis, 299; course of, 172–175, 182; effect on Kennedy-Khrushchev relationship, 300; effect on Soviet arms effort, 288; effect on test-ban negotiations, 176, 199

Darwin, Charles (descendant of naturalist), 237
Dean, Arthur H., 53, 82, 100, 179, 259; comments on VELA findings, 162–163; at ENDC, 144, 168, 176, 177–178; at Geneva Conference, 55–56, 57, 76, 122; at meetings on U.S. policy, 41, 43, 46–47, 55, 60, 64, 75–76, 86, 104, 120, 137, 166–167; Senate testimony on treaty, 255, 274–275
Decoupling, 18–19, 42, 52, 126, 128, 144
Defense, Department of. *See* Joint Chiefs of Staff; McNamara, Robert S.
De Gaulle, Charles, 23, 142–143, 175, 257
Deputies, Committee of, 49–50
De Vault, Don, 62
De Zulueta, Philip, 126
Dillon, C. Douglas, 173
Dirksen, Everett, 83, 138, 259, 279, 280
Disarmament, general and complete: joint U.S.-USSR statement of agreed principles on, 99–102, 135; linked to test ban, 76, 121, 127; U.S. plan for, 96–98
Disarmament Administration, U.S., 94
Disarmament proposals, pre-Kennedy, 4, 5, 6
Dobrynin, Anatoly, 202–203, 260, 261
Dodd, Thomas J., 186–187, 227
DOMINIC test series, U.S. (1962), 150–158; evaluation of, 158; high-altitude tests, 152–157; overall scope, 150–151; public protests, U.S., 151–152. *See also* Testing, atmospheric
Dulles, Allen, 38, 39, 40, 42, 44, 64, 65, 82, 104
Dulles, John Foster, 9, 10, 93
Dunham, Charles L., 31–32
Dutton, Frederick G., 51
Dyson, Freeman, 35, 97n, 102

Economist, The, 223
Eighteen Nation Disarmament Committee (ENDC): concessions offered by West at, 143–144; deadlock at, 161, 176–178, 189; discussion of VELA

findings at, 163; membership, 142–143; opening of, 127, 135; preparation of U.S. position for, 140–142, 187–188; pressure for comprehensive test ban at, 294–295; proposals by eight neutrals, 148–149, 161–162; technical challenge to West at, 144–146
Einstein, Albert, 4
Eisenhower, Dwight D., 8, 10, 18, 117, 280, 298, 299; attitude on arms control, 5, 10, 24; favors resumption of testing (1960), 24–25; meets Khrushchev at Camp David, 20; open-skies proposal (1955), 7; proposes conference of experts (1958), 11–12; proposes test-ban conference (1958), 14; proposes test ban in phases (1959), 17; scientific advice received by, 9–10; and test moratorium, 21, 23, 84; urges reservation on test-ban treaty, 274
Eisenhower, Mamie, 280n
Emelyanov, Vasily, 201, 202
Engle, Clair, 281
Eniwetok Atoll, as test site, 107, 108, 134
Executive Committee of National Security Council (EXCOM), 172–173
Experts. *See* Conference of Experts

Fallout, radioactive, from nuclear tests, 164; Kennedy's preoccupation with, 31–32, 112; scientific uncertainty about, 107, 268; and test-ban treaty, 268–269, 286, 288
Farley, Philip, 133n, 140
Federation of American Scientists, 22, 296
Federov, Yevgeni K., 180–181
Fedorenko, N. T., 181
Finney, John, 45, 106, 107
Fisher, Adrian, 196, 221, 222; on ACDA legislation, 95; on Kennedy's informality, 50–51; at meetings on U.S. policy, 63, 140, 146, 187, 198; at Moscow negotiations, 235, 237, 242, 249, 252; on VELA incident, 162–163
Fisk, James B., 12, 36–37, 74n
Fisk Panel report on Geneva System, 36–37, 43, 45, 46
Foster, John S., 74n, 75, 197, 222, 273, 277
Foster, William, C., 117, 133, 162, 210, 227, 237, 259; at ENDC, 189; at meetings on U.S. policy, 120, 137, 140, 141, 146, 164, 183, 187, 188, 197, 221, 223, 228; named head of ACDA, 95–96; on Plowshare program, 196–197
France: as factor in test-ban negotiations,

21, 47, 55, 84, 110, 122n, 238; nuclear tests by, 23, 55, 78, 84, 194, 286; opposition to test ban, 23; refusal to attend ENDC, 142–143; request for U.S. nuclear assistance, 110—111
Freeman, Orville, 261
Fritsch, Arnold R., 155, 203
Fulbright, J. William, 45–46, 47, 83, 138, 259, 260, 265, 271

Gagarin, Yuri, 66
Galbraith, John Kenneth, 65n
Gallup Poll, 8, 73–74, 268–269
Geneva Conference on Discontinuance of Nuclear Weapon Tests (1958–61): agreement on high-altitude detection (1959), 19–20; early days, 14–25; final adjournment of, 121—122; first sessions during Kennedy administration, 54–60; near agreement, April 1960, 23, 24; preparing Kennedy administration position for, 35–48, 51–52, 53; setback of, by U-2 incident, 24–25; Soviet *Troika* proposal at, 54–55; Technical Working Group II (1959), 20–21; U.S. initiative at, increased by Kennedy, 59–60; Western proposals, 55–59 passim, 76. *See also* Test ban issues
Geneva Summit (Big Four, 1955), 7
Geneva System, for detecting test-ban violations, 13, 15, 19; evaluation of, by Fisk Panel (1961), 36–37; impracticality of, 23, 147; improvements suggested by U.S., 18, 20–21; as recommended by Conference of Experts, 12–13; technical challenge of, by HARDTACK tests, 17
German Democratic Republic, 67, 249, 260, 279
Germany, Federal Republic of, 175, 224–225, 243, 260
Ghiorso, Albert, 203
Gilpatric, Roswell L., 86, 109, 133n, 173, 187
Goldwater, Barry, 281
Gore, Albert, 15, 45, 83
Graham, John S., 30, 31
Graves, Alvin, 73
Great Britain. *See* United Kingdom
Gromyko, Andrei, 4, 143, 238, 243, 245–246, 247, 249–250, 258, 260, 261, 274

Hackes, Peter, 106
Hailsham, Lord (Quintin Hogg), 220, 225, 236, 238, 246, 256
Halleck, Charles, 83

Hammarskjold, Dag, 24, 54, 98
Harriman, W. Averell, 191, 223, 230–231, 264, 298, 301; on comprehensive test ban, 242; evaluation of performance in negotiations, 251–253, 257; instructions to, before negotiations, 228, 229; at Moscow negotiations, 219, 235–259 passim, 274; on Vienna summit, 66, 67
Harris Survey, 269
Haworth, Leland J., 49, 133n, 145, 156, 186
Heath, Ted, 225
Heckrotte, Warren, 21, 41n, 65n, 71, 76–77, 84, 179
Henderson, R. W., 222
Hickenlooper, Bourke B., 45, 46, 65n, 138, 186, 259, 265–266, 270–271, 275
High-altitude tests: DOMINIC test series, 152–157; Geneva agreement on detection system (1959), 19–20; principals accept detection system, 42–43, 56
Hilsman, Roger, 133n
Holifield, Chet, 69–70, 83, 138, 205
Home, Lord (Sir Alec Douglas-Home), 125, 126, 127, 128, 130, 225, 261
Hosmer, Craig, 187, 223–224, 287
"Hot line" agreement (U.S.-USSR, 1963), 206, 207
Humphrey, Hubert H., 10, 22, 56n, 259, 272, 280; meetings with president, 46, 47, 83; views on testing and test ban, 70–71, 94, 227

India, 286, 291
Ink, Dwight, 155
Inspection. *See* Onsite inspection
Interamerican Treaty of Reciprocal Assistance, 173
Interim Agreement (SALT I, 1972), 289
International Atomic Energy Agency, 90, 109, 201, 218, 291
Israel, 291
"Issues and Answers," 163–164
Italy, 226

Jackson, Henry M., 45, 48, 83, 181, 186, 280
Japan, opposition to nuclear tests in, 4, 138, 151
JCAE. *See* Congressional Joint Committee on Atomic Energy
John XXIII, Pope, 226
Johnson, Lyndon B., as president, 49, 287–288

Johnson, Lyndon B., as vice-president: at meetings on U.S. policy, 45, 71, 75, 82, 84, 124, 137, 140, 141, 146, 167, 173, 187, 228; visits Geneva Conference, 55
Johnson, U. Alexis, 173, 237
Johnston Island: test facilities at, 108, 192, 193; tests from, 150, 155, 156, 192
Joint Chiefs of Staff, 277, 288; criteria of acceptability of test ban, 269; national security safeguards proposed by, 269–270; opposition to test ban, 136, 137, 220–223 passim, 227; price paid for support of, 229, 271. *See also* LeMay, Curtis; Taylor, Maxwell

Kadar, Janos, 250
Kastenmeier, Robert W., 95
Kavanagh, George, 145
Kaysen, Carl, 140, 155, 183, 187, 223, 235, 252–253, 256
Keeny, Spurgeon, 37n, 44, 140, 165, 198
Kennan, George, 31, 66, 68
Kennedy, Jacqueline, 126, 151
Kennedy, John F., as president: actions to gain Senate support for treaty, 258, 259–260, 263–265, 279–280; advised by Eisenhower to resume testing (1960), 25; at Bermuda summit with Macmillan (1961), 126–131 passim; comment on Thomas Jefferson dining alone, 151; concern about nuclear weapons proliferation, 48, 171, 193–194, 198–199, 209, 224; consultation with Congressional leaders, 45–48, 50, 83–84, 138, 167, 239; in Cuban Missile Crisis, 172–175 passim; on cutoff date for ending tests, 170–171; on DOMINIC test series, 153–154, 157; "Ich bin ein Berliner" speech, 224–225, 230; importance of test ban to, 134, 265, 282; informality of, 31, 50–51; limits test preparations (1961), 69, 70; at meetings on U.S. policy, 51–52, 63, 64, 65, 71–72, 75, 82–85 passim, 87–88, 124, 136–139 passim, 140–142 passim, 146, 164–167 passim, 183, 187, 188, 223, 224, 228, 229; on need for onsite inspection, 128–129, 146–147, 180, 181; part in Moscow negotiations, 236, 239, 240–241, 246; pessimism about test ban, 198–199, 210, 217, 224, 226, 264; preoccupation with Chinese nuclear program, 181, 182, 188, 217, 239; preoccupation with fallout, 31–32, 112; presents U.S. disarmament plan to UN (1961), 98–99; progress

possible in arms control had he survived, 297–298; and quest for Christmas Island, 117–119 passim; relationship with Khrushchev, 135, 175–176, 207, 240–241, 300; and Seaborg's visit to Soviet Union, 203, 205; signs treaty ratification for U.S., 282; similarity of political position to Khrushchev's, 129, 299–300; and Soviet resumption of testing (1961), 81–82, 84, 85; speech after initialing of treaty, 256–257; trip to Western Europe, 1963, 224–226; and U.S. resumption of testing, 63–66 passim, 88, 105, 115, 117, 124–125, 132–133, 136, 138–139, 192, 193; at University of California on Charter Day, 128n; and Vienna summit with Khrushchev (1961), 66–68, 175; visit to AEC headquarters, 30–32; visit to Macmillan (Birch Grove, 1963), 225–226. *See also* American University speech
Kennedy, John F., as senator: on U.S. lack of preparation in arms control, 36, 92, 93, 96; sponsors legislation on arms-control research, 95; views on need for arms control, 32–33
Kennedy, Joseph P., 125–126
Kennedy, Robert F., 146, 173, 174
Kennedy administration: decision-making in, 49–50; personal relationships in, 182–183
Khrushchev, Nikita: agrees to conference of experts (1958), 11–12; agrees to receive Western test-ban emissaries (1963), 212–213; announces multi-megaton test (1961), 105; becomes premier (1958), 11; conversations with McCloy (1961), 74, 83; correspondence with Kennedy, 135, 178–179, 252; correspondence with Macmillan, 148, 230; in Cuban Missile Crisis, 174; human side of, 250–251; limitations on power of, 208, 298–300; in Moscow negotiations, 238–239, 240–241, 244–245; and onsite inspection quotas, 17, 179–181 passim, 207–208; on peaceful nuclear explosions, 244–245; reasons for support of treaty, 276; relationship with Kennedy, 175–176, 207, 300; remarks on treaty, 257; similarity of political position to Kennedy's, 299–300; on Soviet test resumption (1961), 86–87; speech (7/63) favoring limited treaty, 227–228, 240; and treaty-signing ceremony, 258, 260,

261; and U-2 incident (1960), 24; at Vienna summit (1961), 66–67; visit to U.S.(1959), 20
Killian, James R., Jr., 9, 19, 93, 264–265
King, Cecil, 203
Kissinger, Henry A., 49, 113–114
Kistiakowsky, George B., 19, 74n, 265, 273
Kohler, Foy, 140, 250, 256, 259
Korean War, 5
Kozlov, Frol, 299
Kuchel, Thomas, 83
Kuznetsov, Vasily V., 170, 179, 189, 190–191, 260, 261, 288

Lang, Daniel, 59–60
Latin-American Nuclear-Free Treaty, 288–289
Latter, Albert, 18–19
Latter, Richard, 37n
Lausche, Frank J., 281–282
Lawrence, Ernest O., 6, 8, 12n
LeMay, Curtis, 65, 220, 270–271
Lemnitzer, Lyman B., 38, 44, 45, 75, 82, 104, 137, 140
Life magazine, 70
Limited Test Ban Treaty: arguments for 263–264; compared to 1962 Western draft, 255, 275; effects of, 286–290; first reactions to, 256–257; hopes of proponents, 286; initialing of, 255–256; lack of enthusiasm for in Soviet leadership, 299; ratification by Big Three, 282; Senate amendment to resolution of ratification, 281; Senate floor debate on, 278–280; Senate hearings on 265–277; Senate vote on, 280–282; terms of, 254–255; and use of nuclear weapons in war, 274. *See also* Moscow negotiations
Lodge, Robert, 163
Long, Franklin A., 145, 167, 225, 235–236
Long, Russell, 277
Loper, Herbert B., 37n
Lovell, Sir Bernard, 153
Lovett, Robert A., 167
Lubell, Samuel, 122
Luedecke, Alvin R., 89, 203

McCloy, John J.: and Cuban Missile Crisis, 288; at meetings on U.S. policy, 71, 72, 73, 75, 82, 83, 85, 167; negotiates disarmament statement of principles with USSR, 99–100; proposal for an ACDA, 95; review of U.S. test-ban

policy (1961), 35–37, 38–48 passim, 63; visits Khrushchev at Black Sea, 74, 83
McCone, John: as AEC chairman, 22–23, 30, 33, 34, 201; as CIA director, 124, 133n, 136, 137, 138, 141, 146, 173, 187, 188, 197, 222, 237
McCormack, Mike, 138
McGhee, George, 133n, 140
Macmillan, Harold, 23, 51, 113, 117, 236, 246; at Bermuda summit, 126–131 passim; correspondence with Kennedy, 117–119, 167, 208–209; on Cuban Missile Crisis, 175; on Harriman, 219; importance of test-ban treaty to, 282; initiative leading to Moscow negotiations, 208–209; meeting with Kennedy at Birch Grove, 225–226; and on-site inspection quotas, 17, 41; and U.S. quest for Christmas Island, 117–119 passim
McNamara, Robert: at meetings on resumption of testing, 63, 69, 71, 72, 73, 75, 77, 82, 103, 104, 116, 117, 137, 138; at meetings on test-ban policy, 38–42 passim, 140, 146, 164, 165, 187, 188, 197, 198, 220–223 passim; and Moscow negotiations, 237; Senate' testimony on treaty, 266
McNaughton, John, 225, 235, 249
Makins, Sir Roger, 109, 119
Malinovsky, R. Y., 299
Mansfield, Mike, 83, 138, 259–260, 281
Mark, J. Carson, 37n
Marshall Islands, 4, 108
Martin, Edwin M., 173
"Meet the Press," 105–108, 163
Mendeleev, Dmitri, 203
Menshikov, Mikhail, 47
Mikoyan, Anastas, 178
Miller, Jack, 275, 281
Mills, Mark, 8
M.I.T. Arms Control Project, 84
Moratorium. *See* Test moratorium
Morgan, Thomas E., 46
Morse, Wayne, 280
Moscow negotiations, 235–239; accession to treaty as issue in, 249–250; agreed to by Khrushchev, 210, 211; China as factor in, 238–239; comprehensive treaty, try for, at, 240–242; coordination of Harriman mission and White House, 236–237; designation of Western emissaries, 219–220; East-West nonaggression pact, issue at, 238, 243–244; initial uncertainty about outcome, 229–231; peaceful-explo-

sions, issue at, 244–245, 247–248; preparing U.S. position for, 220–224, 228–229; signing-ceremony, issue at, 228, 258; U.S. delegation to, selection of, 235–236; Western initiative leading to, 208–209; withdrawal from treaty, issue at, 245–247. *See also* Test ban issues
Multilateral nuclear force (NATO), 194, 225, 290
Murrow, Edward R., 38, 82, 86, 133n, 136, 137, 237
Myrdal, Alva, 147, 167

Nehru, Jawaharlal, 4, 8
Neutron bomb, 31, 63, 75, 166
Nevada Test Site, 70, 108, 109, 136, 137
New York test ban talks (1963), 181, 183–185
New York Times, 45, 73, 106
Nitze, Paul H., 44, 104, 121, 140, 165, 166, 173, 187, 188, 222, 223
Nixon, Richard M., 24–25, 51, 94, 122, 182, 250, 295
Noel-Baker, Phillip, 6
Nonaggression pact (East-West): discussed within administration, 224, 228; at Moscow negotiations, 238, 243–244; proposed by Khrushchev, 224, 227.
Nonaligned nations conference (Belgrade, 1961), 75, 85, 88
Non-Proliferation Treaty (1970), 290–292
Northrup, Doyle, 37n
Nuclear arms race: effect of test ban on, 286–288; relative standing of superpowers, 107, 120, 123, 126, 127, 187, 278
Nuclear tests. *See* Tests

O'Donnell, P. Kenneth, 173
Ogle, William, 73, 156
Olson, Loren K., 31
Onsite inspection: chance of detecting violations, 19, 23–24, 147; ENDC neutrals on, 147; Kennedy on, 146–147; procedures for, proposed by West, 184–185, 188, 189–190, 191; in recent test-ban negotiations, 294, 295, 296–297; in U.S.-U.K. draft treaty of 1962, 169–170; U.S.-USSR differences on, in statement of disarmament principles, 100–101
Onsite inspection, annual quotas of: initial U.S. proposal of 12–20 (1961), 20, 22, 40–42, 44, 46, 47–48, 56, 57,

59; misunderstanding about U.S. position, 178–181, 188, 189, 190–191, 240; reduction in number required by U.S., 142, 165, 184–185, 187–188, 189; Soviet offer, of 2–3, 41n, 57, 179–181 passim; Soviet offer of 2–3 withdrawn, 227, 294; Soviets insist "political question," 22, 41, 59; suggested (1959) by Macmillan, 17; U.K. view, 141

Open-skies proposal (Eisenhower, 1955), 7

Organization of American States, 173

Ormsby-Gore, David (Lord Harlech), 15, 41, 57, 126, 129, 130, 183, 210, 225

Outer Space Treaty (1967), 288

Pakistan, 291

Panel on Seismic Improvement. *See* Berkner, Lloyd

Panofsky, Wolfgang K. H., 37n, 74, 154, 296

Panofsky Panel, 74–75

Paris summit (Big Four, 1960), 24

Pastore, John O., 45, 83, 138, 195, 227, 260

Pauling, Linus, 8, 10–11, 151

Peaceful nuclear explosions; applications of, 196, 267; and Limited Test Ban Treaty, 255, 266–268; in recent comprehensive test ban negotiations, 297; U.S. program after 1963, 247–248; USSR program in, 244–245, 247–248; in U.S.-U.K. draft treaties of 1962, 169, 170, 195–197. *See also* Plowshare program

Peaceful Nuclear Explosion Treaty, 296

Pell, Claiborne, 296

Penney, Sir William, 125, 126, 127, 130, 223, 225, 242

Petrosyants, Andronik M., 202, 203, 205, 261

Pillion, John R., 73

Pius XII, Pope, 4

Plowshare program, 144, 196, 197; as factor in Senate review of treaty, 248–249, 267–268, 272, 274, 279; origin of name, 39–40; projects contemplated, 196, 267; Seaborg proposals to save program, 196–198; Soviet demand to inspect devices, 39–40, 45, 46, 56, 57. *See also* Peaceful nuclear explosions; Test-ban issues

Power, Thomas, 277

Powers, Francis Gary, 24

President's Science Advisory Committee (PSAC), 9, 119, 154

Press, Frank, 37n, 74n, 235, 241–242

Price, Melvin, 45, 138

Principals, Committee of: in administration decision-making, 49, 50; meetings, 38–43, 97, 100, 103–105, 120–121, 125, 140–142, 164–165, 193, 197, 198, 220–223; membership, 37–38

Proliferation of nuclear weapons: effect of test ban on, 166, 193–195, 257, 266, 290–292; as factor in test-ban negotiations, 165, 166, 188; Kennedy's concern about, 48, 171, 193–194, 198–199, 209, 224. *See also* Non-Proliferation Treaty

Public opinion, U.S.: focus on fallout, 268–269; on testing and test ban, 8, 48, 73–74, 122

Public opinion, world: courted by U.S., 48, 60, 82–84, 86, 96, 98, 142; on nuclear testing, 4, 118; reaction to DOMINIC, 151; reaction to USSR resumption of testing, 83, 85

Pugwash conferences, 177

Ramey, James T., 45

Read, Benjamin, 229, 236–237

Rockefeller, Nelson A., 32

Roddis, Louis H., 74n

Roosevelt, Franklin D., 60

Rostow, Walt W., 133n

Rusk, Dean, 109, 126, 156, 192, 225, 237, 240, 264; on British having nuclear weapons, 109; and Cuban Missile Crisis, 173, 174, 175; at meetings on U.S. policy, 38, 39, 42, 43, 82, 85–86, 120, 136–137, 140, 142, 146, 183, 187, 197, 220–223 passim, 228, 229; on peaceful nuclear explosions, 197, 198; recommends resumption of atmospheric testing, 135–136; and signing of treaty, 258–261 passim; Senate testimony on treaty, 266; and VELA findings, 162–163

Russell, Richard B., 83, 138, 187, 281

Safeguards, national security: endorsed by Kennedy, 279; implementation of, 287–288; recommended by Joint Chiefs of Staff, 269–270

Salinger, Pierre, 89, 225

SALT I Treaties (1972), 289

SALT II Treaty, 290

Saltonstall, Leverett, 83, 138, 259–260, 278

Sandys, Duncan, 225

Saudi Arabia, 291

Scali, John, 174

Schlafly, Phyllis, 276

Schlesinger, Arthur, M., Jr., 60, 68, 82, 88, 133n, 140, 226, 252
Schweitzer, Albert, 4, 8
Scientists, disagreements among, 34–35, 265–266
Scoville, Herbert, 86, 104, 120
Seabed Treaty (1972), 289
Seaborg, Glenn T.: at Bermuda summit, 126, 127, 128, 130; caught between opposing views on test ban, 35; as chairman of Committee on Atmospheric Testing, 116, 123, 124; and DOMINIC tests, 154–156 passim; favors inspection quotas proportional to events, 42, 44, 47, 48; first meetings with Kennedy, 30–32; on "Issues and Answers," 163–164; at meetings on U.S. policy, 38–48 passim, 51–52, 71, 72, 73, 75–76, 82–84 passim, 85–86, 104, 120, 137, 140, 141, 142, 146, 164, 183–184, 187, 188, 193, 197, 198, 228; on "Meet the Press," 105–108; at Moscow signing ceremony, 259, 260, 261; negotiations with French nuclear officials, 110–111; and People's Republic of China, 217n; and Plowshare program, 40, 195–198, 248–249, 266–268; and quest for Christmas Island, 109–110, 118–119; testimony on treaty by, 266–268, recommends atmospheric testing, 112–113, 114; Senate testimony on treaty by, 266–268; and test preparations, 70, 71, 72, 87–88, 90, 116, 123, 124; visit to Soviet Union (1963), 202–206
Seismic research: advisory group at Geneva Conference, 24; Soviet demand to inspect U.S. devices, 39–40, 45, 46, 51, 56
Senate Armed Services Committee, 259, 265; *See also* Senate Preparedness Subcommittee
Senate Disarmament Subcommittee (Foreign Relations), 10, 94
Senate Foreign Relations Committee, 296; hearings on treaty, 265–276; report on treaty, 277–278. *See also* Senate Disarmament Subcommittee
Senate Preparedness Subcommittee (Armed Services), 221, 265, 276–277, 278
Shulman, Marshall D., 275–276
Skybolt missile, 117
Smith, Bromley, 105
Smith, Margaret Chase, 282
Sorensen, Theodore, 81, 82, 129, 138, 139, 173, 237, 264, 282; and American Uni-

versity speech, 212, 213; on decision-making in Kennedy administration, 49; on opposition to test ban, 220; on relationships in Kennedy administration, 182–183
South Africa, 291
Soviet Union: cooperation agreements with U.S. on peaceful atom, 201–202; fear of espionage, 16, 146, 147, 241; nuclear tests by, 15, 85, 103, 105, 107, 112, 114, 115, 119–120, 163, 168, 288; relations with China, 111, 217, 230, 246, 276; suspected violations of test moratorium (1958–61), 34, 64, 65. *See also* Testing, Soviet resumption of
Spaak, Paul-Henri, 230
Space tests. *See* High-altitude tests
Sparkman, John, 259
Spivak, Lawrence, 106, 107
Sputniks, 9
Stalin, Josef, 5, 251
Starbird, Alfred D., 37n, 155, 156
Stassen, Harold E., 6, 94, 276
Statement of Principles. *See* Disarmament, general and complete
Stelle, Charles, 71, 77, 122
"Stennis Committee." *See* Senate Preparedness Subcommittee
Stevenson, Adlai E., 88, 137, 173, 174, 259; test-ban proposals in 1956 presidential campaign, 7–8; at UN, 105, 106, 294
Strauss, Lewis, 8, 9–10, 273–274
Sullivan, William, 252
Summit conference. *See* Bermuda summit; Geneva summit; Vienna summit
Swedish delegation at ENDC, 142, 145, 147, 177
Sweeney, Walter C., 173
Symington, Stuart, 83, 187, 278
Szilard, Leo, 61

Tape, Gerald F., 203
Taylor, Maxwell D., 82, 87, 140, 173, 221, 222, 269–270
Technical Working Groups (Geneva Conference): Group I, 19–20; Group II, 21–22
Teller, Edward, 8, 10–11, 18, 187, 271–272, 277
Ten-Nation Disarmament Committee, 99, 142
Test-ban issues, Eighteen Nation Disarmament Committee: detecting preparations for testing, 133, 137, 141, 143; gains possible from clandestine underground tests, 142, 188; national vs.

international means of verification, 141, 142, 143, 144–147 passim, 162–166 passim, 167, 184; seismic threshold on underground tests, 141, 143; time lag before beginning inspection, 137, 141–142. *See also* Onsite inspections, annual quotas; Test-ban proposals

Test-ban proposals, Soviet Union: ban of hydrogen tests (1956), 7; three-year moratorium (1957), 8–9, 10, 11; treaties offered at Geneva Conference, 15, 22, 121–122; treaty offered at ENDC, 144

Test-ban proposals, U.S.-U.K.: atmospheric ban (9/61), 85–86, 104, 105, 120, 144–145; Eisenhower moratorium proposal (1958), 14; Eisenhower proposal of ban in phases (1959), 17; phased treaty limited to verifiable tests (1960), 21–22; treaty draft, comprehensive (4/61), 57–59, 120, 136, 137; treaty drafts presented to ENDC (1962), 165, 166, 168–170, 238, 244

Testing, atmospheric, U.S. resumption of: choice of sites, 108, 115; debated within government, 90, 91, 103–105, 111, 112–113, 135–136, 136–137; Kennedy's address announcing, 138–139; Kennedy's guidelines for, 117, 119; preparations for, 105–106, 111, 112, 114, 133–134. *See also* DOMINIC test series; Tests, U.S.

Testing, Soviet resumption of (1961): announced, 77–78; Kennedy's reaction to, 81, 84, 85; meetings to discuss U.S. response, 81–85; motives for, 83–84, 86–87; world reaction to, 83, 85

Testing, underground, U.S. resumption of: debated within government, 43, 62–63, 64, 65, 66, 74–75, 82–84; Kennedy's attitude on, 63, 65, 66, 68; ordered by president, 88; preparations for, 68–73, passim, 87–88. *See also* Tests, U.S.

Test moratorium (1958–61), 43; Eisenhower terminates U.S. obligation, 84; opposition to, by AEC, 33–34; suspected Soviet violations of, 34, 64, 65, 69, 74, 75, 128

Tests, France, 23, 55, 84, 194

Tests, Soviet Union, 15, 85, 87, 163, 168; evaluation of, in U.S., 90, 103, 115, 119–120, 138; multimegaton test (1961), 74, 83, 105, 107, 112, 114; rate of, following test ban, 288

Tests, United Kingdom, 7, 109, 117, 288n

Tests, U.S.: BRAVO (1954), 3–4, 287; first underground test (RAINIER, 1957), 9, 17; HARDTACK series (1958), 15, 17, 20, 21; 1961 series compared with USSR's, 90; plans for 1964 atmospheric series, 192, 193; problems with underground testing (1961), 89, 90, 111, 142; purposes, 63, 123, 152; rate of, following test ban, 288. *See also* DOMINIC test series

Thant, U, 99, 174, 261

Thompson, Llewellyn E., 66, 68, 173, 237, 259

Threshold Test Ban Treaty, 295–296

Time magazine, 108

Tower, John, 281

Tsarapkin, Semyon K., 15, 17, 20, 22, 24, 54–55, 57, 58–59, 76, 93, 144, 177, 237, 260, 261

Tubby, Roger, 133n

Tukey, John W., 74n

Turkey, U.S. missiles in, 174, 175

Twining, Nathan F., 277

Tyler, William, 235, 253

Udall, Stewart, 261

United Kingdom: influence over U.S. policy, 113, 114; opposition to atmospheric testing, 113, 118, 122; tests by 7, 109, 117, 288n. *See also* Bermuda summit; Macmillan, Harold

United Nations: Disarmament Commission, 8, 295; General Assembly, 24, 75, 90–91, 98–99, 103, 104, 166, 176, 294; Security Council, 291

USSR. *See* Soviet Union

U-2 incident (1960), 24, 299

Van Allen, James, and Van Allen radiation belts, 153–156 passim

Van Zandt, James E., 45, 46, 138

VELA seismic research program: early findings, 142, 145, 162–163, 164, 165; premature release of findings, 162–164 passim, 165, 166; progress in late 1960s, 295

Vienna summit (Kennedy-Khrushchev, 1961), 66–68; effect of, on Kennedy, 67, 68; Kennedy's performance at, evaluated, 68, 175

Vinson, Carl, 138

Voroshilov, Klementi, 261

Voss, Earl, 52–53, 59

Wadsworth, James J., 15, 16–17

Walske, Carl, 41n

Webb, James E., 38

Wells, Algie A., 203
Wheeler, Earle G., 86
Wiesner, Jerome B., 32n, 77, 117, 145, 154; and misunderstanding on inspection quotas, 180–181; at meetings on U.S. policy, 30, 38, 42, 44, 45, 48, 51, 75, 82, 140, 146, 166, 183, 187, 197, 222, 223
Wilson, A. Duncan, 252–253
Wilson, Donald M., 173
Wilson, Harold, 179, 227, 240

Wilson, Robert E., 31
Wilson, Woodrow, 60, 258
Wright, Sir Michael, 65n, 122

York, Herbert F., 34, 37n, 273, 290

Zhou Enlai, 23
Zinn, Walter H., 74n
Zorin, Valerian, 74, 99, 167, 168, 175, 261
Zucker, Alexander, 203
Zuckerman, Sir Solly, 225, 242